Postures

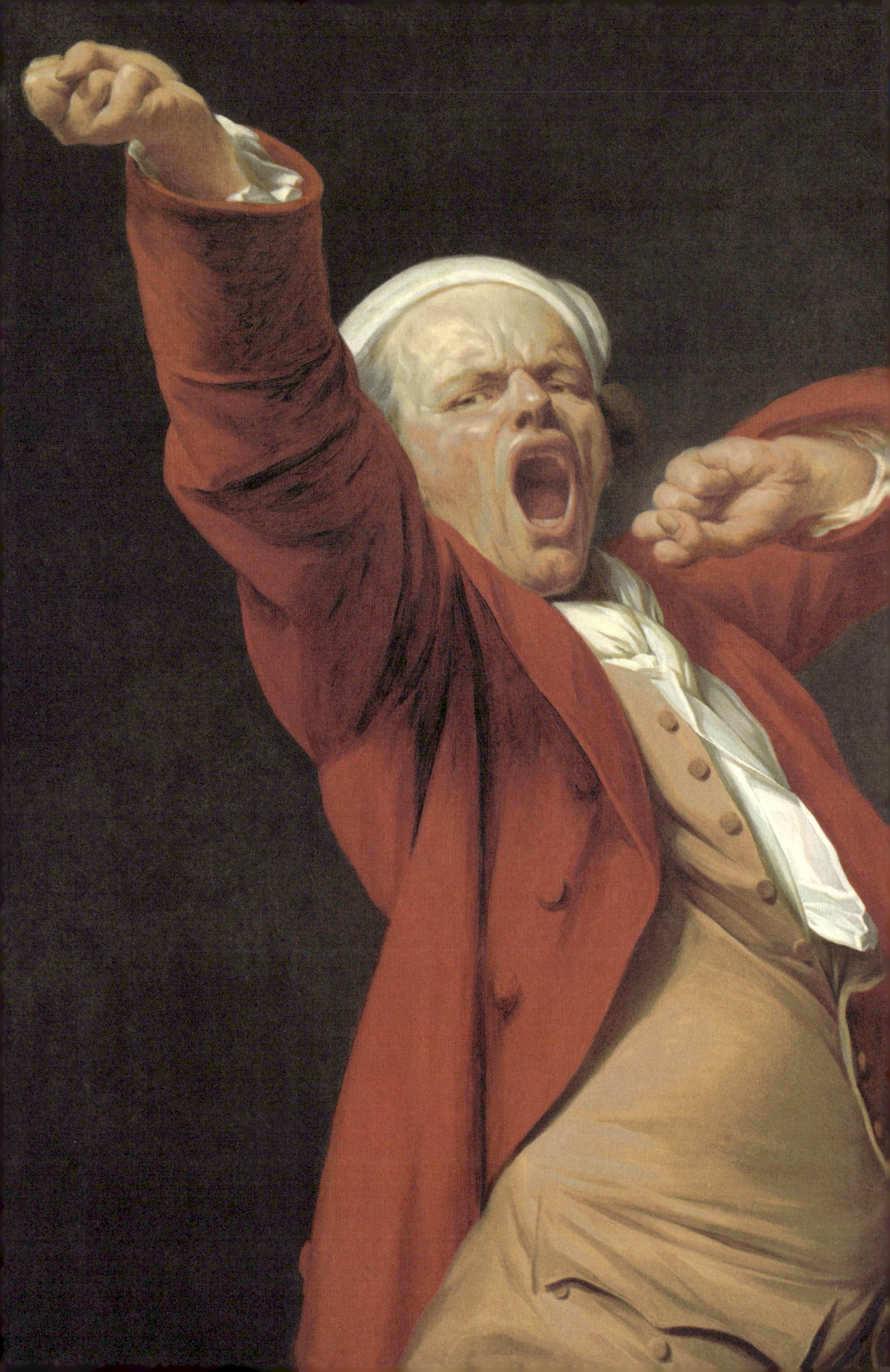

Desmond Morris

Postures

Body Language in Art

Thames & Hudson

Introduction

Every time an artist portrays a human subject, a decision has to be made about the posture of the figure. Will the subject be standing, sitting or reclining? Will they be smiling, screaming or deadpan? Will they be hugging themselves or gesticulating? Will they be making a symbolic sign of some kind? Examining the body language displayed in works of art reveals some unusual traditions and conventions, and tells us a great deal about changing social attitudes and customs throughout history. It provides an exciting new way of viewing art. Even the most familiar paintings are suddenly seen in a fresh light.

When we look at a portrait or the portrayal of a group of human figures in a picture, our attention is usually focused on the identity of the figures, and the style and quality of the painting. We are aware of their postures, gestures and expressions, but we do not study them in detail. It is the same when someone is gesticulating as they speak to us in ordinary conversation. We see that their hands are moving, and their gestures have an influence on our feelings about what is being said, but we do not consciously analyse what they are doing.

In my book *Manwatching* (1977), I introduced the subject of body language and showed how much we can learn by studying human actions rather than just by listening to words. I was focused on social encounters in everyday life, but I did include one or two paintings that showed a particular gesture or posture very clearly. Much later, in 2013, I published a book on the evolution of human art, *The Artistic Ape*, in which I looked at the changes that have occurred over a period of three million years of artistic activity. In this volume, I have put these two subjects together, combining my two separate fields of study for the first time. I have often wondered why Napoleon was always portrayed with his hand pushed into his waistcoat – now, at last, I know the answer. Identifying a posture and then analysing its meaning, not only in terms of basic human behaviour, but also in relation to the customs of the period in which it was depicted, has turned out to be an absorbing story of art detection. For this, my double life – as a scientist and as an artist – has proved invaluable.

On a personal note, I recall that when Francis Bacon and I were examining Pablo Picasso's *Weeping Woman* (1937) at close quarters, we began a discussion of facial expressions in art that made me realize how important the subject of body language was to him. When he died, I was not surprised to see that he had a copy of *Manwatching* in his bedroom. What did surprise me was that he had two copies, one clean and neat, and the other thumbed and grubby. The implication was that he used one for reading at leisure, and kept the other to refer to when working in his studio. He asked me many questions about the facial expressions

of animals, and amused me when he said, with typical modesty, 'I think
I have got the scream, but I am having terrible trouble with the smile.'
The body language of his figures was clearly on his mind. He had recently
done a portrait of a baboon and, knowing that I was a zoologist, he asked
me if he had managed to get the scream of the animal right. I said that he
had, but I was lying. The creature Bacon had portrayed was taken from
a well-known photograph of a yawning baboon, but I did not dare tell
him this because he was notorious for destroying any painting of his that
had what he saw as an imperfection. He kept a Stanley knife in his studio,
and had already slashed to pieces dozens of his paintings. I did not want
his splendid baboon painting to suffer this fate, so I kept quiet about the
yawn. It was obvious to me that the animal was yawning, because when
a baboon screams, it does so in the direction of whatever has provoked
the scream. Yawning is non-directional, and this particular baboon had
its jaws wide open, pointing upwards towards the sky. A man might
scream at the heavens in frustration, but not a baboon. It pleases me to
think that this splendid painting survives because of a small fib of mine.

One way to approach the intriguing subject of human body language
in art is to take each part of the human body in turn, looking separately
at the special finger gestures, the hand movements, the position of the
arms, the tilt of the head, the facial expressions, the set of the legs and
the general postures of the body. But while this has the merit of being
systematic and objective, it is also rather dry and academic. A more
rewarding approach is to look at what a particular form of body language
signals to us. What is its social function? What emotion does it reveal?
This is the method I have employed here. In some cases, it is a matter
of universal human body language that is understood all over the world.
Everyone comprehends a frown or a shaken fist. But other actions are
deeply embedded in a particular phase of history, or in a local culture,
where special rules of conduct have been imposed. So this book is three
things: a study of human body language, a cultural history of social
customs and a survey of changing artistic styles. It covers a vast range
of visual creativity, from prehistoric figurines, tribal artefacts and early
religious art to modern art, folk art and graffiti. And it ranges from Europe
to the Far East, and from Africa to the Americas. Juxtaposing hugely
varied images side by side was often the best way to illustrate a particular
point, and to bring the subject of body language in art vividly to life.

Greetings

When two people meet after a period of separation, they invariably perform some kind of greeting ritual. This involves the display of friendly signals of an exaggerated nature since the many smaller signs of friendship that occur when people are together have been absent. The greeting ritual is intended to make up for this loss. When two old friends meet after a long time apart, they must make a special effort to reassure one another that their friendship has not faded; if the situation involves strangers meeting for the first time, they must show each other that there are no feelings of hostility.

In a meeting between equals, the greeting actions usually mirror one another and are much the same the world over, although cultural differences and preferences naturally occur. They include five common actions. Initially, when the two individuals are at a distance, there is the raised arm of the hail, generally combined with a wave. Then, at close quarters, there is the smile, the handshake, the embrace and the kiss.

In contrast, when an inferior meets a superior figure, their movements usually differ strongly, with the inferior person performing some kind of body-lowering action. Greetings by subordinates involve varying degrees of body lowering, from a slight dip of the head to a full bow from the waist, or a curtsey, and from kneeling down on one knee or both to the ultimate act of subservience – prostration. If leaders wish to appear reassuringly at one with their followers, they may deliberately adopt a greeting of equals to put their subordinates at ease.

The Hail

A common greeting at a distance is the hail, in which one arm is raised high in the air with the palm facing outwards. In cities such as New York and London, it is also the most common gesture when hailing a cab.

An exaggerated, stiff, straight-arm version of the hail became the required form of greeting in Nazi Germany, usually accompanied by the words 'Heil Hitler'. When greeting their leader, the Nazis would hold their right arm rigidly straight, at an angle above the horizontal, with the hand flattened, the fingers tightly together, and the palm facing forwards and downwards. Hitler might respond in the same way, or with a less rigid, bent arm and his hand held vertically, showing the palm. The salute had been introduced within the Nazi Party in 1926 as the formal greeting between its members, but it was borrowed from the Italian Fascists, who had started using the gesture in 1923. The Fascists had claimed that they were adopting a greeting that was popular among their Roman ancestors two thousand years earlier – a notion that appealed to their desire to restore the glories of ancient Rome. As a result, the gesture became known as the Roman salute, or *saluto romano*, and held an obvious attraction for Hitler because it was synonymous with an all-conquering global superpower.

However, if you search the arts of ancient Rome for examples of the Roman salute, it is nowhere to be seen. The Fascists and the Nazis were basing their hail greeting on a misconception – an error undoubtedly perpetuated by famous paintings of the 18th and 19th centuries, in which such artists as Jacques-Louis David [2] and Jean-Léon Gérôme portrayed imaginary events in ancient Rome that incorporated stiff-arm gestures of the kind later adopted by Mussolini and Hitler. In perhaps the best-known example, *Ave Caesar! Morituri te salutant* (*Hail Caesar! We Who Are About to Die Salute You*) [1], of 1859, Gérôme reimagines an incident recorded by the Roman historian Suetonius, in which a group of desperate captives and criminals – faced with death – tried to ingratiate themselves with the emperor Claudius in order to gain clemency. In the painting, the gladiators are shown raising their arms towards the emperor, holding their weapons aloft in their hands. Despite popular belief, there is no authentic record of gladiators customarily hailing an emperor in this way. In reality, if this incident took place at all, it is more likely that the gladiators would have made a palm-up, begging hand gesture. There is also a well-known 19th-century statue at Versailles, showing the French astronomer and mathematician Jean Sylvain Bailly [5] making a stiffly rigid hail gesture, exactly like that employed by the Nazis.

There was considerable confusion at the Olympic Games in the interwar period because the official Olympic greeting consisted of an

arm gesture that was almost identical to the Nazi salute. At the 1936
Olympics in Berlin, it was unclear whether non-German teams were giving
the newly adopted Nazi salute or performing the earlier Olympic greeting.
The original Olympic greeting has since been abandoned, although it is
commemorated in a large bronze statue of an athlete making the gesture.
Man Giving the Olympic Salute [4], created in 1928 by the Dutch artist
Gra Rueb, stands outside the Olympic Stadium in Amsterdam.

The hail gesture also had to be officially abandoned in the United
States, where it had been used for years when greeting the national flag.
In 1892, at a time when the country was still recovering from the ravages
and divisions of the Civil War, the decision was made to encourage a
unified patriotism by insisting that schoolchildren in their classrooms
must start each day by greeting the Stars and Stripes with what was
called the Bellamy salute. In *The Youth's Companion* of the same
year, the gesture was described as follows: 'the right hand is extended
gracefully, palm upward, toward the Flag, and remains in this gesture
till the end of the affirmation'. In the 1930s, the US authorities were
horrified to realize that images of schoolchildren performing the Bellamy
salute could easily be exploited to imply American support for the Nazis.
To avoid this, Congress passed an amended Flag Code in 1942, decreeing
that the Pledge of Allegiance 'be rendered by standing…with the right
hand over the heart.' This is how it has remained ever since, with the
Bellamy salute fading rapidly into history and now largely forgotten.

The strong association of the straight-arm hail gesture with the Hitler
regime meant that, following the Second World War, it could never be used
again in any other context. It is rarely seen in contemporary works of art,
unless they are comical, satirical or scurrilous. The Nazi connection also
presents a problem for anyone wishing to greet a friend or acquaintance
from a distance. The common solution is to add a waving movement
to the raised hand – a combined action that is clearly visible in Thomas
Cowperthwait Eakins's *Salutat* [3], which depicts a boxer waving to the
crowd after a real-life match in 1898. This waving motion was always
absent from the Nazi hail, making the action entirely non-political and
much more friendly.

The typical wave involves moving one's hand from side to side with the
palm showing, but there are several variations. The most interesting one is
the Hawaiian *shaka*, which involves waving the raised hand with only the
thumb and little finger extended. This unique local greeting, which may
have originated as a modified form of a Spanish drinking gesture, can
be seen all over the Hawaiian Islands on carved or painted images.

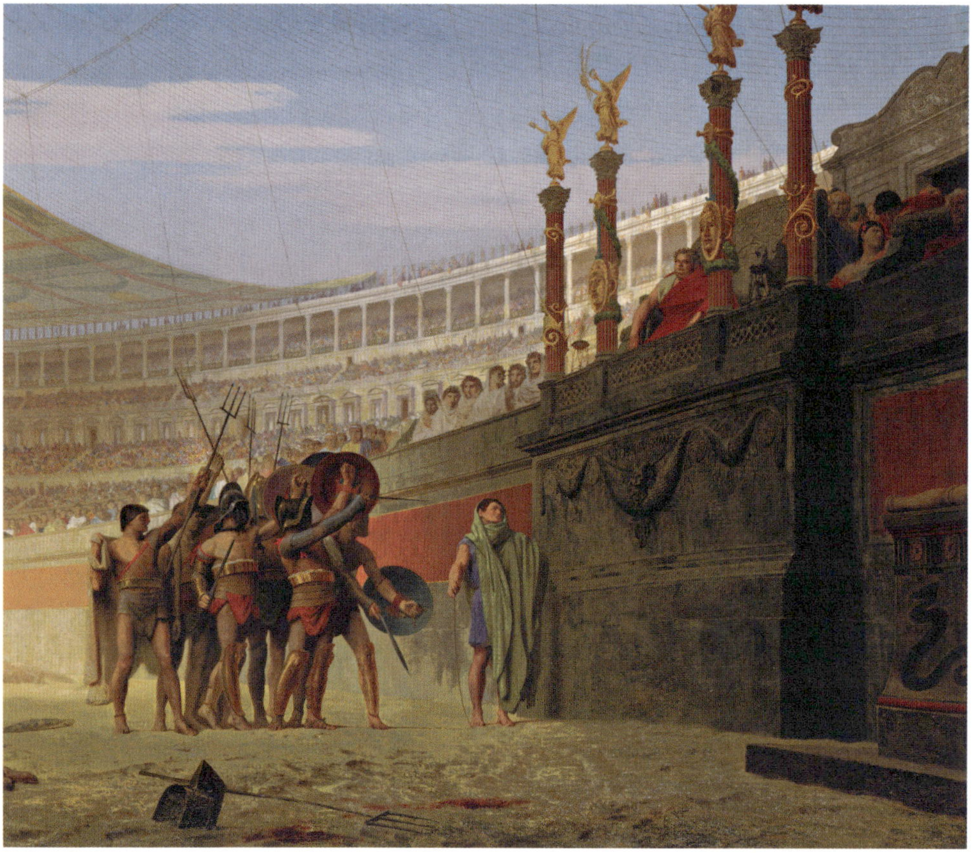

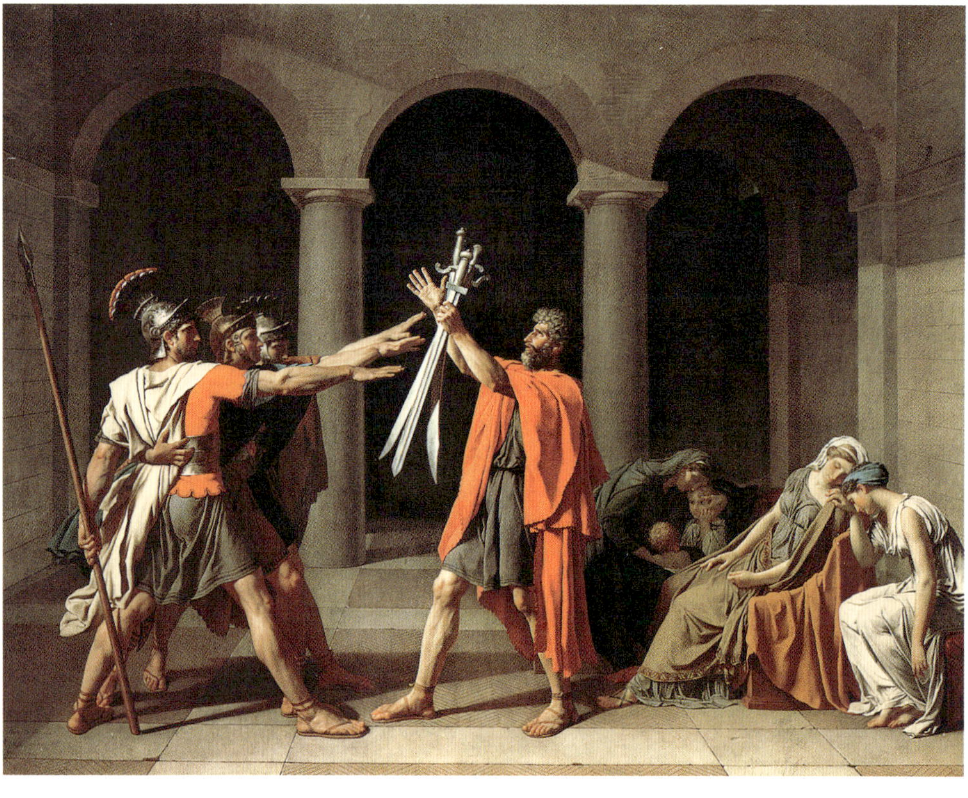

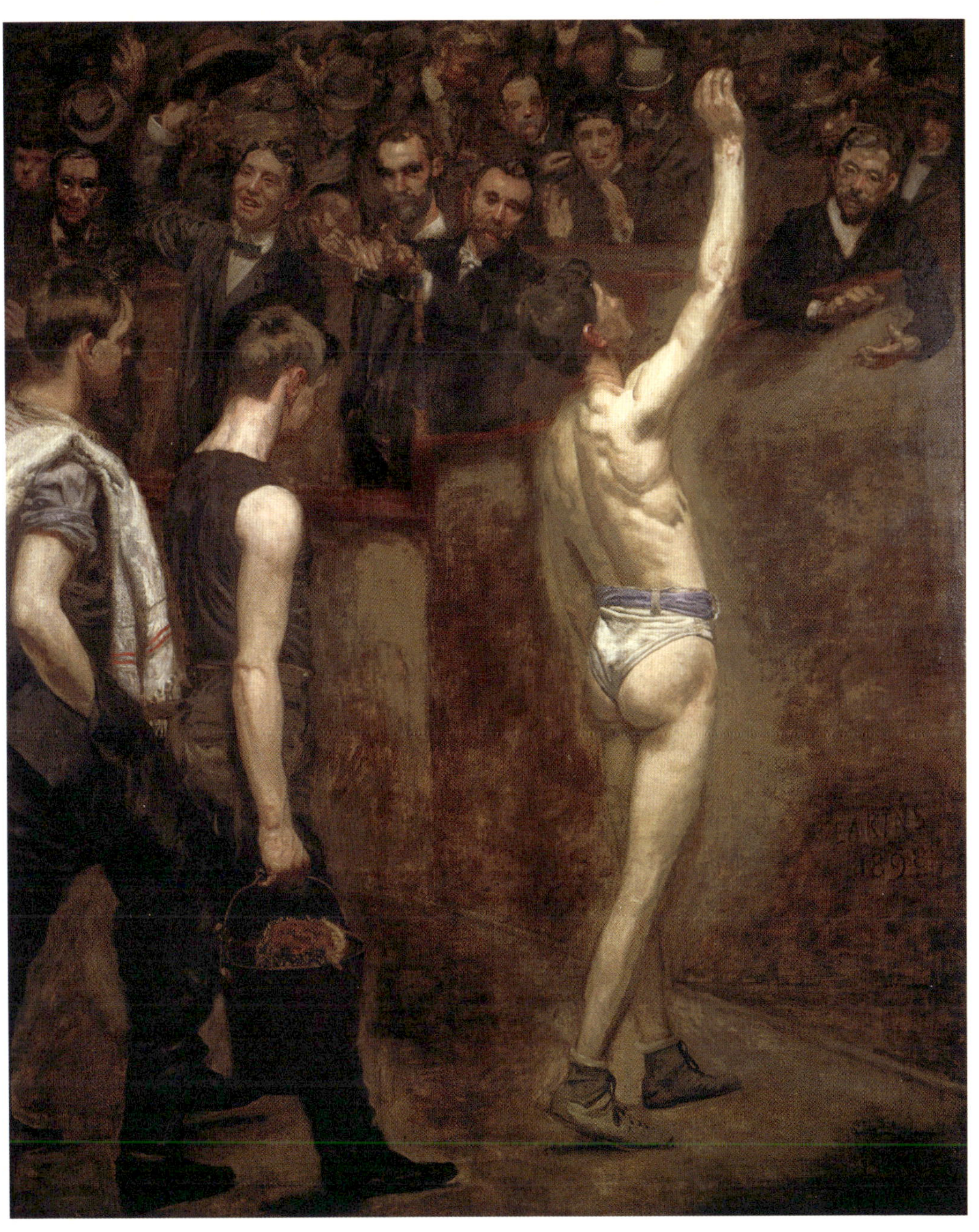

1. opposite, above **Jean-Léon Gérôme,**
Ave Caesar! Morituri te salutant (Hail Caesar!
We Who Are About to Die Salute You)
(detail), 1859, oil on canvas

2. opposite, below **Jacques-Louis David,**
The Oath of the Horatii, 1784, oil on canvas

3. above **Thomas Cowperthwait Eakins,**
Salutat, 1898, oil on canvas

Greetings / The Hail

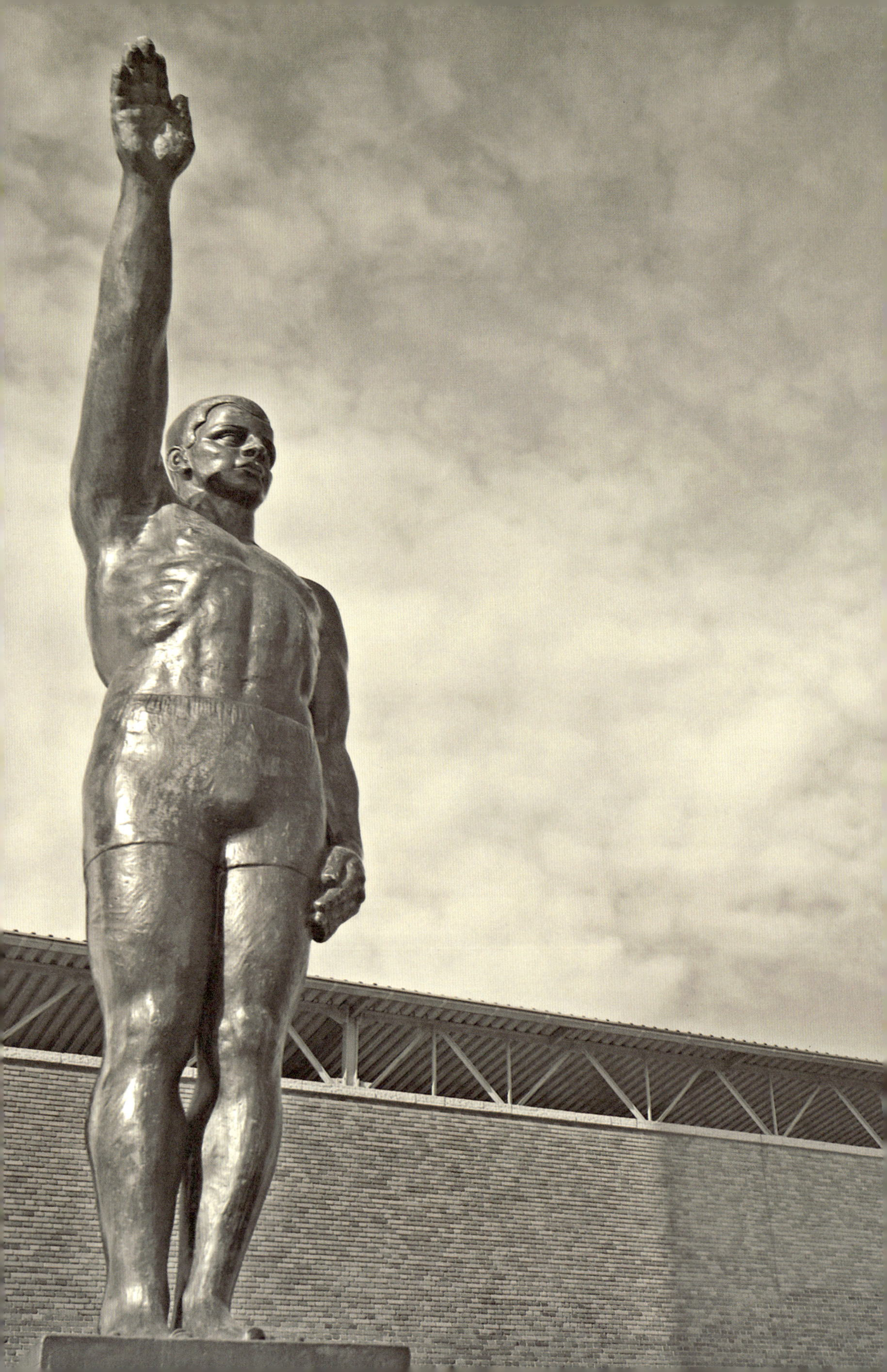

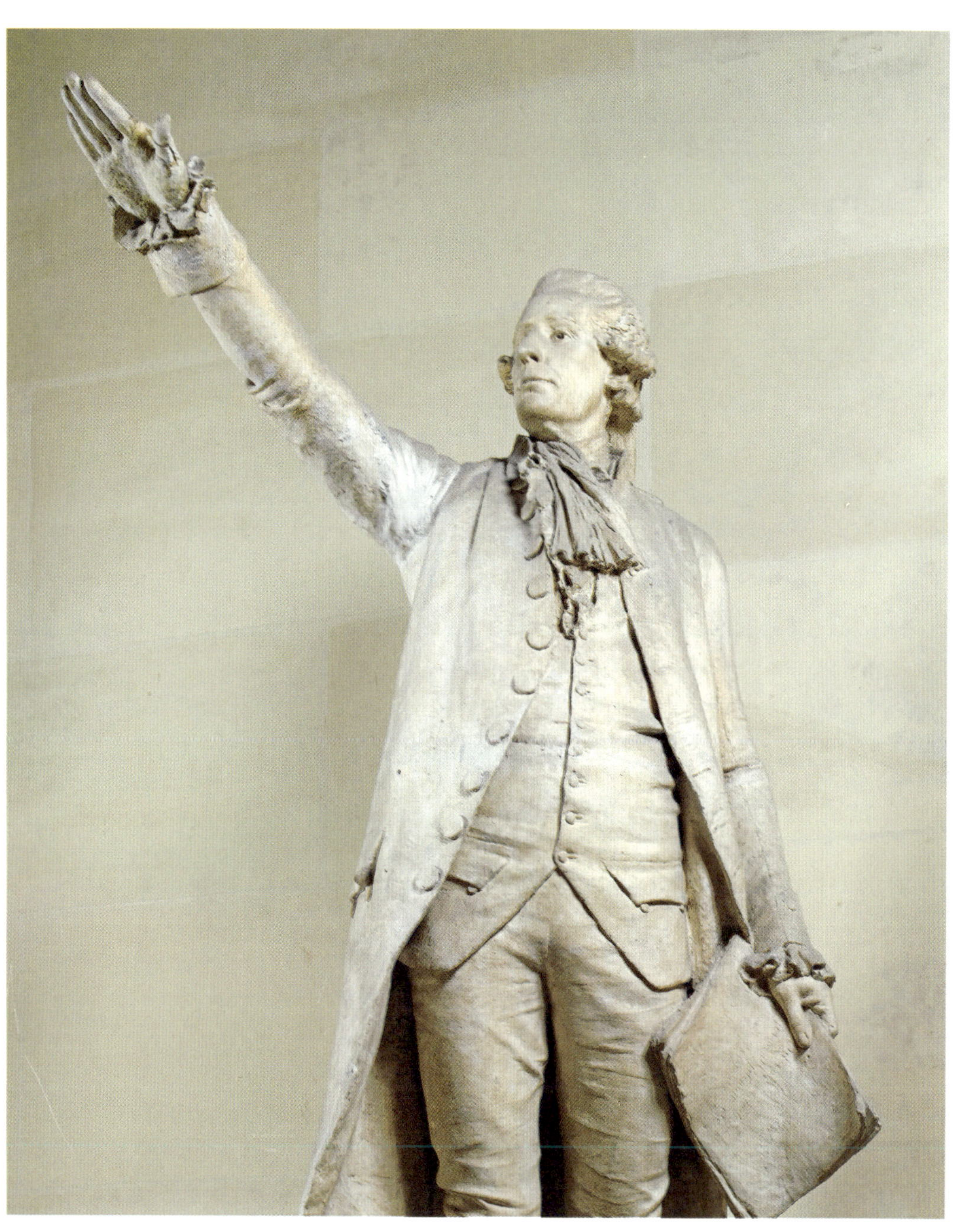

4. opposite **Gra Rueb,**
Man Giving the Olympic Salute, 1928,
**Olympic Stadium, Amsterdam,
Netherlands**

5. above **René de Saint-Marceaux,**
Jean Sylvain Bailly, 1881, plaster,
Château de Versailles, France

The Handshake

Once the long-distance greeting signals – the hail and the wave – have achieved the initial visual contact, there is a pause as the two figures draw closer. Then, when they are near enough to make physical contact, one of two things usually happens: either they embrace or they shake hands. Lovers, close relatives or intimate friends may greet each other with an embrace, holding their bodies close together and wrapping their arms around one another. When greeting a stranger, or a person for whom there is a less intimate attachment, a milder form of the embrace is needed. The answer is the handshake – an action that involves friendly physical contact, but of a minimal kind. One exception to this widespread custom can be found in Japan, where the social touching of another person's body is considered intrusive, and mutual bowing takes its place.

As a common form of social greeting, the handshake is comparatively recent, dating from the early 19th century. Before then, bows, waves, curtsies and flourishes of the hand were the greeting gestures in polite society. The handshake would have been considered too 'egalitarian' and out of place in the highly stratified society of earlier centuries. Today, of course, it fits our modern social attitudes well. If two men meet and one is of much higher rank than the other, they may still perform the reciprocal handshake, in which their actions are identical. The situation is more complicated concerning women, as is discussed later.

To emphasize the importance of a social greeting, there is the amplified handshake, in which the left hand is placed on top of the joined right hands. It has been called the 'politician's handshake' because it is a favourite gesture of public figures who want to come across as ultra-friendly. It is like a miniature hug, with the companion's hand embraced as intimately as possible. The effect is to give a powerful friendship signal while at the same time retaining the formality of this type of greeting.

There is one way in which the 'equality' aspect of the handshake can be subverted. The initiator of the greeting offers their hand in a palm-down position, which forces the other person to respond with their palm turned upwards. This is the handshake of a dominant person who wishes to 'gain the upper hand'. By offering the hand in the palm-down position, they present a challenge. Either the hand posture is accepted, in which case the egalitarian quality of the greeting is lost, or an uncomfortable incident is provoked by the refusal to cooperate. In an ordinary handshake, the two people involved perform identical actions – each with a 'thumb-above' hand position – regardless of their relative status. But in the palm-down handshake, the initiator rejects this and expresses their high status in a subtle way.

Certain differences between the sexes remain to this day. In some countries women do not offer their hands for shaking, while in others it is customary. This has sometimes led to confusion. Also, in most Islamic countries, men who are not closely related to a woman may not touch her in any way; if a male visitor offers his hand for shaking, his action may be considered an insult. In the Middle East and Asia, more ancient forms of greeting, such as the *salaam*, the *namaste*, the *wai* and the bow, are often still preferred.

Although the handshake as an everyday social greeting is a relatively recent phenomenon, a few ancient works of art reveal that, as a formality on special occasions, it was in use in earlier civilizations. The oldest known example is found on a relief from the 9th century BC [6], showing the Assyrian king Shalmaneser III shaking hands with the Babylonian ruler Marduk-zakir-šumi I. This relief commemorates the close bond that existed between the two kingdoms, a friendship that was bolstered by intermarriage.

A few centuries later, the handshake is clearly depicted in the art of ancient Greece, for example on an Attic red-figure vessel from 470 BC [7] showing Theseus being received with a welcoming handshake in the undersea palace of his father, Poseidon. There are also a number of funerary reliefs from Greece dating from the 5th and 4th centuries BC, in which the deceased is depicted clasping the hand of a close relative or companion. The term *dexiosis* is used to describe this handshaking motif on Greek gravestones, where it has a specific meaning and symbolism. It is essentially a farewell gesture between the deceased person and close family members, emphasizing the importance of strong family bonds.

In ancient Rome, coins were struck with a pair of disembodied hands performing a symbolic handshake. The artist who designed one of these coins, a Caesarea Cappadocia silver coin of AD 112, took great care to show the exact position of the fingers and thumbs as the hands clasp each other. In imperial Rome at this time, the ceremonial joining of right hands was given a special name – *dextrarum iunctio* – and images of it appear on some funerary reliefs. A modified form of the Roman handshake, in which two soldiers grab one another's forearms to ensure that there are no weapons concealed in the sleeves, has become a popular form of military greeting in Hollywood epics set during this period, although there are no records of it ever having occurred.

After the fall of Rome, the handshake largely disappeared from artworks until the 17th century, when a painting by the Dutch artist Bartholomeus van der Helst called *Banquet at the Crossbowmen's Guild in Celebration of the Treaty of Münster* (1648) [8] made a feature of it. At a banquet at the Crossbowmen's Guild, the mayor of Amsterdam is seen shaking hands with his lieutenant as a sign of peace and close friendship. This is a rare example from this period, and it is clear that the handshake was still reserved for special occasions. One such occasion was the wedding ceremony: a number of 17th-century marriage portraits show the newlyweds performing a handshake, a sign of greeting in their new status as husband and wife.

In the following century the situation seems to have been much the same, with the handshake reserved for important occasions. An early 20th-century painting by Jennie Augusta Brownscombe [9] depicts George Washington greeting the Marquis de Lafayette with a handshake at his plantation home, Mount Vernon, in 1784. The rich young Frenchman commanded American troops in the American Revolutionary War and helped Washington and the Continental Army to overcome British rule. The painting portrays the handshake at the moment of the comrades' emotional reunion following the war.

It was not until the 19th century that the handshake evolved into an everyday greeting in the West. Victorian etiquette books were full of instructions to guide the emerging middle classes on key aspects of conduct, including the best way to shake hands. This might explain why some young people today find the gesture too traditional and have replaced it with the high-five and the fist-bump. It has to be said, however, that the fist-bump is more hygienic than the palm-to-palm contact of the traditional handshake, and is favoured by some public figures who are required to meet and greet large numbers of people.

Recent scientific research at the Weizmann Institute in Israel has shown that an important side-effect of everyday handshaking is that the gesture acts as a means of transferring social chemical signals between two parties. Following a handshake, whenever the hand of one of the participants comes near to the face, the nose picks up scent information about the other person. This occurs unconsciously, but gives the participant a better understanding of the person they have just met. The Maori custom of nose-pressing or nose-touching, known as the *hongi*, is a localized greeting ceremony that also involves chemical exchanges. It is designed to create a moment of mutual inhalation – described as 'sharing the breath of life' – with the other person.

A final word about the handshake. It is an action that consists of two elements: the clasping of palms, and an up-and-down movement of the joined hands. It has been suggested, however, that the second element was not a prominent feature in ancient times. There may have been only slight movement of the joined hands – just enough to emphasize the strength of the emotion involved. It is thought that a vigorous up-and-down shaking of the clasped hand was introduced at some later date as a deliberate attempt to dislodge any weapons that might be concealed in the sleeve of the other person. It is an attractive idea, and may even be true, although the evidence for it seems rather slender.

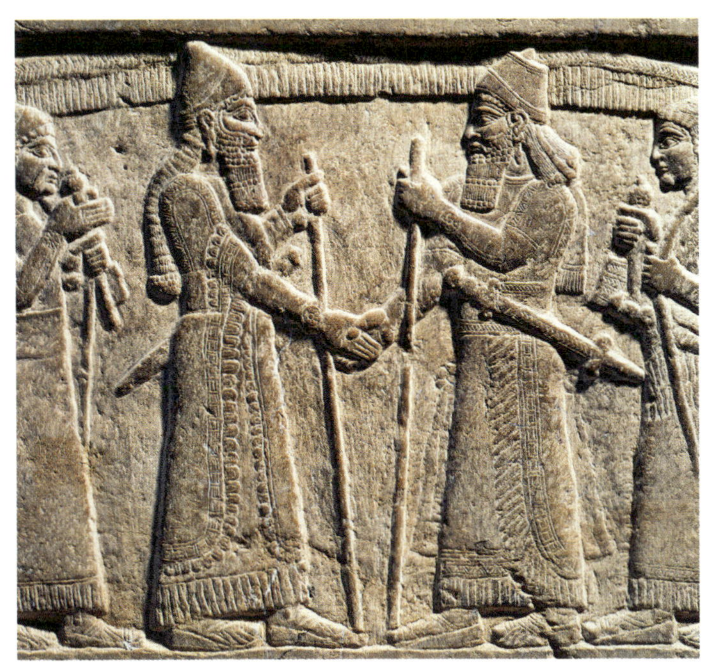

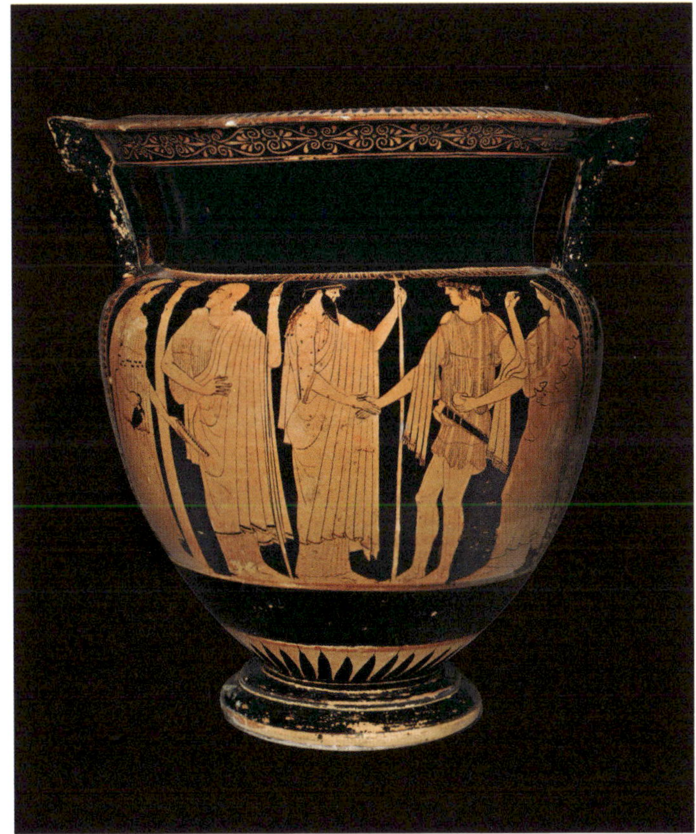

6. above **Relief on throne pedestal, showing King Shalmaneser III of Assyria greeting King Marduk-zakir-šumi I of Babylon, 9th century BC**

7. right **Attic red-figure vase, depicting Theseus being received by Poseidon, 470 BC**

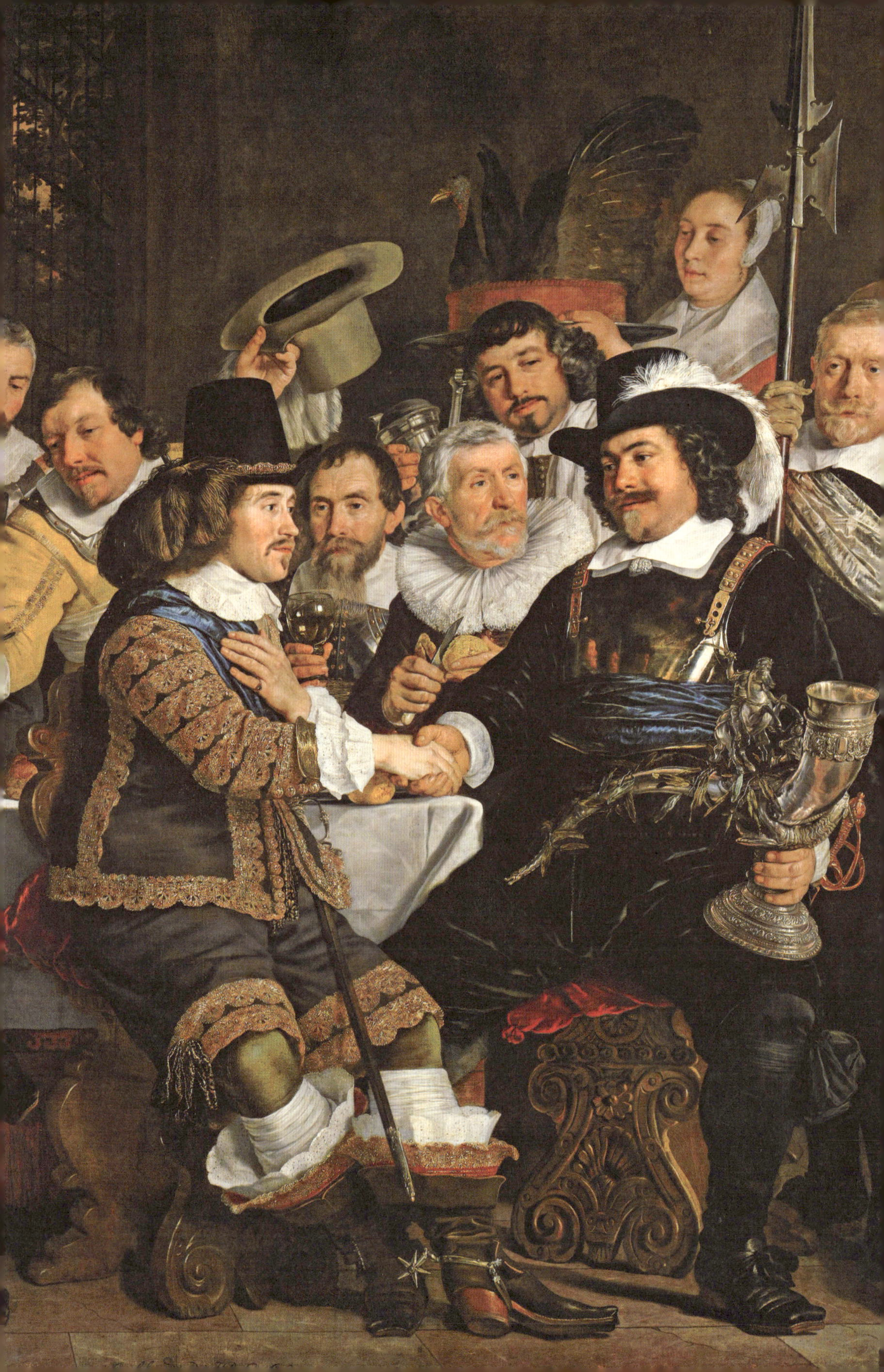

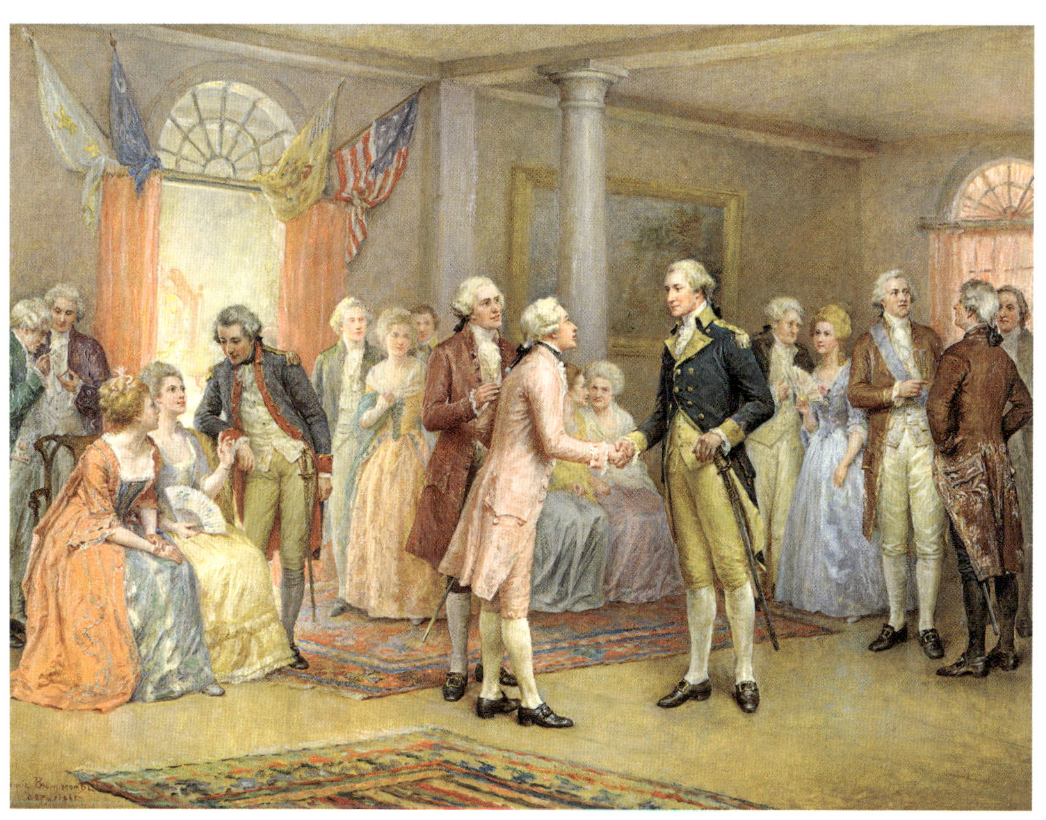

8. opposite **Bartholomeus van der Helst,**
Banquet at the Crossbowmen's Guild
in Celebration of the Treaty of Münster
(detail), 1648, oil on canvas

9. above **Jennie Augusta Brownscombe,**
Washington Greeting Lafayette at Mount
Vernon, early 20th century, oil on canvas

Greetings / The Handshake

The Embrace

The primary form of greeting between relatives, lovers or very close friends who have been separated for a while is the full embrace. This gesture has its origins in childhood when a parent holds their small child lovingly or protectively. As adults we recreate this 'clinging together' action to express our strongest feelings of attachment when meeting someone. Compared with other forms of greeting, the embrace is poorly represented in the visual arts. There is a simple reason for this. When two people hug each other, they tend to present a rather shapeless lump that lacks visual appeal. As a result, when an embrace has been made the subject of a painting, it is usually depicted in its incipient phase, as the two people reach out towards one another before making full contact.

An early religious scene demonstrates this very clearly. It shows the parents of the Virgin Mary, Joachim and Anne, meeting at the Golden Gate of Jerusalem. An angel had told each of them, separately, that their prayers for the gift of a child had been answered, and that this infant would be very special. The angel instructed them to meet at the Golden Gate of Jerusalem, and when they arrived, they greeted each other with an emotional embrace, celebrating their new-found joy. This scene became a popular subject for early artists, including Giotto, who showed the embrace itself (1305) [13], and Filippino Lippi, who portrayed the couple in a semi-embrace with their heads touching (1497) [12].

This encounter between the parents of the Virgin Mary was by no means the only depiction of a greeting embrace by early artists. In 1452, the Florentine Benozzo Gozzoli showed an embrace between St Dominic and St Francis [14]. According to legend, when St Francis was praying in a church in Rome in 1215, a man came up to him and embraced him, telling him that they would work together to convert sinners. St Francis recognized him as a man he had seen in a vision the previous night; the other man, St Dominic, had had a similar vision. The artist depicts the pair in a rather stiff embrace, but with the tips of their noses touching – a detail that would appeal to any Maori.

A Cretan icon of around the same date [11] shows an emotional encounter between the apostles Peter and Paul. They are engaged in a full embrace, but instead of being nose to nose, they are illustrated cheek to cheek. The intimacy of this posture is such that some critics have suggested, rather rashly, that they may have been lovers. The reality is that the icon was a symbolic work in favour of the union of the Western and the Eastern Church, with Peter symbolizing the former and Paul the latter.

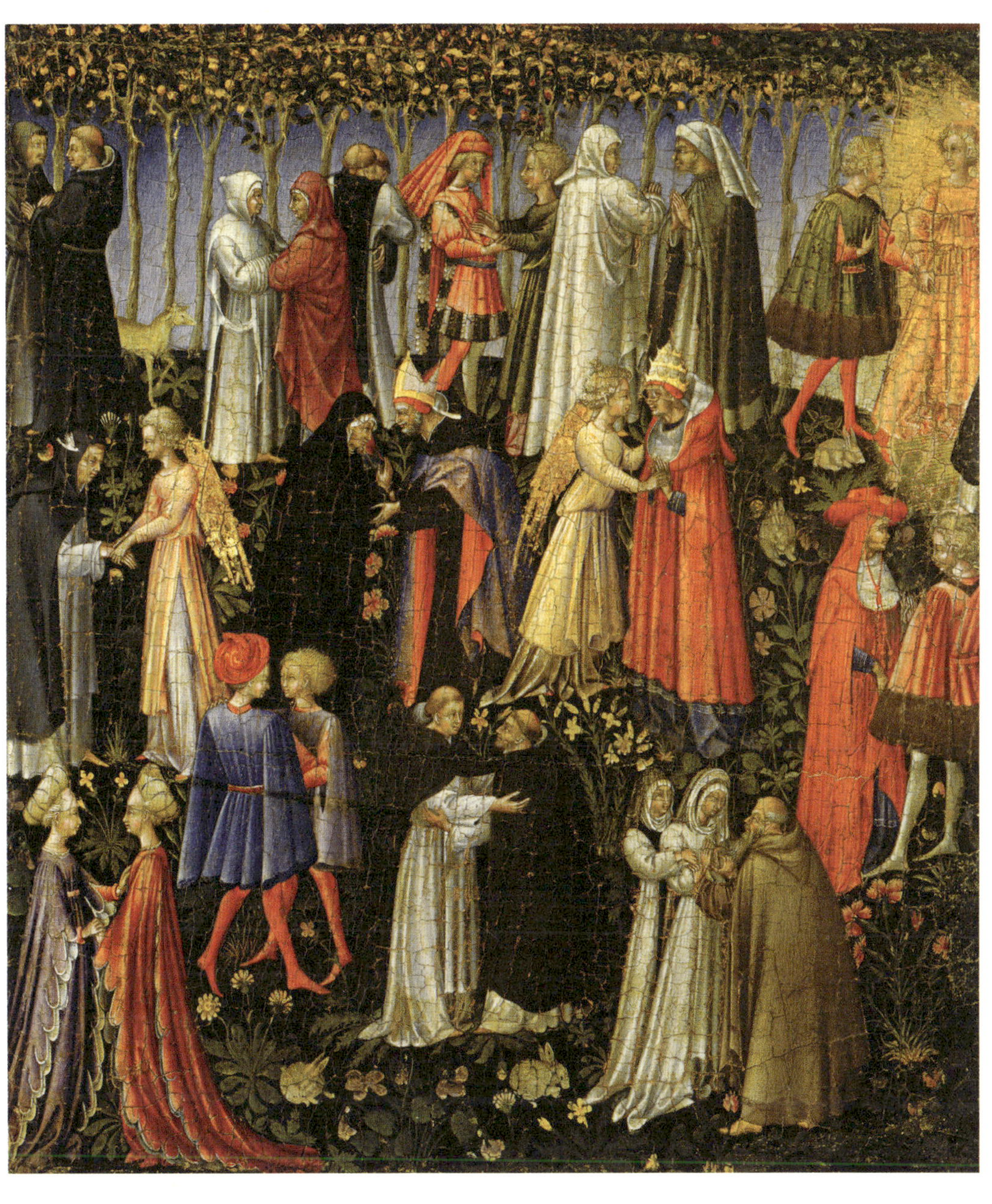

10. **Giovanni di Paolo,** *Paradise*, **1445, tempera and gold on canvas, transferred from wood**

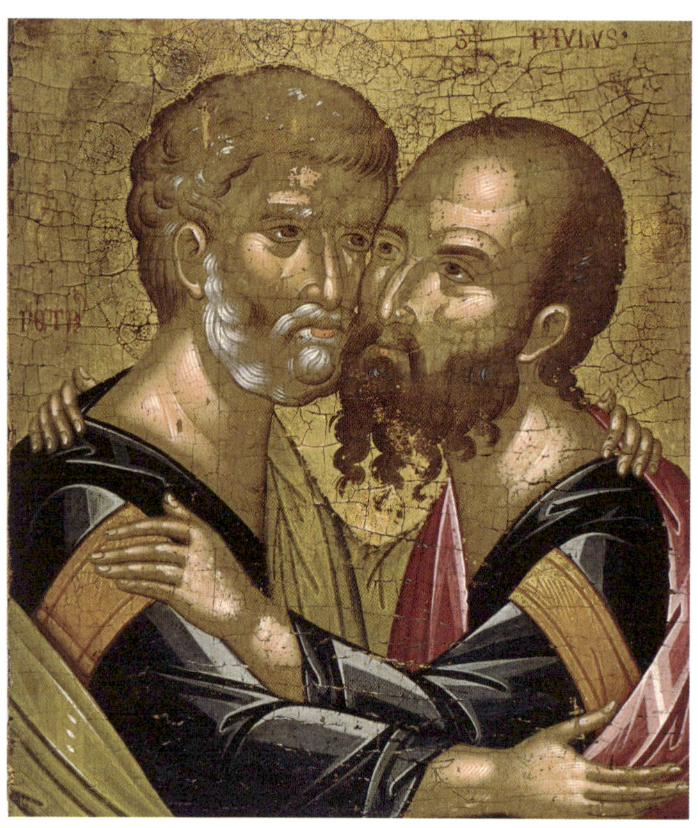

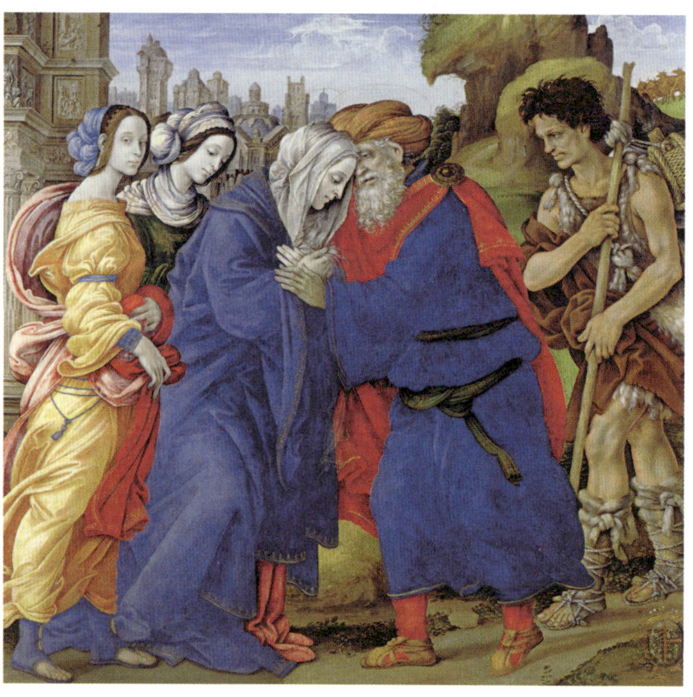

11. above **Angelos Akotantos, icon of *The Embrace of the Apostles Peter and Paul*, 15th century, oil on canvas on panel**

12. left **Filippino Lippi, *Meeting of Joachim and Anne outside the Golden Gate of Jerusalem*, 1497, tempera on panel**

13. opposite, above **Giotto, *Joachim and Anne Meeting at the Golden Gate*, 1305, fresco, Cappella degli Scrovegni, Padua, Italy**

14. opposite, below **Benozzo Gozzoli, *Meeting of St Francis and St Dominic*, 1452, fresco, Church of San Francesco, Montefalco, Italy**

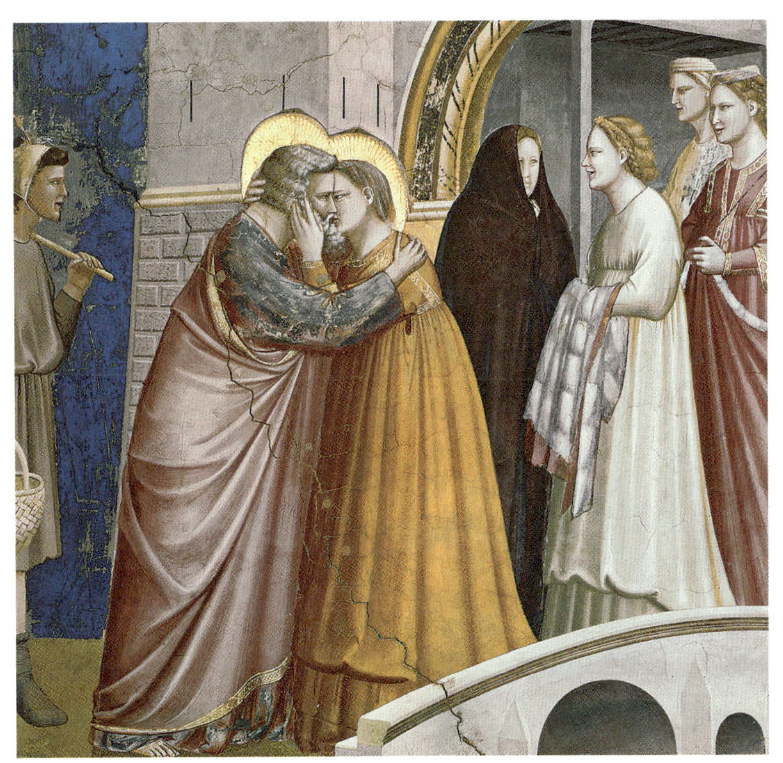

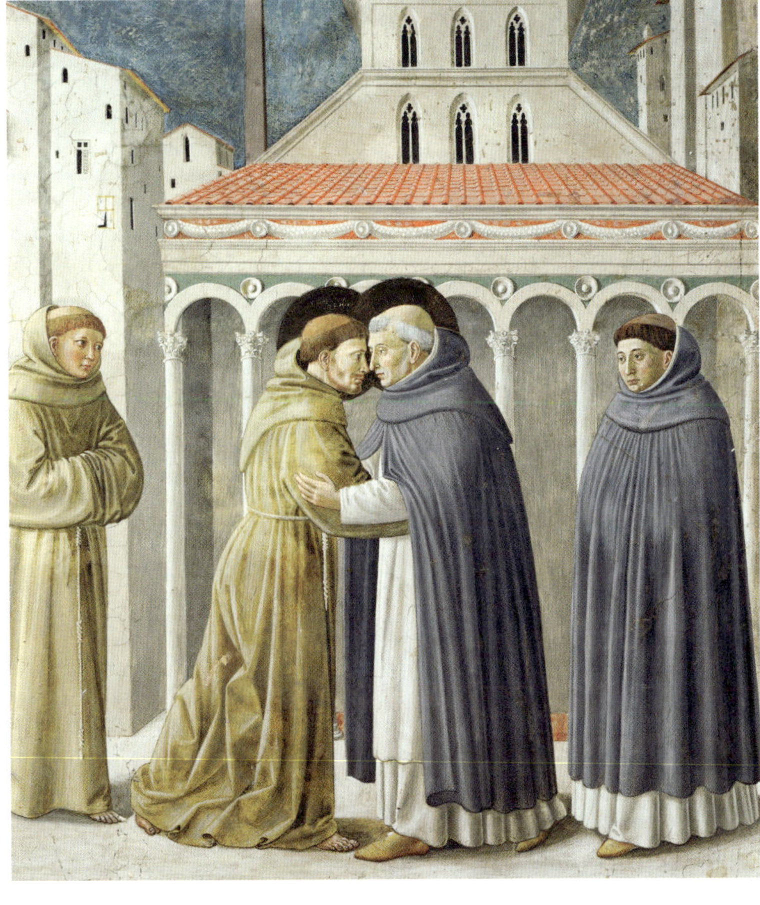

The Bow and the Curtsey

The hail, the handshake and the embrace are typical greetings among those of equal status, but when the encounter is between a superior and an inferior, the body language generally changes. Here, the key element is the lowering of the inferior's body. There are four characteristic displays: the bow, the curtsey, kneeling and, in extreme cases, various forms of prostration. In this respect, these are primeval actions that we share with many other animal species, where a submissive or subordinate animal will lower itself in front of a dominant individual to signal non-aggression and avoid being attacked.

In Western cultures, the bow is understood as a predominantly male action, in which the individual bends the head or the upper part of the body as a greeting or sign of respect. The female equivalent, the curtsey, is essentially a half-kneel – a brief bending of the knees, with one foot taken back a short distance. If the descending movement were continued, the individual would end up kneeling, but she stops halfway, pauses for only a second and then straightens the legs again. Historically, the distinction between these two actions has not been clear-cut. In earlier centuries, there was no difference between what today we call the bow and the curtsey; in medieval times, for example, a man would have bowed by bending only his knees and keeping his body straight [15]. Indeed, before Shakespeare's day, the male action was called a curtsey, not a bow. Gradually, the bending of the head and trunk was added to the bending of the legs and the genders separated, with men bowing and women curtseying. It is this history of bowing that makes the depiction of the bending of the upper body so rare in early works of art.

In many Southeast Asian countries, and also Japan, bowing is the typical form of greeting for both sexes. In a country where social touching is avoided, the bow is the perfect action for a display of respect when encountering another person in public or even in private. In general, the degree to which the upper body bends forwards indicates the level of respect: someone of very high status is greeted with a deep bow, while a less exalted individual is given only a slight dip of the head. A woodblock print of about 1767–68 by the Japanese artist Suzuki Harunobu [16], in which pilgrims bow to the famous courtesan Chozan of the Chojiya, shows this distinction to great effect: the bald man in the foreground amplifies his bow by falling to his knees. Extreme bowing of this kind was not uncommon in earlier centuries, and it sometimes went even further. The bow given to high officials in Japan could involve not only the bending forward of the upper body and lowering of the head, but also the extreme bending of the legs to lower the body into a crouching position that created the impression of semi-prostration.

In present-day Britain, the bow and the curtsey are observed usually only in very formal contexts, such as meeting royalty [18]. The ritual of curtseying in particular was formalized during the Victorian era. There were four annual events at which ambitious social climbers would compete with one another for the honour of being presented to the queen. The successful débutante went through the following procedure, as described by the novelist and historian Evangeline Holland: 'Her name was announced as she curtsied before the Queen, so low as to almost kneel, and while doing such, she kissed the royal hand extended to her, underneath which she placed her own ungloved right hand... After passing Her Majesty, the débutante curtsied to any of the Princesses near her and retired backwards in what may be called a succession of curtsies until she reached the threshold of the doorway. The official in attendance replaced her train upon her arm and the presentation was complete.' Etiquette experts at the time went into even more detail – enough to scare the life out of any untutored, nouveau-riche young woman with social aspirations!

The other context in which the bow and the curtsey can be seen today is when a stage performer is acknowledging the audience's applause at the end of a performance. Although it has become common practice for actresses to bow to their audience rather than curtsey, the full curtsey has managed to survive in certain traditional performing arts, such as the ballet or the opera. It is interesting that, in the ballet in particular – an art form so specifically concerned with the quality of body movements – the curtsey has been preserved. The French Impressionist Edgar Degas caught this moment in several of his paintings, in which the leading ballerina is seen curtseying to her audience having received the traditional bouquet of flowers [19]. Sometimes he portrays the curtsey without the bow, but in other works he shows the two combined.

In other artworks the curtsey is sometimes hard to discern beneath the subject's clothing, and the quick dip of the body is almost impossible to distinguish. A portrait of a little girl by the French artist William-Adolphe Bouguereau, titled *The Curtsey* (1898) [21], is interesting because it shows the moment before the curtsey is made. Historically, the first act performed, when a curtsey was about to be given, was to gently lift the skirt a little on either side, in preparation for the bending of the legs. This small girl is holding her skirt as if to curtsey, but it is clear from the position of her feet that she has not yet started to make the leg movement itself. Her head is tilted slightly to one side, suggesting the start of a bowing movement – a remnant of the time when the curtsey and the body-bow were part of a single gesture.

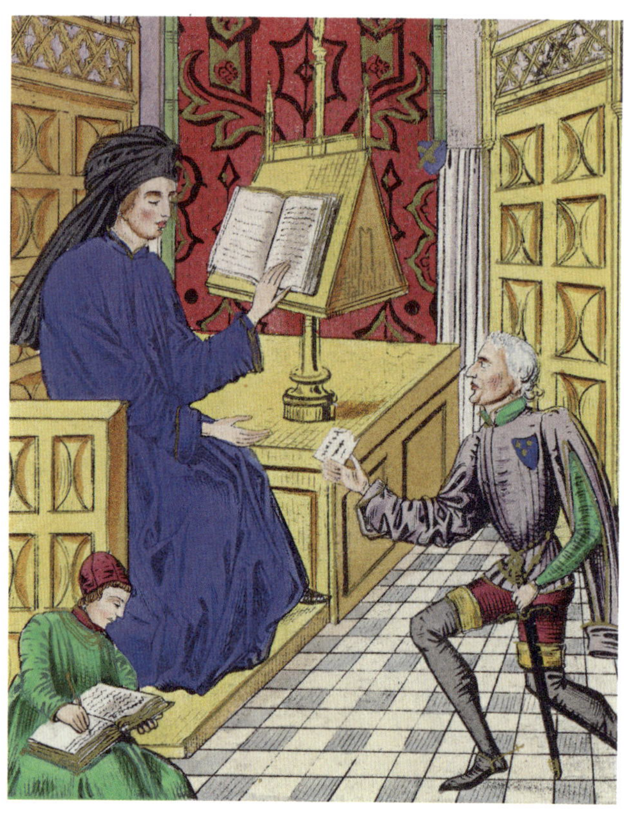

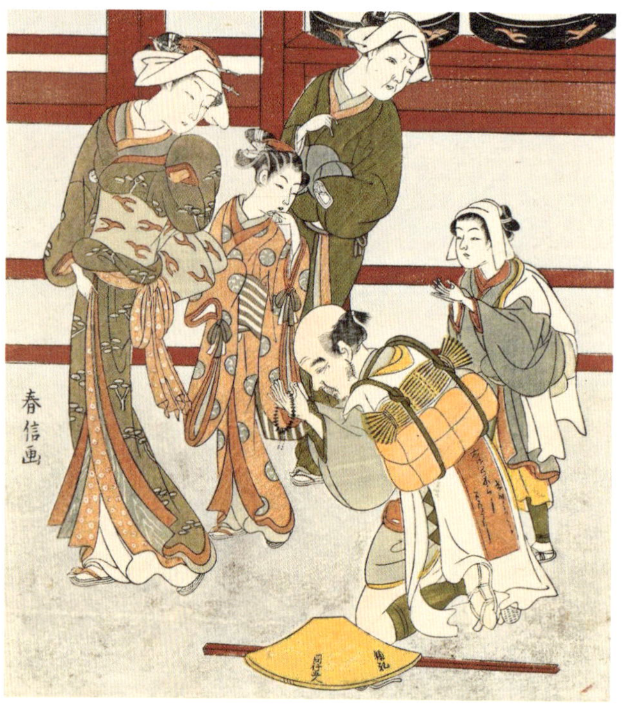

15. above **Detail from a 19th-century edition of Jean Froissart's** *Chronicles* **(written in the 14th century), showing Froissart being greeted by a messenger**

16. left **Suzuki Harunobu,** *Pilgrims Bowing to Courtesan Chozan of the Chojiya* **(detail), c. 1767–68, woodblock print**

17. opposite, above **Henry Gillard Glindoni,** *Fan Flirtation,* **1908, oil on canvas**

18. opposite, below **Unknown artist, a débutante performs a curtsey to King George V in 1914**

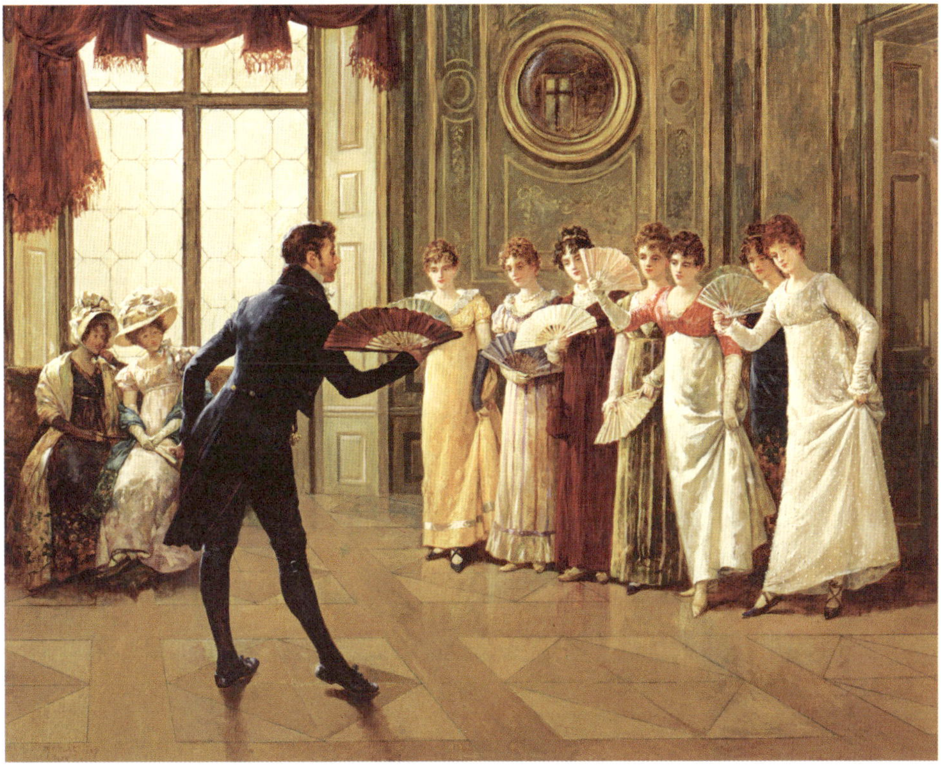

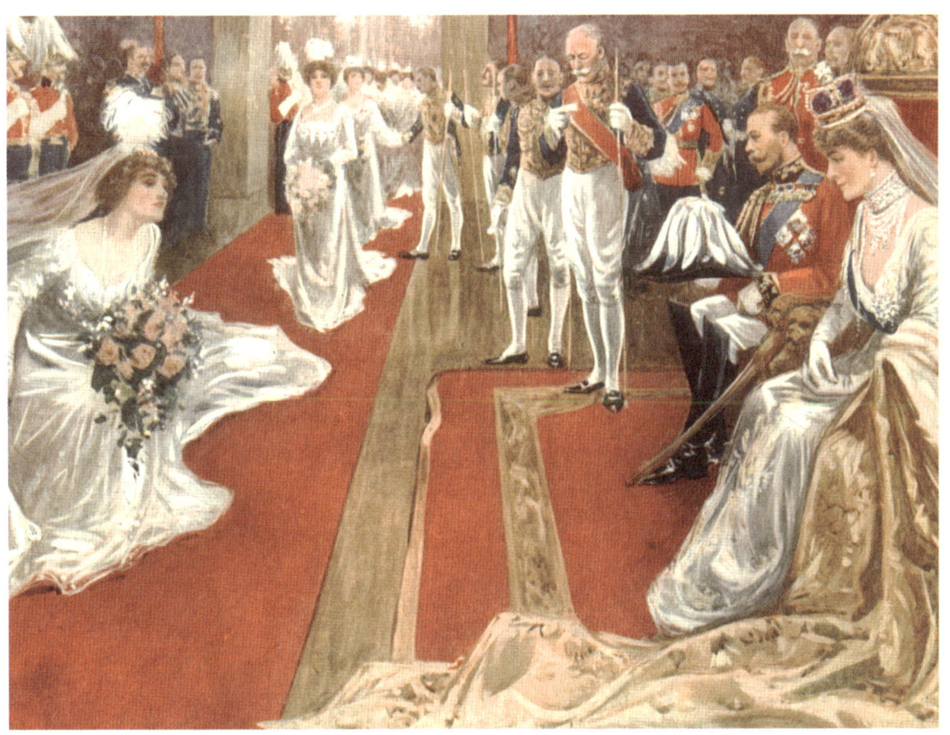

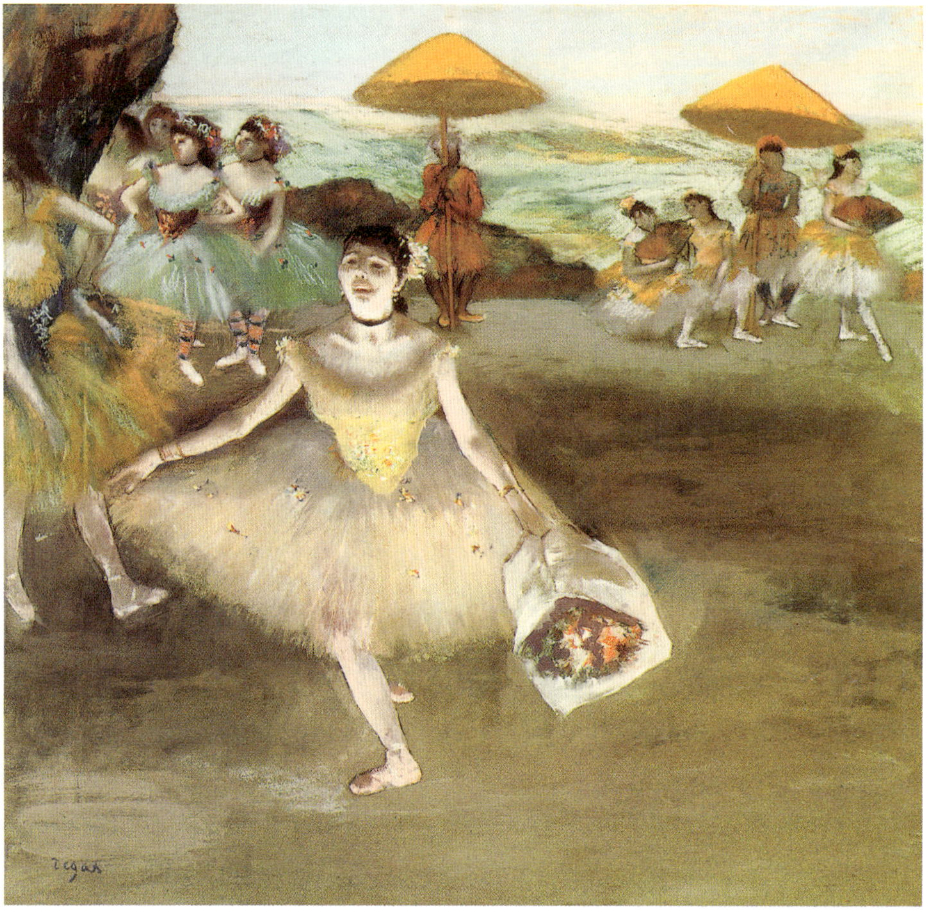

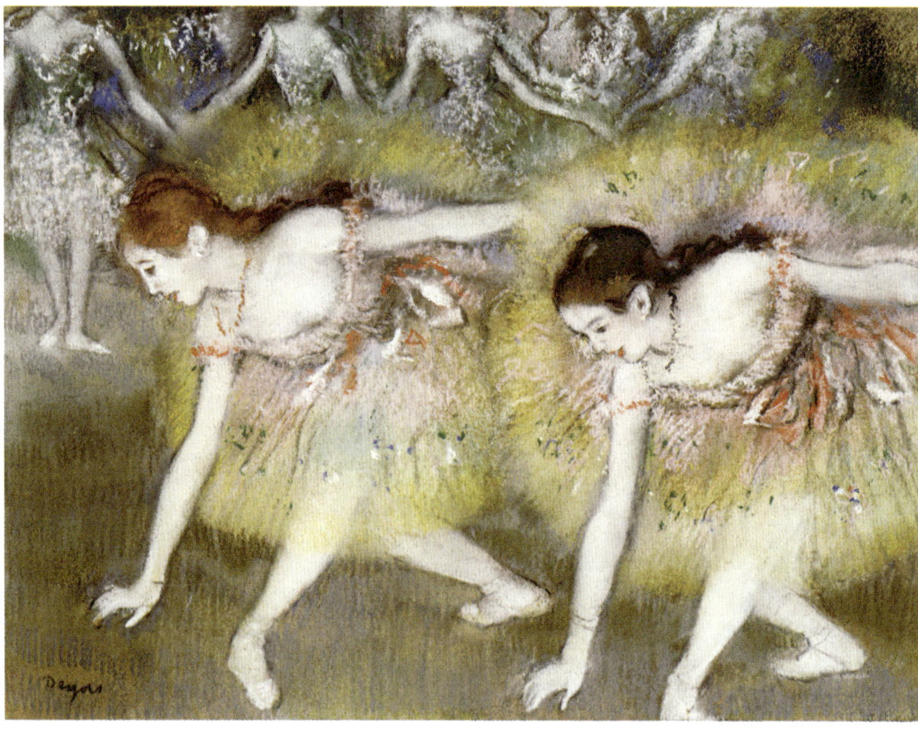

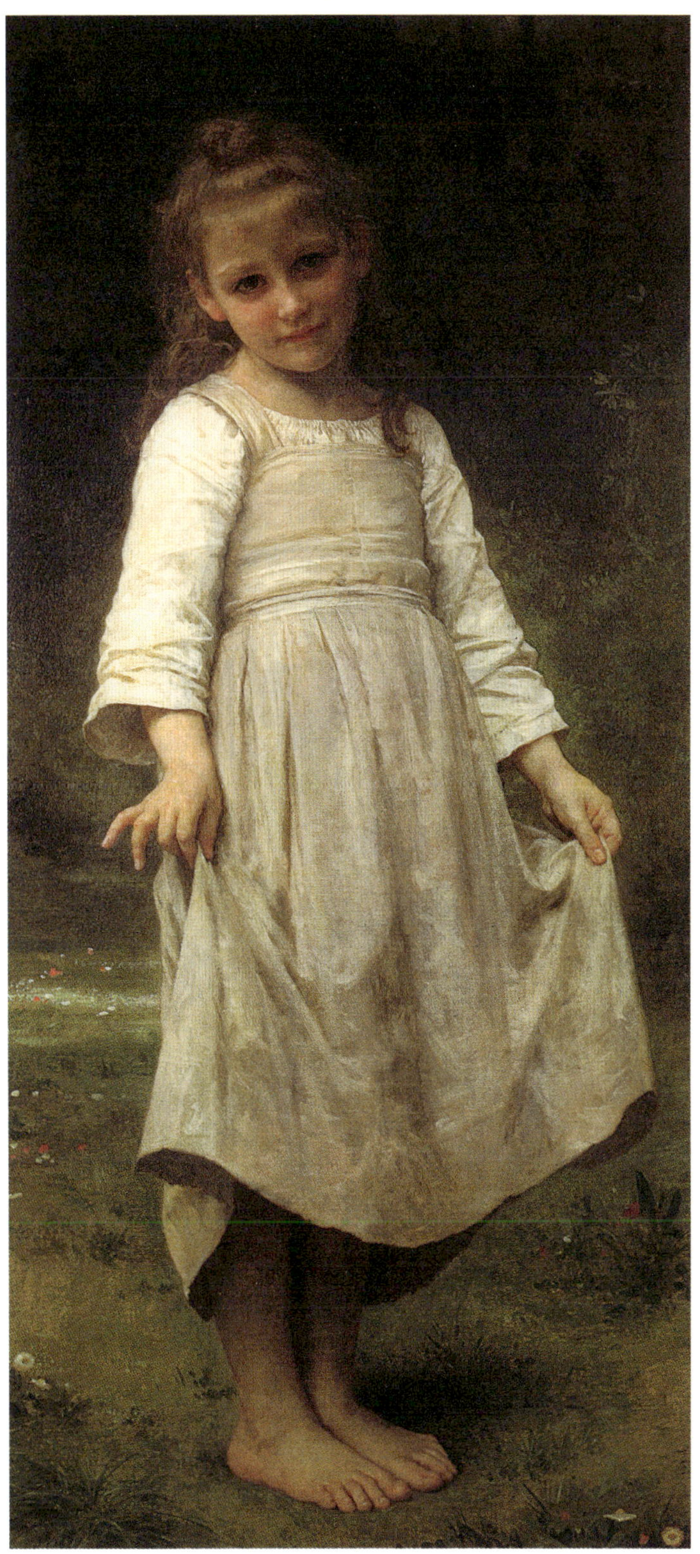

19. opposite, above **Edgar Degas,
Dancer with Bouquet, Curtseying,
1877, pastel on paper**

20. opposite, below **Edgar Degas,
Dancers Bending Down, 1885,
pastel on paper**

21. right **William-Adolphe
Bouguereau,** *The Curtsey* (detail),
1898, oil on canvas

Kneeling

It was mentioned earlier that the curtsey is a kind of half-kneel, with the legs bending as if to place the right knee on the ground, but with the action remaining incomplete. The one-knee kneel sees that action completed, and is therefore a more extreme display of subordination.

In the West, there are generally just two situations in which the one-knee kneel occurs today. The first is when a man goes down on one knee to ask a woman to marry him. This is the traditional posture for a proposal, but it is becoming increasingly rare. The second is the one-knee kneeling position that must be adopted when British royalty is bestowing a knighthood. The recipient is aided by the use of a royal kneeling-cushion, complete with a handle to grasp as the right knee is lowered onto it. Even so, to avoid any embarrassing incidents on the day, Buckingham Palace always sends out a note with the question, 'Can you kneel?' In a high-profile exception to this general rule, in recent years the one-knee kneel has been used by American football players during the national anthem as a form of protest against racial inequality and injustice.

An early example of the one-knee kneel can be seen in a painting by the 15th-century German Renaissance artist Konrad Witz. In *Abishai Kneeling before David* (*c.* 1435) [25], the famous warrior Abishai kneels – in full armour, and no doubt with some difficulty – on his left knee to greet his uncle, the biblical King David, and offers him an elaborate bottle containing water for him to drink. It is recorded in the Bible that when David was in his stronghold he developed a craving, saying: 'Oh that someone would give me water to drink from the well of Bethlehem, which is by the gate!' So three mighty warriors, including Abishai, broke through the camp of the Philistines, who were garrisoned in Bethlehem, and drew water from the well. When Abishai brought this water to David, the king was so shocked that the warriors had risked their lives for him that he refused to drink it and instead poured it on the ground as an offering to the Lord.

A painting after Hendrick Danckerts [26] shows a delightful scene in which John Rose, the royal gardener, kneels on his right knee to present a pineapple – a great rarity in the 17th century – to King Charles II. In England at the time, the pineapple had become a symbol of wealth and luxury, with a single fruit costing the equivalent of £5,000 in today's money. Indeed, pineapples were so valuable that you could even rent one to show off on your dining table. Christopher Columbus had 'discovered' the pineapple in the Caribbean, but it would generally become rotten when transported to Europe by ship. It was not until the 17th century that European gardeners successfully managed to cultivate the fruit. Having at last grown one in the royal gardens, John Rose makes a formal presentation to the king, kneeling ceremonially to mark the occasion.

In the 18th century, polite society required a young gentleman to kneel on his right knee when asking for his loved one's hand in marriage. Henry Singleton's painting *The Proposal* [27] captures this moment – when the male suitor makes himself dramatically subordinate to the female. If she «had accepted him, however, she would soon have found herself socially and domestically in a far less dominant position. In this context, the gesture of kneeling was something of a sham, little more than a formality. Nowadays, of course, the act of going down on one knee, though still a formality, may prove to be the herald of a genuine marital relationship.

Although in modern times the one-knee kneel has become something of a rarity, the eccentric surrealist Salvador Dalí was rather fond of depicting it in his paintings. In one work, the elaborately titled *Dalí, Nude, Entranced in the Contemplation of Five Regular Bodies Metamorphosed in Corpuscles, in Which Suddenly Appears Leonardo's 'Leda', Chromosomatized by the Face of Gala*, painted in 1954, a naked Dalí is shown kneeling on his right knee in front of a strange vision. Bizarrely, his knee is resting on a venomous stingray, an action that would likely have disastrous consequences. Portraying himself in such a subordinate posture looks at first sight like an act of extreme modesty, but Dalí was anything but modest. Rather, what the painting does is to elevate Dalí to the level of a saint experiencing a sacred revelation.

An unusual example of the one-knee kneel appears in the art of ancient Egypt. The vast majority of kneeling figures in Egyptian art are shown on both knees, paying their respects to one of their many gods or to their pharaohs, who were regarded as living gods. A handful of figures, however, are shown kneeling on one knee with their arms in a fixed position – the right arm raised and the left arm pressed against the chest – and their hands clenched into fists [24]. There is nothing submissive about these arm gestures, and they make an odd companion for the downbeat body-lowering of the kneel. The explanation is that in ancient Egypt this particular pose symbolized praise or jubilation. In this, it is curiously reminiscent of the kneeling 'skid' performed by a modern footballer when he has scored an important goal. He slides across the grass on his knees with his arms raised and his fists clenched. His action is a simultaneous demonstration of respect for the massed supporters and a triumphant celebration of his goal.

Short of prostration, kneeling on both knees has always been seen as the most extreme form of subordination in front of a dominant figure. Today, the two-knee kneel is most commonly seen in a religious context, during prayer, in which the dominant figure is the deity. It may also be used in a comic situation, where someone is down on their knees, theatrically begging for forgiveness. On very rare occasions, the full kneel is seen when convicted criminals or hapless victims of extremists are forced to adopt the pose before being executed. Historically, however, kneeling on both knees was much more common, and was seen in many contexts as a sign of deep respect. As a result, it appears frequently in the artworks of past centuries.

When rulers believed they were divine beings, they expected their subjects to kneel before them on both knees. A typical example of this can be seen in a miniature from John Lydgate's *Troy Book* and *Siege of Thebes* [22], of 1475, where Sir William Herbert and his wife, Anne Devereux, perform a full kneel to an enthroned king as his courtiers look on. Later, when royalty accepted that they were merely human, a distinction was made between kneeling on two knees or one: it was two knees for God, and one for other people. An English etiquette book made this clear: 'Be courteous to God, and kneel down on both knees with great devotion. To man thou shall kneel upon the one, the other to thyself thou hold alone... Kneel but on one knee to your sovereign or lord, whoever he be.'

One notorious work depicts the two-knee kneel in a deeply disturbing manner. Created by the Italian conceptual artist Maurizio Cattelan, *Him* (2001) [23] is a life-size wax figure dressed in a 1930s suit. When approached from behind, the work appears to be the figure of a small, innocent schoolboy kneeling devoutly at his prayers. However, as you walk around to the front of the figure, you discover that it has the unmistakable face of Adolf Hitler. The idea of an innocent figure of Hitler greeting the Almighty with a prayer is so unsettling that the artist has said: 'I wanted to destroy it myself. I changed my mind a thousand times, every day. Hitler is pure fear; it's an image of terrible pain. It even hurts to pronounce his name. And yet that name has conquered my memory, it lives in my head, even if it remains taboo.' When the piece was sold at auction in 2016 for more than $17 million, New York journalists, intrigued by the motives of the anonymous buyer, began an unsuccessful investigation to uncover their identity.

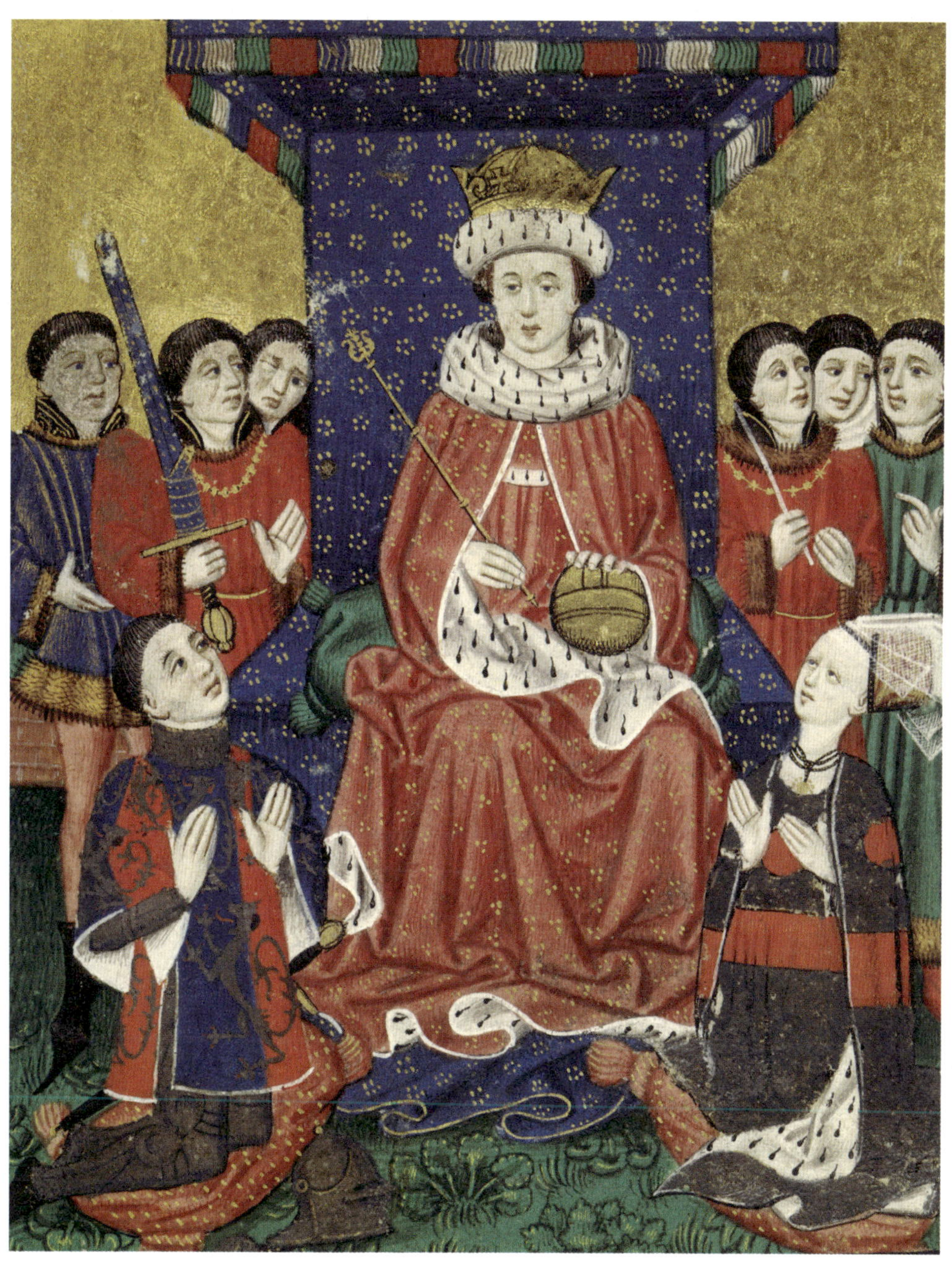

22. **Sir William Herbert and his wife, Anne Devereux, kneel before the king, from John Lydgate's *Troy Book* and *Siege of Thebes*, 1475**

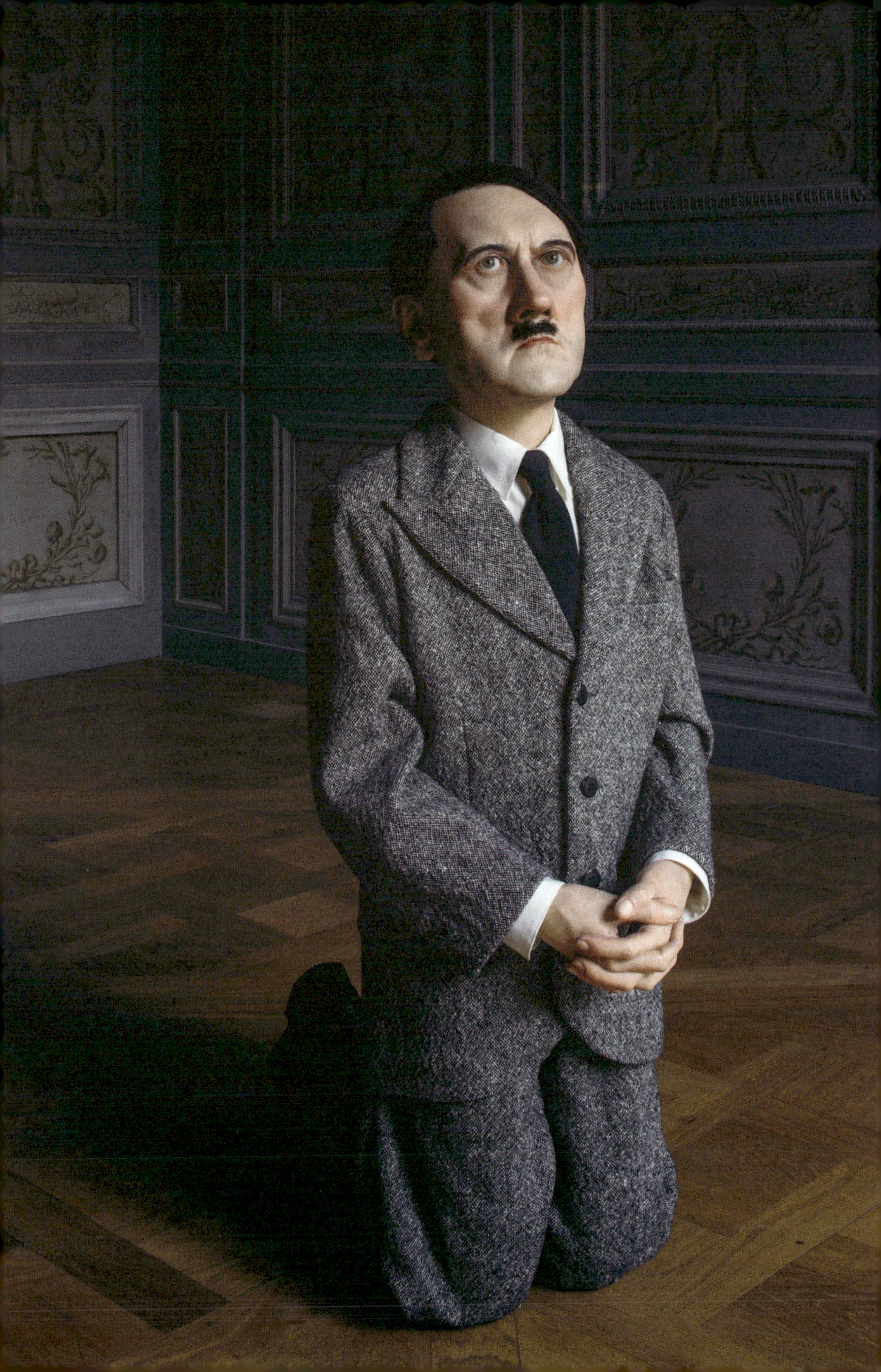

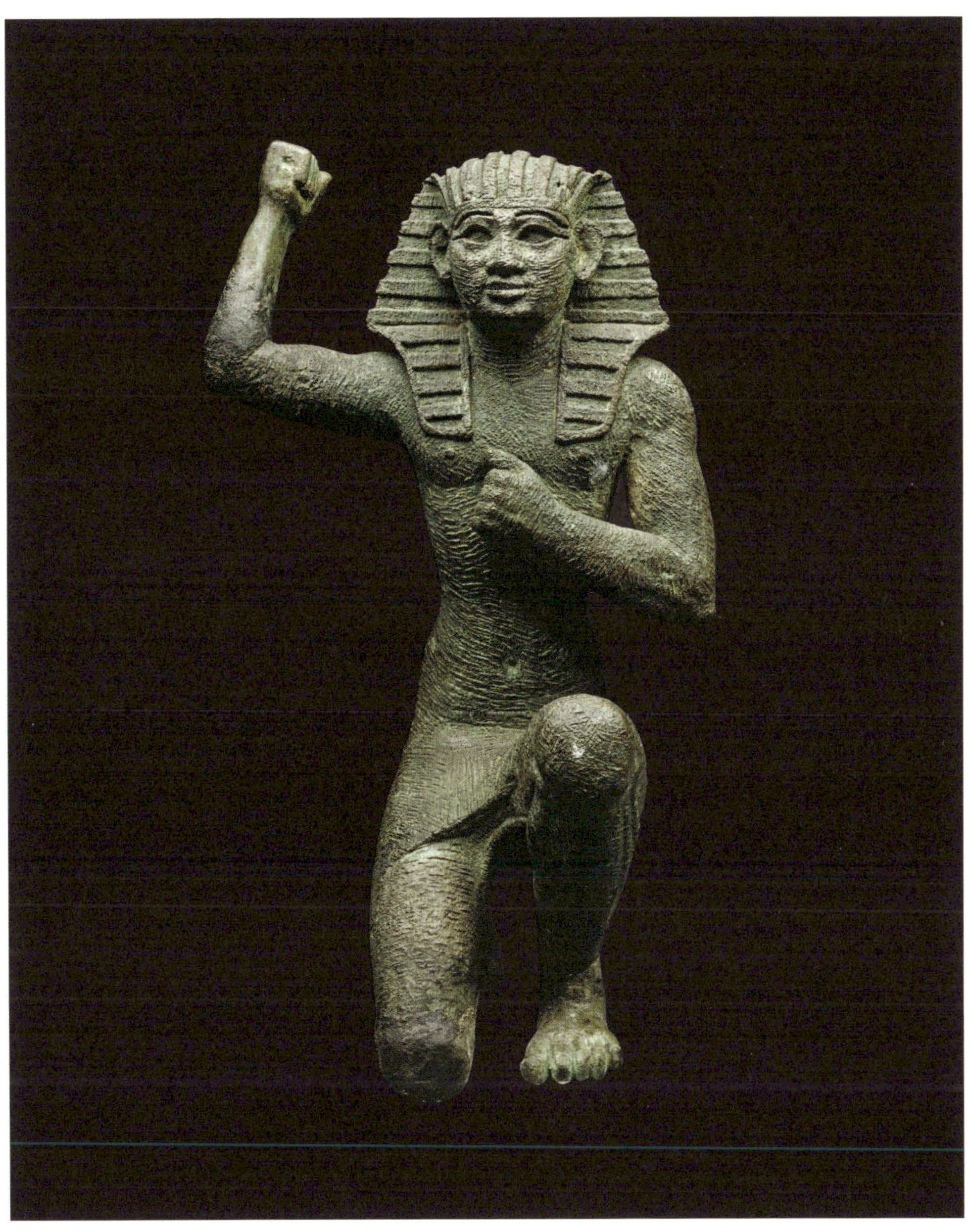

23. opposite **Maurizio Cattelan,**
Him, **2001, wax, human hair,**
suit and polyester resin

24. above **Egyptian bronze of**
a kneeling man, probably a king,
Late Period, *c.* **712–323 BC**

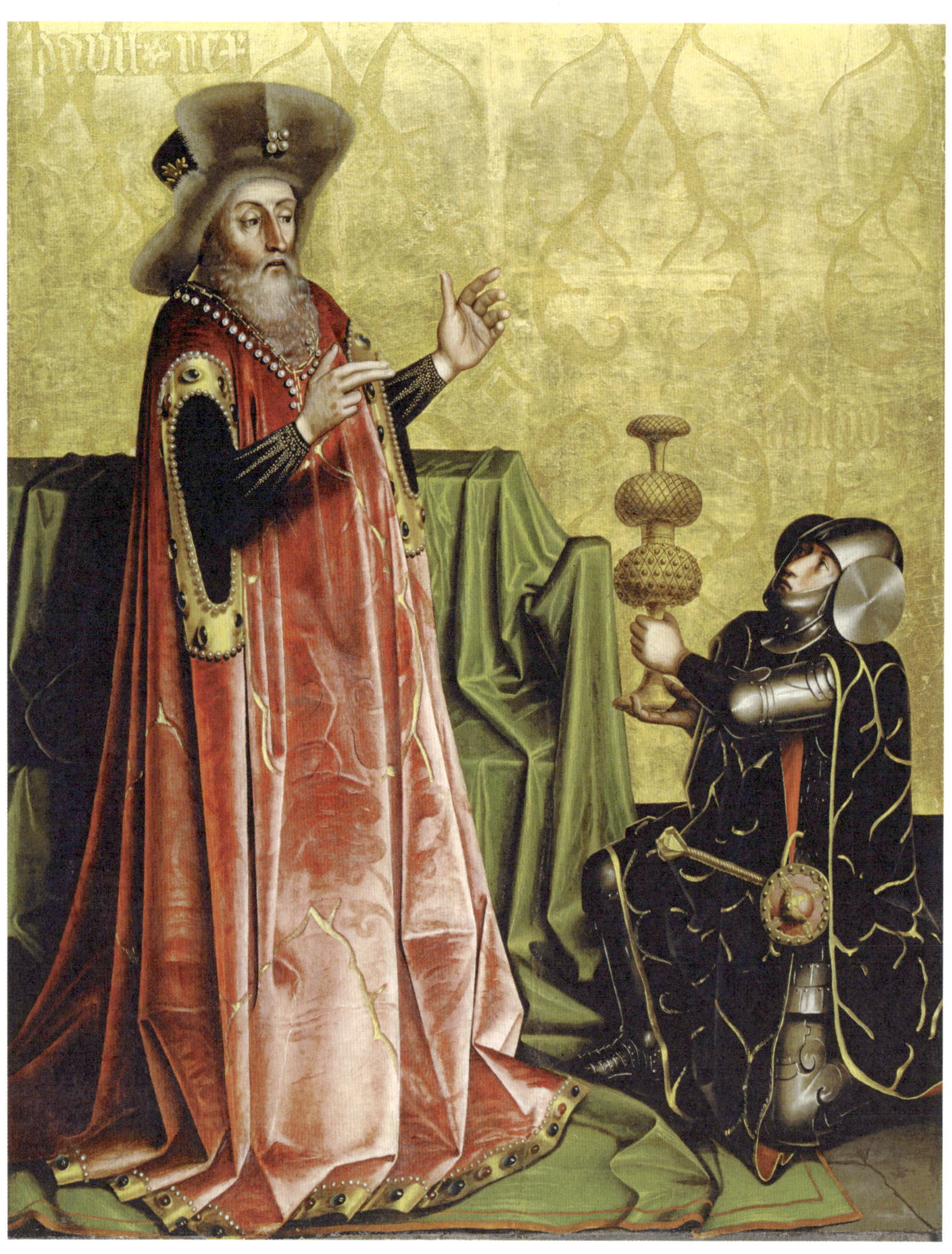

25. **Konrad Witz**, *Abishai Kneeling
before David*, c. 1435,
Mirror of Salvation altarpiece

     Greetings / Kneeling

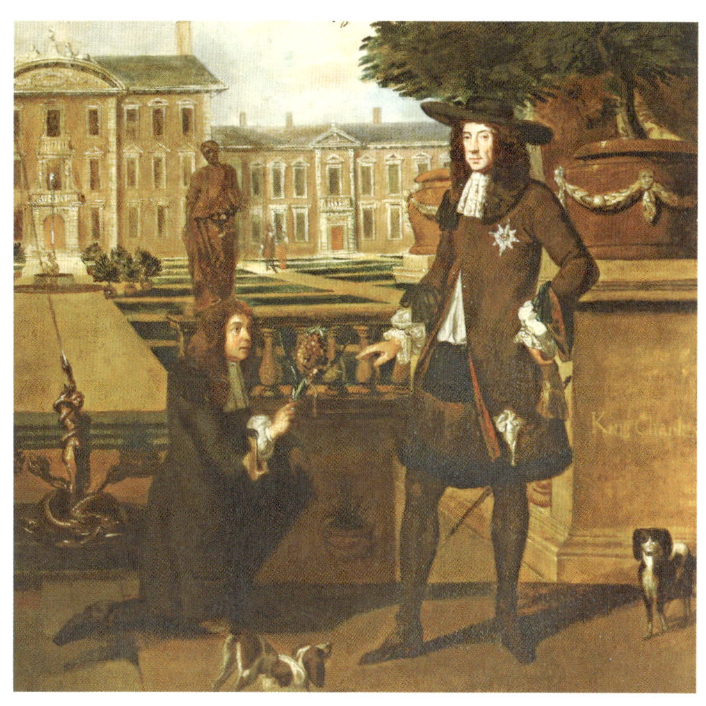

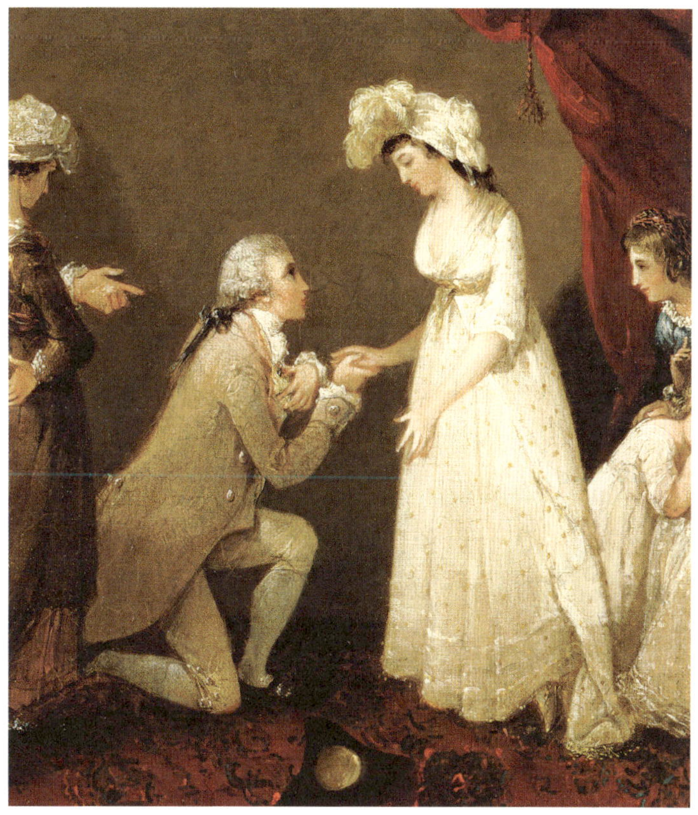

26. above **Thomas Stewart (after Hendrick Danckerts),** *John Rose, the Royal Gardener, Presenting a Pineapple to King Charles II* (detail), 1787, **oil on canvas**

27. right **Henry Singleton,** *The Proposal* (detail), late **18th century, oil on canvas**

Prostration

The most reverential and submissive form of greeting is prostration, in which the body is lowered to the point where the hands are placed on the ground. At its most extreme, the entire body is laid out flat; in a modified form, the body is kneeling, with the hands and sometimes also the forehead pressed to the ground. In the past, prostration was quite common when greeting an all-powerful ruler, but it has become increasingly rare and is today largely confined to religious ceremonies or rituals, or where a deity is being honoured.

One of the earliest examples of prostration before a king can be seen on a black obelisk from 825 BC [28], originally erected in the ancient Assyrian city of Nimrud but now in the British Museum, London. In those days, if you vanquished your rivals you did more than simply erect a monument to commemorate your victory; you adorned it with reliefs depicting your rivals grovelling at your feet. The victorious ruler in this case was the Assyrian king Shalmaneser III. In five separate relief panels, the obelisk shows the five local kings that he had subdued, including Jehu, the king of Israel, prostrating before him and offering tributes of gold, silver and tin.

In *The Soldier of Marathon* (1869) [31], Luc-Olivier Merson depicts the celebrated scene, in 490 BC, when the Greek runner Pheidippides arrived in Athens to announce victory over Persia at the Battle of Marathon. The runner's reverent prostration before the leaders of Greek society is mixed with exhaustion after his 26-mile run (indeed, the story goes that he died shortly after delivering his news). Modern runners who take up the challenge may be surprised to learn, however, that there never was such a run in 490 BC. It is a world-famous event that never happened. In reality, Pheidippides ran a much longer distance, from Athens to Sparta, before the battle, to seek the Spartans' help.

Most depictions of prostration do not centre on important human figures, but on the act of submission to a holy being, such as a saint, a god or a goddess. Each of the major religions has its own version of prostration, and most give it a special name. Christian prayers are generally offered in the kneeling position, with both knees on the ground, and full prostration is mostly restricted to special ceremonies, such as ordination or the consecration of virgins. In the 13th century, an illustrated manuscript was produced showing nine ways in which St Dominic positioned himself for prayer. The second way is described as follows: 'Saint Dominic used to pray by throwing himself outstretched upon the ground, lying on his face. He would feel great remorse in his heart and call to mind those words of the Gospel, saying sometimes in a voice loud enough to be heard: *O God, be merciful to me, a sinner.*'

In Islam the act of prostration is called the *Sujūd* or *Sajdah* [29], and – as the common posture of prayer – involves a set, seven-stage sequence, performed five times a day by the devout. Specific instructions are given to Muslims for adopting this posture correctly: 'Go down to a kneeling position by placing both hands on knees, lowering oneself slowly and easily onto knees, then touch the head upon the ground so that the following seven body parts are in contact: forehead, two palms, two knees, toes of both feet.' The posture differs from the Chinese kowtow (see below), in which the hands are positioned further from the head.

In the various forms of Buddhism, prostration is known as *panipāta*, *namas-kara*, *li-pai* or *raihai* [30]. In Theravada Buddhism, detailed instructions are given as to how to adopt the position, here taken from Bhikkhu Khantipalo's *Lay Buddhist Practice* (1974), for example: 'In the kneeling position, one's hands in *añjali* [palms together, fingers flat out and pointed upward] are raised to the forehead and then lowered to the floor so that the whole forearm to the elbow is on the ground, the elbow touching the knee. The hands, palm down, are four to six inches apart with just enough room for the forehead to be brought to the ground between them. Feet are still as for the kneeling position and the knees are about a foot apart.'

In Hinduism, the gesture is known as *Pranama*. This Sanskrit word is derived from *Pra*, meaning 'forward' or 'in front of', and *Anama*, meaning 'bending' or 'stretching'. There are several types of *Pranama*, including *Ashtanga* (touching the ground with knees, belly, chest, hands, elbows, chin, nose and temple); *Shastanga* (touching the ground with toes, knees, hands, chin, nose and temple); *Panchanga* (touching the ground with knees, chest, chin, temple and forehead); and *Dandavat* (bowing the forehead down and touching the ground).

Dandavat is a Sanskrit word that literally means 'to lie on the floor like a stick'. People lie fully prostrate on the ground with their arms stretched out towards the *murti* (idol of a deity). It is a symbol of complete submission that reminds devotees to respect the Divine and cultivate humility. Specific parts of the body should touch the floor: *Jānubhyām* – thighs; *Padabhyām* – feet; *Karābhyām* – hands; *Urasā* – chest; *Shirasā* – head; and *Drushtyā* – eyes.

In imperial China, the act of prostration known as the kowtow [33], or *ketou* – a term that has been absorbed into the English language – was required in the presence of the emperor. There were several degrees of prostration depending on the solemnity of the occasion. For example, at the coronation of a new emperor, it would be necessary to perform the grand kowtow, called the ceremony of the 'three kneelings and nine kowtows'. It involved kneeling from a standing position three times, and performing the kowtow three times with each kneel.

In the late 18th and early 19th centuries, there were major diplomatic disagreements when leaders of British delegations refused to kowtow

in the traditional manner at the Chinese court [32]. Their refusal cost
them dearly in lost commercial enterprises, but they had no intention
of performing what they saw as an act of submission to the Chinese
emperor. The result was growing hostility, war and, ultimately, the
cession of Hong Kong Island to the British. It is fascinating to think
that the teeming modern metropolis of Hong Kong grew out of a
single gesture – or, rather, the lack of one.

In the Shinto religion, the Japanese perform the *dogeza*, which
involves kneeling directly on the ground – in the position known
as *seiza* – and then bowing so low that the head touches the floor.
The *dogeza* has been used not only in a religious context, but also
domestically as a sign of deep respect for and submission to the
elder members of a family, honoured guests, revered samurai and,
of course, the emperor.

In modern times, the most widely practised form of prostration,
by far, is the Muslim *Sujūd* (described above), which is performed
millions of times every day during *salat* (daily prayers). Research
has shown that it may have an added benefit: during the prostration
phase of the *salat*, there are significant rises in the brain's alpha wave
activity, in volunteers' parietal and occipital cortices. Interestingly,
this only occurs at the moment of full prostration when the head
is on the ground, and it makes no difference whether the person
is silent or praying. There is no such increase in alpha wave activity
during the other phases of the praying ritual, which suggests that
it is the physical act of prostration that has the biggest impact. A rise
in alpha wave activity can help to increase relaxation, reduce tension
and focus the mind.

28. Relief on an Assyrian black obelisk,
showing Jehu, King of Israel, prostrating
himself before the Assyrian king
Shalmaneser III, 825 BC

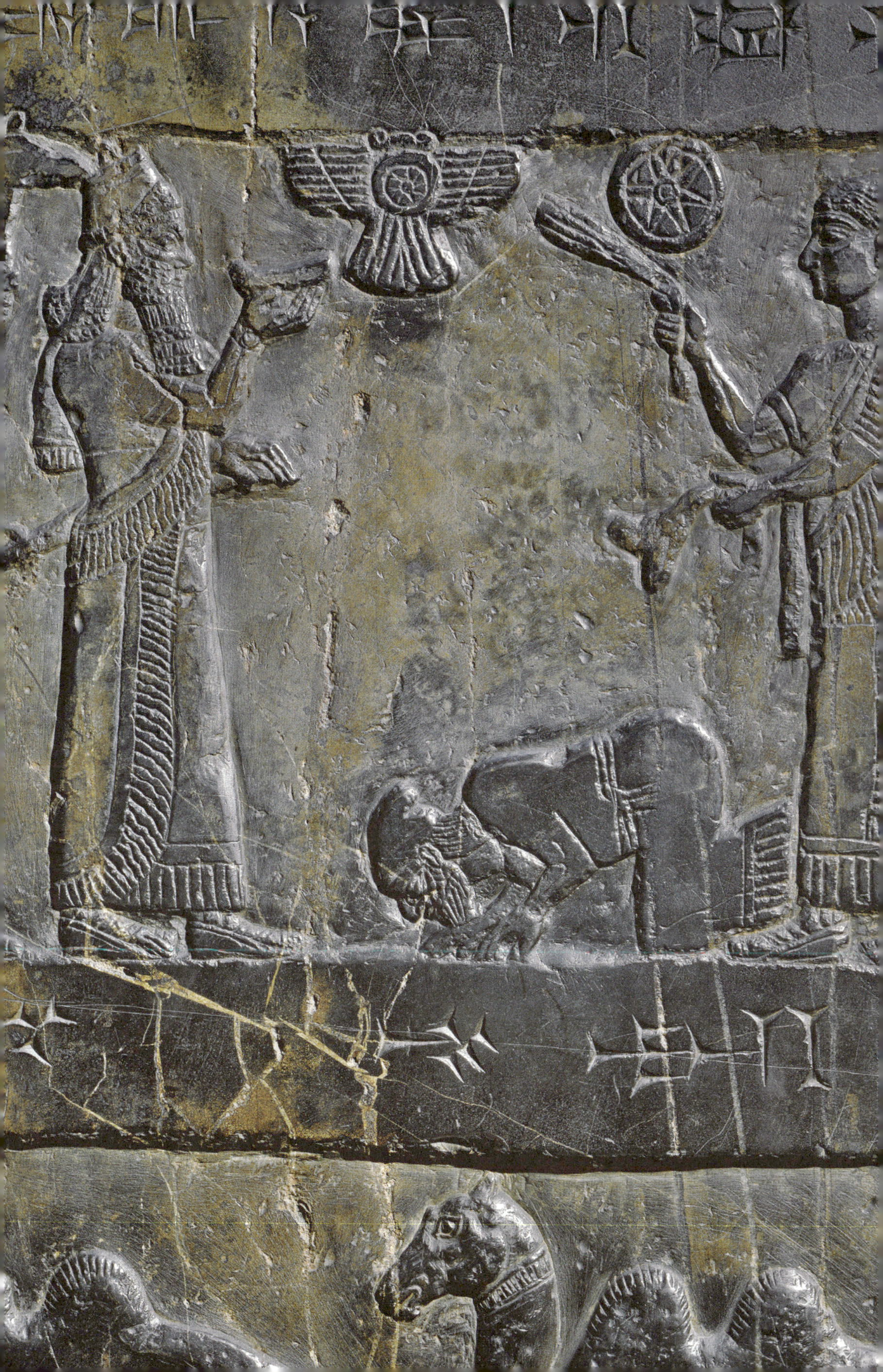

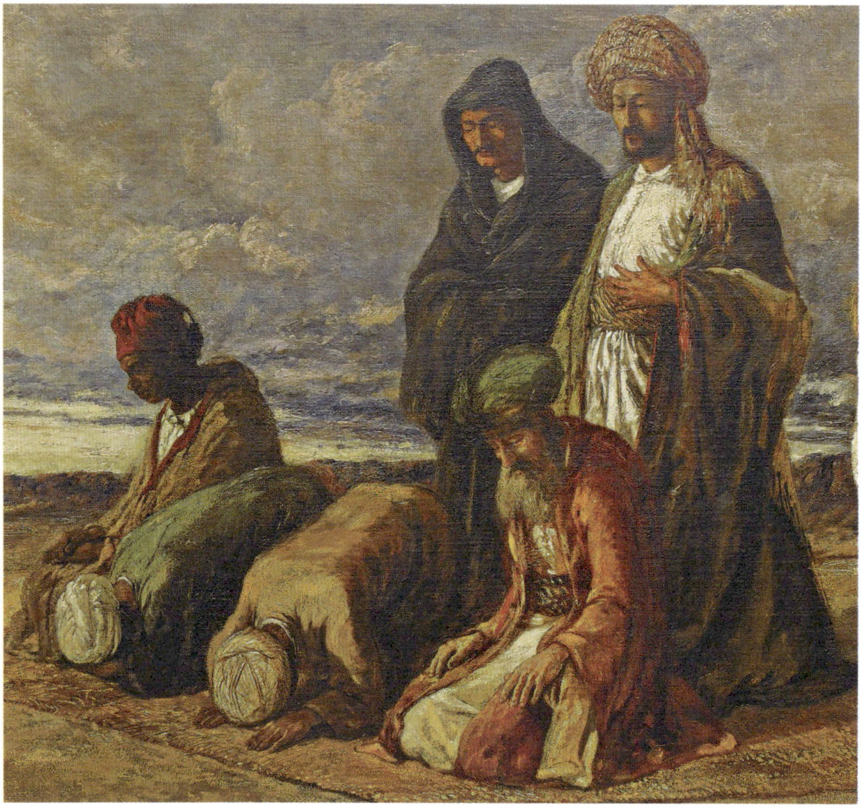

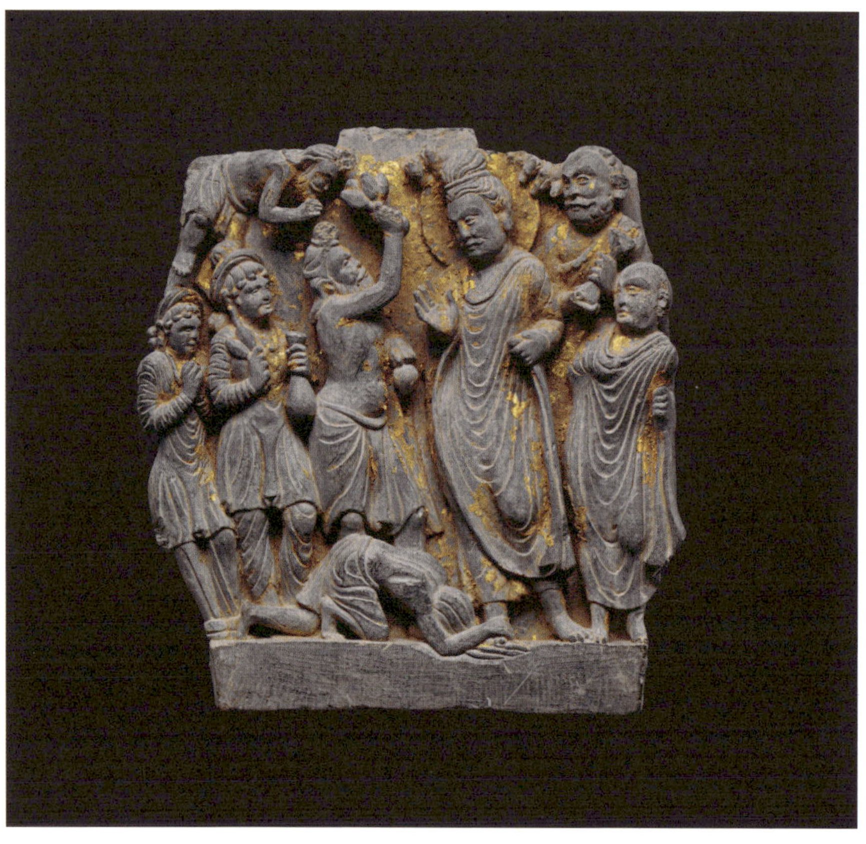

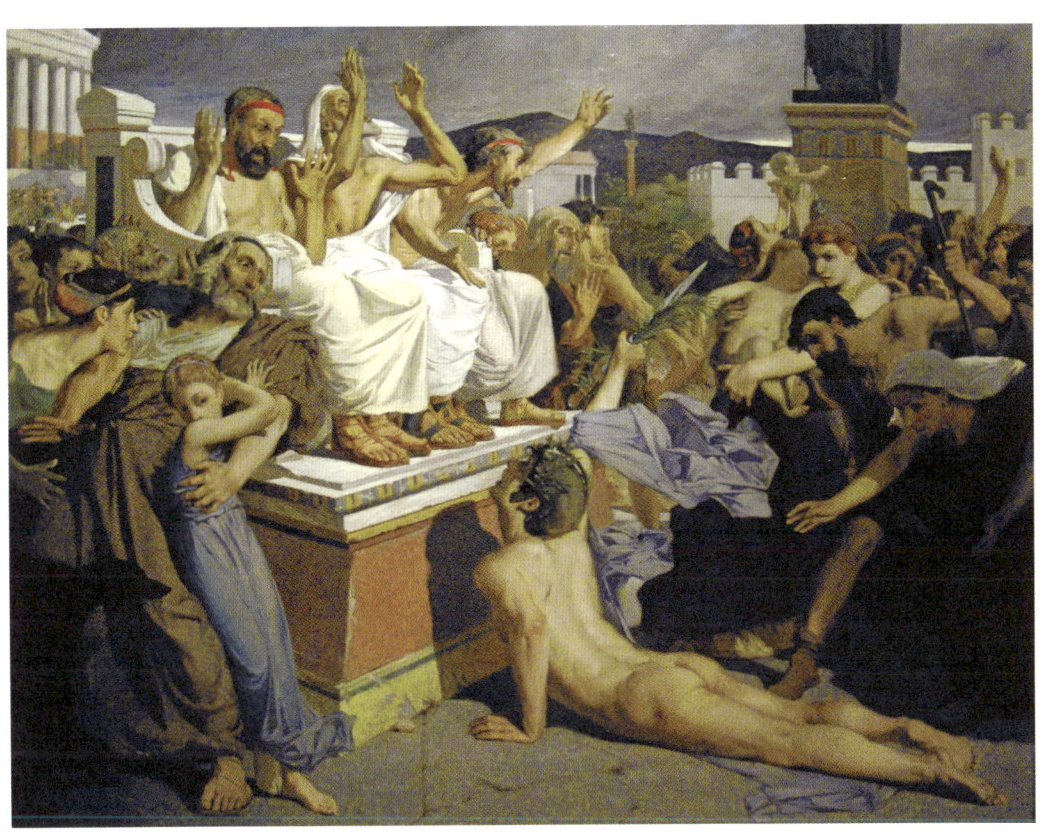

29. opposite, above **William James Müller, *Prayers in the Desert* (detail), 1843, oil on canvas**

30. opposite, below ***Dipankara Jataka (The Story of the Ascetic Megha and the Buddha Dipankara)*, c. 2nd century AD, schist panel with gold leaf, Pakistan**

31. above **Luc-Olivier Merson, *The Soldier of Marathon*, 1869, oil on canvas**

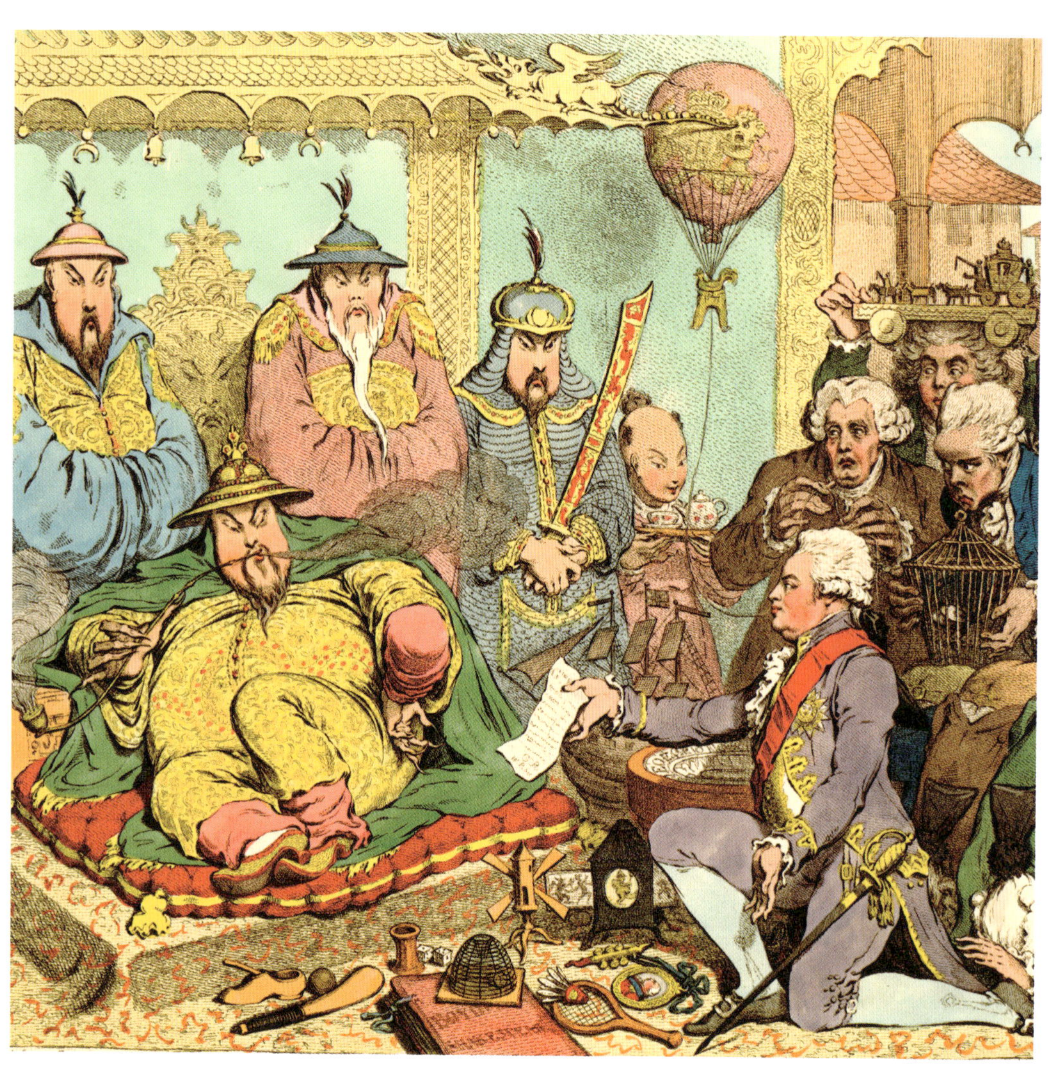

32. **James Gillray**, *The Reception
of the Diplomatique and his Suite,
at the Court of Pekin* (detail),
1792, hand-coloured etching

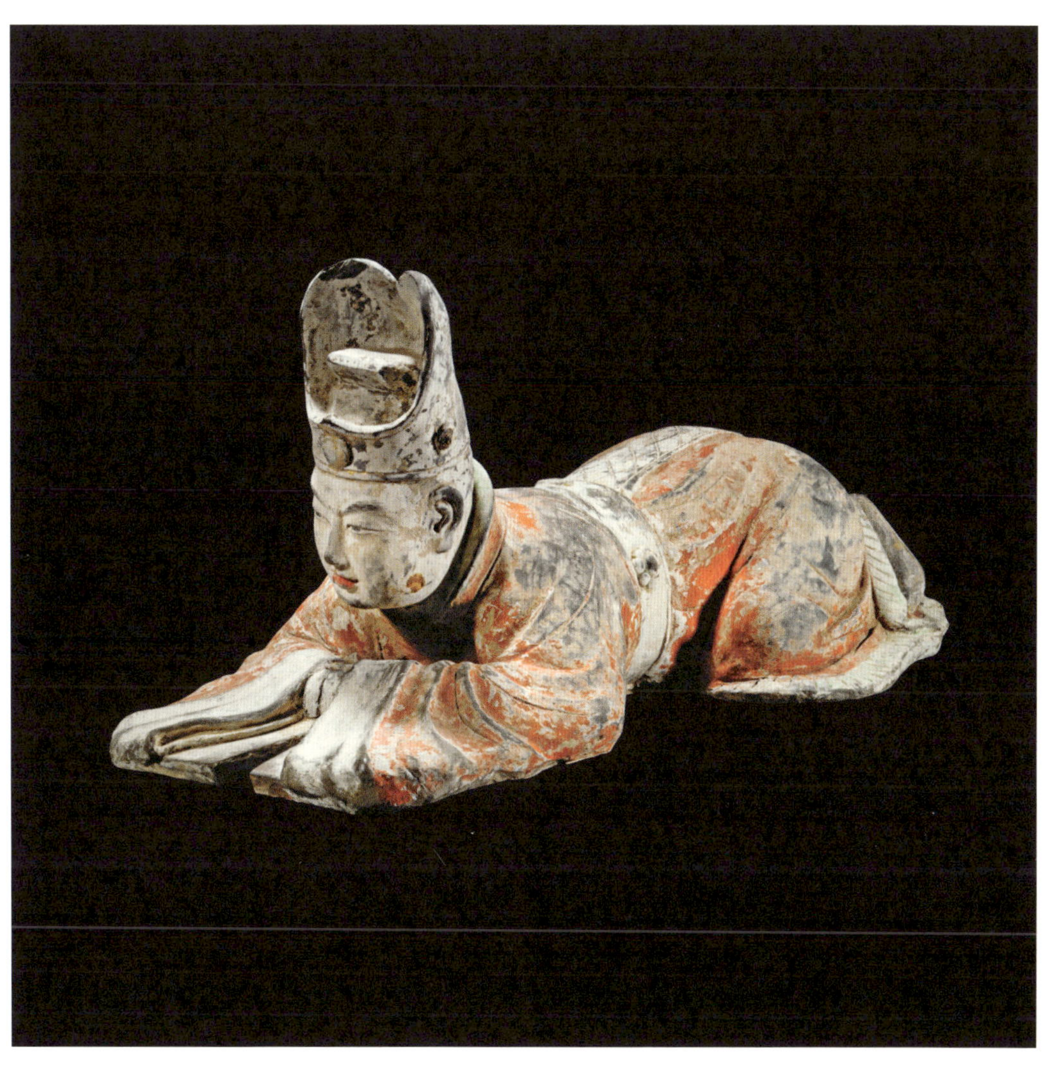

33. **Kowtowing court official,
early Tang Dynasty, 7th–8th century,
painted ceramic, China**

Blessings

Today, the act of giving or receiving a blessing plays little part in everyday life and is largely restricted to religious ceremonies. It does, however, feature widely in the artworks of earlier centuries, where it appears in several forms that often cause confusion due to the subtle differences in the gestures involved in performing the action.

The most basic form of blessing is the laying on of hands, a practice most commonly associated with Christianity. As this involves physical contact on a one-to-one basis, it was perhaps inevitable that a modified form of blessing would be developed that could operate on a larger scale, so that a whole group could be blessed with a single action. This was achieved by starting to perform the laying on of hands but then halting the action before physical contact was made. In other words, the hand or hands would reach out towards the recipients, but the movement would not be completed. The palm or palms would be raised towards them, and then the verbal blessing would be given while the arm or arms were held aloft. Perhaps, because this was too much like a friendly greeting rather than a solemn benediction, the shape of the hand had to be modified in some way – by holding some of the fingers erect while others were slightly bent, or tightly curled – to make the action more specific.

In a religious context, complications developed when distinct Christian groups adopted slightly different finger positions. In early works, artists paid great attention to these small differences. Further confusion arose with the use of similar gestures in other religions, where the same arrangement of the fingers might have a completely different meaning.

The Laying on of Hands

The laying on of hands (*cheirotonia* in Greek) is an ancient form of blessing. The palms of the hands (or palm of one hand) of the person giving the blessing are placed gently on the top of the head of the person receiving it. In Christianity, the person giving the blessing is acting as an agent of God and believes that he is passing on His favour to the recipient of the blessing.

In the 17th century, Govert Flinck, a student of Rembrandt, depicted one of the earliest examples of the laying on of hands [35], taken from a story in Genesis. When Isaac was old and blind, he had to bestow a blessing on his elder son, Esau, to endow him with his inheritance of goods and position. His younger son Jacob, however, had done a deal with Esau, offering him a bowl of lentil soup in exchange for his birthright. Esau was hungry and accepted the offer. Flinck's 1638 painting shows the moment when Jacob, pretending to be Esau, tricks their blind father into bestowing Esau's rightful blessing on him.

In 1656, Rembrandt himself portrayed the now elderly Jacob blessing the children of Joseph [34], again by performing the action of the laying on of hands. In this painting, and in a number of others, the artist shows the moment when the hand is just about to touch the person who is being blessed. The arm reaches out, but the palm has yet to make contact with the top of the head.

In the works of this period, the act of laying on of hands is usually depicted at moments of special importance, such as when John the Baptist is baptizing a naked Christ. In some portrayals of this event, John is seen pouring water over the head of Christ, but in others the later part of the ceremony is shown, when John's hand comes to rest on top of the head as a blessing [36].

The laying on of hands can also be seen in depictions of the disciple Ananias restoring the sight of St Paul. A 12th-century mosaic [37] shows Ananias baptizing St Paul and completing the ceremony with a blessing in which he lays his hand on Paul's head. In a much later work [38], from the 17th century, Pietro da Cortona shows Ananias blessing Paul three days after his conversion on the road to Damascus, during which a great light had cost him his sight. Paul's eyes are closed, but his sight will soon be restored by the sacred blessing. In *The Conversion of St Paul* (*c.* 1786), Benjamin West adds a dramatic intensity to this moment by showing the hand of Ananias clasped on Paul's head with the tip of the forefinger pressed onto the eye of the blind man, the moment before he miraculously regains his sight.

This form of blessing appears again in the Bible when Christ himself is performing acts of healing, with the contact of his hand appearing to bestow miraculous benefits on the recipients. After Christ's time, the apostles continued to perform the laying on of hands, and the practice was then handed down from generation to generation. It is still performed by Christian clergy today, most commonly during the act of confirmation.

A special form of the laying on of hands, known as the king's (or royal) touch, was popular in England and France from medieval times up until the 18th century. Rulers frequently performed the laying on of hands with victims of disease, in the belief that they had the divine gift of healing. In particular, it was thought that the king's touch could cure the disfiguring form of tuberculosis known as scrofula, or the King's Evil. Victims of the disease, suffering from an unsightly swelling of the lymph nodes in the neck, would kneel before their monarch to receive his blessing. Because the king believed that his right to rule was God-given, it followed that the power of the Almighty could be transmitted through the palm of his hand and into the body of the sufferer.

Some monarchs took part in grand ceremonies during which they would touch the heads of hundreds of sufferers. Henry IV of France was said to have touched as many as 1,500 sufferers at one such event, while Louis XIV, who started performing the ceremonies when he was a small boy, exceeded this with 1,600 blessings at Easter in 1680. Louis XVI outdid them both by giving the king's touch to 2,400 people at his accession in 1774. The practice continued in France until 1825, but in England it was abandoned a century earlier. The last English monarch to perform the laying on of hands was Queen Anne, who died in 1714. There is a famous print showing her performing the royal touch on the head of a young Samuel Johnson, later renowned as the creator of *Dr Johnson's Dictionary*. The reason why this piece of regal quackery, masquerading as divine intervention, lasted for hundreds of years is that scrofula underwent natural periods of remission, which gave the impression that the king's touch really did work.

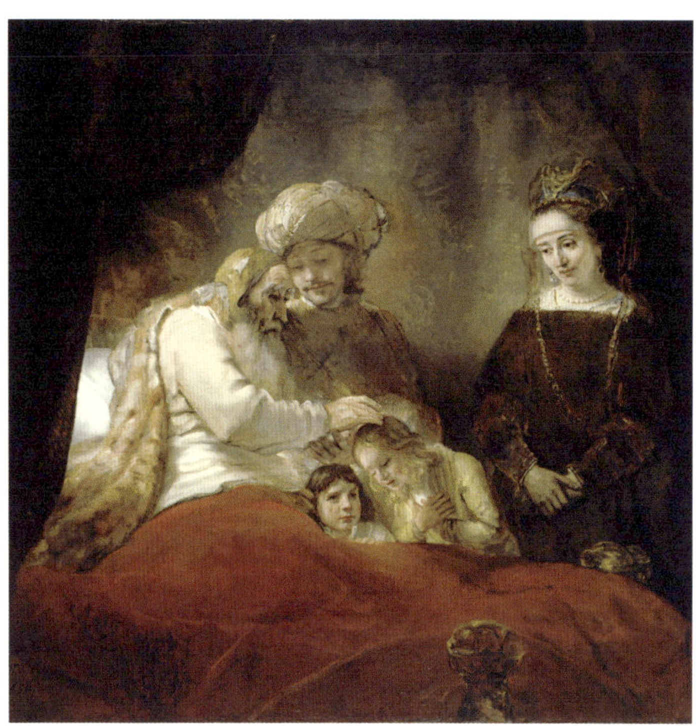

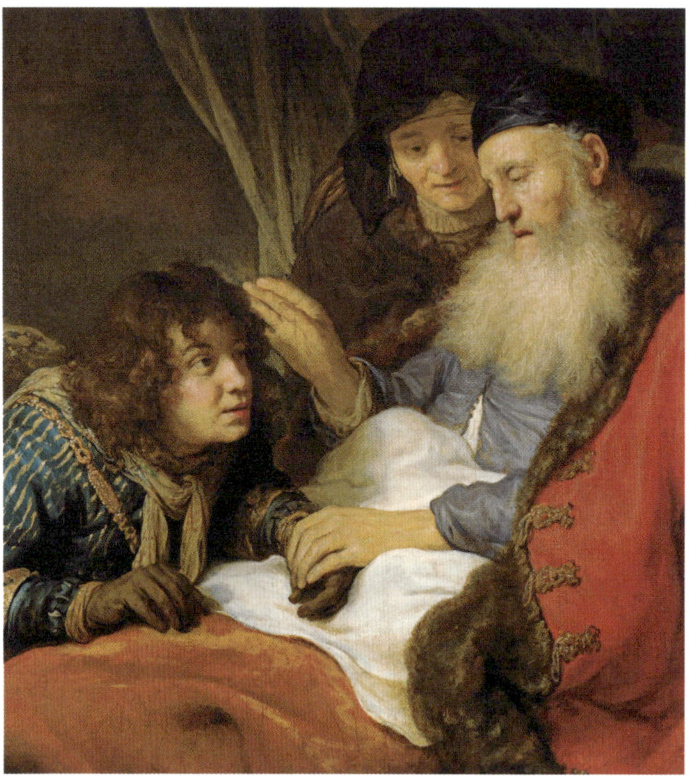

34. above **Rembrandt,** *Jacob Blessing the Sons of Joseph* (detail), 1656, oil on canvas

35. left **Govert Flinck,** *Isaac Blessing Jacob* (detail), 1638, oil on canvas

36. opposite **Icon of** *The Baptism of Christ* (detail), late 18th–early 19th century, painted gesso on wood, Volga region, Russia

     Blessings / The Laying on of Hands

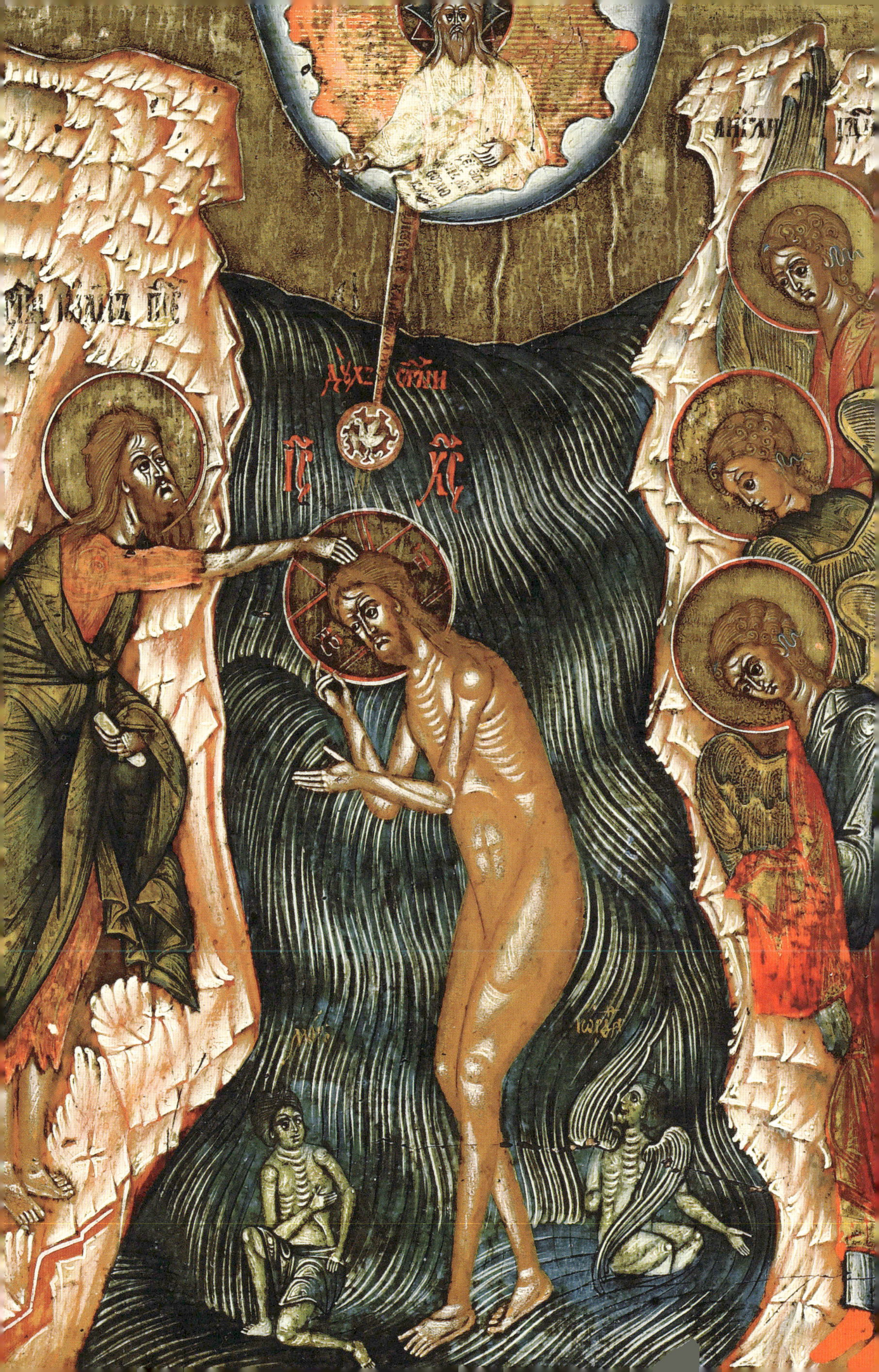
ДУХЪ СТЫИ
ІС ХС

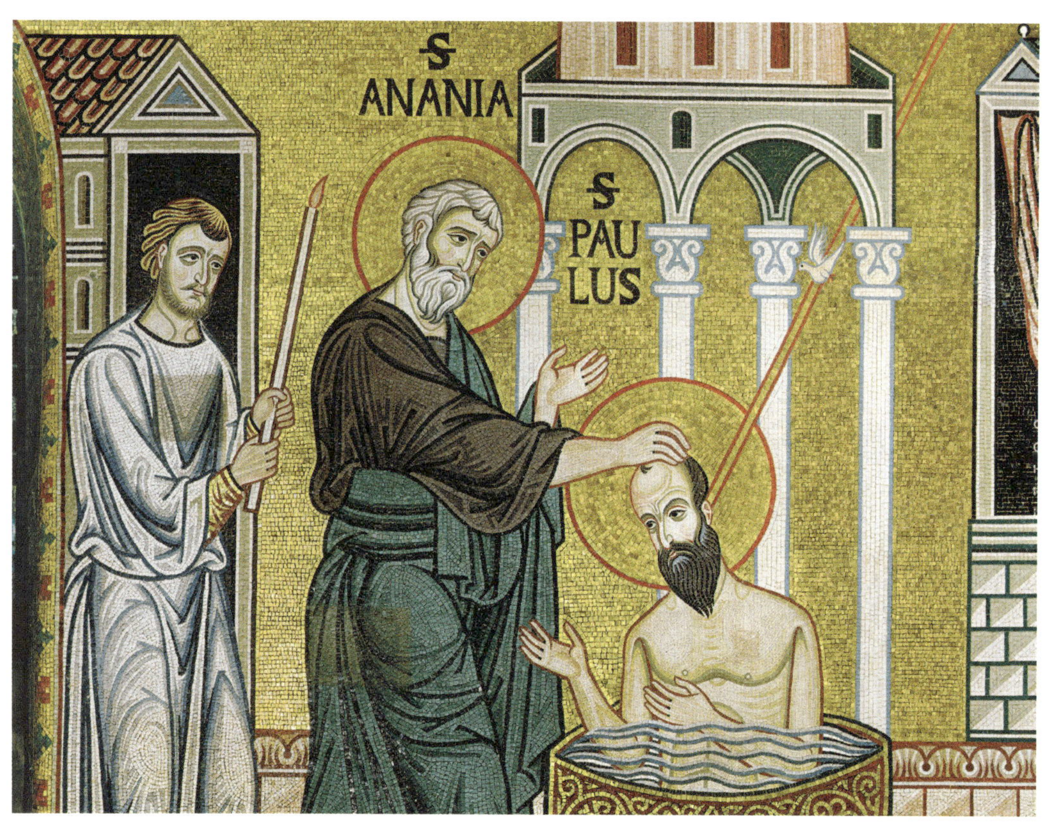

37. above **Ananias baptizing Paul,
12th century, mosaic, Cappella
Palatina, Palermo, Sicily**

38. opposite **Pietro da Cortona,
*Ananias Restoring the Sight of
St Paul*, 1631, oil on canvas**

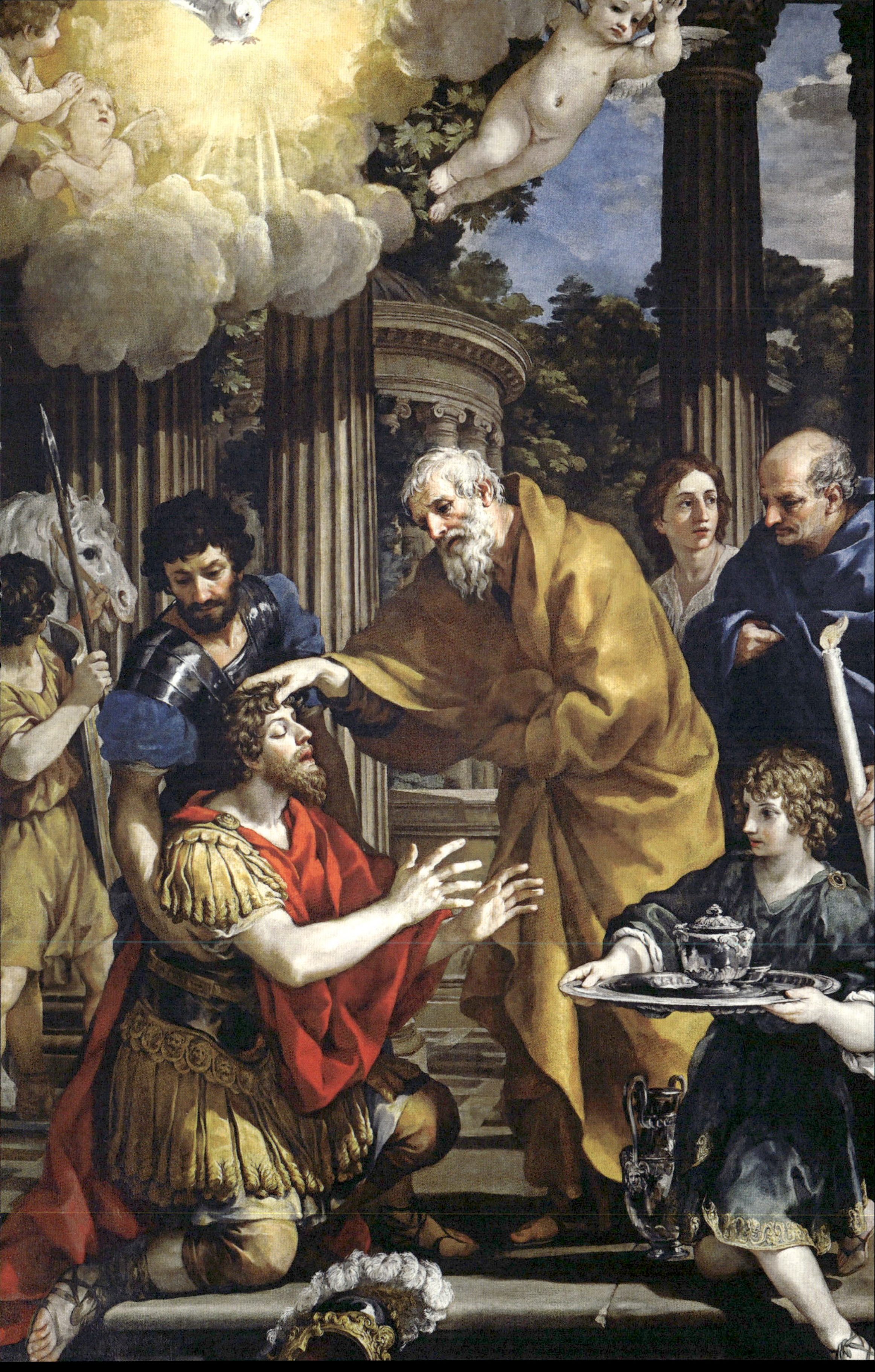

The Latin and Orthodox Blessings

When the Christian Church split into two factions – East and West, Orthodox and Latin – in the 11th century, the Western faction, the Roman Catholic Church, adopted a blessing sign that consisted of keeping the thumb and the first two fingers erect, with the fourth and fifth digits bent and the palm facing forward [39, 42]. The official explanation of this gesture was that the three erect digits represented the Holy Trinity – the Father, the Son and the Holy Spirit. This gesture is still in use today by Catholic priests when giving a benediction.

Recently, an alternative explanation of the origin of this gesture has been put forward, suggesting that it has a medical basis. An American professor of anatomy, Bennett Futterman, claims that the first pope, St Peter, assumed this gesture because a nerve injury prevented him from fully opening his hand. In his opinion, the early Christians would have copied the flat-handed blessing gesture employed by the Jewish high priests. Futterman points out that ulnar nerve damage prevents a hand from extending its fourth and fifth fingers away from the palm, and believes that Peter suffered from this type of nerve injury to his right hand. Later popes, out of respect for Peter, would then have adopted the same form of hand blessing. If Futterman is correct, the official explanation – that the three erect digits represent the Trinity – would have been a later invention introduced to give the blessing gesture a sacred (rather than medical) meaning.

Futterman's idea seems plausible enough, but it does not explain why, on a Greek red-figure vase dating from the 4th century BC [41], Demeter, the goddess of the harvest, is shown extending her hand in a benediction that clearly shows the first two fingers extended and the other two bent into the palm, in the same arrangement as the Latin blessing. This suggests that the two-finger blessing was an ancient gesture that was later adopted by the Christians, although the significance of Demeter choosing to use it remains unclear.

It has also been suggested that the nails driven brutally into Christ's wrists during the crucifixion caused nerve damage to his hand, making the fourth and fifth digits curl into the palm. Those who believe in this theory see St Peter copying the hand of Christ when he makes a blessing.

Following the split of the Christian Church, the Eastern faction, the Orthodox Church, adopted its own version of the blessing sign [40]. It was a complex one, in which each digit was positioned in a special way to spell out a coded monogram for 'Jesus Christ'. This monogram is IC XC –

an abbreviation of the Greek name for Jesus. The code is signalled
in the following way:

   I = erect forefinger
   C = curved middle finger
   X = crossed thumb and ring finger
   C = curved little finger

Christian scholars tend to see this gesture as heavy with meaning, perhaps slightly more than is justified. It has been suggested that the three fingers of Christ – as well as spelling out 'I' and 'X' – are a symbol of the Trinity, while the touching finger and thumb represents the Incarnation, the embodiment of God the Son in human flesh as Jesus Christ.

In practice, this gesture seems to have been too elaborate for everyday use and, judging by the way it is often represented in the art of the Greek Orthodox Church, it became simplified to a ring gesture made by touching the tips of the thumb and ring finger [43]. This rather negates the idea of making an 'X', while the straightened form of the little finger eliminates the final 'C' required to spell out the coded name of Jesus. What we see in art is a reduced version of the ancient coded signal, but one that still distinguishes it from the Latin blessing.

In Asia, depictions of the Buddha performing the Prithvi mudra show him with the tips of the thumb and the ring finger touching, in a gesture that looks identical to the Orthodox Christian blessing. In Buddhism, however, this particular arrangement of the fingers transmits a different and quite specific meaning. It is used to increase the earth element within the body and to decrease the fire element. The earth element is the underlying component of the tissues and organs of the body and, when it is increased, it improves a person's vitality, strength and endurance. Decreasing the fire element brings down the body temperature and helps to reduce fever. In this sense it is a kind of blessing because it is meant to boost the well-being of the body, but it lacks the spiritual element of the Christian version.

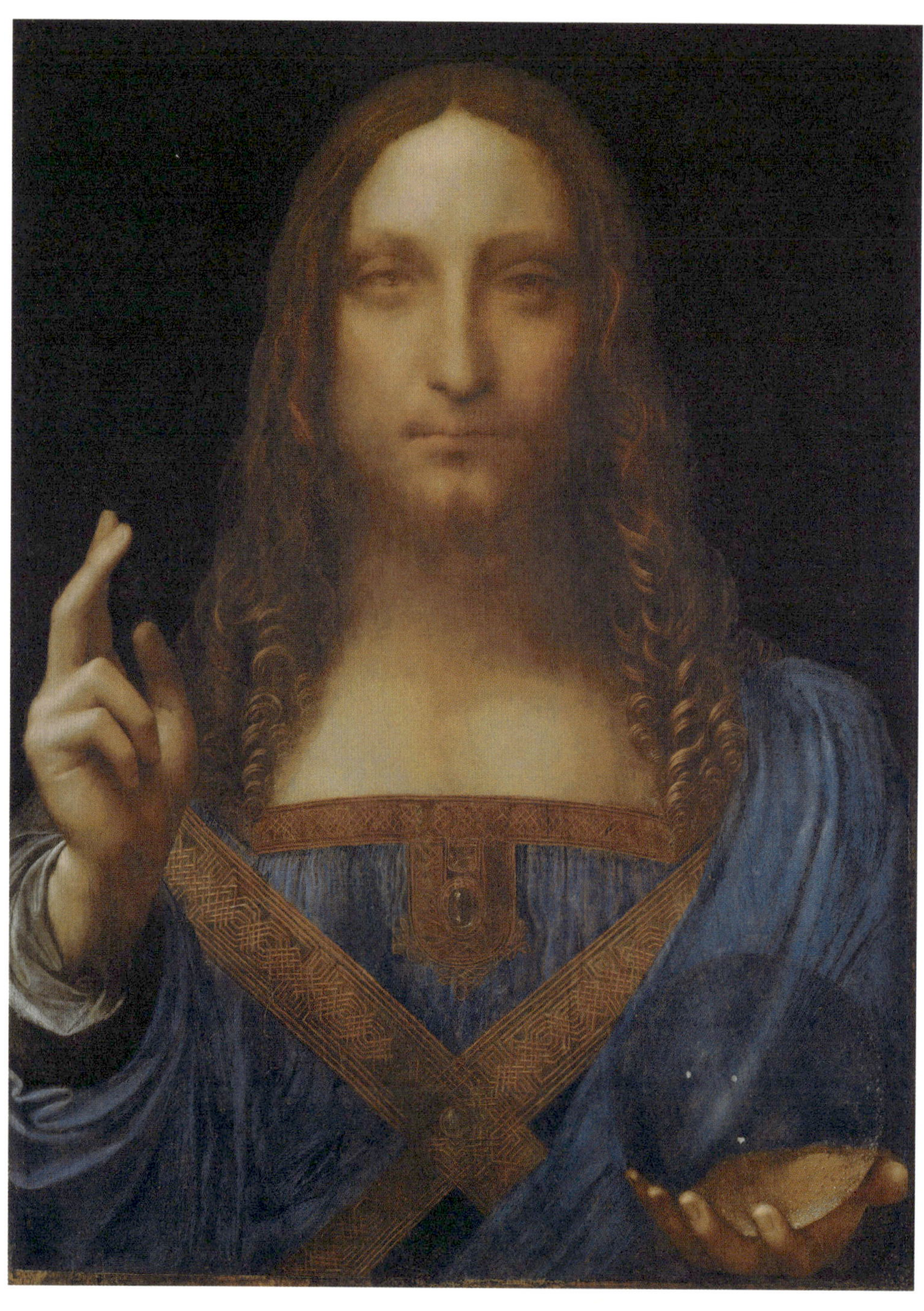

39. **Leonardo da Vinci,**
Salvator Mundi (detail), c. 1490,
oil on walnut (Latin blessing)

    Blessings / The Latin and Orthodox Blessings

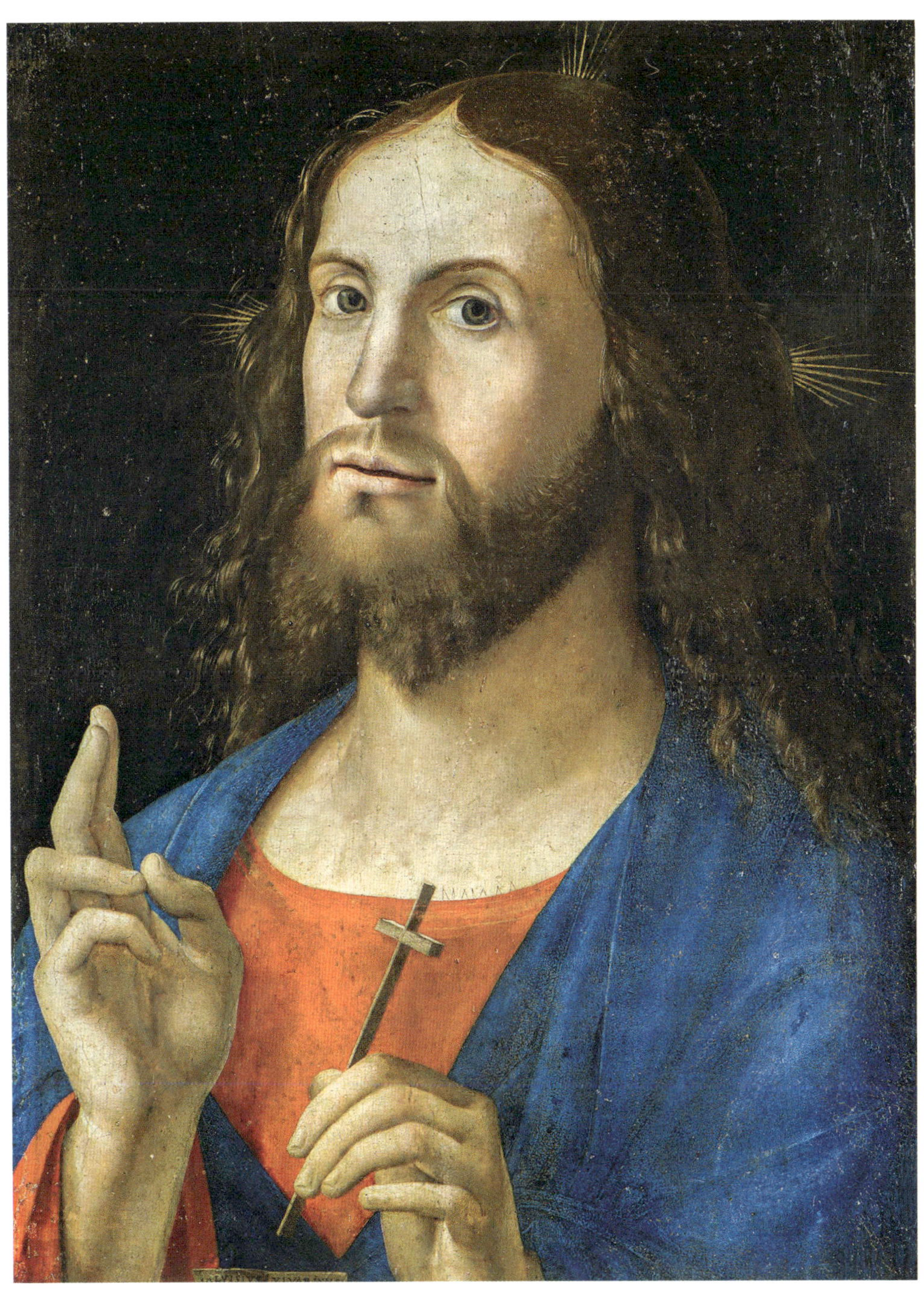

40. **Alvise Vivarini,** *Christ Blessing*
(detail), 1498, oil on panel
(Orthodox blessing)

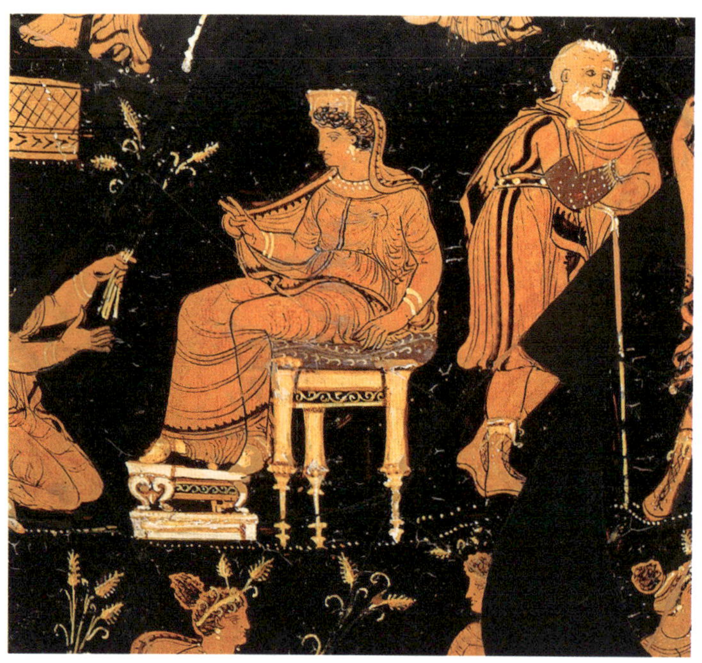

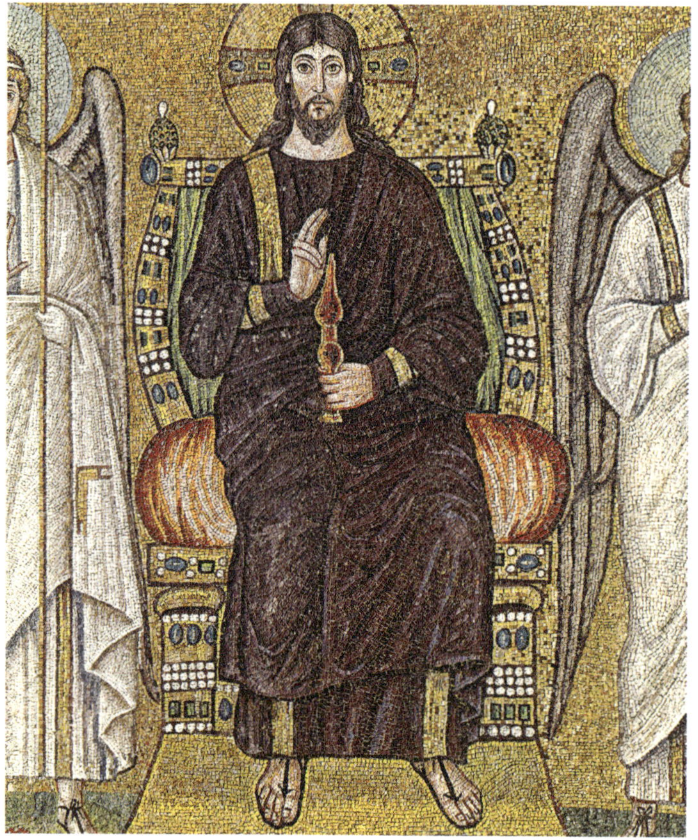

41. above **Varrese Painter,
vase depicting scenes from Greek
mythology, 340 BC, Puglia, Italy**

42. left **Christ Pantocrator,
mosaic, 6th century, Basilica
of Sant'Apollinare Nuovo,
Ravenna, Italy (Latin blessing)**

43. opposite **Christ Pantocrator,
Cypriot icon (detail), 18th century
(Orthodox blessing)**

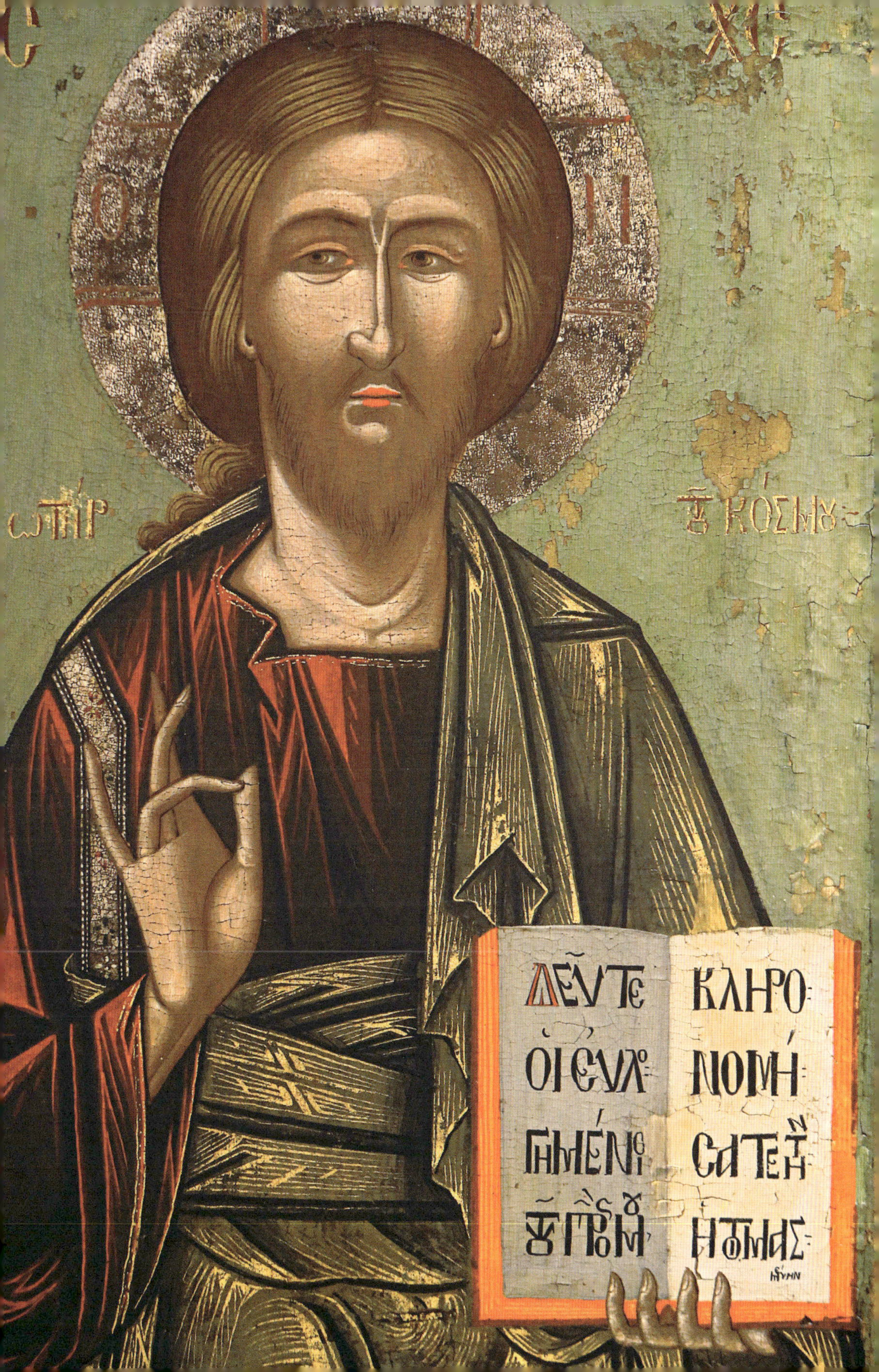
Ο ΩΝ
Ω ΠΑΤΗΡ
Ω ΚΟCΜΟΥ
ΔΕΥΤΕ ΚΛΗΡΟ
ΟΙ ΕΥΛΟ ΝΟΜΗ
ΓΗΜΕΝΙ CΑΤΕ Τ
ΤΟΥ ΠΡΟΜ ΗΤΟΙΜΑC

Buddhist Blessings

In Buddhist art, figures are nearly always shown performing hand gestures that have a specific meaning. These gestures are called mudras, and there are at least twenty of them. One of them, the Abhaya mudra, is a blessing. It is a simple gesture, superficially similar to the hail greeting of the Western world. The right forearm is raised so that the hand is roughly at shoulder level. The hand is held vertically with the palm facing away from the body. It is said to have been a blessing employed by the Buddha immediately following his enlightenment, and is believed to provide the energy of protection, peace and a sense of strong, deep inner security. It is a blessing that has been portrayed on Buddhist statues for more than 2,000 years.

This Buddhist blessing is seen at its most impressive on the giant Buddhas that have been erected in such countries as Malaysia, Thailand and Japan. A particularly dramatic example – 9 metres (30 ft) high – looms over the temple of Wat Mahathat, which was founded between 1292 and 1347 and forms part of the Sukhothai Historical Park in northern Thailand. Adopting the same gesture but even more imposing is the Lingshan Grand Buddha [44] near the city of Wuxi, on the northern bank of Lake Taihu in eastern China. Unveiled in 1997, the bronze statue stands 88 metres (289 ft) high and is one of five giant Buddhas that have been built in China – in the east, west, north, south and centre of the country. The hand alone is several times taller than a human being, which surely makes this the biggest blessing of any artwork in the world.

The blessing has been expressed verbally in *The Dhammapada*, a collection of verses attributed to the Buddha: 'A blessing in the world: reverence to your mother. A blessing: reverence to your father as well. A blessing in the world: reverence to a contemplative. A blessing: reverence for a brahmin, too. A blessing into old age is virtue. A blessing: conviction established. A blessing: discernment attained. The non-doing of evil things is a blessing.'

44. **Lingshan Grand Buddha, unveiled 1997, bronze, Jiangsu Province, China**

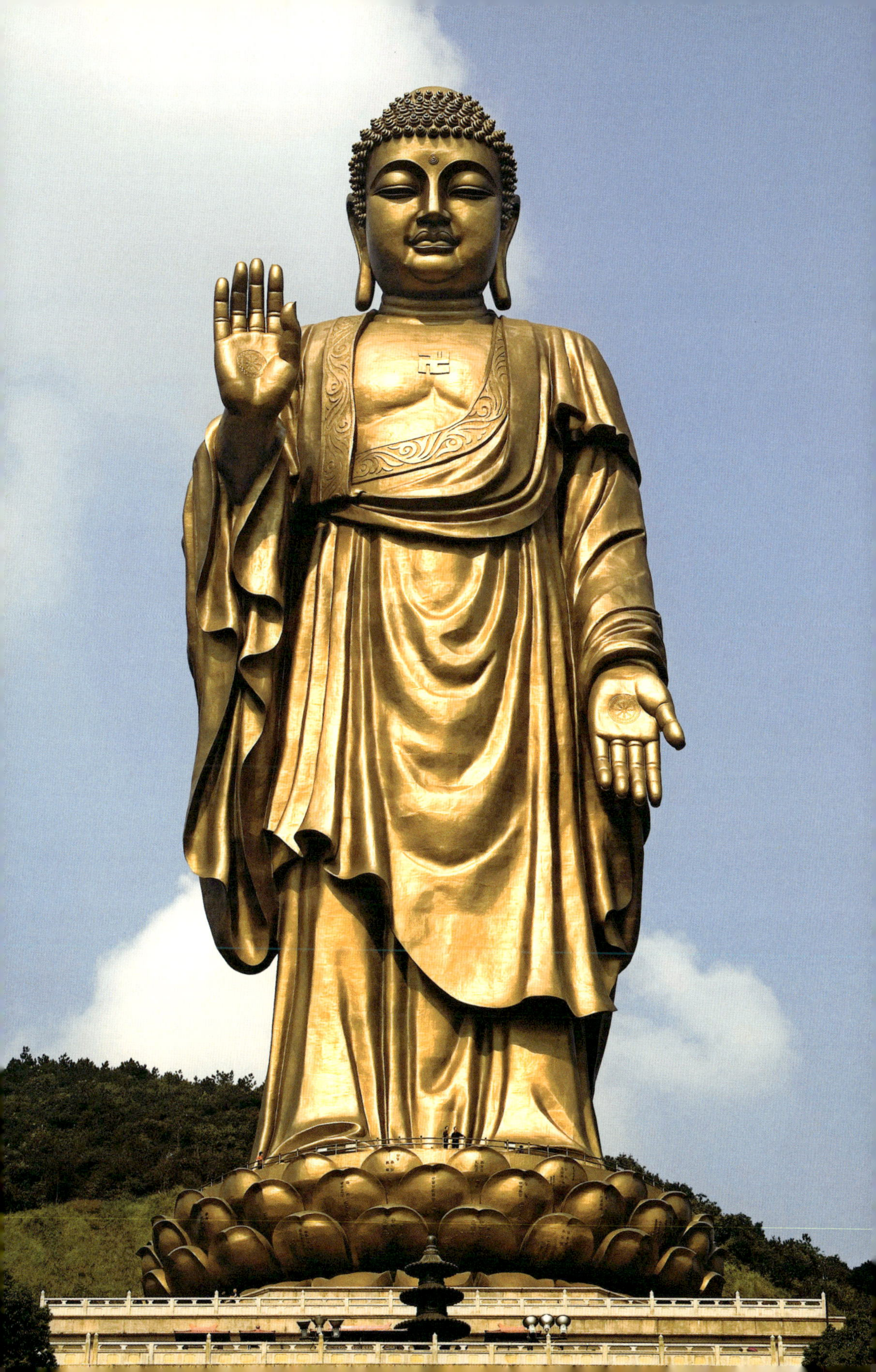

The Vulcan Blessing

The Vulcan gesture, in which the hand is held up with the four fingers divided to form a V shape, has acquired its name from the science-fiction television series *Star Trek* [47]. Mr Spock, the science officer of the starship *Enterprise*, played by Leonard Nimoy, is of mixed heritage – half-human, half-Vulcan. When he bestows his Vulcan blessing 'Live long and prosper', he does so with his right hand held in the split-V position. The huge success of the series made this blessing gesture universally recognizable.

When Nimoy was asked about the origin of the gesture, he explained that he had borrowed it from a Jewish ritual that he had observed as a child, when his grandfather took him to an Orthodox synagogue. There, he saw the blessing performed by the *kohanim* (priests) using both hands at once, with the thumbs touching [45] – an action that is sometimes replicated on Jewish tombstones, where it can indicate a priestly lineage. This form of the gesture creates the Hebrew letter 'Shin', which stands for 'El Shaddai', meaning 'Almighty God'. It is accompanied by the verbal blessing: 'May Adonai bless you and guard you. May Adonai make His face shed light upon you and be gracious unto you. May Adonai lift up His face unto you and give you peace.'

Nimoy used this as the basis for his Vulcan salute, modifying it from a two-handed to a one-handed action. In 2015, following Nimoy's death, the astronaut Terry Virts tweeted an image of his hand forming the Vulcan blessing as a tribute to the actor. The photograph was taken from the International Space Station as it flew over Boston, the city of Nimoy's birth.

By an extraordinary coincidence, there is a Nazca textile panel [46], dating from the 2nd or 3rd century AD, that depicts a strange monster with sharply pointed ears making the split-fingers gesture. One could be forgiven for imagining that Nimoy had seen this textile and committed it to memory, were it not for his own account of the gesture's origin.

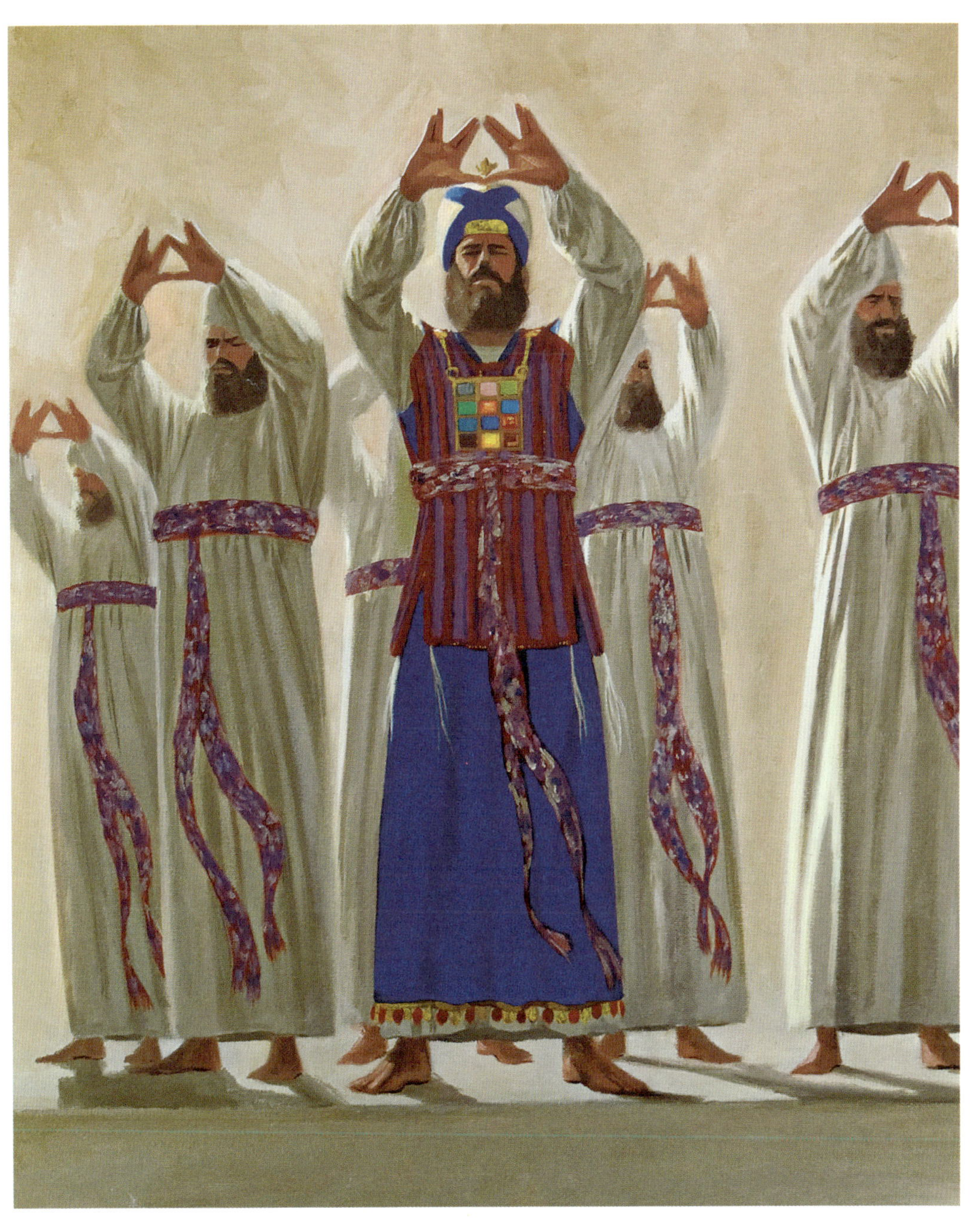

45. **Balage Balogh,**
Priestly Benediction (detail),
21st century

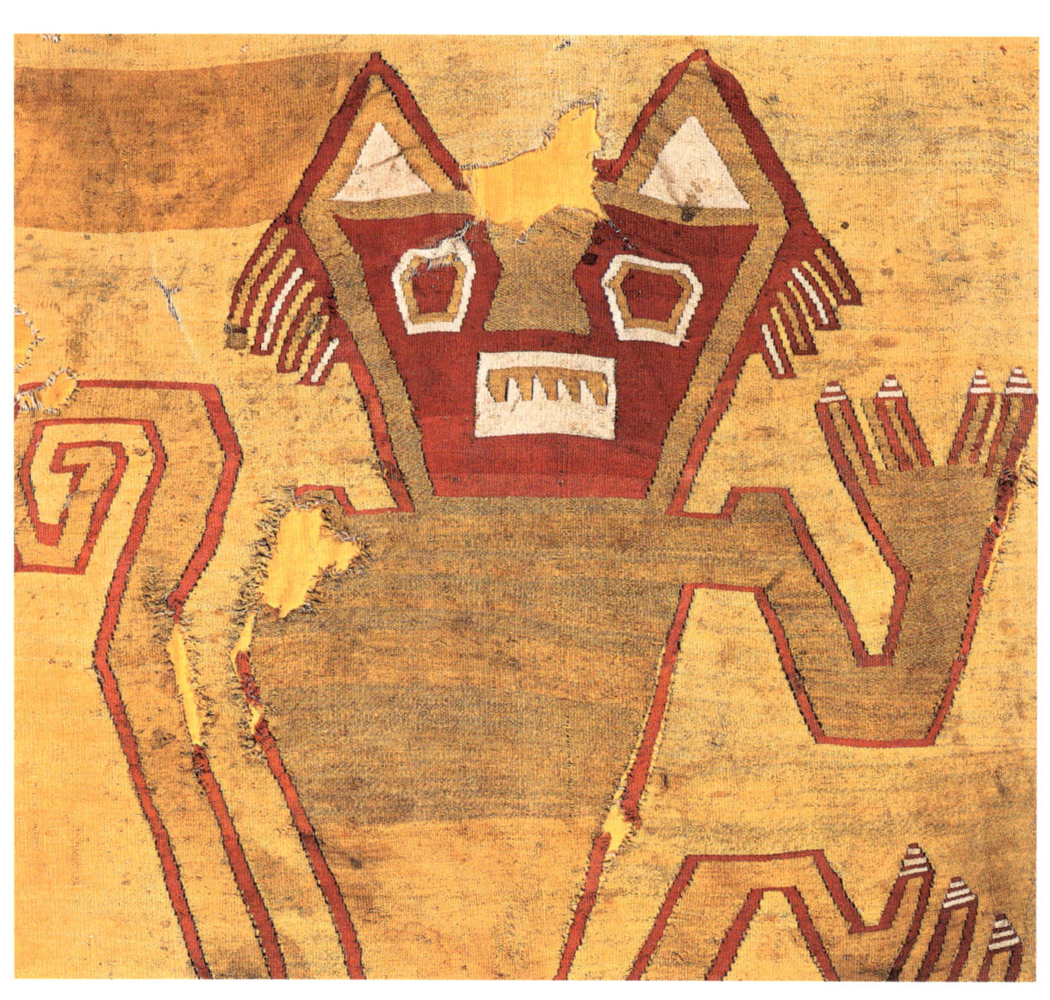

46. **Nazca textile panel,
2nd–3rd century AD, Peru**

    Blessings / The Vulcan Blessing

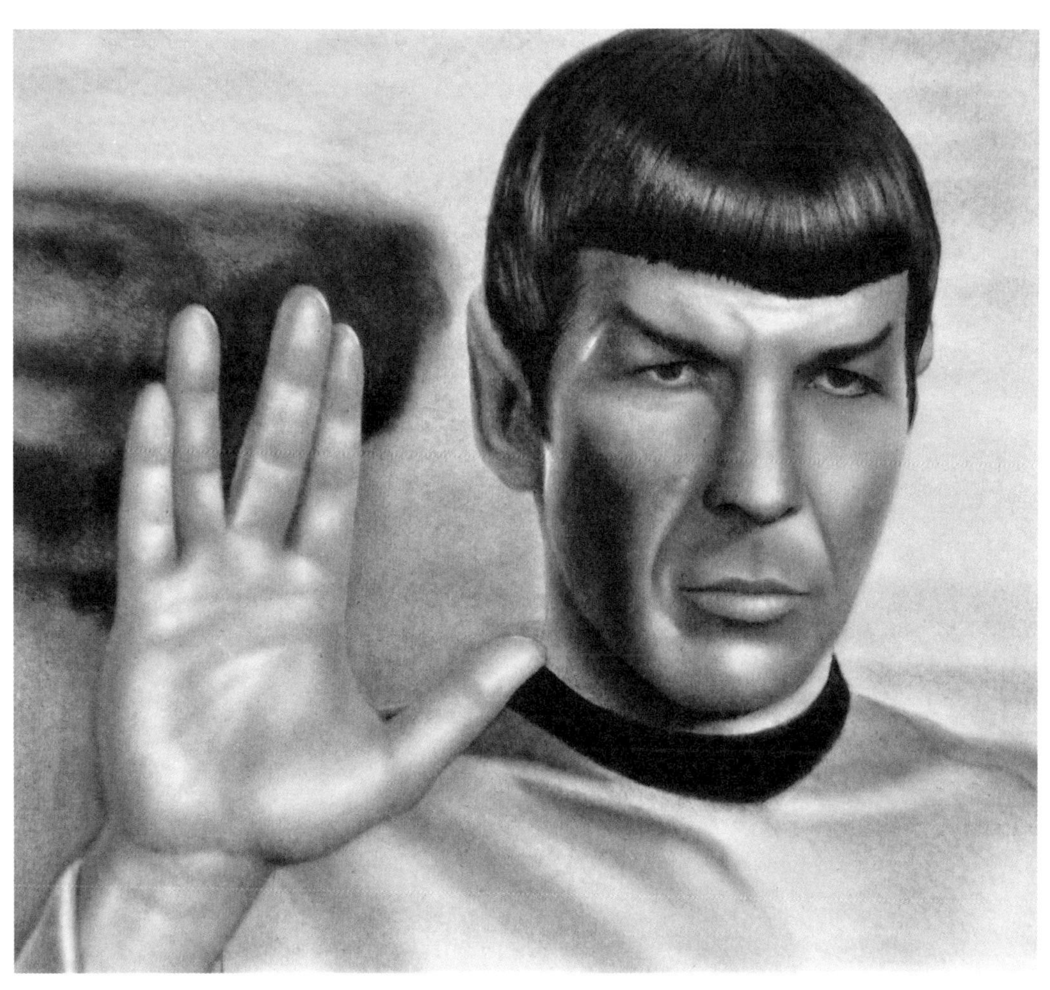

47. **Stefan Pabst,** *Spock
(Leonard Nimoy)* **(detail),**
2015, drawing

Status

Historically, if your portrait was painted or a sculpture was made in your likeness, it indicated that you were likely a person of considerable repute. The body language of those who were portrayed was itself a display of high status. Subjects were shown standing or sitting, elegantly clothed and in postures of solemn restraint. Intense expressions, active postures and uninhibited behaviour were all taboo. Certain details helped to signal a superior social position, including an erect stance, a hand tucked into clothing or a special arrangement of the fingers, a protruding elbow and a pointed foot.

A few artists rebelled against this tradition, choosing to portray ordinary people of low status – often as a deliberate affront to the ruling classes. Some preferred to show working people bent over in toil and labour, while others depicted peasants enjoying themselves with the sort of ribald abandon that was notably absent from high-status portraiture. A number of painters made a point of portraying the squalor of low-status existence as a comment on the social inequalities of their day.

The Erect Posture

A vertical posture with the head held high has always been associated with a display of high status. In portraits through the centuries, it is clear that the costumes of the elite members of society have frequently acted as aids to keeping the body erect. It would be hard to slouch when wearing an Elizabethan ruff collar, and portraits of Elizabeth I [49], for example, always show the great queen standing stiffly erect. The high collars of early military uniforms also forced their wearers into postures of aloofness and swagger.

The English language is full of phrases such as 'We look up to him', and a person who has rounded or hunched shoulders or is slumped in their seat may be seen as passive or indecisive. Portrait artists have always been aware of the importance of posture, and the paintings they have created of the aristocracy and other leading members of society have generally done their sitters the favour of raising their heads, lowering their shoulders, stretching their necks, and straining their backs slightly more than either nature or custom intended. In the best cases, this has been done with a subtle touch that is barely noticeable, but occasionally it has been overstated so that the sitter begins to look just a little too self-important.

Historically, this did not matter unduly because the social customs of the day accepted the fact that leading figures would display themselves in an arrogant and flamboyant manner. However, increasing egalitarianism over the past century has seen a decline in the more blatant forms of high-status posturing. Holding oneself erect may still be considered a display of superior status, but with today's leading figures, postures of dominance have had to become more subtle and rather muted. In Graham Sutherland's famous portrait of the author Somerset Maugham [48], from 1949, he manages to convey the high standing of his sitter by the backward tilt of his head.

A Harvard University study has shown that the body posture we adopt influences the levels of our hormones, specifically testosterone and cortisol. Participants were divided into two groups: the first was instructed to relax in casual, lounging positions, while the second was asked to stand tall and adopt vertical 'power poses'. The results of the experiment were summed up as follows: 'high-power posers experienced elevations in testosterone, decreases in cortisol, and increased feelings of power and tolerance for risk; low-power posers exhibited the opposite pattern.' This is a remarkable discovery, revealing the hidden impact of our everyday postures.

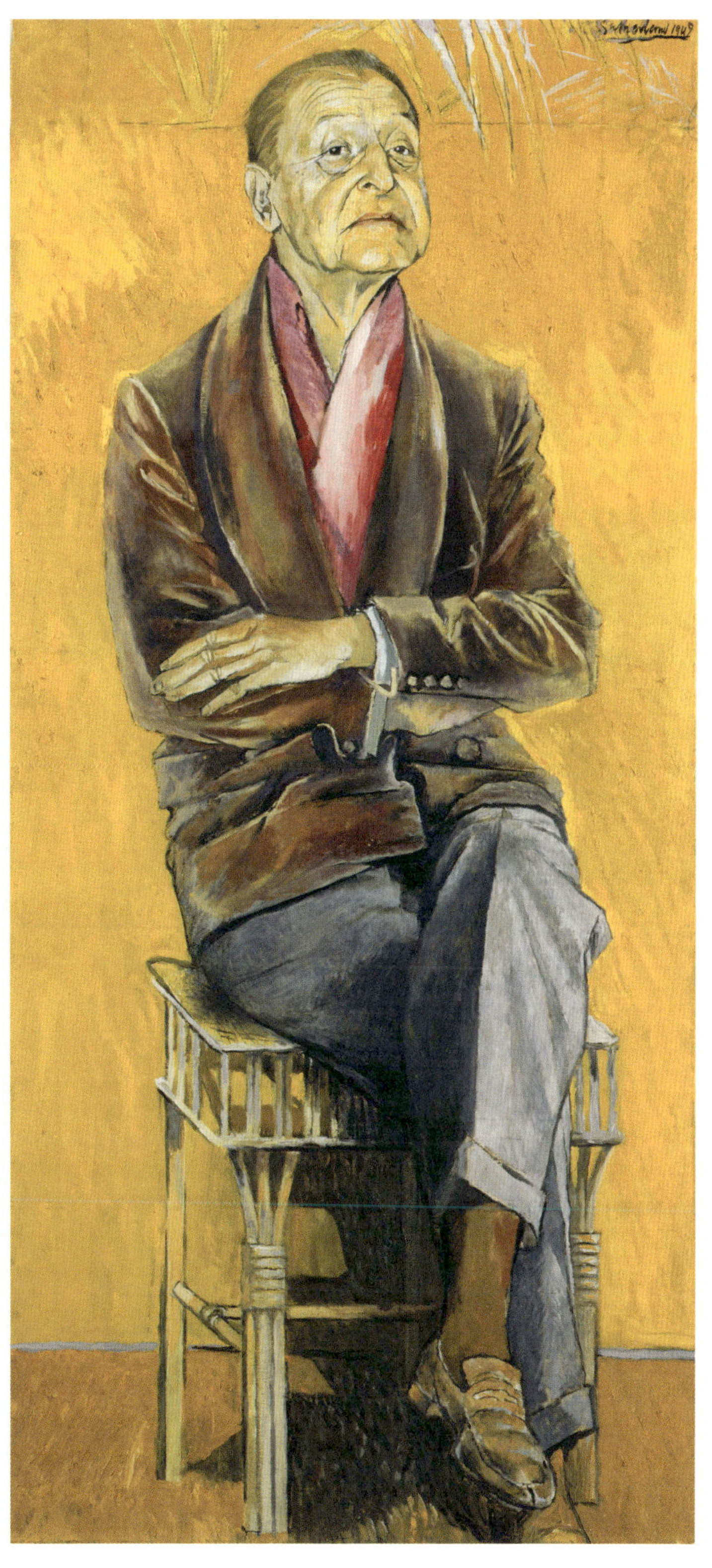

48. **Graham Sutherland,**
Somerset Maugham, 1949,
oil on canvas

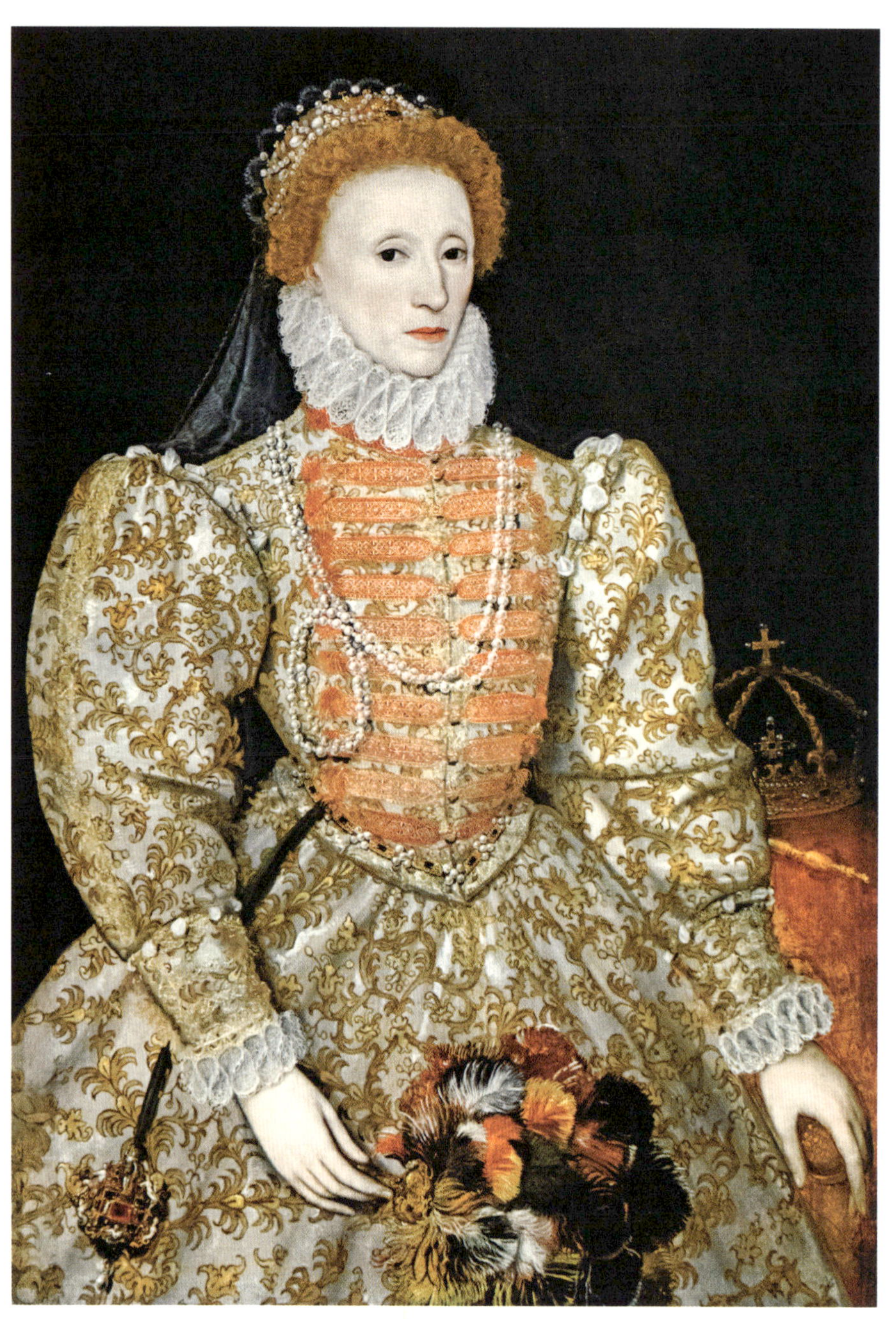

49. above **Unknown Flemish artist,**
***Queen Elizabeth I*, c. 1575, oil on panel**

50. opposite **Gerard ter Borch,**
***Memorial Portrait of Moses ter Borch**
(1645–1667), **1667–69, oil on canvas**

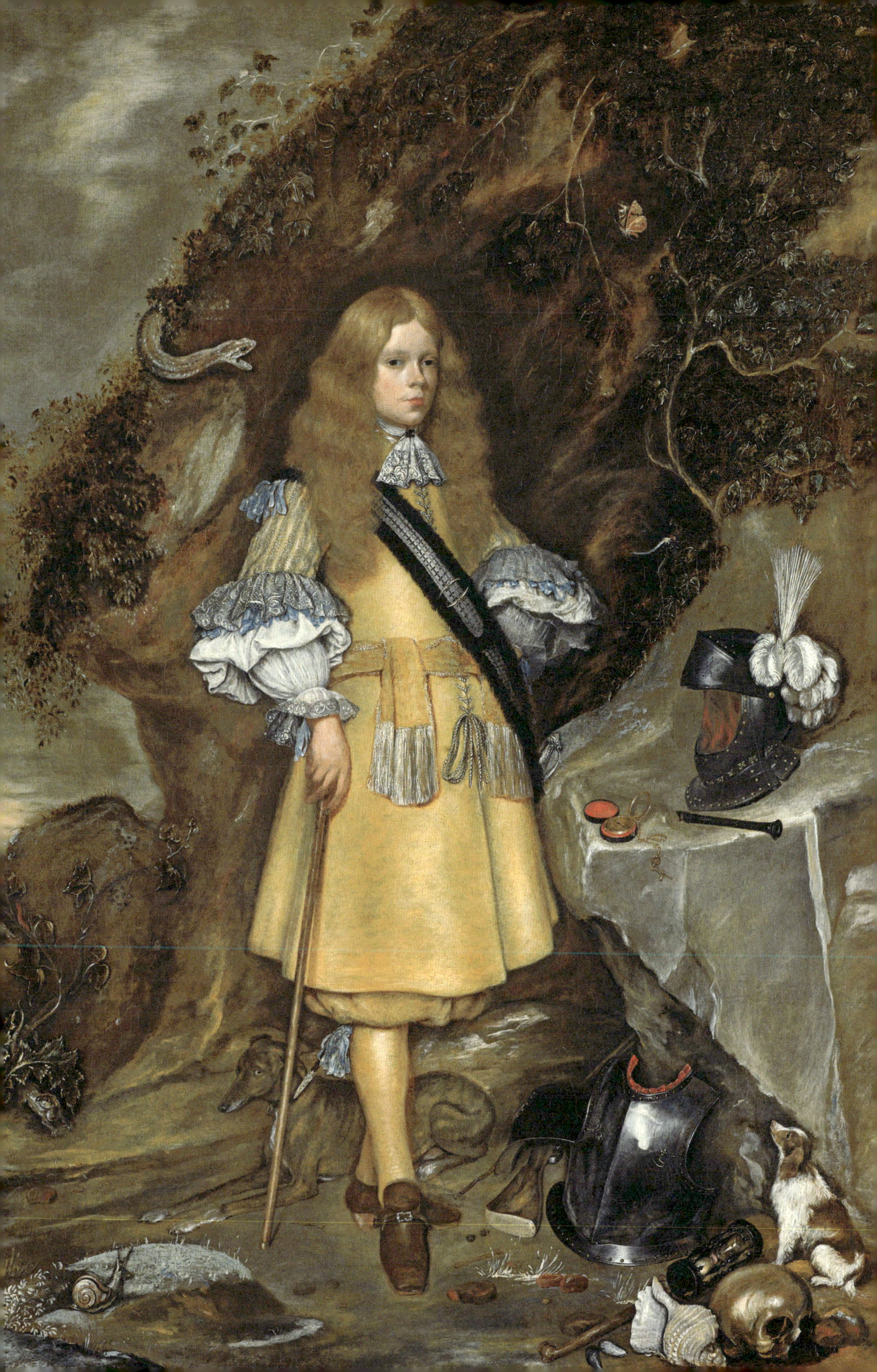

The Double-split Hand

A strange and highly specific hand gesture can be seen in a number of high-status portraits from earlier centuries, especially the 16th. The palm of one hand – usually the right – is placed gently on the chest, with the fingers positioned in a particular way. The middle fingers are held close together, while the forefinger and little finger are spread. It is an arrangement that has to be created consciously. If the hand is placed on the chest without thinking, there are only two arrangements of the fingers that occur naturally: in the first the fingers are closed, and in the second they are open and spaced equally. So what we are dealing with here is a deliberate, contrived finger gesture that must have a meaning.

Over the centuries the significance of this gesture has been forgotten. Indeed, it is only when its oddity and frequency in earlier portraits are pointed out that it becomes the focus of interest. The artists, and the sitters who have arranged their fingers in this way, must have known what it meant, but it seems never to have been recorded.

Thomas Kunesh of Minnesota University decided to investigate the gesture's history, giving his 188-page study of the double-split hand the wonderfully ornate title of *The Pseudo-zygodactylous Gesture of the Lactating Goddess* (1990). He borrowed the word 'zygodactylous' from ornithology, where it refers to a bird having the toes of each foot arranged in pairs, with two toes in front and two behind. One has some sympathy with Kunesh's choice of words, because it is a finger arrangement that defies a simple name. However, the double-split hand is not strictly zygodactylous because all four fingers are pointing forwards in the same plane. In a truly zygodactylous gesture, the hand would be pushed into the clothing with the two central fingers showing and the other two hidden beneath the fold of the garment.

Kunesh takes as his starting point the most conspicuous display of this gesture in a portrait, El Greco's *The Nobleman with his Hand on his Chest* (*El caballero de la mano en el pecho*) [51], of about 1580. At first sight, Kunesh's proposal that the mysterious finger arrangement can be linked to 'the breastfeeding of goddesses, then progressively to their ability to bestow eternal life through their milk, to the gradual evolution of the gesture away from the naked breast, and its migration to men for their use in seeking maternal salvation' seems rather far-fetched, but he goes on to make a very strong case for it.

Kunesh begins by rejecting two previous explanations of the gesture's meaning:

1. that it is a secret sign indicating that the gentleman is a 'Marrano' – a crypto-Jew who accepted Christian baptism in order to remain

in Spain after the Catholic kings' order of 1492 that all practising
Jews must leave Spain; and

2. that it indicates a Loyola/Jesuit spirituality that calls for the sinner
    to place their hand on the chest after committing a sin as a sign
    of moral pain.

The first explanation – that the double-split hand gesture is a secret
Jewish signal – is the result of poor observation. It has been suggested
that the gesture is borrowed from Jewish ritual because Sephardic Jews,
when they are reading sacred prayers or pronouncing a blessing, 'hold
their hands in this curious way', but this is not strictly correct. It is true
that they employ a split-hand display (see the discussion of the Vulcan
gesture, p. 64), but theirs has a central split, not a double one. Proponents
of this theory would argue that when the Jewish priests are making their
special hand gesture, they always do it with both hands and the tips of
the thumbs touching. This means that if you view the two hands together
as a single gesture, they are indeed making a double split. The case
collapses, however, when it emerges that the finger gestures depicted in
the El Greco portrait can also be seen in many other paintings, including
those with no Jewish connection whatsoever. A wider explanation must
be sought.

The same is true for the second explanation, which introduces a
Loyola/Jesuit element. It has been suggested that the El Greco gesture is
somehow connected to one of the spiritual exercises of St Ignatius Loyola
in which he advises that, each time a sin is committed, one should place
one's hand on one's chest 'whilst inciting one's inner self to grief'. This
explanation also falls short because it contains no reference to the special
positioning of the fingers.

A third explanation puts forward the idea that the man in El Greco's
portrait had a deformed hand. There is a condition known as syndactyly,
a kind of webbing of the hand, in which two or more fingers are attached
to one another along their lengths. Again, the presence of this mysterious
gesture in many other portraits undermines this theory. Indeed, El Greco
depicts the same gesture in around twenty other paintings, including
portraits of Jesus, the Virgin Mary, Mary Magdalene, St John, St Dominic
and St Francis of Assisi.

If these theories all fall short, where can we look for a possible
explanation for this somewhat awkward arrangement of the fingers?
The surprising answer, Thomas Kunesh believes, is in the act of
breastfeeding. Support for this idea comes from a study of the finger
positions in portraits of the Madonna where she is depicted breastfeeding
the infant Jesus. Her forefinger is placed at the top of the breast and
her little finger is beneath it. The two middle fingers are kept together
to support the breast. Examination of a 16th-century *Nursing Madonna*
(*Madonna Lactans*) [53] by an anonymous master of Bruges clearly shows

the Madonna employing the double-split hand for practical reasons, rather than as a symbolic gesture. The same is true of a number of other paintings that show the Madonna breastfeeding.

Kunesh makes a convincing case for the origin of the hand gesture displayed in El Greco's portrait of the nobleman and in other similar cases. All that remains is to explain the connection between breastfeeding and the symbolic gesture. Kunesh argues that 'the gesture's occurrence can be seen in paintings of the Virgin Mary in a nursing attitude but without a child, in a position of maternal care for mortals seeking heavenly salvation. The gesture later appears in art without a nursing context, used by saintly characters and, ultimately, secular figures such as El Greco's *Caballero*.'

The gesture, argues Kunesh, is therefore essentially a protective one, rather like keeping your fingers crossed as a covert way of making the sign of the cross to defend yourself against hostile elements. The double-split hand imitates the action of sacred breastfeeding, and the placing of the hand on the chest with this particular configuration of the fingers, by either sex, summons up the nurturing power of the mother goddess. Unlike the sign of the cross, however, the double-split hand did not survive into modern times and its symbolic meaning was lost. Only the ingenuity of Kunesh's painstaking research has resurrected it for us.

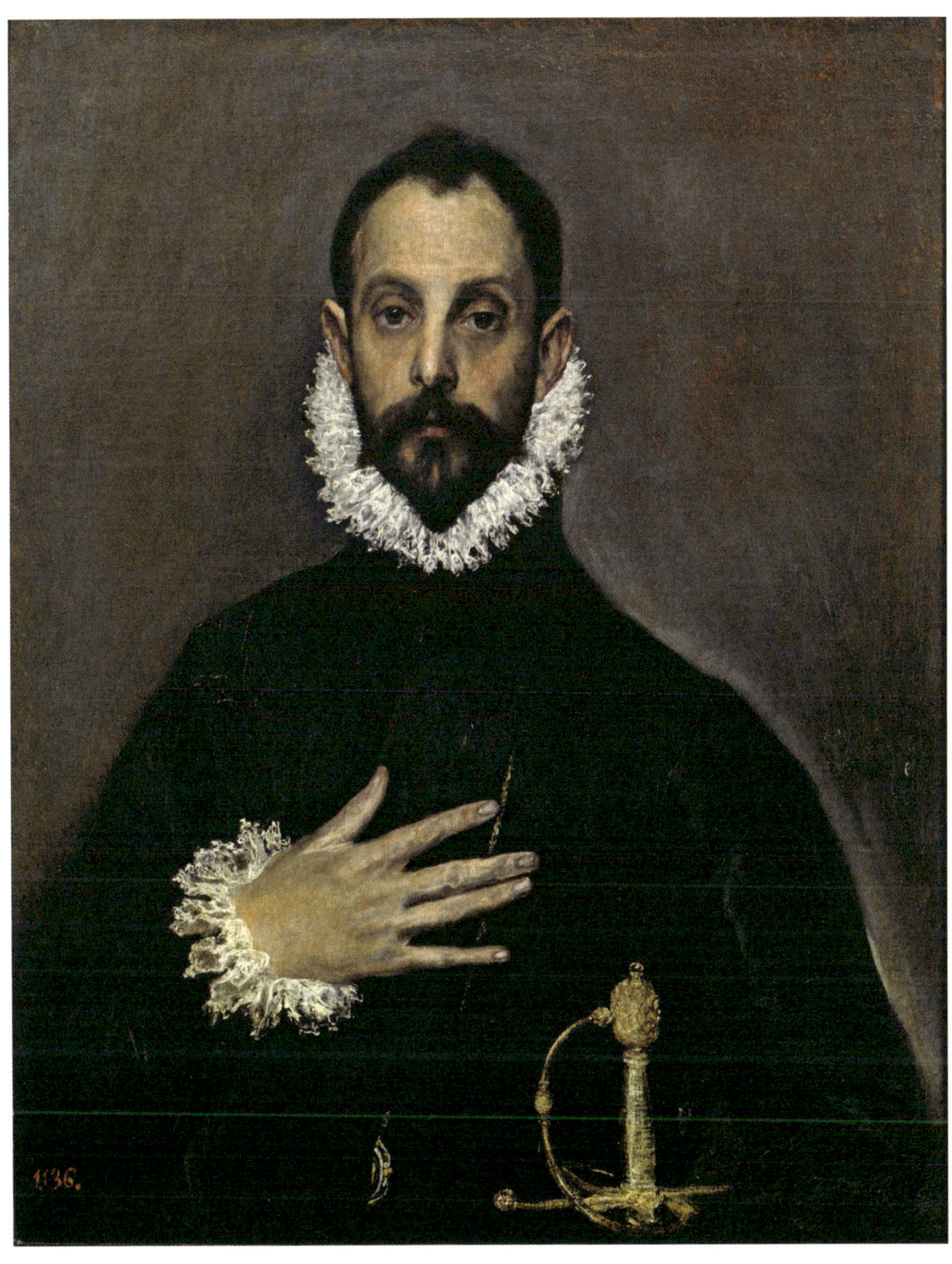

51. **El Greco,** *The Nobleman with his Hand on his Chest,* **c. 1580, oil on canvas**

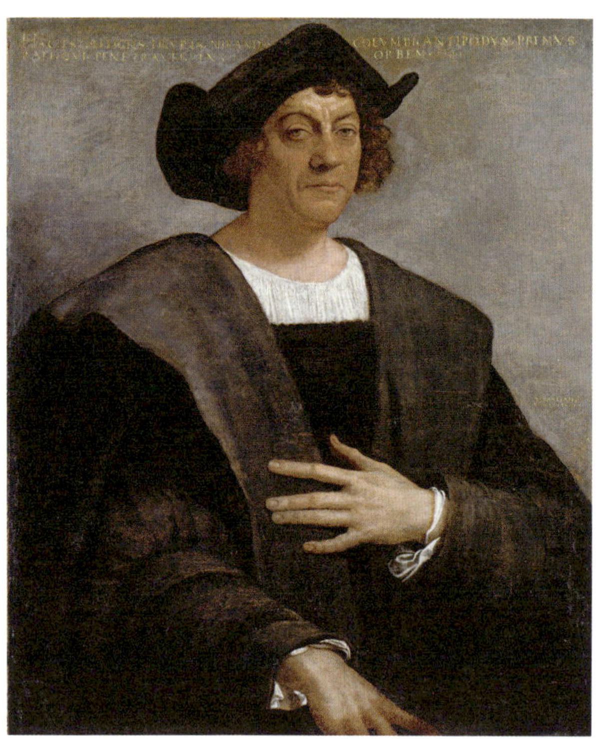

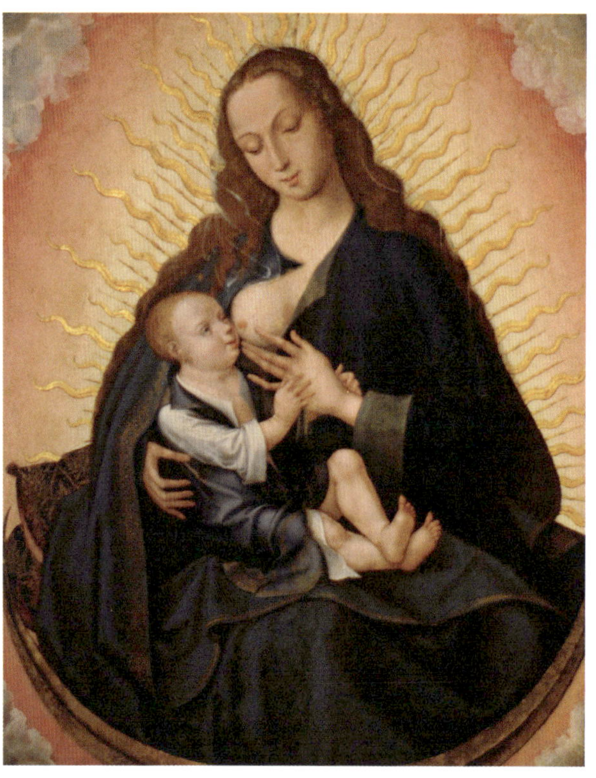

52. above **Sebastiano del Piombo,**
Portrait of a Man, Said to be
Christopher Columbus, 1519,
oil on canvas

53. left **Unknown master**
of Bruges, *Nursing Madonna*
(*Madonna Lactans*), **16th century**

54. opposite **Agnolo Bronzino,**
Maria de' Medici, 1551, **tempera**
on wood

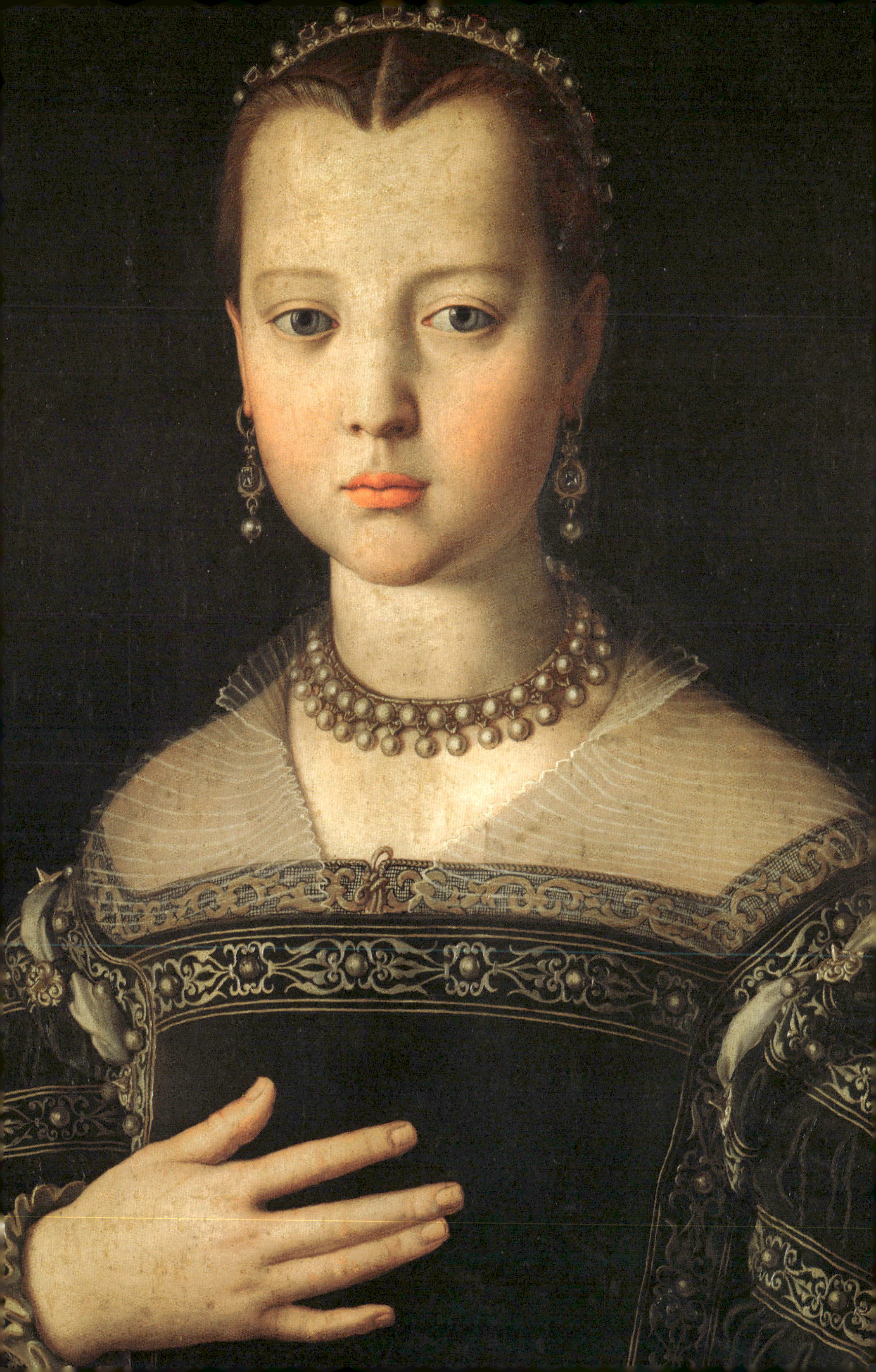

The Hidden Hand

One of the best-known gestures in historical portraits is Napoleon's hidden hand [58]. The emperor stands proudly erect with his right hand thrust deeply into his bulging white waistcoat. Many reasons, some of them verging on the ridiculous, have been offered to explain this characteristic posture: he had a stomach ulcer; he was winding his watch; he was scratching an itch; he had breast cancer; he had stomach cancer; he had a deformed hand; he had a shoulder injury that he wished to conceal; he kept a perfumed sachet in his vest that he would sniff surreptitiously; he was wearing a ring given to him by a secret lover that he had to hide from Josephine; he was giving a secret Masonic sign; and, finally, that artists do not like to paint hands.

The truth is rather different. To start with, all the explanations that relate specifically to Napoleon are discredited when it emerges that many other portraits from the same period also depict the hidden-hand gesture. In other words, it was not a personal idiosyncrasy of the emperor, but instead a fashion of the day. If you were an important person of high status having your portrait painted in the 18th century, it seems that standing with a hand thrust into your clothing was a popular pose.

The origin of this gesture can be traced back to ancient Greece and Rome, which rules out the Masonic explanation. As far as we can tell, two contrasting styles of oratory were used in these ancient civilizations. In one, the orator is seen gesticulating openly with his right hand to emphasize the points he is making. In the other, brandishing the arm was considered bad manners; instead, the orator spoke with his right arm thrust into his toga.

There are Greek and Roman statues portraying both these postures [57], and we have early writings that tell us how a speaker with a gesticulating arm was looked down upon. Writing in the 4th century BC, Aeschines of Macedon, an actor, orator and the founder of a school of rhetoric, condemned the use of excited gestures and urged the necessity of restraint, insisting that an orator should, while speaking, hold his hand within his robe. In a famous speech of 346 BC, he commented:

> And so decorous were those public men of old, Pericles, Themistocles and Aristeides...that to speak with the arm outside the cloak, as we all do nowadays as a matter of course, was regarded then as an ill-mannered thing, and they carefully refrained from doing it. And I can point to a piece of evidence which seems to me very weighty and tangible. I am sure you who sail over to Salamis have seen the statue of Solon there. You can therefore yourselves bear witness that in the statue...Solon stands with his arm inside his cloak. Now this

is a reminiscence, fellow citizens, and an imitation of the posture
of Solon, showing his customary bearing as he used to address the
people of Athens.

In the 18th century, the Grand Tour of classical locations became
extremely popular with wealthy young upper-class men, who grew
familiar with the costumes and conduct of the inhabitants of ancient
Greece and Rome. This knowledge seems to have spread the idea that
it is more dignified to conceal your right hand when striking a pose
[55, 56]. The artists of the day soon began to suggest to their sitters that,
when having a portrait painted, it would benefit them to stand with
the right hand thrust into their clothing. In 1737, in an etiquette guide
entitled *The Rudiments of Genteel Behavior*, the author, François Nivelon,
remarked that the hidden-hand pose signified 'manly boldness tempered
with modesty'. Increasingly, the pose came to be considered a sign of
good breeding.

There was another feature of the hidden hand that added to its
appeal: it symbolically incapacitated the sword arm. Placing the right
hand inside clothing was the opposite of holding it ready to grasp one's
sword. It therefore said to the onlooker, 'I am being benignly non-
aggressive', as well as, 'I am too dominant to worry about any threat
or the need to defend myself. I am a firm leader who is also calm, cool
and collected.'

The popularity of the gesture declined in the 19th century, but it did
not disappear altogether, and there are isolated examples of it even in the
20th century. One leader who favoured it was the Soviet dictator Joseph
Stalin [59], as can be seen in certain portraits of him. It also survived into
the days of early photography, but it was then being used for a special
reason. With the early cameras, the exposure-time was so long that sitters
found it hard to keep their hands still. Some photographers suggested
that their sitters use the hidden-hand pose, simply because it helped
to prevent the arm from moving.

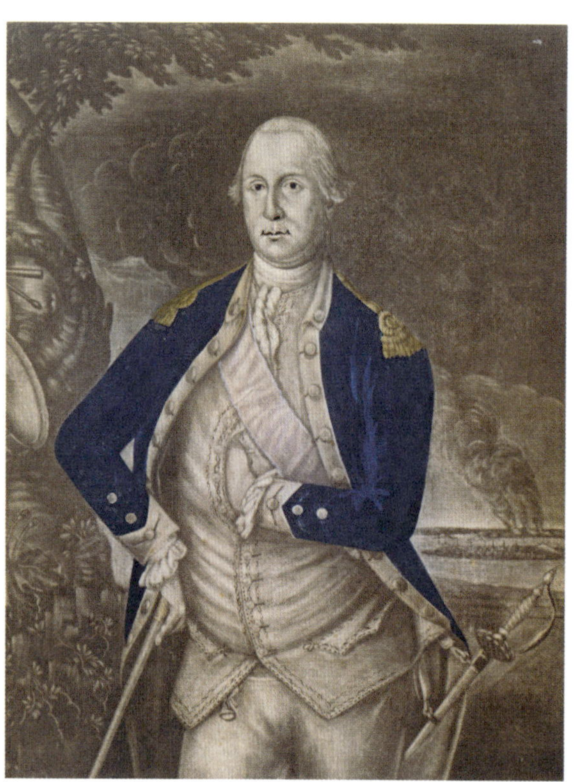

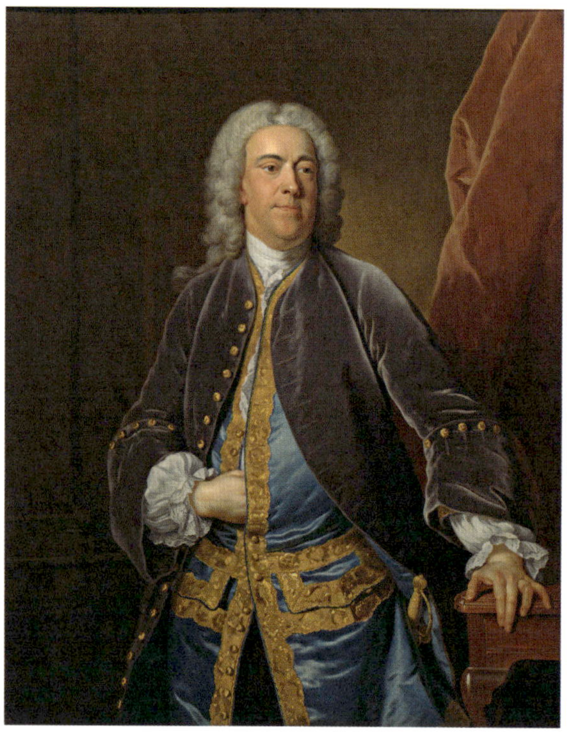

55. above **Joseph Hiller, Sr (after Charles Willson Peale),** *His Excellency George Washington Esq-r,* c. 1777, **mezzotint**

56. left **Jean-Baptiste van Loo,** *The Rt Honorable Stephen Poyntz, of Midgham, Berkshire,* c. 1740, **oil on canvas**

57. opposite **Attributed to Johann Heinrich von Dannecker,** *Polyhymnia, Muse of Lyric Poetry,* c. 1785–89, **marble (reduced copy of a statue discovered in 1774 in the Villa Cassia in Tivoli, Italy)**

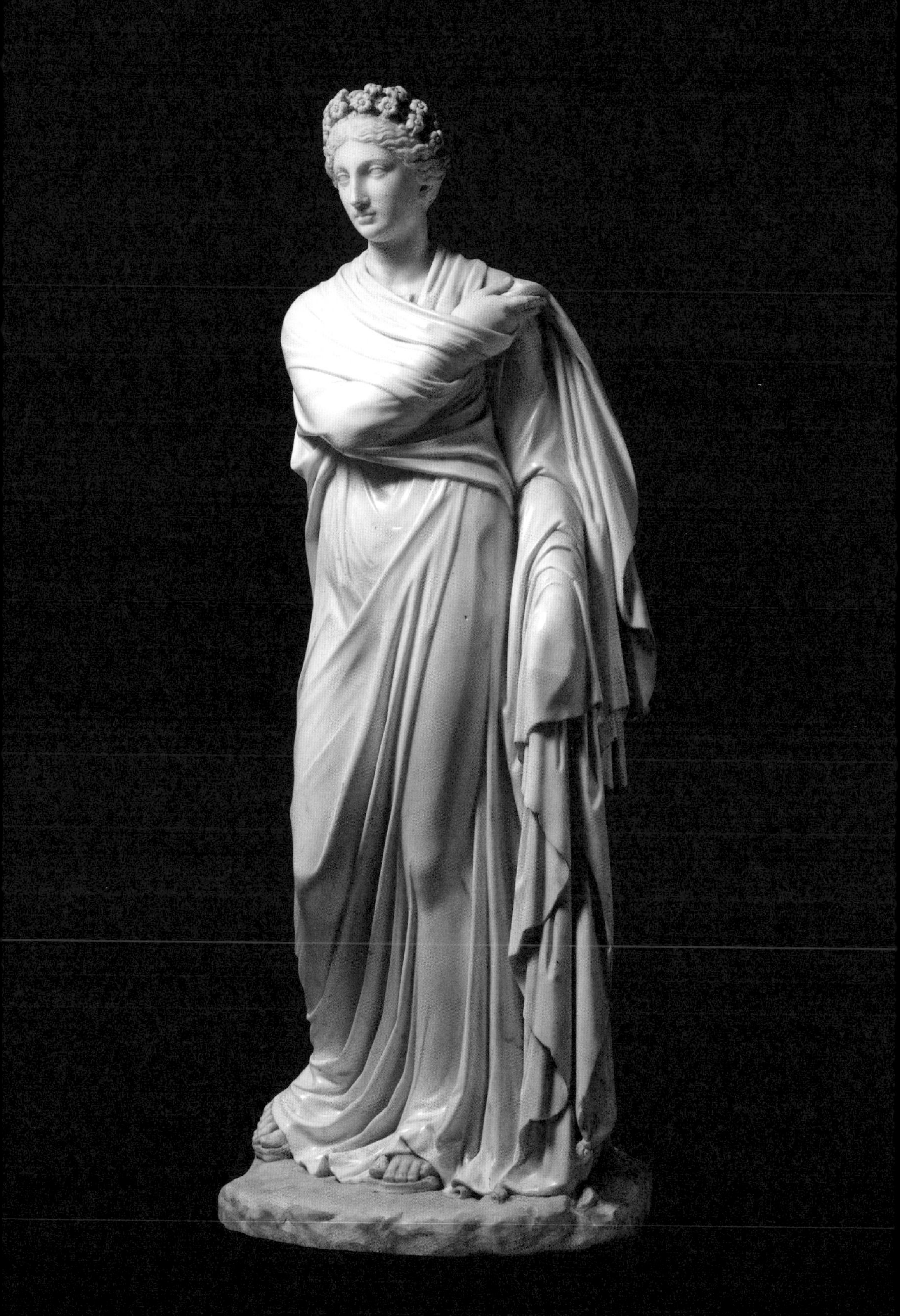

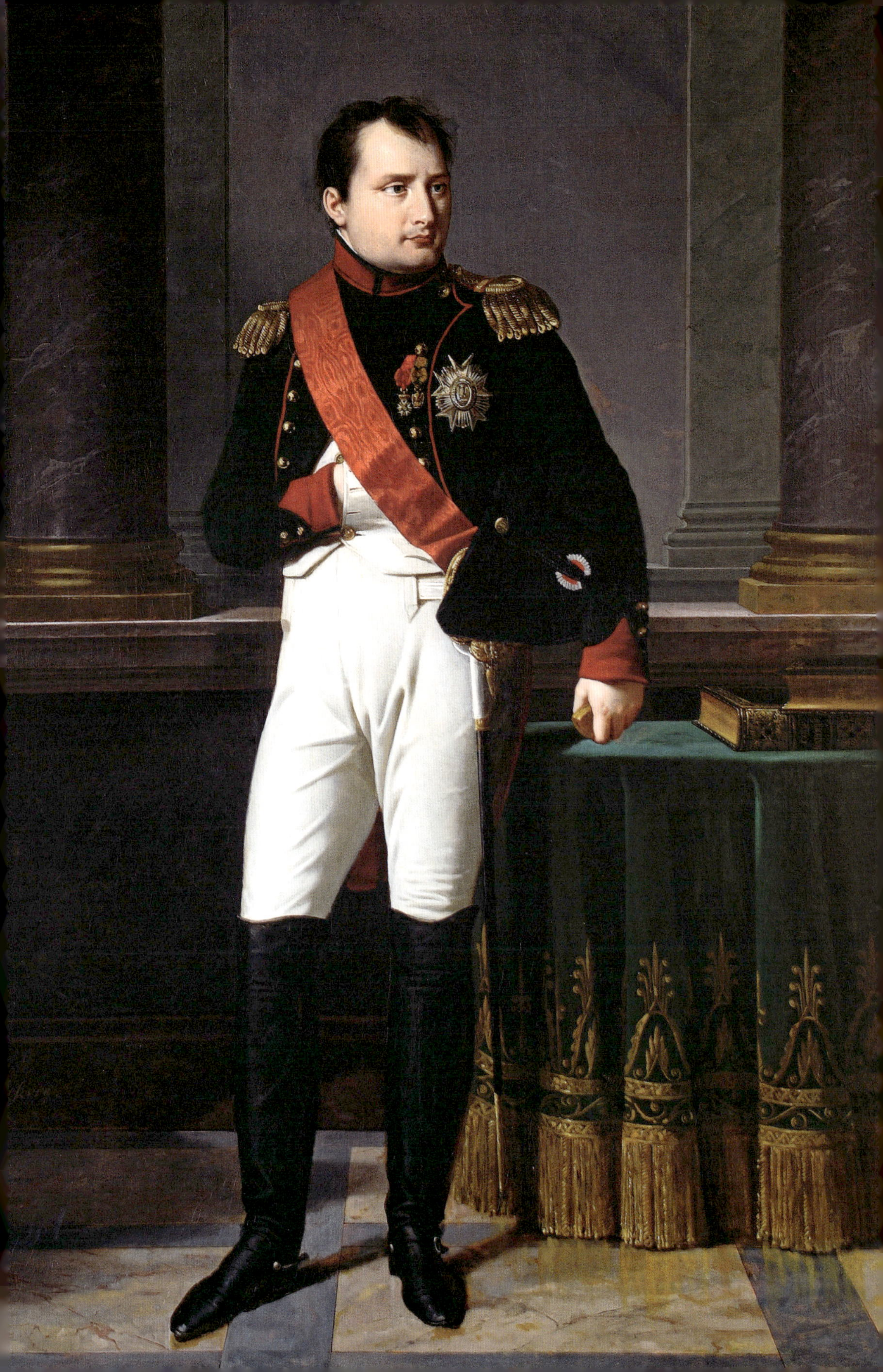

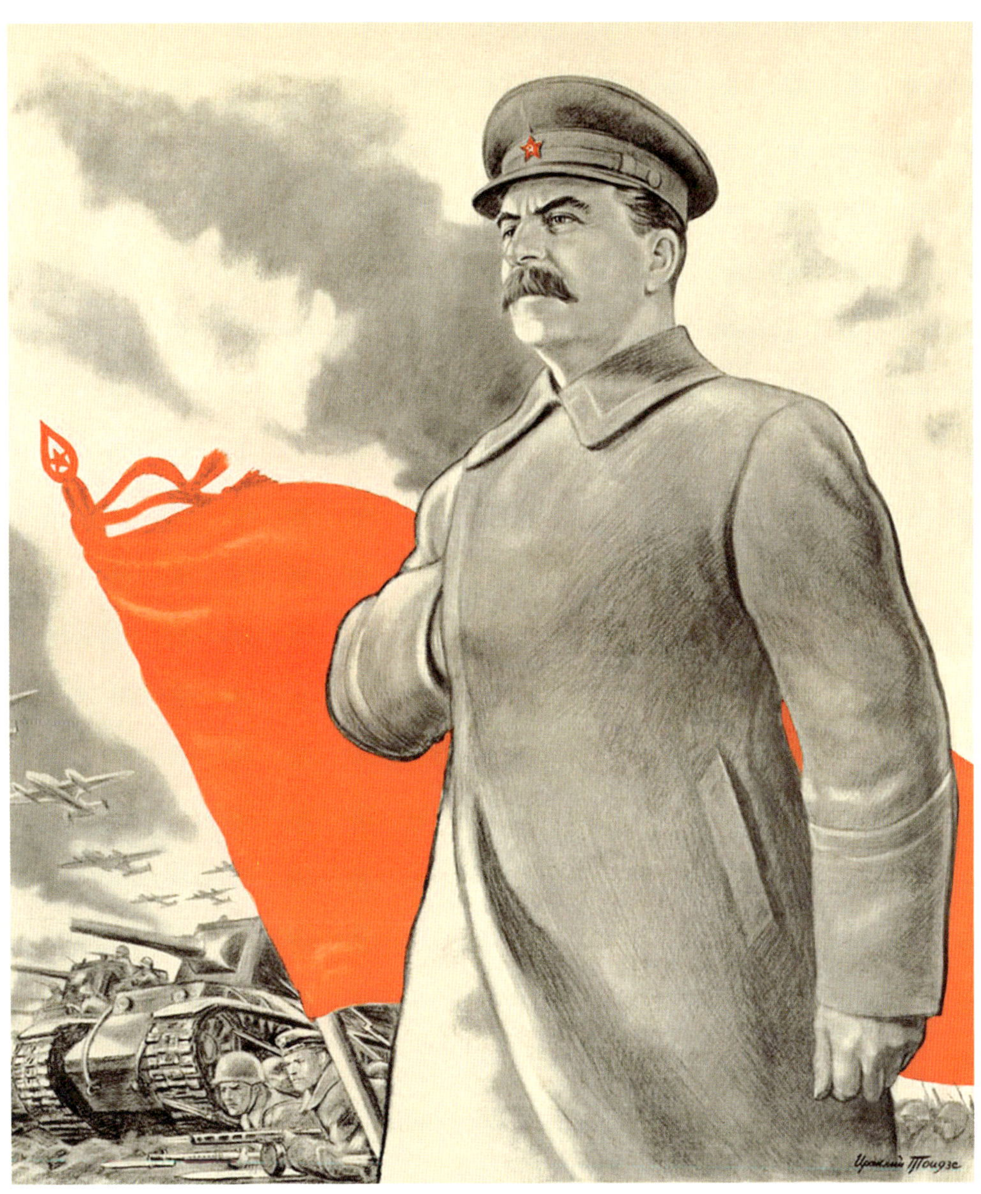

58. opposite **Robert Lefèvre,**
Napoleon Bonaparte **(detail),**
1812, oil on canvas

59. above **Irakli Toidze,**
Stalin Is Leading Us to Victory,
1943, Soviet poster

The Dominant Elbow

The posture known as 'arms akimbo', in which the hands are placed on the hips and the elbows point out sideways, is essentially an unfriendly gesture. It is as if the arms are arrows pointing away from the body, saying 'keep away from me'. Arms held forward invite an embrace, but arms held akimbo are anti-embrace.

In ordinary social encounters, the akimbo posture is often performed unconsciously. There is nothing calculated about it, and the person performing it is unaware of their actions. It can occur in two different contexts. The first is when something has gone wrong and the perpetrator feels uncomfortable. They would like to be somewhere else, but because they are trapped where they are by social pressures, they stand their ground and display the 'keep away from me' signal.

The second context is when the person concerned adopts the posture as a display of arrogant superiority, transmitting the signal 'you are not worthy of coming into close proximity with me'. Although the two situations are very different, they carry the same message: keep away from me. Where works of art are concerned, especially portraits, it is usually the second context that is involved. A high-status sitter sticks out his (for it is usually a man) elbow to suggest he is so important that he is not to be closely approached or, heaven forbid, embraced. He is above such things.

It is not clear whether important people sitting for their portraits displayed the dominant elbow automatically, or whether the artists, who were skilled in depicting their subjects advantageously – to make them look as grand as possible – would consciously pose their sitters in a special way. The latter seems more likely.

In the history of portraiture, the depiction of the akimbo posture was most popular in the 16th and 17th centuries. The art historian Joaneath Spicer pointed out in her essay 'The Renaissance Elbow' (1991) that in portraits from about 1500 to 1650 [61], the increased importance given to the male elbow is 'indicative essentially of boldness or control – and therefore of the self-defined masculine role, at once protective and controlling, in contemporary society'.

Although Spicer's detailed study ends in the 17th century, the elbow display does not stop then. It still appears, often in an exaggerated form with a protruding hip, in the 18th century, and is almost always confined to male subjects, with females adopting a more demure posture. When the upper classes were commissioning portraits of their children, even tiny boys were posed in this arrogant, cocksure fashion.

It is possible to find examples of the dominant elbow in works from the early 19th century, but it subsequently began to decline and

is rarely seen in modern portraiture. A number of works by Kehinde
Wiley, including *Big Daddy Kane* (2005) and *John Wilmot, 2nd Earl
of Rochester* (2013) [60], prove the exception, but there is a special reason
for the elbow pose in these particular paintings. The artist, who is known
for his portraits of young African American men, has stated that he likes
to portray his subjects 'fashioned in urban attire, within the field of power
reminiscent of Renaissance artists'. In other words, these paintings are
a deliberate imitation of the power portraits of earlier centuries and the
poses that the sitters assumed. As with all dominant-elbow displays, they
certainly succeed in endowing the subject with an air of lofty arrogance.

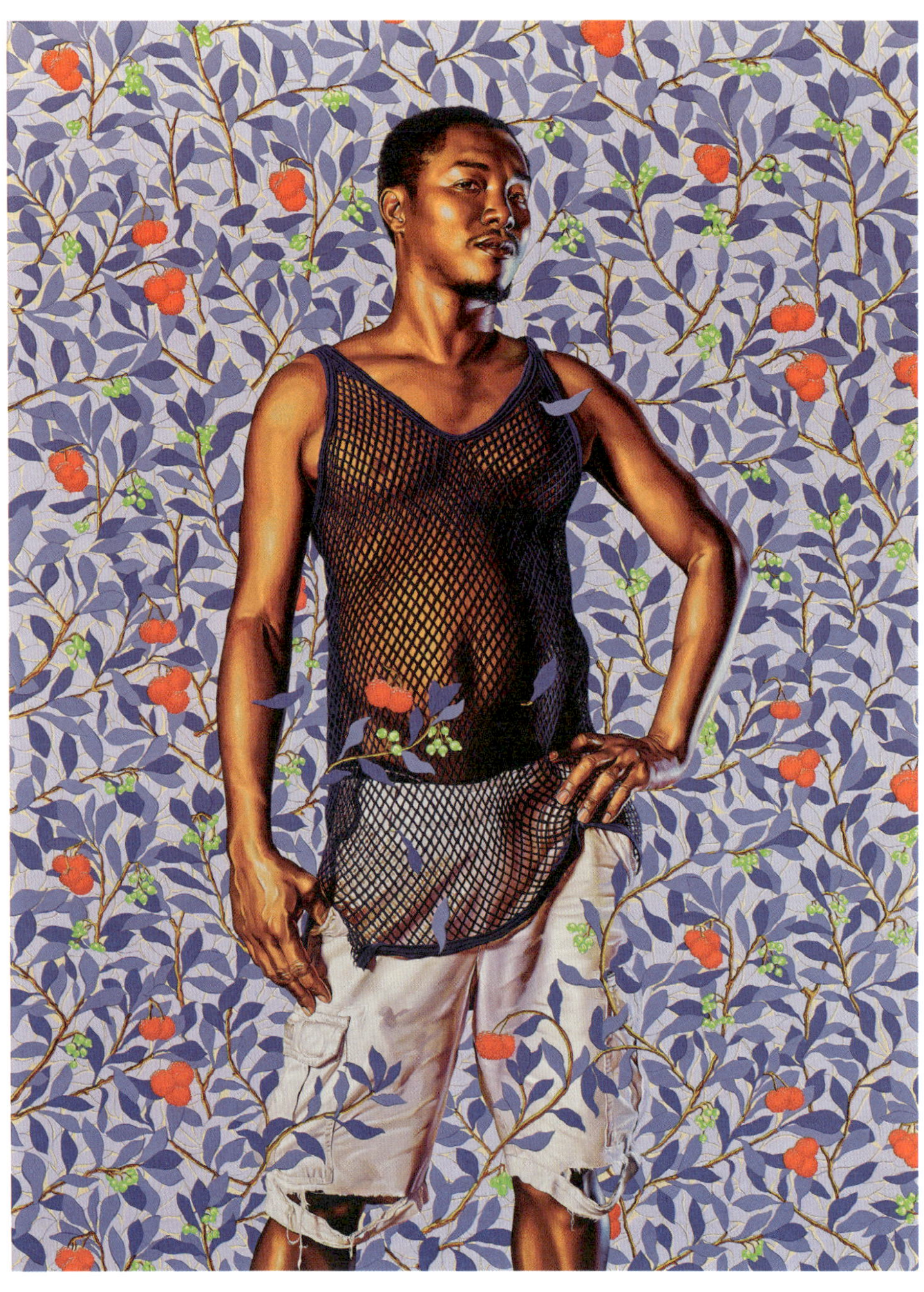

60. **Kehinde Wiley,** *John Wilmot,*
2nd Earl of Rochester, 2013,
oil on canvas

    Status / The Dominant Elbow

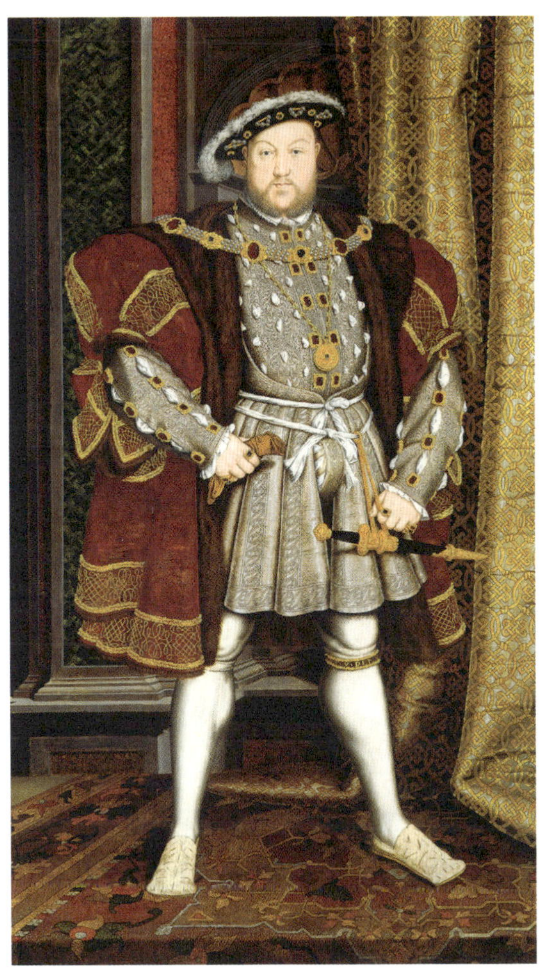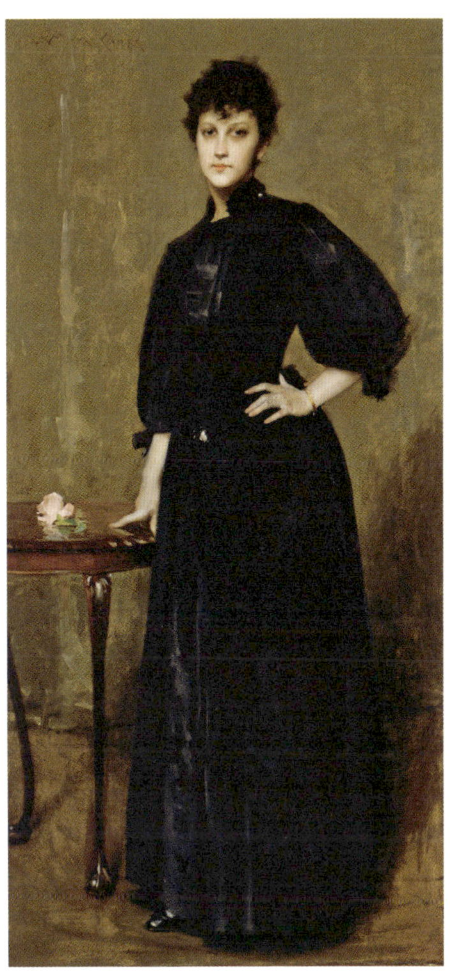

61. above left **Workshop of Hans Holbein the Younger**, *Henry VIII*, c. 1537, oil on panel

62. above right **William Merritt Chase**, *Lady in Black*, 1888, oil on canvas

The Codpiece

One of the most surprising instances of body language to be recorded in the history of traditional European art is the erection of the penis. Yet it is to be found blatantly and proudly displayed in the form of the medieval codpiece. One might have expected such a display to be confined to secretly collected examples of the pornographer's art, but the opposite is true. It appeared publicly in official portraits of kings and nobles [64, 65] right through to the peasant scenes of the Bruegels, and at the time was widely recognized as a socially acceptable, masculine status display indicating a high level of virility.

It began modestly enough, as a way of concealing the male genitals rather than displaying them. In the early 15th century, there had been a modification of male clothing that threatened to expose 'a gentleman's privy parts'. His costume consisted of a tunic or doublet above a pair of leggings. The leggings were fastened onto the tunic, but when fashion determined that the tunic should become shorter, the male genitals were ill-concealed and caused outrage among the more prudish members of society.

In a sermon given by an Italian priest in 1429, parents were criticized for dressing their sons in 'a doublet that reaches only to the navel [and] stockings with a little piece in front and one in back, so that they show a lot of flesh for the sodomites'. A little later, in 1463, the situation became so serious that the English Parliament issued an order making it compulsory for a man to cover 'His privy Members and Buttokes'.

Something had to be done. The answer was an addition to the male costume: a triangular piece of cloth that was stitched into the stockings below and the tunic above. Although the codpiece was intended to preserve modesty, it was soon being enlarged with padding to make it more comfortable. Over time, as more padding was added, the temptation to decorate it with silks, velvets, jewels and embroidery proved irresistible. As well as growing in size, it also became more conspicuous in shape, and began to thrust itself upwards in a phallic display. By the mid-16th century, it had reached epic proportions and was even being built into suits of armour – a trend that amused the French author François Rabelais, who commented that men's soft parts needed to be protected in battle, just as nature had protected nuts with their shells.

The idea of presenting such a blatantly phallic display in polite society may seem odd to us today, but at the time virility was so closely linked to ideas of masculine power and military prowess that the upstanding codpiece seems to have escaped the attentions of the establishment's moralists. Its popularity continued well into the latter part of the 16th century, but by the beginning of the 17th it had been overtaken by other fashions. Fast-forward to the 19th century and the codpiece had become such an embarrassing costume appendage that one Victorian museum classified the surviving examples in its collections under the heading 'shoulder pads'.

It would not be seen again in the Western world until 1971, when Stanley Kubrick's film *A Clockwork Orange* [63] featured a gang of rapist thugs wearing cloth codpieces and, on special occasions, a long phallic nose. This theme was later taken up by some heavy metal rock groups, notably GWAR, who appeared on stage wearing huge, elaborately decorated codpieces, although the fashion was short-lived.

On the other side of the world, in New Guinea, high-status males in the villages of the Sepik region have been wearing tribal codpieces for centuries. These so-called 'phallocrypts' are held taut by strings attached to their waists, giving the impression of a permanent erection. Many phallocrypts are elaborately decorated and have become works of art in their own right.

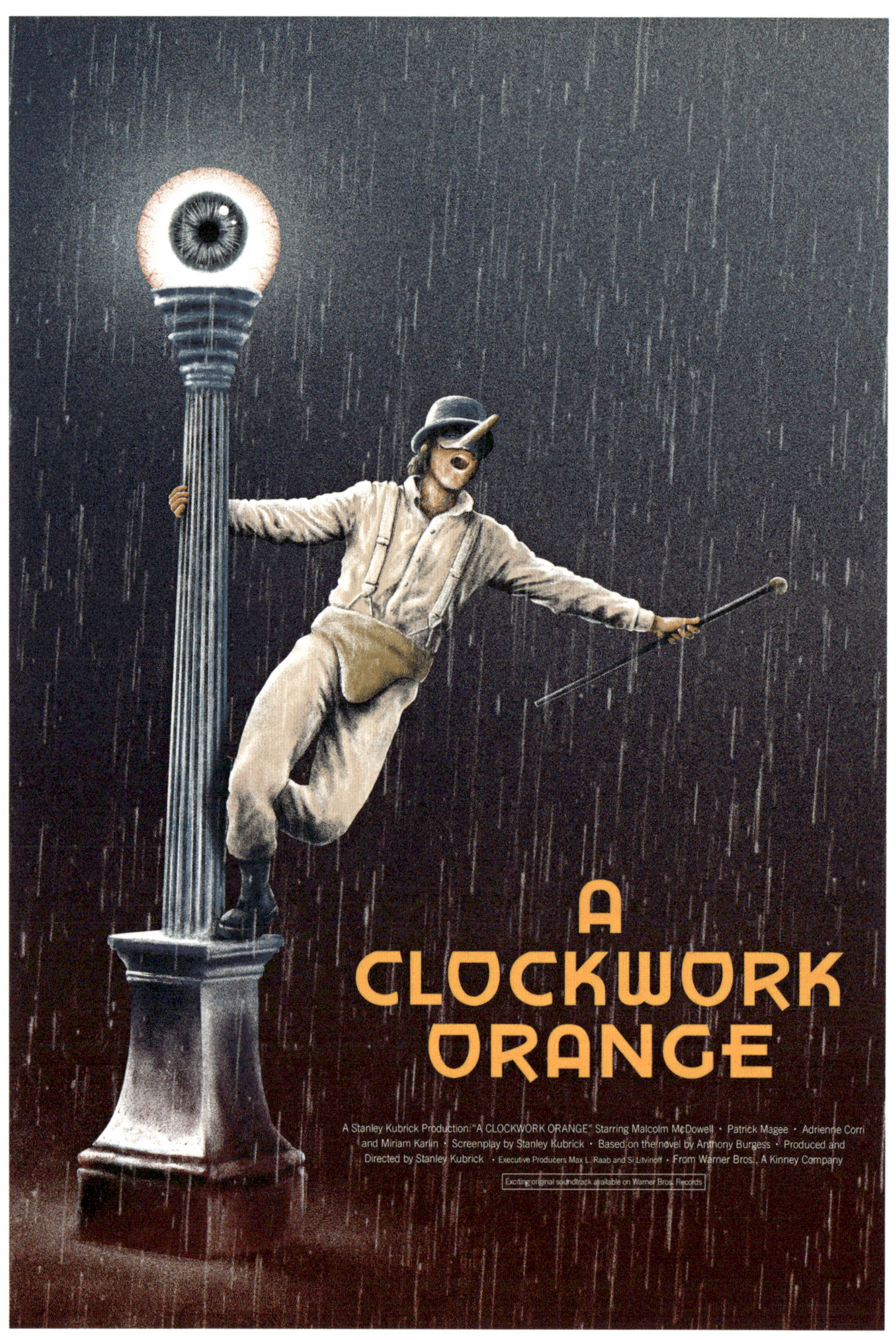

A
CLOCKWORK
ORANGE
A Stanley Kubrick Production: "A CLOCKWORK ORANGE" Starring Malcolm McDowell · Patrick Magee · Adrienne Corri
and Miriam Karlin · Screenplay by Stanley Kubrick · Based on the novel by Anthony Burgess · Produced and
Directed by Stanley Kubrick · Executive Producers Max L. Raab and Si Litvinoff · From Warner Bros., A Kinney Company
Exciting original soundtrack available on Warner Bros. Records

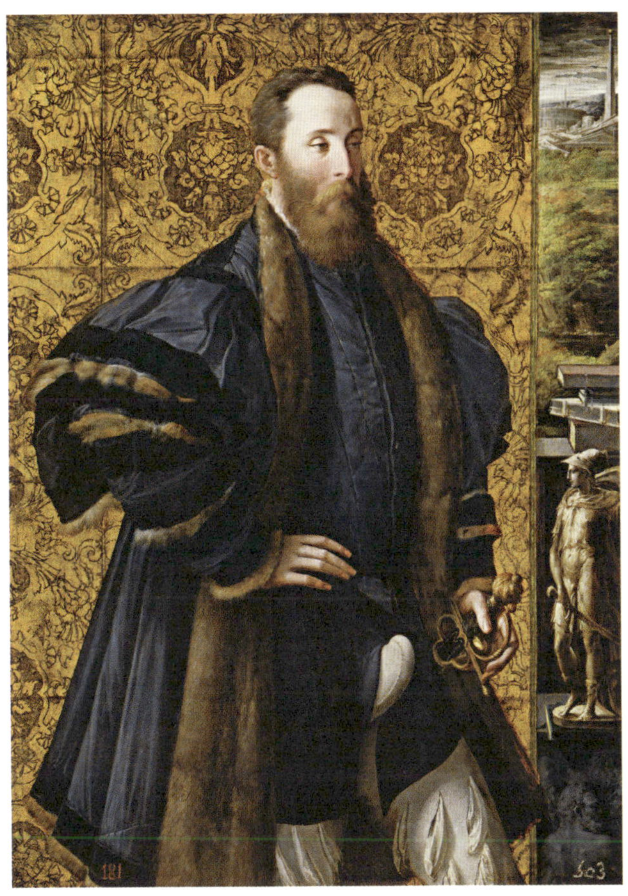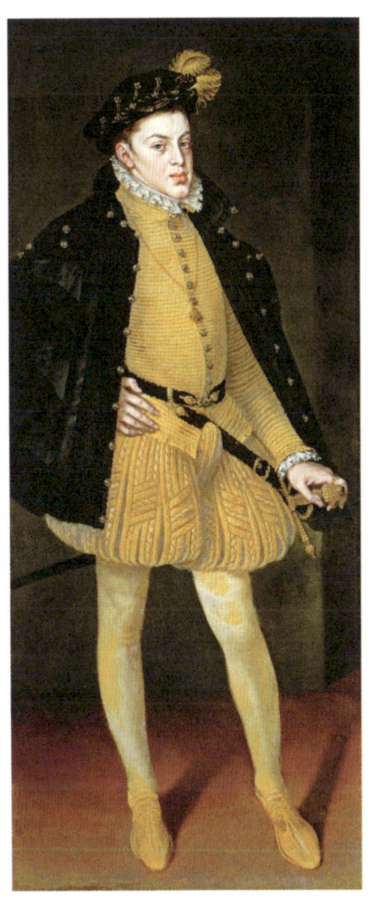

63. opposite **Adam Rabalais, *Cinematic Psychopaths – A Clockwork Orange*, 2015**

64. above left **Parmigianino, *Pietro Maria Rossi, Count of San Secondo*, 1535–38, oil on panel**

65. above right **Alonso Sánchez Coello, *Infante Don Carlos*, 1564, oil on canvas**

The Pointed Foot

When a royal portrait is being painted, the position of the subject's legs is carefully considered. High social status demands that the feet should be placed in a particular way. Standing with the feet together – or to attention, in military terms – is a dutiful position associated with people of low status and is avoided at all costs. This leaves two alternatives: to stand with the feet placed wide apart, or to have one foot pointing in front of the other. The preference in Tudor times was to stand with a balanced posture and the feet apart, the favourite stance of Henry VIII. In fact, it is hard to imagine him being portrayed in any other position.

This all changed with the Sun King, Louis XIV of France. His most famous portrait, painted in 1701 by the French artist Hyacinthe Rigaud [68], depicts him with one foot in front of the other, in a highly contrived posture. The forward foot is pointing directly at the onlooker, as though it is taking aim in his direction. The rear foot is at right angles to it and is seen in profile. It has been suggested that this pose was developed, consciously or unconsciously, as a way of displaying an erotic zone of the male body, namely the inner part of the thigh.

This portrait presents a striking contrast between the king's head and his legs. The puffy face is that of an ageing 63-year-old man, while his slender, elegant legs – fully exposed by the way he has swept back his coronation robes – are those of a young ballet dancer. His shoes have diamond buckles and conspicuous, bright-red heels. The king was a brilliant dancer, capable of performing complicated moves, all of which were noted down by his dancing master. When these were codified and published in 1700, a new term was coined – choreography. This was the start of a new phase of dancing that would eventually see the birth of the ballet.

The high-status posture adopted by the Sun King was repeated in official portraits, not only of himself but also of later generations, throughout the 18th century [67]. The only variation was that sometimes it was the right foot that was put forward, rather than the left. It is amusing to note that modern celebrities still follow this tradition when being photographed on the red carpet at premieres and film festivals. Some of them are never photographed in any other way and must consciously adopt the pointed-foot pose whenever they see a photographer aiming a camera at them.

There is another, completely different version of the pointed-foot display that is associated with high status. In medieval times it became fashionable for young upper-class men to wear extremely long, pointed shoes called *poulaines* [66]. Reaching its height in the late 14th and early

15th centuries, this fad may have been inspired by the Crusades, when returning soldiers brought back exotic curiosities including oriental slippers with pointed, upturned toes. Over time, the length of these shoes was exaggerated until they became so cumbersome that it was difficult to walk. At their most extreme, they had points that extended 61 cm (24 in.) beyond the wearer's feet and had to be supported by wires connecting the tip of the shoe to the knee. It was, of course, this inefficiency that gave them their high-status appeal; they were so impractical that physical labour could not be performed while wearing them. This meant that they could only be worn by the wealthy leisure class, which puts them in the same category as the tradition of feet-binding among high-status women in the Far East. In the West feet were made artificially long, and in the East they were crushed to create the desired shape – in both cases making it difficult to walk and signifying the individual's separation from the working classes.

This high-status display was repeatedly portrayed by the artists of the day, and *poulaines* became so notorious that the more conservative elements in society began to disapprove, calling the new fashion ridiculous and disgraceful. They were concerned that if it spread to the lower orders, it could interfere with work efficiency. Church leaders condemned *poulaines* as Devil's Fingers, but it seemed as if nothing could dim their popularity. As a result, in the mid-14th century, the English king Edward III had to introduce a law to control the length of the shoes. The working classes could wear only a 15 cm (6 in.) toe, while gentlemen could display a toe of 38 cm (15 in.) and the nobility even longer. Despite the disapproval of the authorities, the high-status pointed-toe display managed to survive for another half-century. It was not until 1410 that the extreme forms began to disappear, with *poulaines* eventually falling out of fashion in the 1480s.

Today, we may laugh at the exaggerations of the medieval pointed foot, but the people of that time would perhaps find the modern-day fashion for stiletto heels equally ridiculous in the way they create an extreme form of downward pointed foot. Modern males have largely managed to escape the pointed foot display, except for brief periods in the 1950s and 1970s, when 'winklepickers' were in vogue in rock 'n' roll culture.

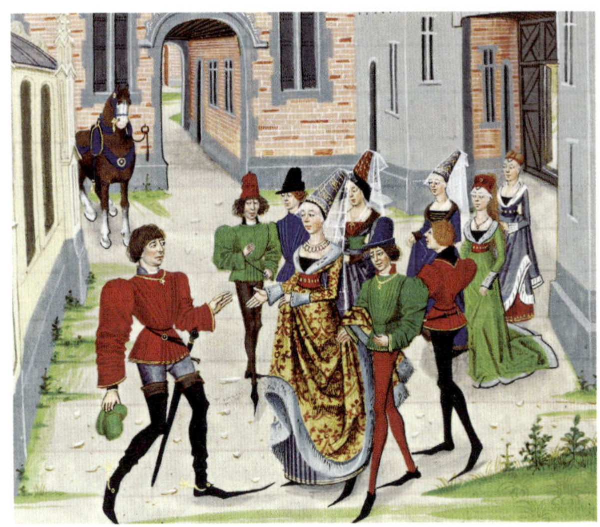

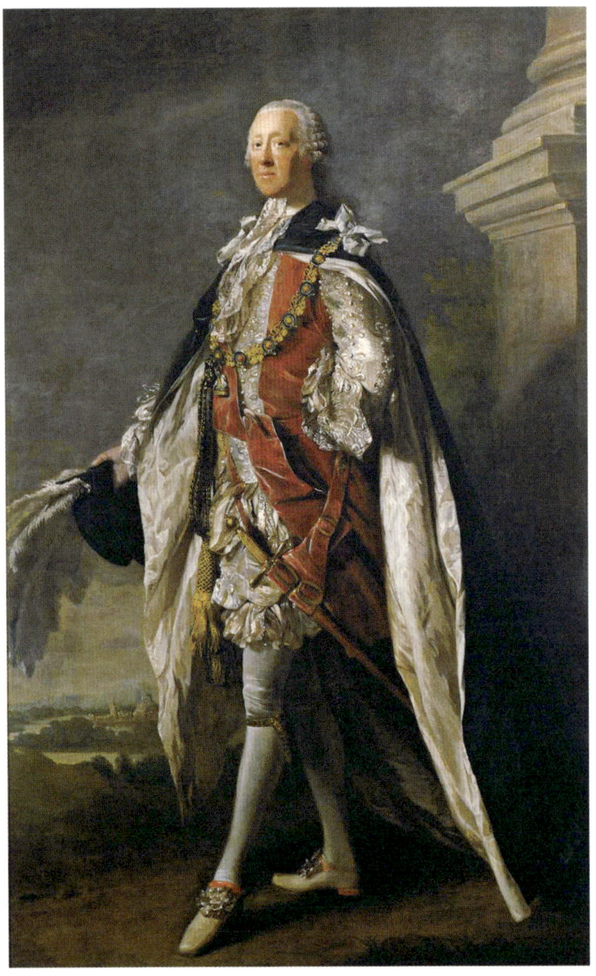

66. above **Loyset Liédet, wedding scene with the groom wearing long _poulaines_, c. 1470, miniature**

67. left **Allan Ramsay, _Richard Grenville, 2nd Earl Temple_, 1762, oil on canvas**

68. opposite **Hyacinthe Rigaud, _Portrait of Louis XIV (1638–1715), King of France_, 1701, oil on canvas**

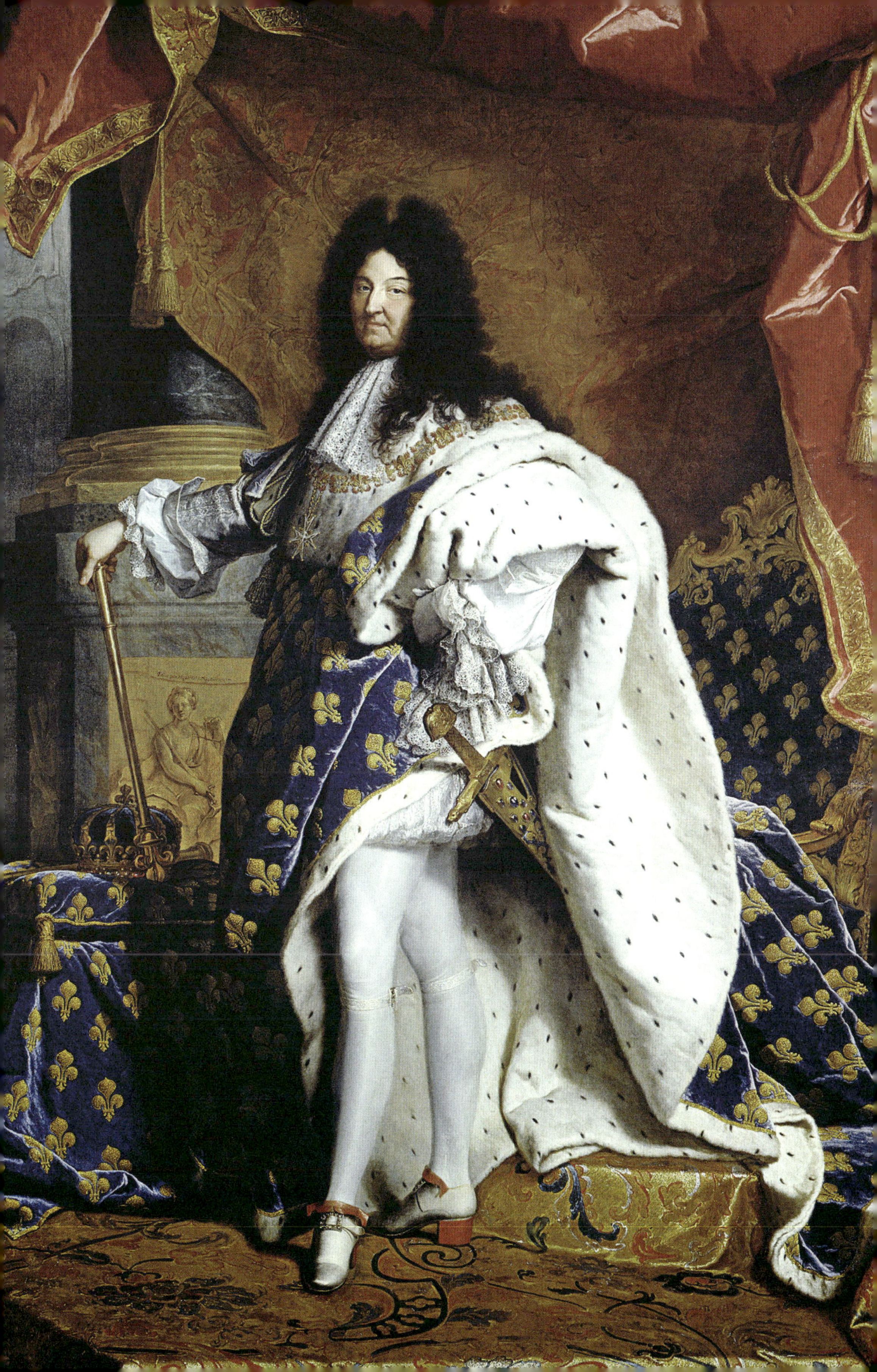

The Bent Body

Historically, high-status members of society would never have allowed themselves to be depicted in a bent-over posture. In paintings, the vertical, stiffly erect bodies of the social elite contrast vividly with those of working people, who are shown in positions of hard toil. Even when high-status individuals were depicted performing some kind of energetic activity, the paintings would nearly always show them in a swaggeringly upright posture, wielding a sword or riding high in the saddle. The words 'high' and 'low', when discussing status, apply not only to power but also to body language.

In the illustrated manuscripts of the 14th and 15th centuries, a popular subject was the construction of cathedrals or towers by hard-working stonemasons. They were nearly always shown labouring with their bodies bent low, sometimes watched by their superiors who, in sharp contrast, were seen standing stiffly erect.

In Flemish art of the 16th century, it became popular to portray the lower classes performing various menial tasks, often bent forward, crouching or kneeling. Gone were the artificial poses and pompous posturings of the social elite; in their place came vigorous muscular activity or perhaps physical exhaustion. A typical example is found in the work of the northern Italian artist Vincenzo Campi, who worked in the Flemish style. In his painting of a busy kitchen [69], of 1590–91, he shows us the toils and drudgery of the low-status members of society as the servant women bend over their tasks.

After the French Revolution, low-status members of society were sometimes viewed with more respect, but even as late as the 19th century, it was important – often self-important – figures who were more likely to be found on the canvases of professional artists. When, at the Paris Salon in 1857, Jean-François Millet exhibited his painting *The Gleaners* [70], depicting three peasant women at work in a field with their bodies bent over, it caused outrage. How could a serious artist make these women, from the lowest ranks of rural society, the central figures in a major oil painting? Salon paintings were always mythological or religious scenes or high-status portraiture, yet here was this sympathetic treatment of a trio of nobodies. One critic complained that Millet's 'three gleaners have gigantic pretensions, they pose as the Three Fates of Poverty...their ugliness and their grossness unrelieved.' What this remark reveals, of course, is the uncompassionate, callous way in which the 19th-century upper classes so often viewed and treated the lower classes. The strong reaction to Millet's painting stemmed, in part, from the reverberations of the French Revolution: the upper classes, looking nervously over their shoulders, were wondering whether the lower classes might start to rise up against them. Glorifying them in this large oil painting might only encourage them, and that made the social elite uneasy.

The Gleaners had a powerful influence on the younger artists of the day who, in the second half of the 19th century, started to rebel against the rules of traditional Salon art and portray all levels of society, relegating mythological and religious subjects to an increasingly minor role. Bent bodies, hard-working labourers, toiling servants and rural peasants featured more and more as the 19th century drew to a close. And something else was beginning to happen: artists were showing ordinary people having fun. The working classes were depicted drinking in bars, dancing in clubs, performing in theatres and strolling in the streets. Haughty posturing and pompous posing were being edged out as a new era of body language in art began to gain momentum.

In England, at about the same time that Millet's painting was causing an uproar in Paris, a London-born artist called John Linnell was quietly painting country scenes that were also populated by the bent figures of rural workers. He seems to have avoided controversy by making these figures slightly less dominant in his compositions. His paintings were primarily scenes of the British countryside, and the figures working there were smaller and more integrated into the general composition. It was clear that he was fascinated by the details of rural life, but in his later years he became known simply as a landscape painter, rather than someone who shone a spotlight on working people.

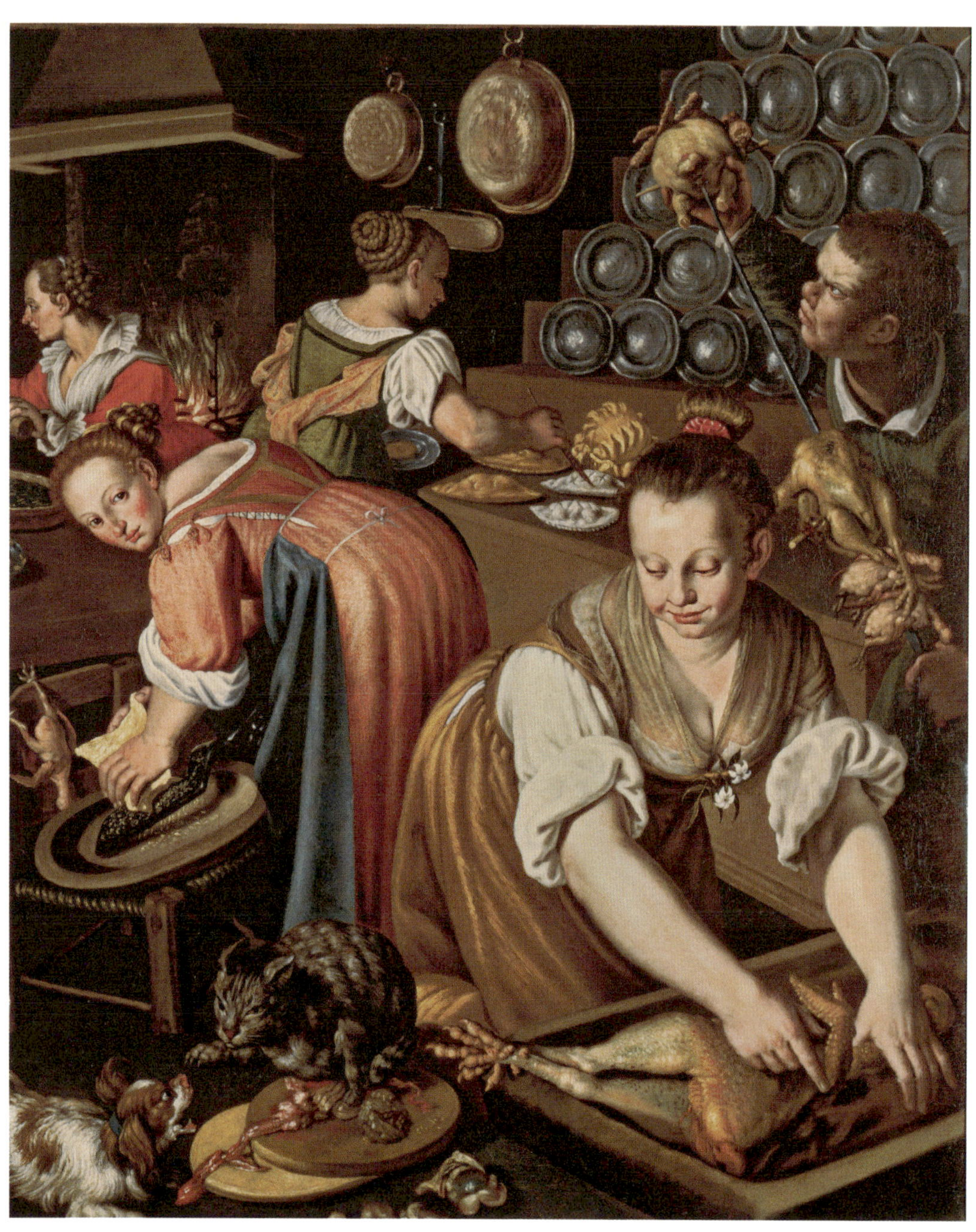

69. above **Vincenzo Campi**, *Kitchen*
(detail), 1590–91, oil on canvas

70. opposite, above **Jean-François Millet**,
The Gleaners, 1857, oil on canvas

71. opposite, below **Gustave Caillebotte**,
The Floor Planers, 1875, oil on canvas

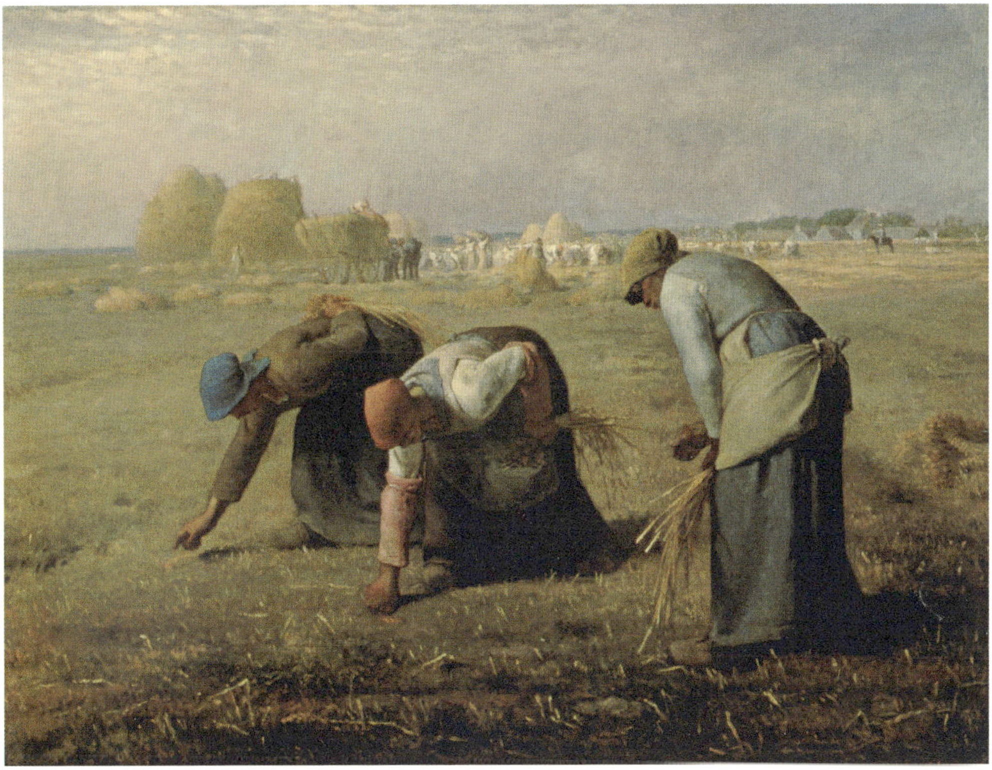

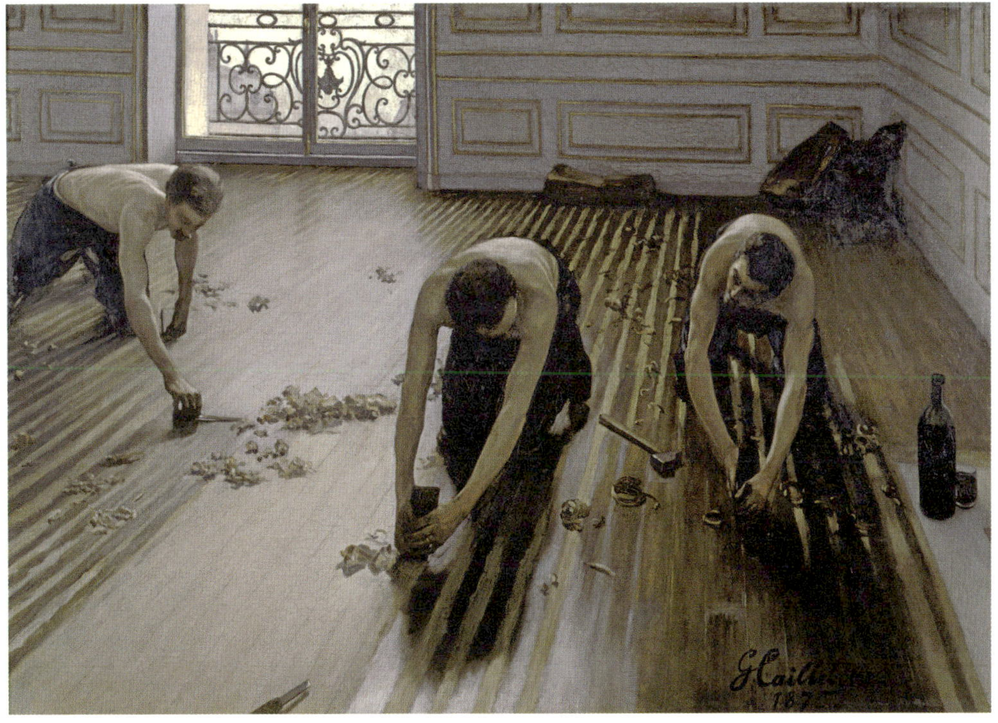

Uninhibited Actions and Urban Squalor

When we look at historical portraits of the social elite, their body language is inhibited, restrained and suppressed. By contrast, low-status subjects tend to show little restraint. If depicted at work, their actions are vigorous and muscular; if at play, they are ribald and disinhibited.

The Bruegels were masters of painting peasants enjoying themselves. Working in the Low Countries in the mid-16th century, Pieter Bruegel the Elder was so obsessed with recording the joyful excesses of village life that he acquired the nickname 'Peasant Bruegel'; it was also believed (incorrectly) that he himself must have come from a working-class background. His sons Pieter the Younger and Jan also depicted peasant scenes, as did a few other artists of their generation, although this was not a phase in the history of art that was to last long or to spread wide. It was an isolated instance of artists celebrating the joy of uninhibited amusements and excesses in rural working life.

The Bruegels' down-to-earth depiction of peasant feasts, dances, celebrations and games was devoid of sentimentality or criticism. Their pictures did not portray village life as quaintly charming or repulsively vulgar, but simply said: this is how it is. The result was an honest account of how the lower classes made life as enjoyable as possible, without the advantages – but also the restraints and restrictions – of high status. In Pieter Bruegel the Elder's wedding scenes [72], villagers dance with wild abandon, their limbs kicking and waving, pulling and pushing. Some are shown stuffing food into their mouths or drinking alcohol, others are kissing. In the wonderfully composed *The Land of Cockaigne* (1567) [73], the well-fed men are sprawled out on the ground in postures of abandoned relaxation. A more vivid contrast with the stiffly upright subjects of aristocratic portraits is difficult to imagine.

In his day, Pieter Bruegel the Elder was sometimes misinterpreted: his work was seen as poking fun at the loutish peasantry because his choice of subject matter was so at odds with earlier traditions. People found it hard to believe that he was simply celebrating village life and assumed that his work must contain some sort of moral condemnation of the clumsy fun and games portrayed. In the 19th century, Baudelaire was particularly critical, saying: 'I defy anyone to explain the diabolical and ribald curiosity-shop of Bruegel the Droll.' Today, we have a clearer picture. We see Bruegel as an acute observer, recording in his small notebooks – with great precision – every gesture and posture, in order to create an accurate depiction of the ordinary people that he loved, and to celebrate their daily lives through his paintings.

The rural poor could usually scratch a living from the countryside, but penury for the city-dweller was often a much more brutal experience. The lowest levels of urban existence all too often presented scenes of squalor, starvation and disease. For those who could obtain it, cheap alcohol was the only escape. In 18th-century London, William Hogarth captured this sad situation in such works as *Gin Lane* (1751) [74]. The central figure is a slouching, drunken woman, sprawled at the top of some steps; her legs are covered in sores, and she is so busy taking a pinch of snuff that she fails to notice her baby is tumbling headfirst to the ground below. Lower down the steps is a skeletal soldier holding an empty glass. To the left of the scene, a figure is seen sharing a bone with a dog. To the right, a woman is pouring alcohol down the throat of her child. In the background, other children can be seen drinking alcohol. Hogarth's brutally frank depiction was intended to draw attention to the child neglect that was commonplace in the city slums; indeed, Hogarth was one of the reformers involved in setting up the Foundling Hospital in London, which was established in 1739. His interest in this cause was personal: when he was a child, his family's business had gone bankrupt and he spent time in a debtors' prison – a traumatic experience that had left him with the lifelong determination to improve society.

During the Victorian era, while city slums still existed, concern was mounting over the appalling conditions, and the number of influential people demanding reforms began to grow. A French artist, Gustave Doré, was given the task of visually recording different aspects of London, including the slums and the working poor. The four-year project, a collaborative effort with the writer Blanchard Jerrold, resulted in the publication of *London: A Pilgrimage* (1872). Doré's depictions of poverty are haunting. The human figures in the slums display the body language of dejected resignation, boredom and misery. There is no liveliness in their postures, no excitement on their faces. When describing a rag-merchant's home, Jerrold makes the telling point that 'The extremes lie close together', with the magnificent homes of the rich not far from the wretched streets of the poor. The elderly rag-merchant is shown glumly examining fragments of cast-off clothing, and 'The old clothesman's children are rolling about upon his greasy treasure, while he...takes up each item, and estimates it to a farthing.'

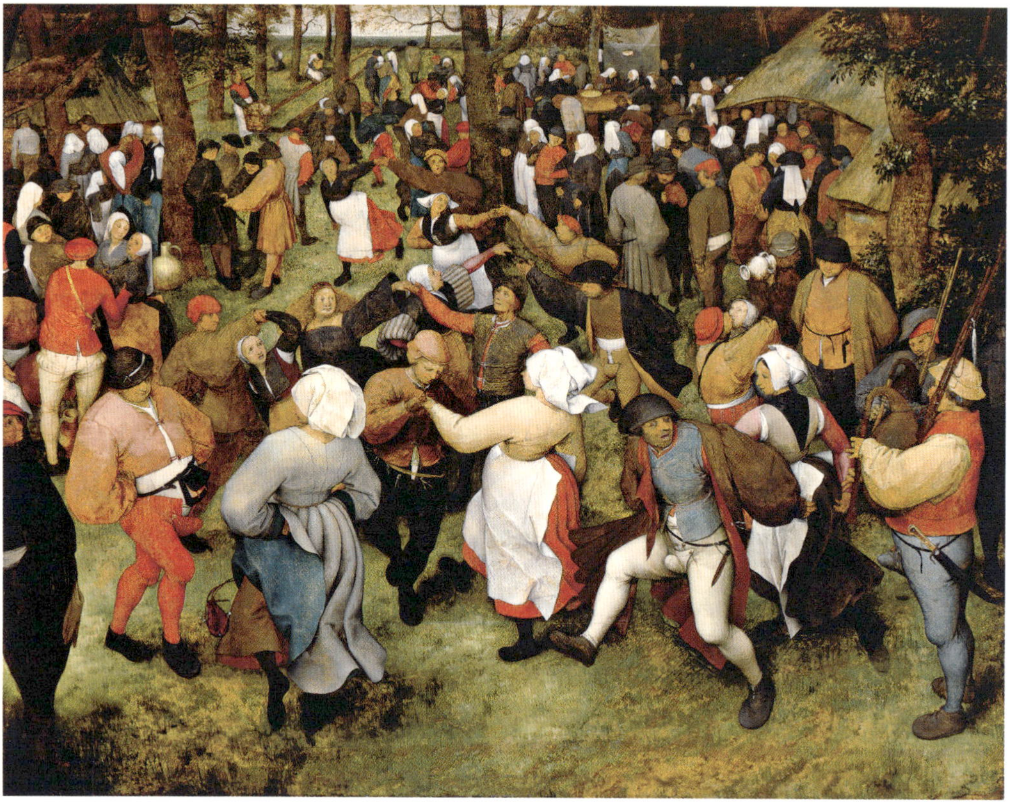

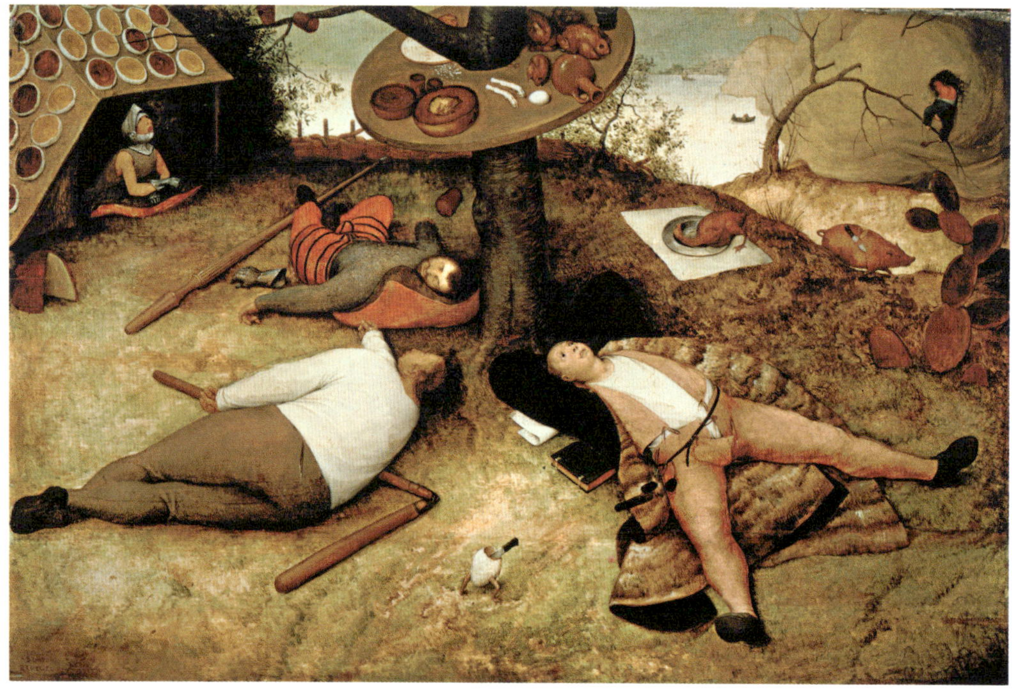

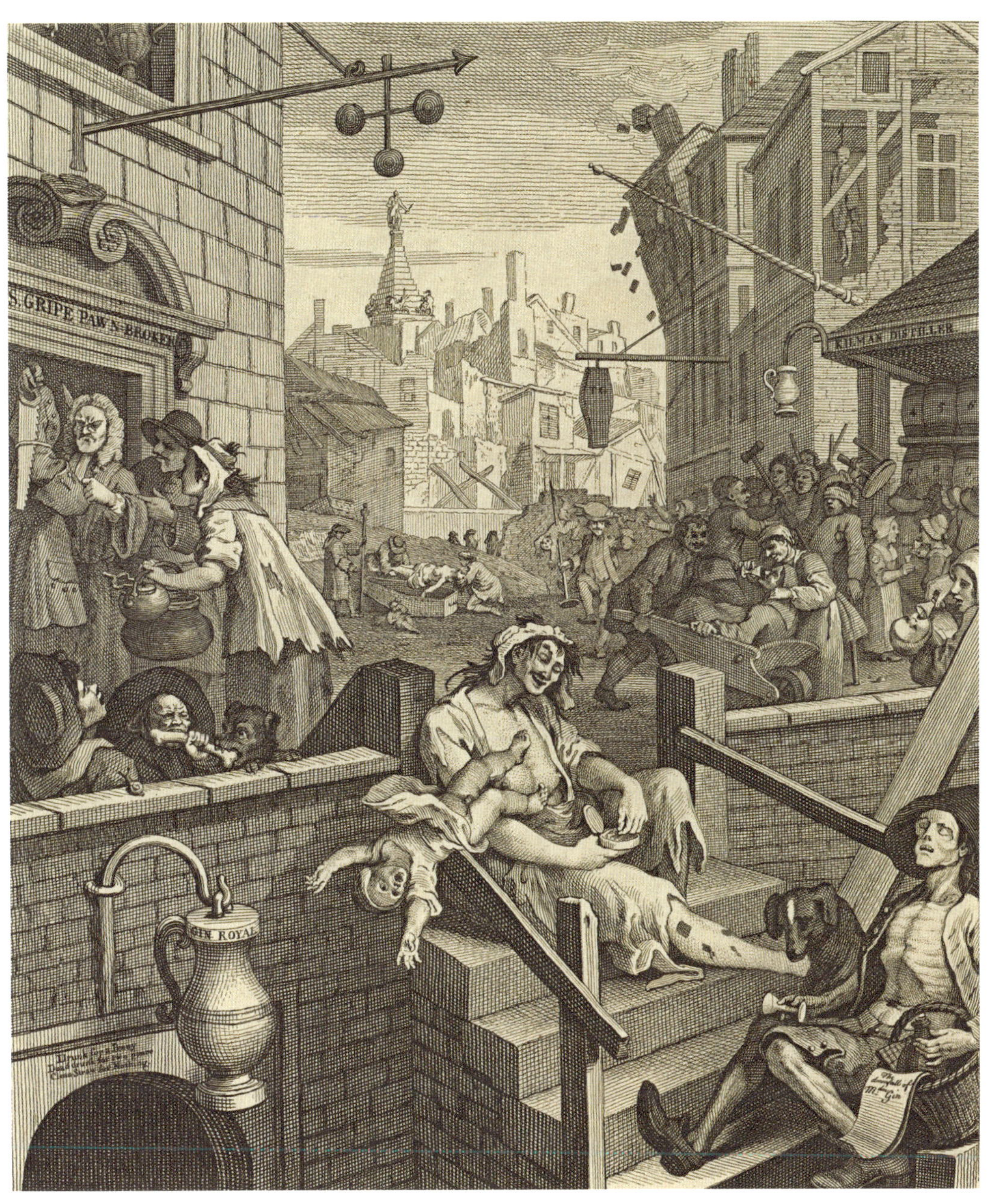

72. opposite, above **Pieter Bruegel the Elder,**
The Wedding Dance, 1566, oil on panel

73. opposite, below **Pieter Bruegel the Elder,**
The Land of Cockaigne, 1567, oil on panel

74. above **William Hogarth, *Gin Lane*, 1751,**
etching and engraving

Insults

When human beings feel the need to insult one another, verbal abuse is often insufficient, especially where distance intervenes. On these occasions, to show their anger, irritation or disdain, they are likely to display their feelings with a hostile gesture. Some of these actions are understood only locally, but a few have spread to become internationally familiar. It is the latter that occasionally appear in works of art.

Sometimes these visual signals are seen as mildly insulting or even amusing, but on other occasions they have been known to cause such deep offence that they have led to the gesticulator being attacked or even losing his life. Arguably, the most lethal of these insult gestures has been the Italian *mano cornuta* ('horned hand'), with its suggestion that the victim's wife has been unfaithful. Although it is rare for an insult such as this to provoke a full-blown assault, the power of these simple hand gestures should not be underestimated. They have sometimes led to explosive 'road rage' situations, or have seen the offender punished in some other way.

Making a Face

Mocking is primarily a verbal assault but is often accompanied by a scornful facial expression, of which the sneer is perhaps the most obvious example. The sneer is a subtle expression, in which the upper lip curls at one side, and, if over-emphasized, it can quickly become a comic caricature. This may explain why it has been so rarely attempted in the fine arts. Of course, there is also little appeal in having a sneering face staring at you from the wall.

Joseph Ducreux's *Self-portrait in the Guise of a Mocker* (1793) [77] demonstrates how difficult it is to capture the true sneer. Even the great Hieronymus Bosch, when he painted an evil throng crowding around Jesus on the day of the crucifixion in *Christ Carrying the Cross* (c. 1510) [75], was unable to capture the subtlety of the sneer. His savage, ugly faces snarl at one another in a hideous manner, and despite the painting having an enormous impact, the nuances of human mockery are lost. Perhaps the best example of a mocking face is to be found in a small work by a 20th-century artist. Despite the level of abstraction, which reduces the sneer to little more than a meandering line, *Or The Mocked Mocker* (1930) [76], by the Swiss artist Paul Klee, is more successful. You can feel the annoyance of the sneering man, who is used to jeering at others, when he suddenly finds himself the subject of mockery.

In extreme cases, mocking is accompanied by a grotesque facial expression, typically by using the hands to pull at the sides of the mouth and make it as wide as possible. This popular form of visual insult between children, and sometimes adults in a light-hearted context, appears frequently in historic paintings but is rarely seen in more recent art. It seems to have been most popular in the 14th and 15th centuries, when it was commonly included in the irreverent miniature images that decorate the margins of important illustrated manuscripts [79]. It also appears in the primitive murals found on the walls of a number of medieval churches in Europe, as well as on the faces of the stone gargoyles that adorn many Christian buildings of the same period [80].

Dutch Golden Age artists enjoyed creating scenes of daily life, some idealized, others humorous. The crudely insulting figure in Adriaen Brouwer's *Youth Making a Face* (c. 1632/1635) [78] looks directly at the viewer as he makes his rude gesture. It has been suggested that the dishevelled youth in Brouwer's painting could represent the artist himself, privately mocking the polite gallery-goers inspecting his work. In life, Brouwer was notorious for his unkempt appearance. He once bought an elegant and expensive suit for a wedding, but then, at the reception, started smearing pies all over his clothes, declaring eccentrically that 'it was the suit, rather than the man wearing it, that had been invited'.

It is worth asking why, historically, pulling this wide-mouthed face, with the lips dragged away from the teeth, should have been such a popular insult, and why it has now largely disappeared from serious artworks. The answer may have something to do with the advance of dentistry. In the past, it was considered courteous to avoid open-mouthed expressions because they would, all too often, expose a row of rotten teeth, probably accompanied by bad breath. Polite society restrained their lip movements and kept their mouths as closed as possible. A gaping mouth was associated with 'base character' or even evil, which made the deliberately wide-mouthed gesture a powerful visual insult. Today, in modern society, it has lost its impact and simply looks infantile.

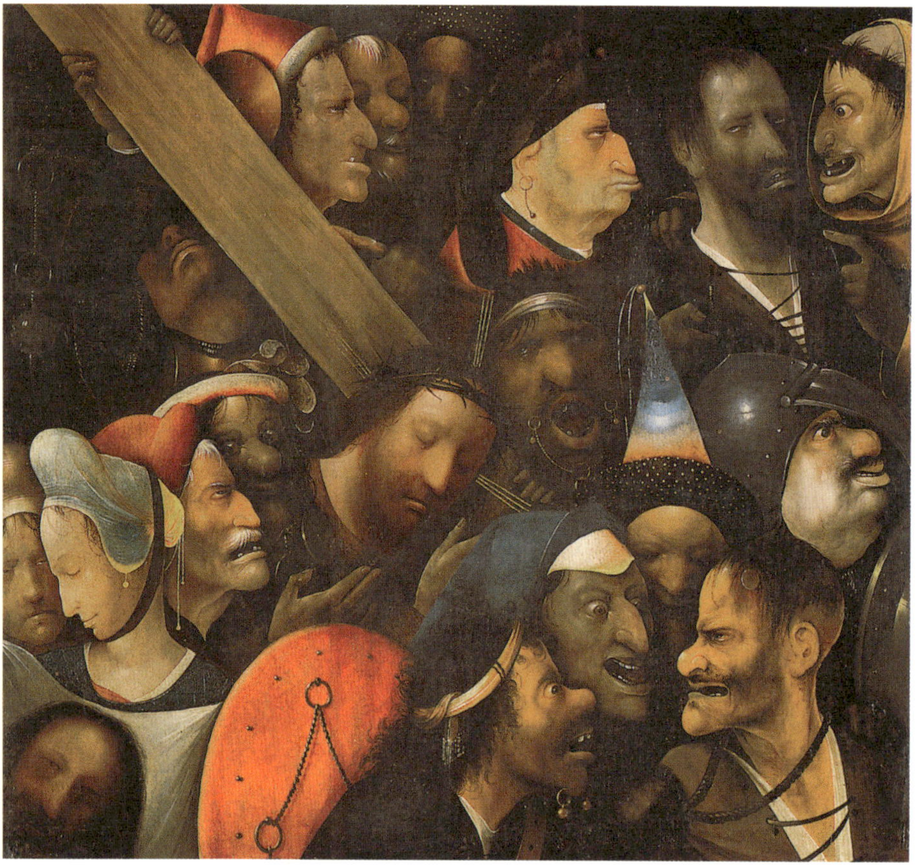

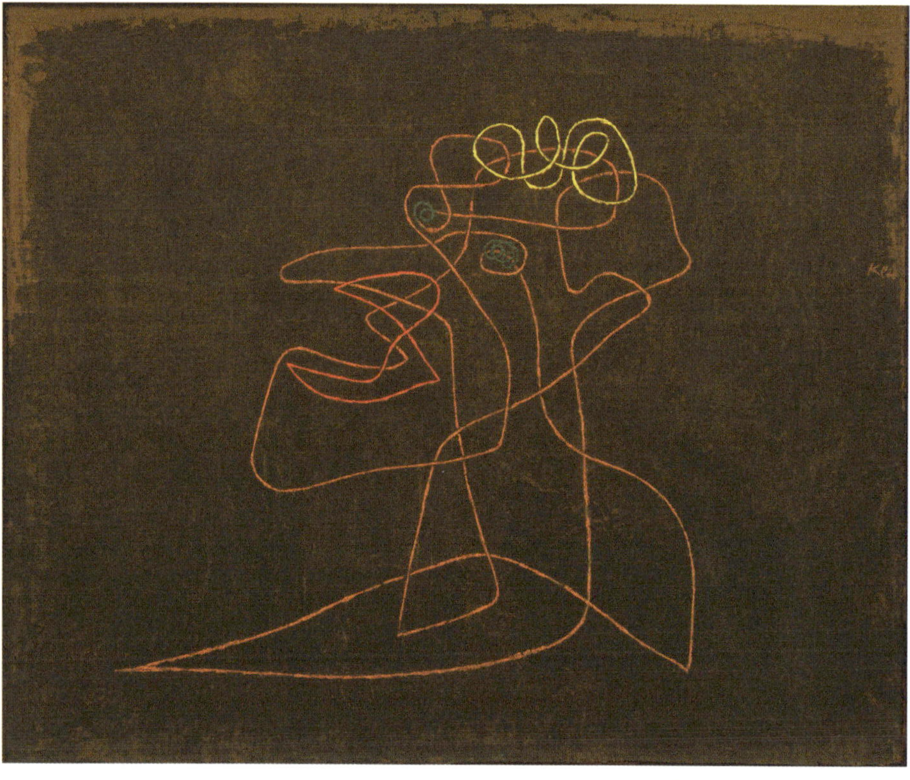

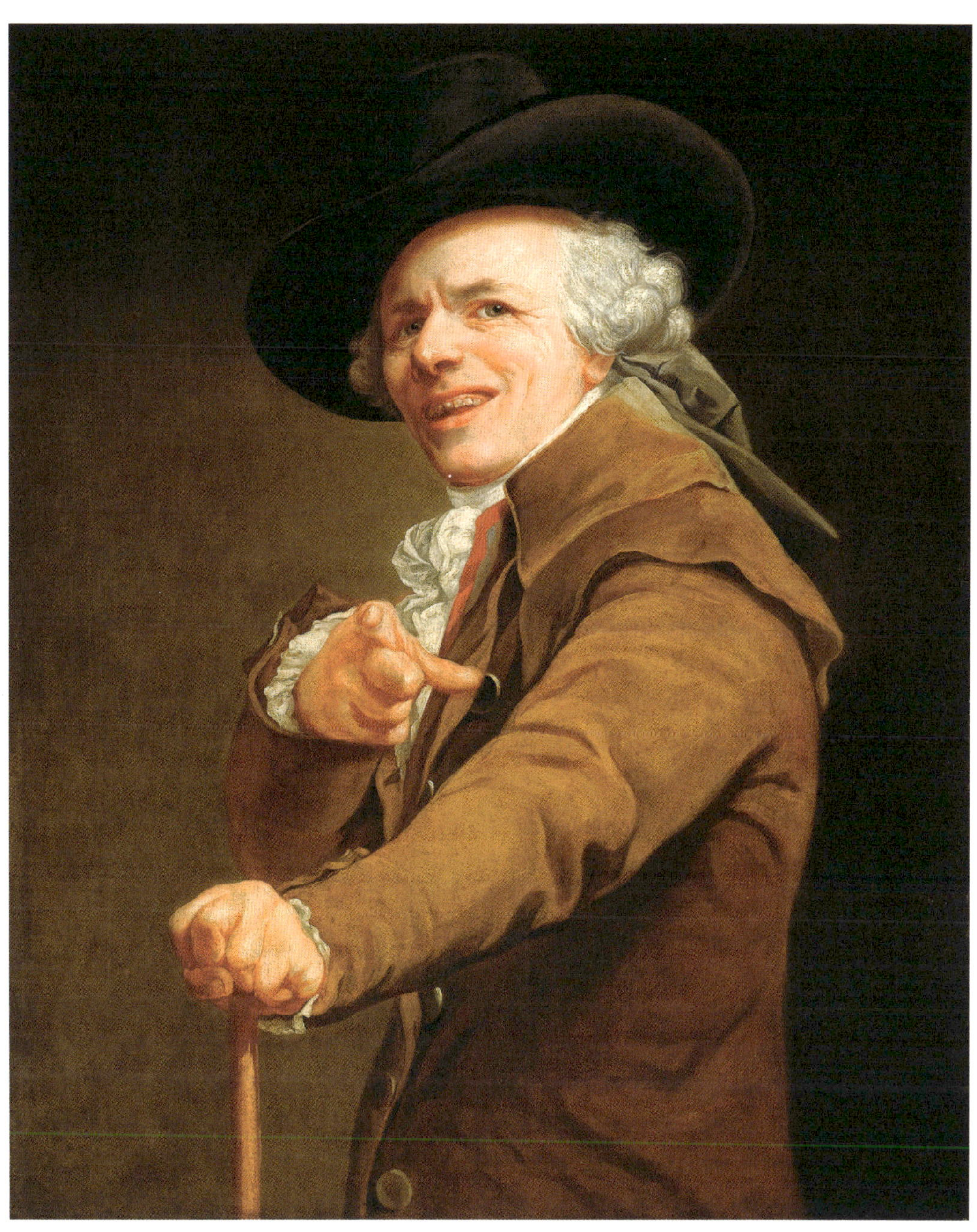

75. opposite, above **Hieronymus Bosch,**
Christ Carrying the Cross, c. 1510, oil on panel

76. opposite, below **Paul Klee,**
Or The Mocked Mocker, 1930, oil on canvas

77. above **Joseph Ducreux,** *Self-portrait in
the Guise of a Mocker,* 1793, oil on canvas

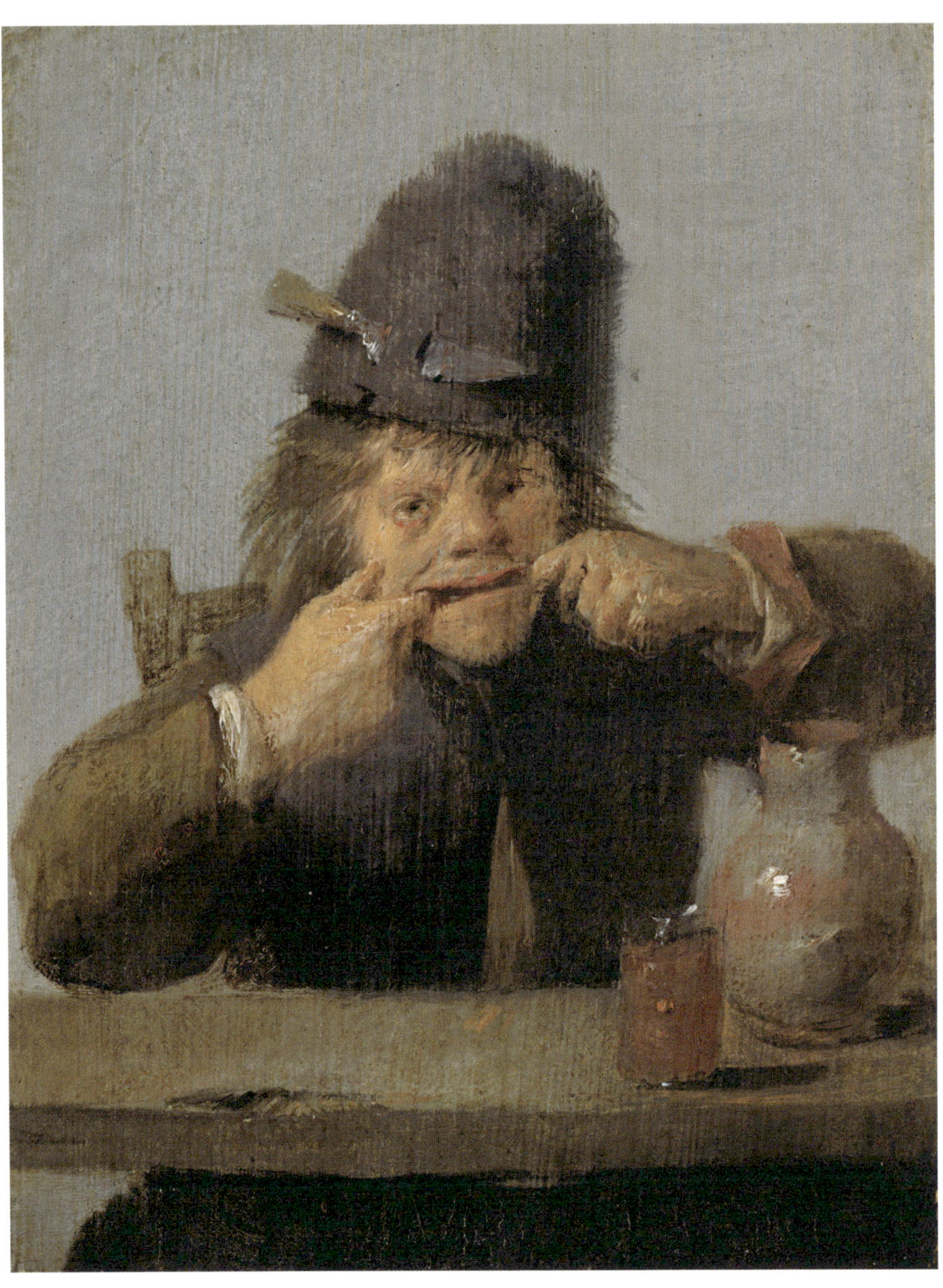

78. **Adriaen Brouwer,**
Youth Making a Face,
c. 1632/1635, **oil on panel**

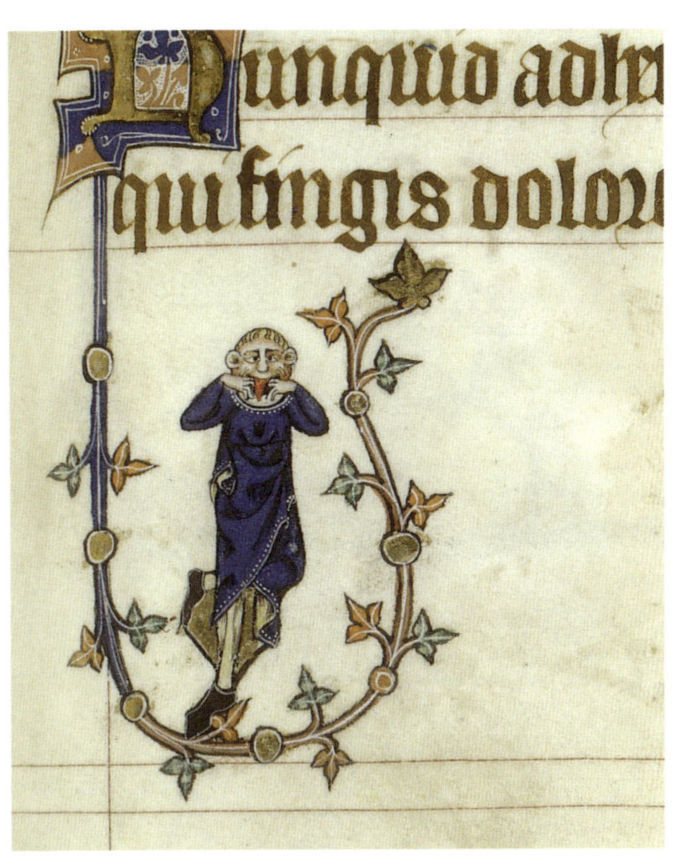

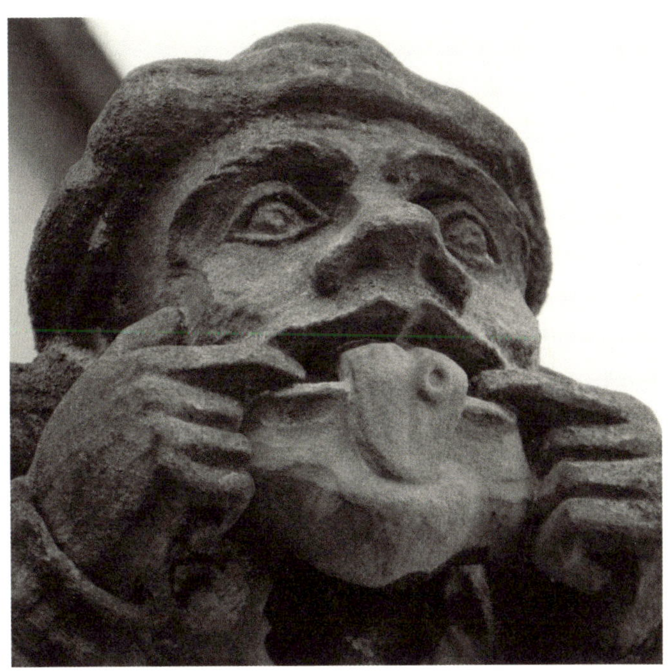

79. above **Miniature from the**
***Gorleston Psalter**, 14th century*

80. right **Gargoyle, 14th–15th century, Guild Chapel, Stratford-upon-Avon, England**

The Tongue-out

In the West, sticking the tongue out is considered a childish insult, although it does have quite different meanings around the world. As an insult, it is what's known as a relic gesture – one that has survived long after its original, primary context has vanished. Its origins can be traced back to infancy, when a baby rejects its food by pushing it away with its tongue. The child is too young to say 'No more!', so it must forcibly push out the food with the tip of its tongue. Tongue protrusion and rejection therefore become linked at a very early age and this connection survives into adulthood. If someone is focusing on a difficult problem and does not wish to be disturbed, they can often be seen to protrude their tongue slightly between their lips. Unconsciously, they are rejecting any outside interference that might disturb their concentration.

When schoolchildren want to perform a simple, rude gesture, they will often unthinkingly stick out their tongue. Again, this is an echo of infantile rejection. When adults do it, knowing that it is the typical reaction of an impudent child, they do so jokingly and it is rarely taken seriously. However, they have to be careful to make an ugly facial grimace when they perform this action, to make it clear they are being rude, because otherwise there is a risk that the protrusion of the tongue could mistakenly be interpreted as an erotic invitation.

Historically, in addition to being associated with childish rudeness, the protruding tongue had a more sinister role to play in a special context. It was sometimes referred to as 'Satan's Tongue', and the Devil was often portrayed with an evil, long, pointed – or even forked – tongue hanging from his mouth. In a charming medieval fresco in the village church of Tingsted on the Danish island of Falster, there is a scene in which a black, horned devil is depicted sticking out his long red tongue at an innocent woman churning butter [81]. This late 15th-century work was later piously covered in whitewash and lay hidden until 1877, when it was rediscovered and restored.

The horned demon Krampus, a folkloric figure with affinities to Satan, is also frequently depicted lolling out his tongue [82]. According to European tradition, he appears on the night before the Feast of St Nicholas; while St Nicholas visits the good children and rewards them with gifts, Krampus punishes the bad children. He greets them by sticking out his exceptionally long red tongue and showing them his instruments of punishment. The idea that all children, both good and bad, should receive gifts at Christmas is a comparatively recent one.

In art, there is a classic example of the 'impudent child' action in a 17th-century work attributed to the Dutch Golden Age painter Roeloff van Zijl, called *Elisha Mocked by Boys* (*c.* 1625–30) [83]. A small boy points both his forefingers at the prophet Elisha and sticks out his tongue as far as it will go. He and his friends are mocking Elisha because of his baldness. Since Elisha is God's prophet, God will not tolerate this and punishes the boys by sending two she-bears from the forest. The bears promptly attack, and, according to the Bible, tear to pieces forty-two of the boys – another example of a simple gesture having a lethal consequence.

In modern times, there have been several examples of a simple tongue protrusion becoming a famous image. On 14 March 1951, Albert Einstein was celebrating his seventy-second birthday and was receiving a great deal of press attention. Over and over again, he was asked to smile for the camera. At the end of the day, when a photographer called Arthur Sasse asked him for one more smile, he stuck out his tongue. Sasse caught the moment on film – the world's cleverest man making the silliest of insults. The contrast was irresistible, and the photograph became world-famous. Several artists have since transformed the photograph into a painting, including a number of street artists [84].

Although, at the time, Einstein's action seemed to be no more than a trivial, impromptu response to a moment of boredom, he himself would later add a darker flavour to it. In 1953, he signed a copy of the now-famous photograph as a gift for a journalist and political commentator whose work he admired. On it, he wrote a message that translates as: 'This gesture you will like, because it is aimed at all of humanity. A civilian can afford to do what no diplomat would dare.' It seems as though what started out as a humorous, spontaneous reaction to excessive press attention had somehow grown in Einstein's mind to become a loaded statement concerning his attitude towards humankind.

Several contemporary artists have incorporated tongue protrusion in their work. One of the most extraordinary examples is *Self-portrait with Tongue* (2010) [85] by the African American artist Trenton Doyle Hancock, whose wide-ranging influences include comic books and graphic novels. Perhaps the most famous example of a protruding tongue in an artistic context, however, is John Pasche's iconic 'tongue and lip' logo for the Rolling Stones, which was first used on the album *Sticky Fingers* in 1971. Although the initial design brief centred on the Indian goddess Kali, it was Mick Jagger's own mouth that inspired Pasche. A symbol of friendly rudeness tinged with an erotic flavour, 'Hot Lips' – as the logo became known – captured the rebelliousness of the band perfectly.

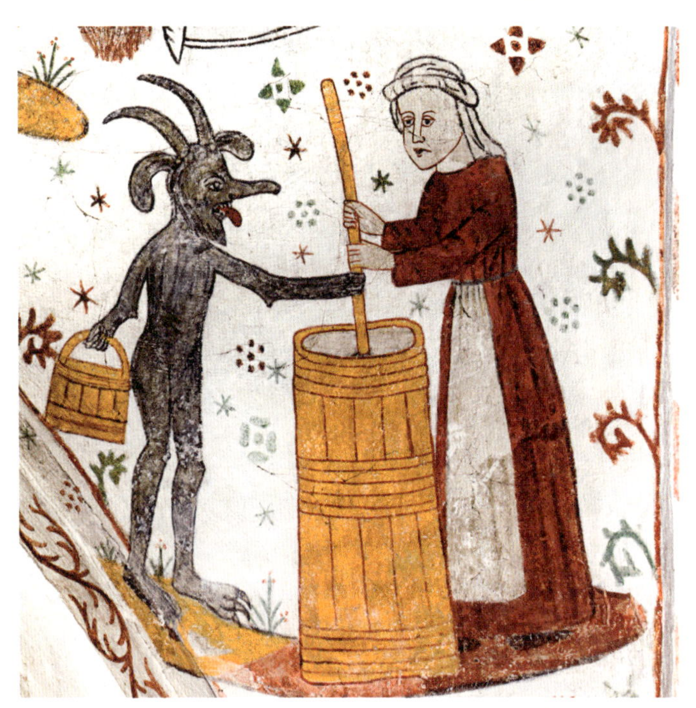

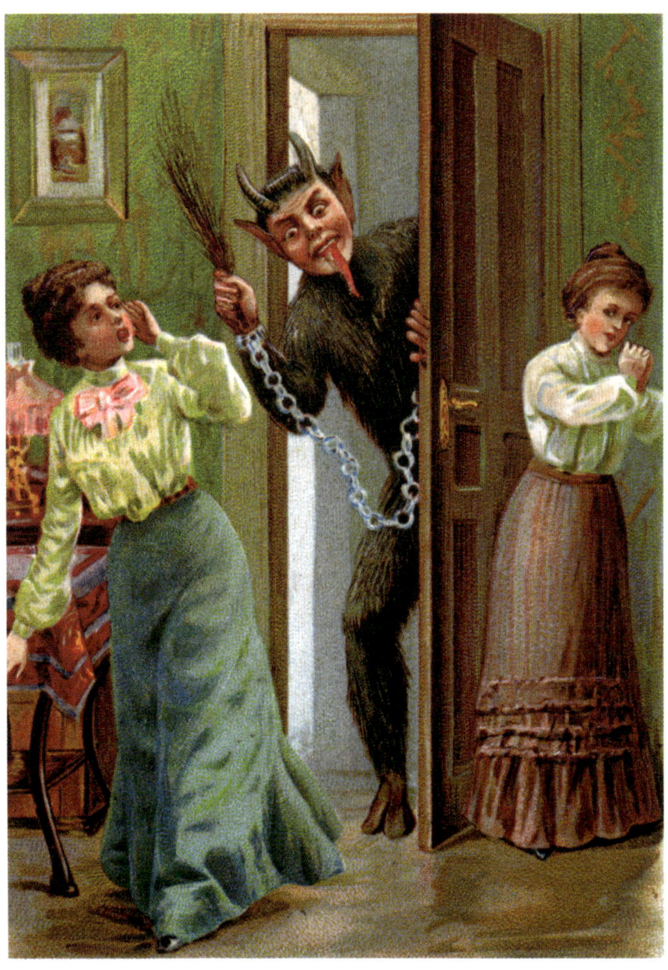

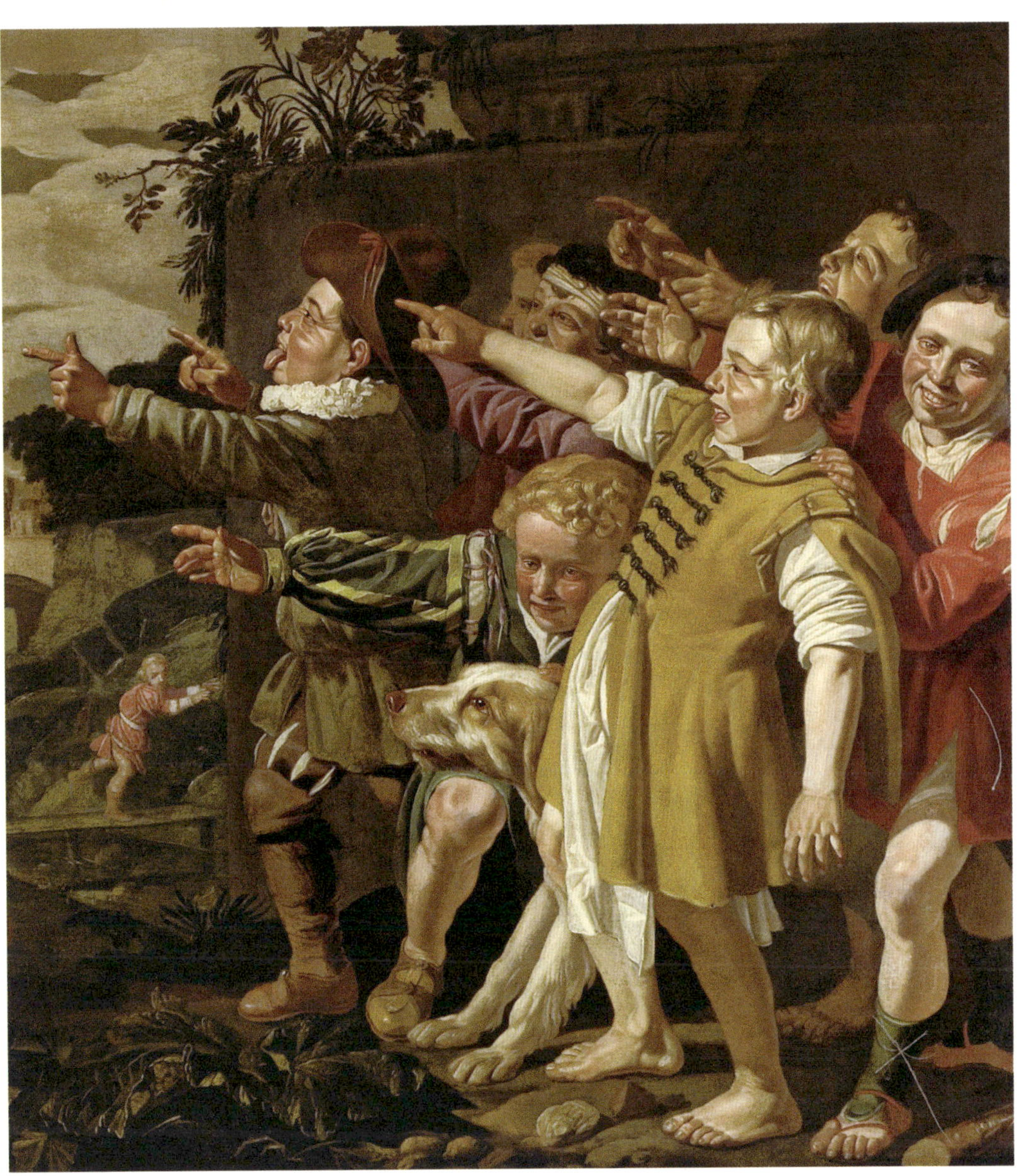

81. opposite, above **A woman churning butter with the Devil, fresco, late 15th century, Tingsted Church, Denmark**

82. opposite, below ***Saint Nicholas's Day. The Krampus (Incubus in Company of Saint Nicholas)*, c. 1904, Hungarian illustration**

83. above **Attributed to Roeloff van Zijl, *Elisha Mocked by Boys* (detail), c. 1625–30, oil on canvas**

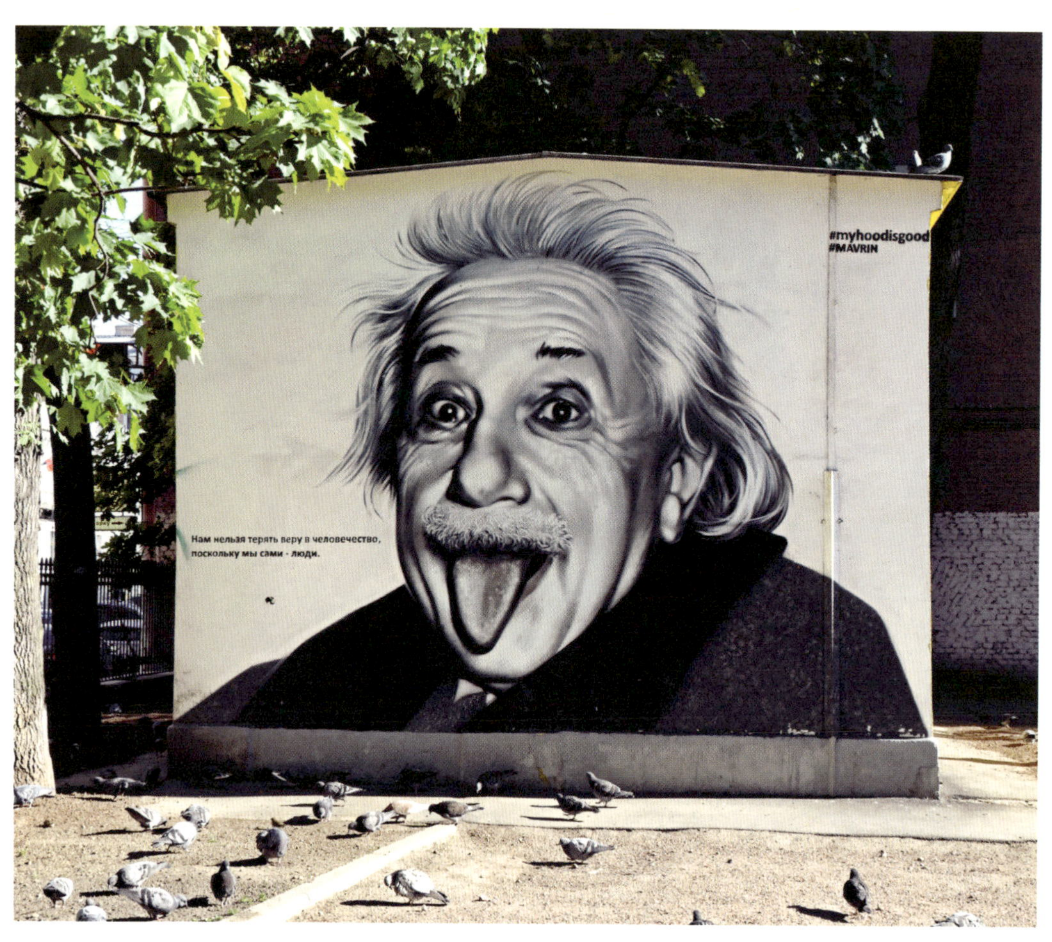

84. **HoodGraff team,** *Albert Einstein*, **2014, spray paint on wall, St Petersburg, Russia**

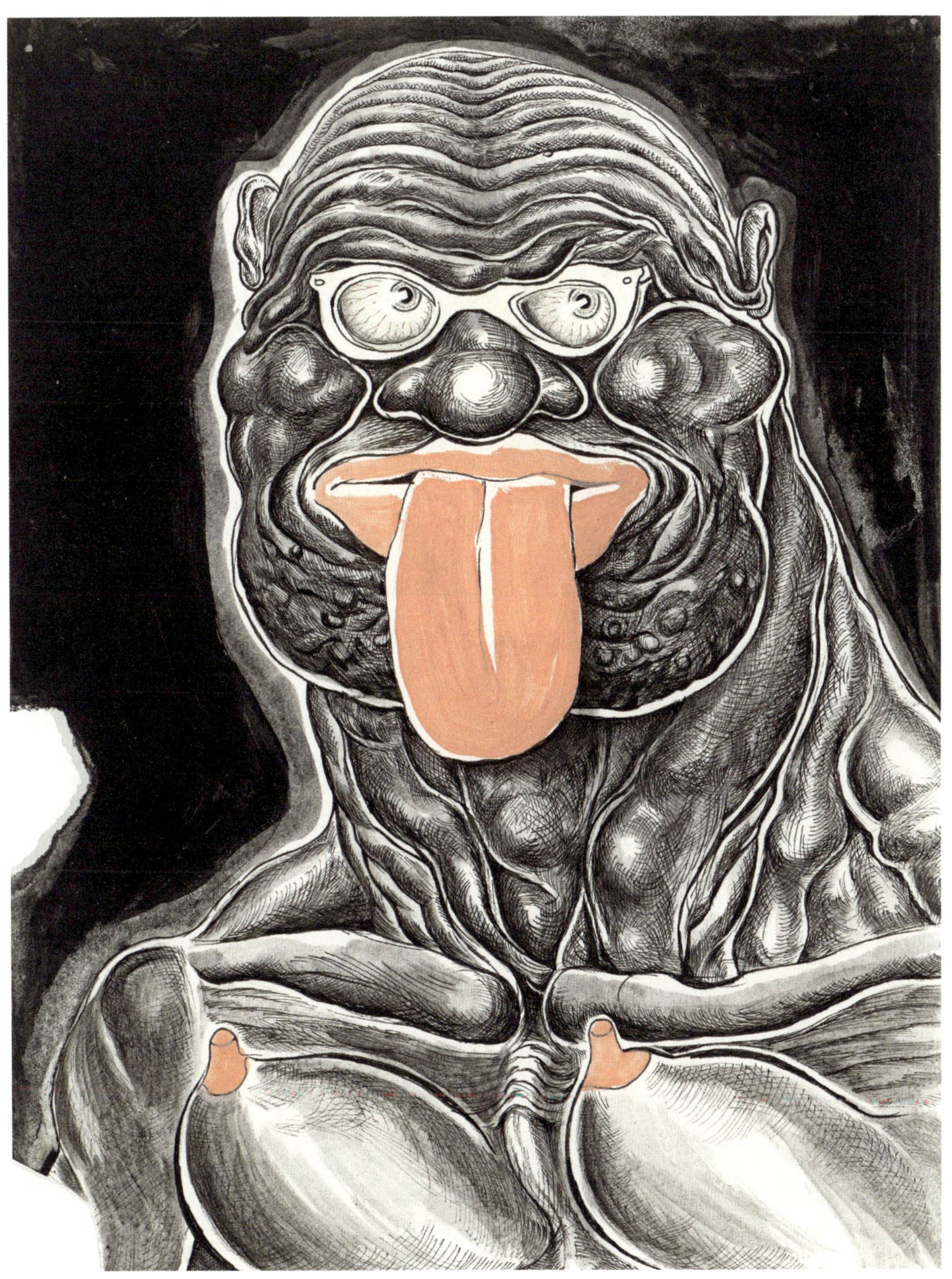

85. **Trenton Doyle Hancock,**
***Self-portrait with Tongue**, 2010,
acrylic and mixed media on paper

The Nose-thumb

Thumbing the nose is usually performed as a joke and is not taken seriously. An adult may do it to a small child, or one child to another. As a light-hearted insult it is widely known over the whole of Europe and has been used for at least 500 years, possibly longer. Because of this, it has acquired a large number of names. There are no fewer than fourteen names in the English language alone, including cocking a snook, making a long nose, pulling long bacon, the five-fingered salute, Queen Anne's fan and the Shanghai gesture. This last example was once so popular that it became the title of a play by John Colton. One theory about the origin of the name draws a comparison between the nose-thumb gesture and the action of firing a catapult, which is otherwise known as a 'shanghai' in Australia.

There are almost as many explanations concerning the origin of this insult as there are names for it. The most popular account sees it as a distorted salute. The hand, instead of being raised to the forehead to make a proper salute, is brought up to the nose as a parody of the serious version. This might explain why it was once given the name of the five-fingered salute.

Another explanation is that the thumb is making contact with the nose to flick snot at the victim. Supporting this argument is the earliest reference to the gesture in literature, which appears in François Rabelais's *Gargantua and Pantagruel*. Writing in the 16th century, Rabelais describes a spectacularly complex display of nose-thumb insults that are performed in a gestural contest between Panurge, acting on behalf of the giant Pantagruel, and Thaumast, a scholar who has travelled from England to Paris to see if Pantagruel is as brilliant as he is supposed to be. The contest soon descends into a series of derogatory hand gestures:

> Panurge suddenly lifted up in the air his right hand, and put the thumb thereof into the nostril of the same side, holding his four fingers straight out, and closed orderly in a parallel line to the point of his nose, shutting the left eye wholly, and making the other wink with a profound depression of the eyebrows and eyelids. Then lifted he up his left hand, with hard wringing and stretching forth his four fingers and elevating his thumb, which he held in a line directly correspondent to the situation of his right hand, with the distance of a cubit and a half between them. This done, in the same form he abased towards the ground about the one and the other hand. Lastly, he held them in the midst, as aiming right at the Englishman's nose... Then made the Englishman this sign. His left hand all open he lifted up into the air, then instantly shut into his fist the four fingers

thereof, and his thumb extended at length he placed upon the gristle
of his nose. Presently after, he lifted up his right hand all open, and
all open abased and bent it downwards, putting the thumb thereof in
the very place where the little finger of the left hand did close in the
fist, and the four right-hand fingers he softly moved in the air. Then
contrarily he did with the right hand what he had done with the left,
and with the left what he had done with the right.

Another explanation of the nose-thumb insult arises from the idea that
having a disproportionately long nose is grotesque, and therefore making
it longer by attaching a hand – or two – is effectively saying: I think
you are as ugly as this. A variation of this explanation is that the gesture
is meant to form a phallic nose, bringing this insult into line with other
popular phallic gestures. A more convincing explanation suggests that
the gesturer is imitating a cock's comb, and is acting rather like a fighting
cock in leaning forward to make the insult.

In truth, we will probably never know for certain how this insult first
arose or what its precise symbolism is. But for the small child who brings
a hand up to the nose and makes a suitably rude noise, these historical
considerations mean nothing; the gesture is simply a light-hearted way
of being impertinent without being taken too seriously.

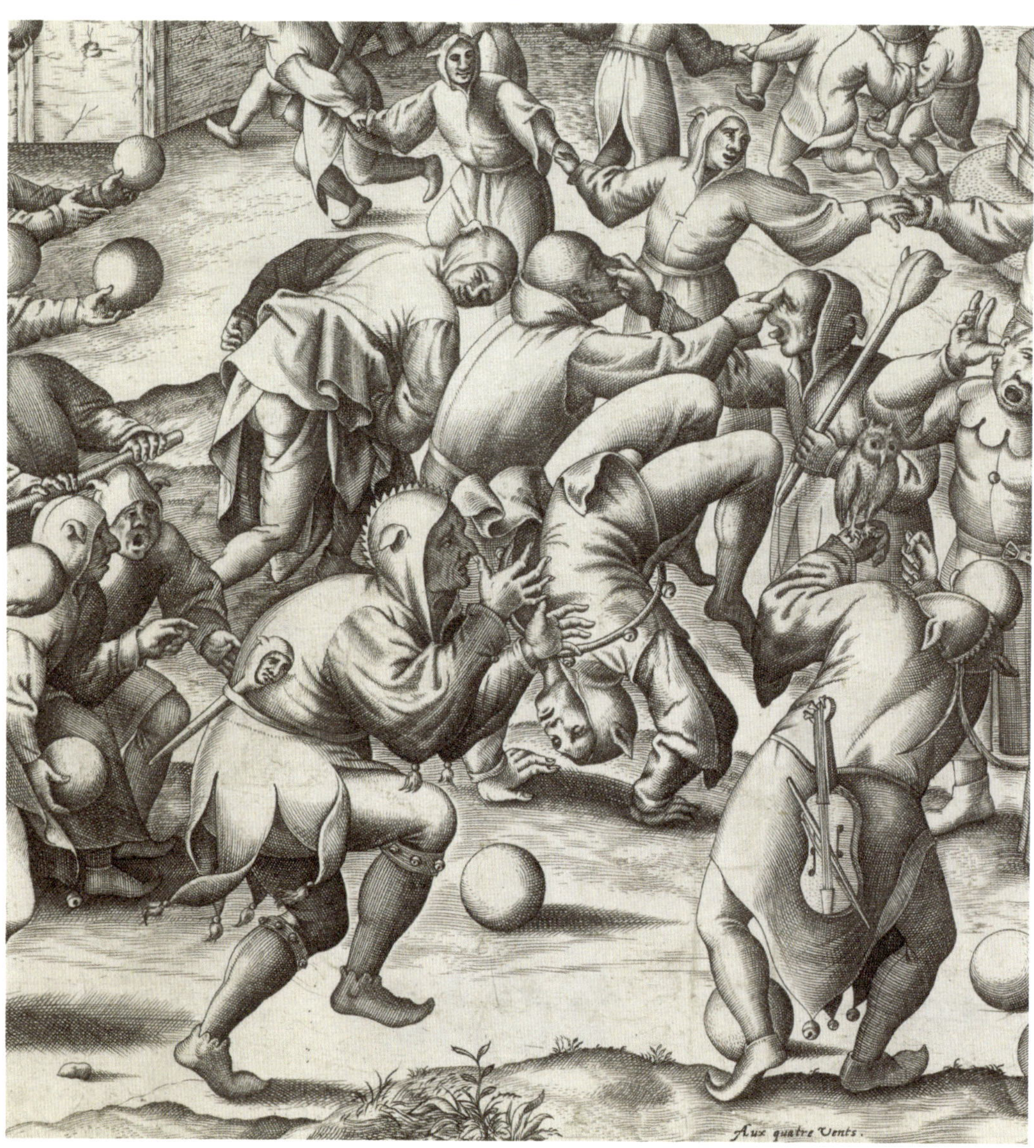

86. above **Pieter van der Heyden
(after Pieter Bruegel the Elder),
The Festival of Fools (detail),
1559, engraving**

87. opposite, above ***Trial by Battle*,
mid-19th century, colour lithograph,
American school**

88. opposite, below ***Thumbing one's
Nose from the Motor Tricycle*, 1900,
advertisement for Automobiles de
Dion-Bouton (illustration by Wilhio)**

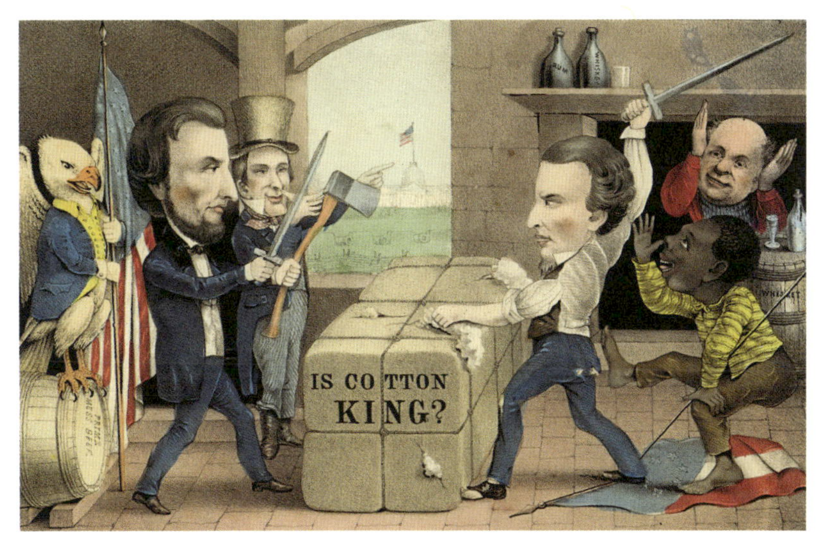

IS COTTON KING?

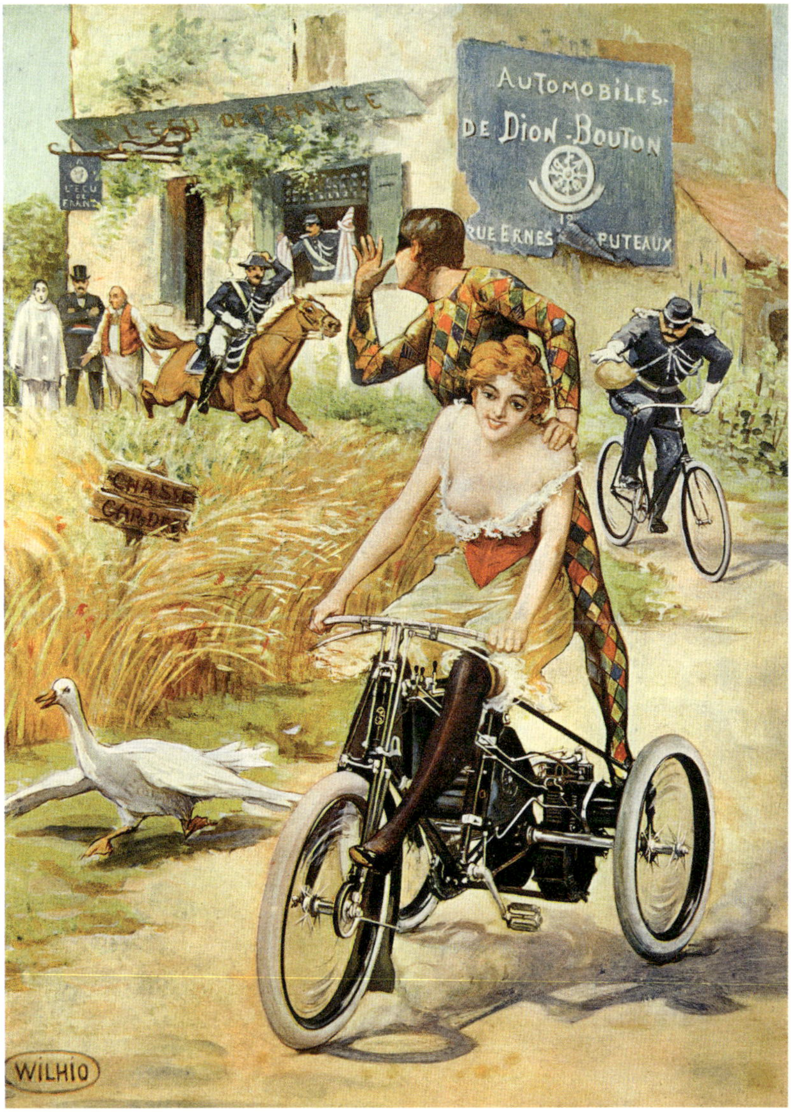

Finger Gestures

In the West, the 'middle finger' seems to have become an increasingly popular insult. Its symbolism is obvious enough: the erect middle finger represents the penis and the other digits, curled up on either side of it, are the testicles. Making the gesture transforms the hand into male genitalia, and if the hand is jerked upwards it symbolizes the insertion of the penis.

This insult has a long history. It was popular in ancient Greece and Rome, and references to it occur in the work of classical authors. It was so notorious that the middle finger became known in Roman times as the *digitus impudicus* – the indecent finger. It is said that the emperor Caligula, when offering his hand to be kissed, would sometimes extend only his middle finger, keeping his other fingers bent. It presumably amused him to think that he was forcing his subjects to kiss his symbolic penis.

Around the turn of the 20th century, when large numbers of Italians emigrated to the United States, they took with them their rich body language. Some of the gestures remain uniquely Italian, but the middle-finger insult became so popular that it spread across the whole of North America. Since then, it has also spread to other parts of the world, and its meaning is now understood almost everywhere. In the USA, it is known simply as 'the finger'.

The overtly sexual symbolism of the middle finger means that it is rarely seen in historic paintings, although a number of modern artists have enjoyed depicting it. In 2008, the pop surrealist Marion Peck played on the perverse contrast between a sweetly elegant, innocent girl and her obscene hand action in a work entitled *Fuck You* [93]. Perhaps the most famous example in recent years, however, appears in a work of street art. The stencilled *Rude Copper* [92] by Banksy, from about 2002, shows the gesture being made by a British policeman.

A handful of high-profile sculptors have also chosen the middle finger as a theme. In 2010, the controversial Italian artist Maurizio Cattelan unveiled a massive, 11-metre-tall (36 ft) sculpture of a middle finger [89] in front of the Milan Stock Exchange as part of a retrospective of his work; the other fingers of the hand look as though they have been sawn off. The provocative piece, which was intended for public display over a two-week period only, still stands in its original location. The official title of the work is *L.O.V.E.*, which stands for *Libertà, Odio, Vendetta, Eternità* ('Freedom, Hate, Vengeance, Eternity'), although the artist has commented that 'everyone can read between the lines and take away the message they see for themselves'. The Czech sculptor David Černý went even further than Cattelan, creating an outsized purple hand with an extended middle finger, which he then mounted on a barge on the

Vltava river, opposite Prague Castle. It stood there as a political comment
concerning the pro-Kremlin president of the Republic, Miloš Zeman.

As an insult, the V-sign – in which the first two fingers are held
erect, with the back of the hand facing outwards – is an amplified
form of the middle finger, theoretically doubling the impact of the 'Up
yours!' gesture. It is sometimes done with the two erect fingers touching
one another, but it is much more common to see them separated in
a V-shape. Although considered highly offensive in the UK and some
Commonwealth countries, it has other meanings depending on the
cultural context and the position of the hand. It should not be confused
with the 'V for Victory' sign that is done with the palm of the hand facing
away from the body – a gesture that is now, of course, also associated
with the peace movement. When Winston Churchill first used the 'V for
Victory' sign during a speech on 19 July 1941, he appeared to be unaware
of the rude version of the gesture and was photographed doing it the
wrong way round, although in later shots – having presumably been
informed by his advisors – he is seen doing it correctly.

It has been suggested that the idea of the V-sign as an insult
originated at the Battle of Agincourt in 1415. The story goes that the
French threatened to cut off the bow-fingers of the English archers
when the battle was over. When the English won, and French prisoners
of war were being taken away, the English archers enjoyed insulting
them by holding up their two bow-fingers and jerking them in the
air to demonstrate that they had not been amputated. There are
figurines demonstrating this, but they seem to have been made many
centuries later. It is an ingenious explanation, and does help to answer
the question as to why this gesture should be used predominantly
in the UK. Unfortunately, there is no historical evidence to support
the Agincourt theory.

The earliest evidence we have of the existence of this gesture as
a savage insult appears in Rabelais's *Gargantua and Pantagruel*. As we saw
earlier, Rabelais describes in great detail a ridiculous gestural duel that
takes place between Panurge, acting on behalf of the giant Pantagruel,
and the English scholar Thaumast (see p. 120). Instead of using words,
Panurge and Thaumast throw increasingly disgusting gestural insults
at each other. At one point in the battle, Panurge 'then stretched...out the
forefinger and middle finger or medical of his right hand, holding them
asunder as much as he could, and thrusting them towards Thaumast...
Thaumast began then to wax somewhat pale, and to tremble.'

Strangely, in this encounter, it is the French contestant who makes
the insulting V-sign to the Englishman, rather than the other way round.
This suggests that the French did understand the gesture as an insult at
that time, and it is clear from Thaumast's reaction that he understood it
too. Since then, for some reason, the action has disappeared in France but
thrived in England. It is apparent from studies of early slang that the two

fingers being thrust into the air were meant to symbolize their insertion into a woman's vagina. It is mentioned in several 17th-century English writings as 'to make V' or to 'fork your fingers'. Sadly it does not appear in any works of art from that period, no doubt because it was based on an obscenity, and even in modern times the gesture is largely confined to the work of rebellious graffiti and street artists [91].

In an entirely different context, a similar, very aggressive gesture appears in early Japanese armoured warrior sculptures [90]. The figures are shown with the first two fingers extended, and with the thumb and other fingers clenched. The two erect fingers are touching each other, instead of being spread out into a V-shape. This gesture is known as the knife-hand strike mudra, and is meant to represent the sword of enlightenment, which 'cuts away all delusions'. Despite its superficial similarity to the two-fingered insult, it has no sexual connotation and simply mimics a knife thrust.

89. **Maurizio Cattelan,** *L.O.V.E.,*
2010, hand: Carrara marble,
base: Roman travertine, Piazza
degli Affari, Milan, Italy

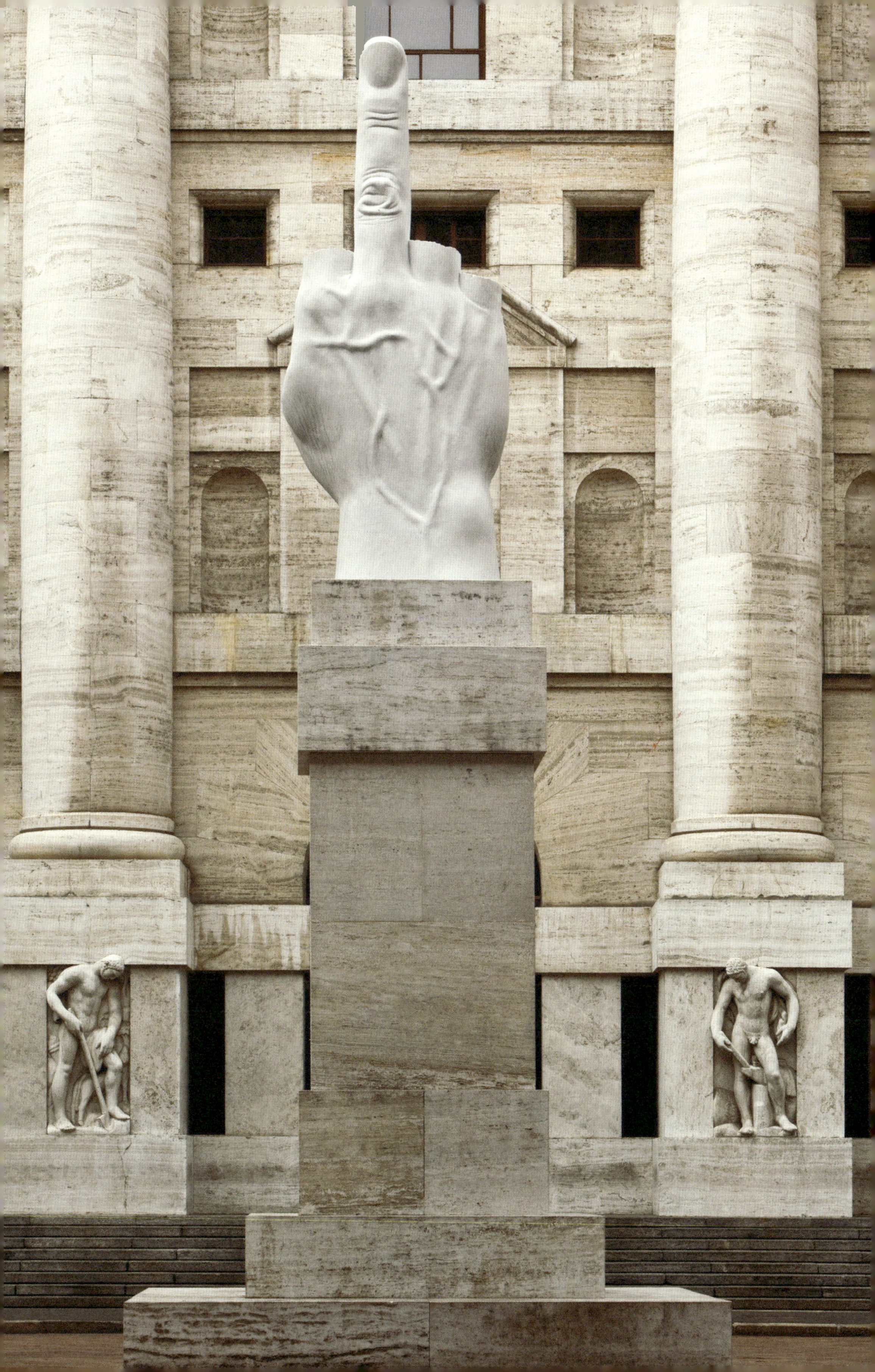

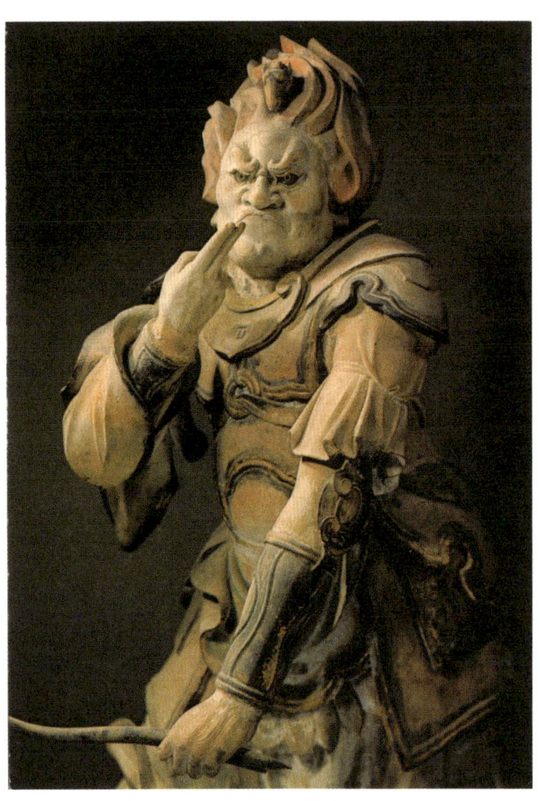

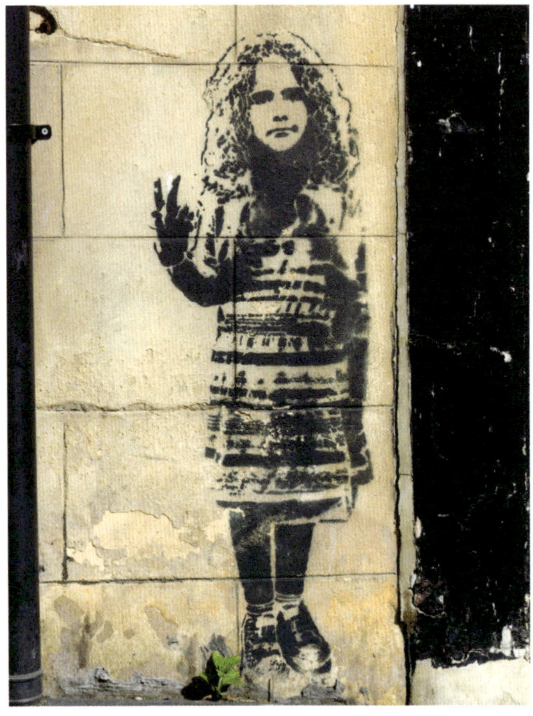

90. above *Statue of General Anira, one of the Twelve Divine Generals,* Kamakura period, 12th–14th century, Japan

91. left **Dotmaster,** *Rude Kids,* 2016, spray paint on wall, London

92. opposite, above **Banksy,** *Rude Copper,* c. 2002, print with spray paint

93. opposite, below **Marion Peck,** *Fuck You,* 2008, oil on canvas

     Insults / Finger Gestures

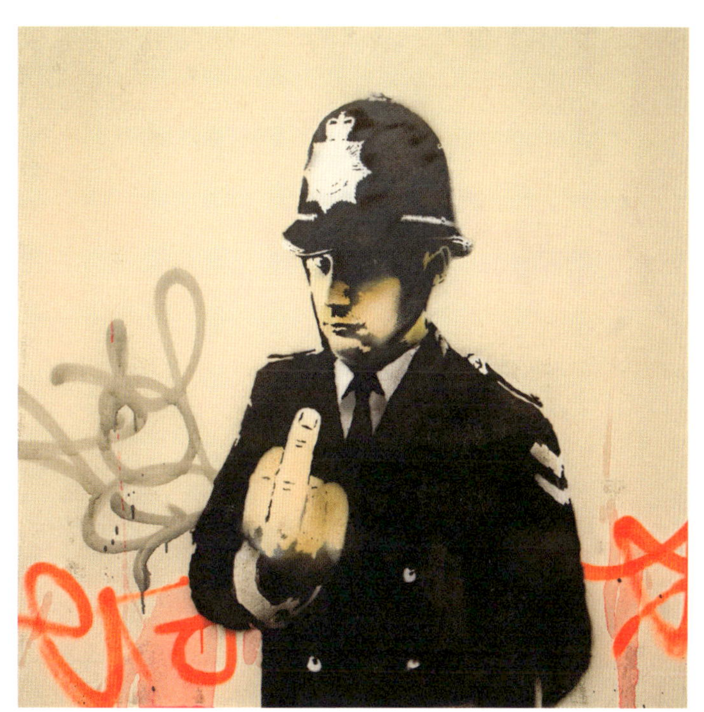

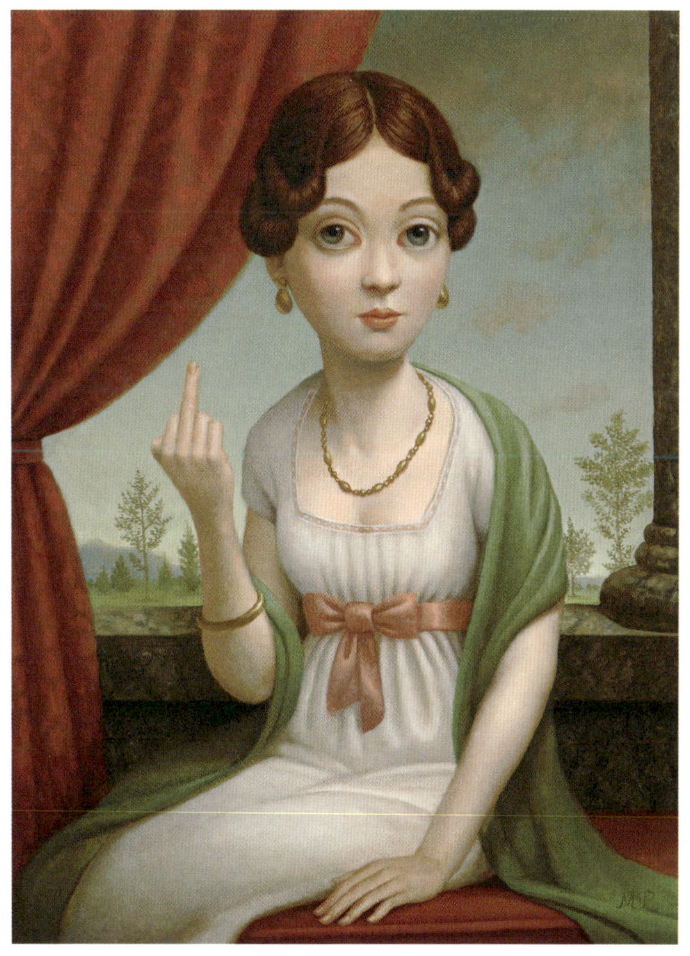

Hand Gestures

The fig sign – in which the hand makes a fist, with the tip of the thumb protruding between the first and second fingers – symbolizes the penis pushing through female labia. It is sometimes used simply as a sexual comment, meaning 'This is what they are doing', 'She is sexy', or 'This is what I would like to do'. A more common use, however, is as a sexual insult – another version of the 'Up yours!' – particularly in such countries as Turkey, Greece and central France.

Known as the *mano fica*, or 'vulva hand' (the Italian word 'fica' being slang for female genitalia), the gesture has been used as an insult for at least 2,000 years. Roman soldiers going into battle would often wear (or carry) a fig-and-phallus amulet [96] – with a phallus at one end and a fist making the fig sign at the other – as a lucky charm. It was thought to bring good luck by offering a double insult to evil spirits, keeping them at bay.

The early Christians called the gesture the *manus obscena,* or 'obscene hand'. It has been suggested that it may have a connection to the early Hindu religion, in which it symbolizes the (male) *lingam* and the (female) *yoni* – symbols of divine procreative energy. There is a *linga* mudra in which both hands are used, wrapped around a protruding, phallic, vertical thumb.

Despite the fact that the fig sign was clearly known in ancient times, there are some that insist it originated from a bizarre incident in the 12th century. This clearly isn't possible, but it may well be that the fame of this incident helped to boost the popularity of the gesture and its use. The legend of Barbarossa and the mule concerns a public humiliation that occurred in the city of Milan in 1162. The Holy Roman Emperor, Frederick Barbarossa, was faced with Milanese rebellions that cost him the city. The victorious rebels had grossly insulted his wife, Empress Beatrice, by forcing her to ride out of the city on a mule, seated backwards so that she faced the animal's rump. This so angered the great Barbarossa that he besieged the city with an army and, after retaking it, imposed an extraordinary punishment on his prisoners, forcing each of them, on pain of death, to extract a fig from the anus of the aforementioned mule, using their teeth. Once they had performed this action, they had to shout out *Ecco lo Fico!* – 'Behold the Fig!'

It would be easy to discount this incident as imaginative fiction, were it not for the fact that Barbarossa was notorious for imposing strange forms of punishment. For example, when two of his nobles had been squabbling, he punished them by condemning them to carry dogs on their shoulders from one country to another. So it does seem possible that the incident really did occur, and that the act of making the fig sign

now had an additional obscene meaning, with the thumb representing
the fig protruding from the anus of the mule.

Whatever the truth, the story became immensely popular across
Europe, and in the 16th century Rabelais penned an amusing retelling
of the incident:

> The inhabitants of Milan…had rebell'd against [Barbarossa]…and
> turn'd the Empress out of the city, mounting her a Horse-back on
> a Mule called Thacor, with her breech foremost towards the old
> Jaded Mule's Head, and her face turned towards the Crupper. Now
> Frederick being return'd…found and got to the famous mule Thacor.
> Then the Hang-man, by his Order, clap'd a Fig into the mule's
> Jim-crack, in the Presence of the enslaved Citts that were brought
> into the middle of the great Market-place, and proclaimed, in the
> Emperor's Name, with Trumpets, that whosoever of them would
> save his own Life, should publickly pull the Fig out with his teeth,
> and after that put it in again in the very individual cranny whence
> he had draw'd it, without using his hands; and that whosoever refused
> to do this, should presently swing for 't, and die in his Shoes. Some…
> chose honourably to be hang'd…and others…resolved to have at the
> Fig, and a Fig for 't, rather than…die in the air…accordingly when
> they had neatly picked out the Fig with their teeth from old Thacor's
> Snatch-blatch, they plainly showed it to the Heads-man, saying *Ecco
> lo Fico!*

The depiction of this form of insult in art stretches back hundreds
of years. One of the earliest examples is a 15th-century drawing of a
disembodied hand by the German artist Albrecht Dürer [97]. In 1566, the
Flemish artist Jan Massys composed an amusing domestic scene called
The Ill-matched Pair [98], in which the fig sign plays an important role.
The painting shows an elderly husband clasping the breast of his beautiful
young wife and gazing at her with senile lust. Her facial expression, as she
caresses his cheek, subtly suggests that she will welcome the day when
she becomes a rich widow. The couple are unaware that, behind their
backs, their plump maid is offering them an obscene fig insult with her
right hand, to the amusement of another servant. The gesture was also
depicted in a number of 17th-century works, including Jusepe de Ribera's
The Mocking of Christ (*c.* 1620) and Godfried Schalcken's later etching
Man Making an Obscene Gesture (*c.* 1660–80).

The fig sign is rarely seen in modern works of art, but makes a
spectacular appearance in a 1961 painting by the French surrealist Felix
Labisse. Entitled *La Fille d'Yemanja* [99], the painting shows a nude
woman on a seashore, performing the fig sign with her raised right hand.
The title is a clue to the work's meaning. A deity of the African Yoruba
people, Yemanja is a mother spirit, a patron spirit of all women, and

worshipped wherever there is flowing water. Her name is derived from
the Yoruba words *Iye omo eja*, meaning 'Mother whose children are like
fish'. She is popular in Brazil, where there is an annual celebration in her
name on Copacabana beach, with thousands of her followers throwing
offerings into the sea, in the hope of gaining her help in the year ahead.
Labisse chose to portray Yemanja's fecundity and her role as a procreative
force by showing a figure performing the fig sign, with the male thumb
inserting itself between the female fingers. Yemanja is shown wearing
a necklace, the pendant of which is a fig-sign amulet of the kind that is
still worn today in some Mediterranean countries as a protective charm.

Even older than the fig sign, the cuckold sign, or *mano cornuta*
('horned hand'), is another common insult in many Mediterranean and
South American countries. The hand forms the shape of a horned head by
keeping the forefinger and little finger erect, while the thumb holds down
the other two fingers. The cuckold sign suggests that a man's wife has
been unfaithful to him, and implies sexual inefficacy or even impotence
on his part. In cultures where male virility is highly valued in connection
with social status, this is one of the worst insults a man can receive, and
has sometimes led to physical retaliation and even murder.

This ancient gesture is thought to be at least 2,500 years old. While
its origin is obscure, there are many theories that attempt to explain the
symbolic link between a horned hand – suggesting a bull's head – and
cuckoldry. The most plausible are as follows:

- The hand sign is meant to be ironic, saying, 'What a great
  bull you are', but meaning the exact opposite.
- The hand sign symbolizes the castrated condition of the
  victim of the insult. The connection here is that many bulls
  had to be castrated in ancient times to make them docile.
- The hand sign represents the rage of a maddened bull,
  which is how the husband will behave when he discovers
  that his wife has been unfaithful.
- The hand sign represents the virility of the wife's lover,
  and holding up the 'horned head' in front of the man
  is meant to remind him forcibly of the way in which the
  lover is behaving like a rutting bull with his wife.

Typically, the cuckold sign is performed with the hand held vertically
and the 'horns' pointing upwards, but it may also be done with the hand
in a horizontal position, with the horns being jabbed towards the victim.
This horizontal version has a double meaning, however, because it is
also employed, especially in Italy, as a protection against the evil eye.
Here, it symbolizes the protective bull, the all-powerful Horned God of
the ancients. In this form, the horned hand is often worn as a protective
amulet. Owing to the potential for misunderstanding, one can only

be certain that the horned hand gesture signifies the cuckold insult when the hand is held in a vertical position, as this is never done as a protective sign.

In modern times, there have been two further points of confusion concerning this particular gesture. Also known as 'the Devil's horns', it has a strong association with satanic cults, and has crossed over into mainstream culture through heavy metal groups in particular (although the man generally credited with popularizing the gesture, Ronnie James Dio of Black Sabbath, said he borrowed it from his grandmother, who used it to ward off the evil eye). Because of this satanic association, people were surprised to see President George W. Bush and his family repeatedly using the gesture at public events. Could it be that a Christian American president was in league with the Devil? No, the answer was simply that Bush and his family hail from Texas, and the famous Longhorn cattle of that state are an emblem of Texas University, whose vertical 'Hook 'em Horns' hand sign has come to represent Texas as a whole.

One of the earliest known images of a vertical horned hand gesture in a work of art can be found on an Etruscan wall painting at Tarquinia [94], dating from 520 BC. In a scene showing dancers and musicians, one of the dancers is holding the left arm high, with the first and fourth fingers erect, as if giving a playful insult to the adjacent figure. A much later miniature in the *Libro de los juegos* (*Book of Games*) [95], dating from the late 13th century, shows a chess-player with a horned hand. The chess-player appears to be aiming the gesture at his opponent, but it is not clear whether he is insulting the man or trying to protect himself from him.

A French satirical print of 1815 pokes fun at the knightly orders of Europe. Entitled *The celebration of the Order of Cuckoldry before the throne of her majesty, Infidelity*, it is based on the idea that those married individuals who have sexually unfaithful partners must wear the horns of the cuckold on their heads. It is this imagined condition that the horned hand insult suggests. The person who is holding up a horned hand is saying, in effect: you should be wearing horns like this upon your head, you sad cuckold. An interesting feature of this cartoon is that the horns of infidelity may also take the form of branched antlers. This may be an attractive idea for the artist, but it is beyond the scope of anyone trying to mimic a horned head with a human hand.

In modern times, graffiti and street artists have enjoyed playing with the horned hand insult. While some examples are crude, others show remarkably skilful paintwork.

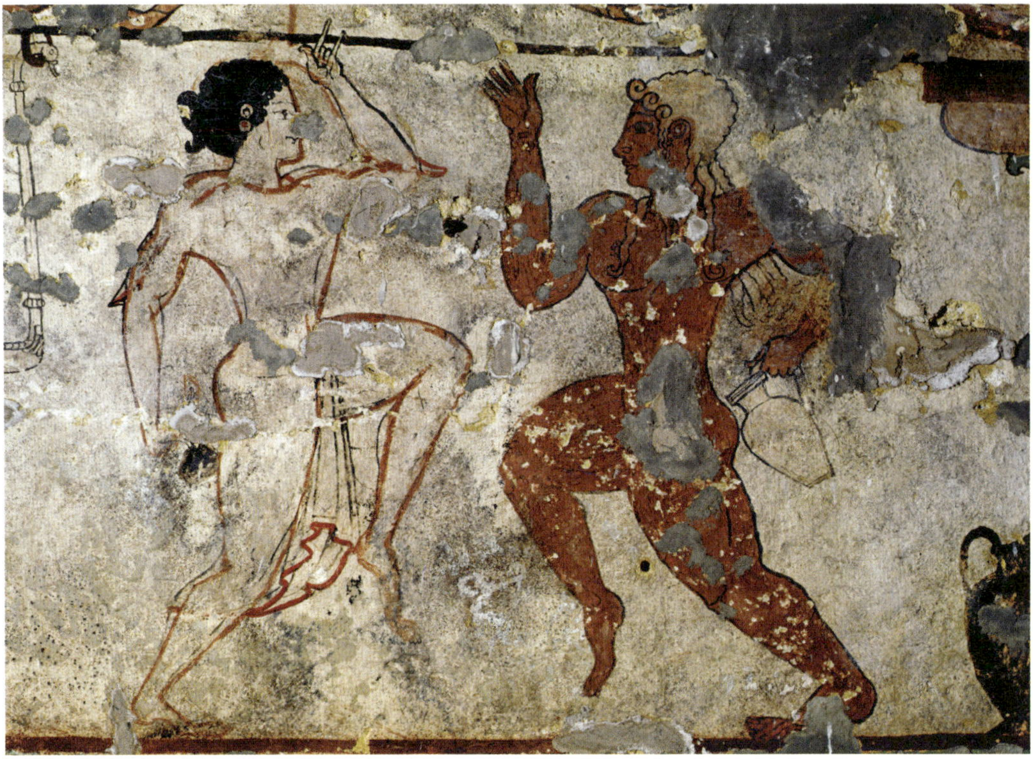

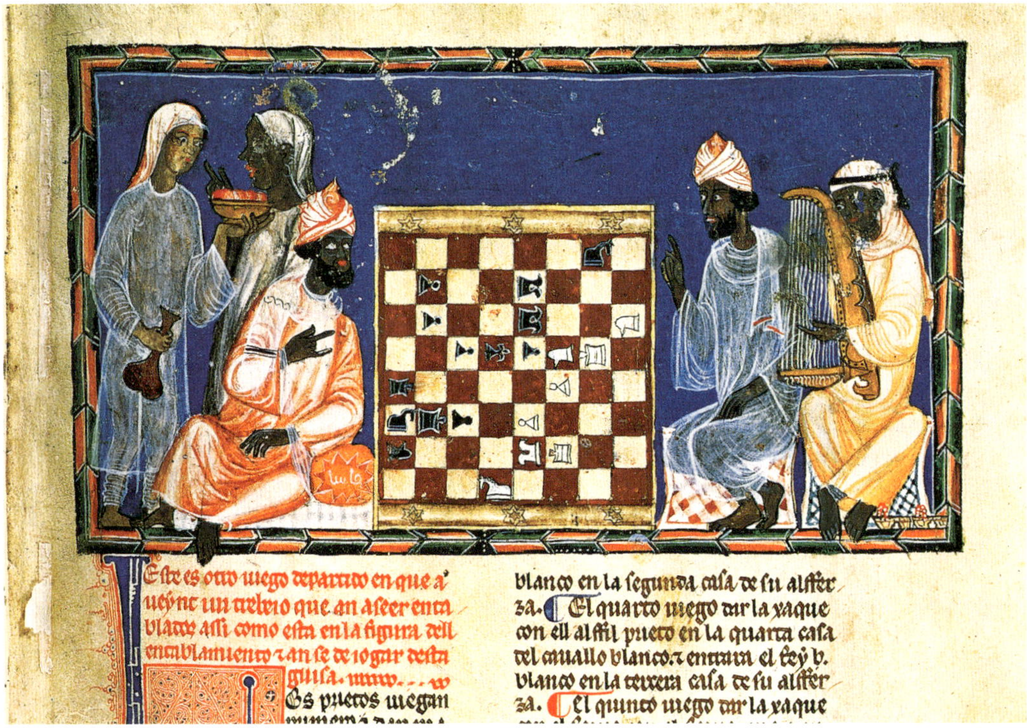

  Insults / Hand Gestures

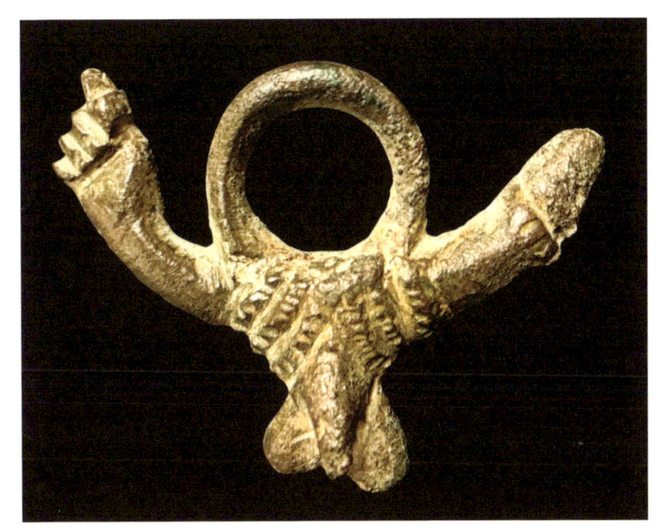

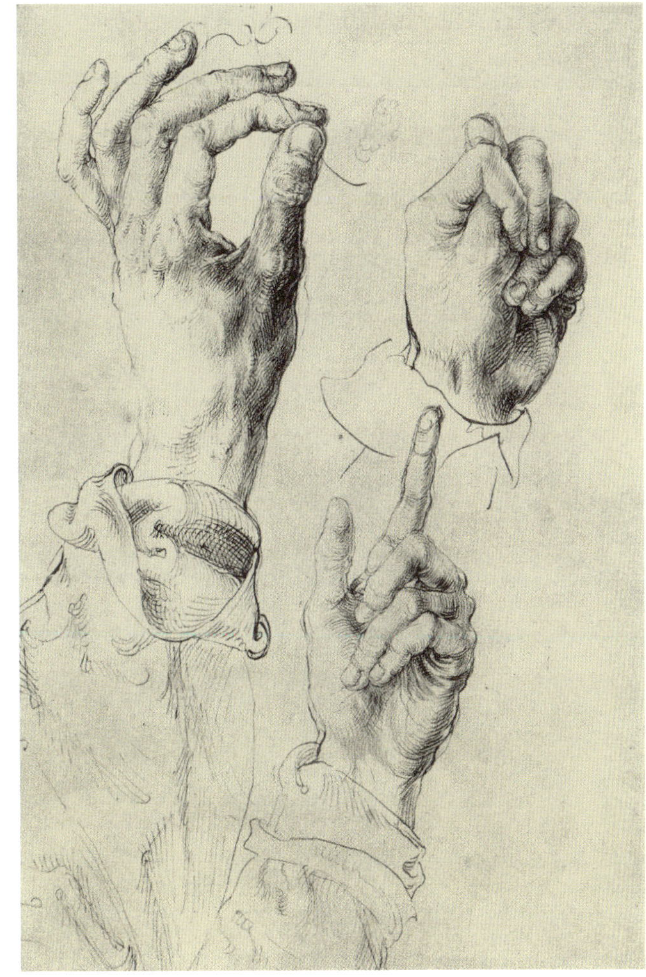

94. opposite, above **Etruscan fresco from the Tomb of the Lionesses, 520 BC, Necropolis of Tarquinia, Lazio, Italy**

95. opposite, below **A game of chess, from the *Libro de los juegos* (*Book of Games*), commissioned by the Spanish king Alfonso X and completed in 1283**

96. above **'Fig-and-phallus' Roman amulet, bronze**

97. right **Albrecht Dürer, *Studies of Dürer's Left Hand*, 1493–94, pen and ink on paper**

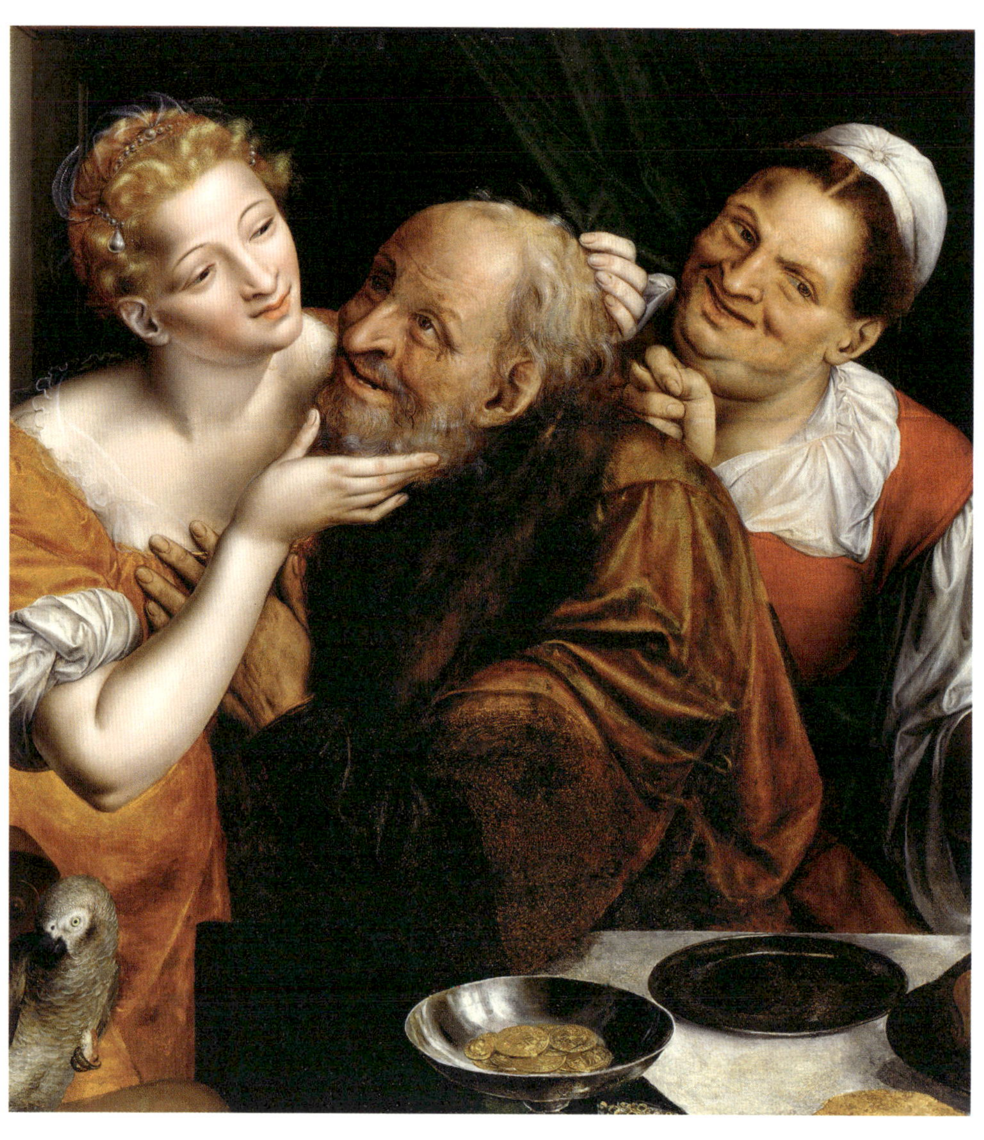

98. **Jan Massys,**
The Ill-matched Pair (detail),
1566, oil on panel

      Insults / Hand Gestures

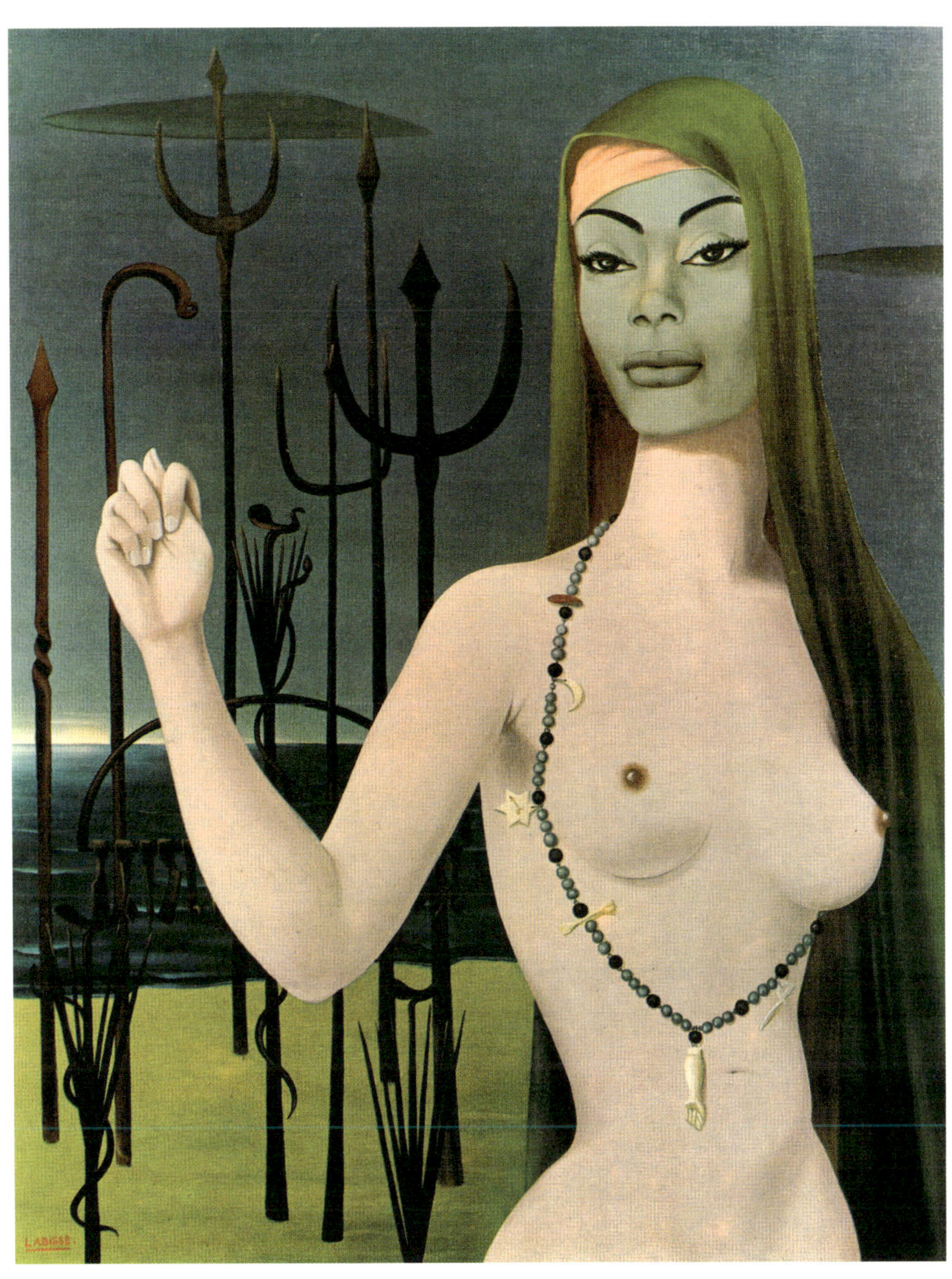

99. Felix Labisse,
La Fille d'Yemanja,
1961, oil on canvas

The Forearm Jerk

The forearm jerk is a crude phallic insult that is well known in France and other Mediterranean countries, but less common in northern Europe. Generally it is the right arm that is raised, with the right hand forming a fist; as the right arm jerks up, the left hand slaps down on the upper arm. In France it is known as the *bras d'honneur*, the 'arm of honour'. By giving it this name, the French are equating a man's honour with his virility. It is a curiously old-fashioned title for such a gesture, which suggests that, in France at least, it has been in use for a very long time.

In a sense, the forearm jerk is like an enlarged version of the middle finger gesture. In both cases, the part of the body that is being jerked upwards symbolizes the thrusting phallus. Historically, the obvious vulgarity of the forearm jerk has meant that it has largely been restricted to male groups, where one man insults another, although nowadays it is not unknown among women.

There are several minor variations of this insult. In one, the arm swings sideways across the front of the body, and in another the forearm is thrust straight out in front of the body. In Spain, there is a miniaturized version of the gesture called the 'peseta', in which the two forefingers mimic the action of the two arms. It is used jokingly when two men are sitting close to one another in a bar or a restaurant. In Portugal, there is an amplified version of the insult in which the gesture combines the forearm jerk with an erect middle finger – giving two insults simultaneously. In some countries, the gesture is considered to be so obscene that you can be arrested for performing it in public. This has led to the development of a cryptic version that can be used at close quarters but is not conspicuous at a greater distance. In this, the left hand is placed on the right upper arm and simply rubs back and forth.

Proof that this gesture still carries a powerful message in some parts of the world comes from an unlikely source. When the popular videogame *Mario Kart 8 Deluxe* was updated, Inkling Girl's victory pose was changed from an 'Up yours!' gesture to a fist pump. The forearm jerk was also removed from the videogame *Super Mario RPG*, where it was Bowser's victory pose. The move reflects an interesting shift in social mores, as the liberal attitudes that gained such momentum in the second half of the 20th century start to feel the effects of a new wave of social sensitivity sweeping across the Western world in the early part of the 21st century.

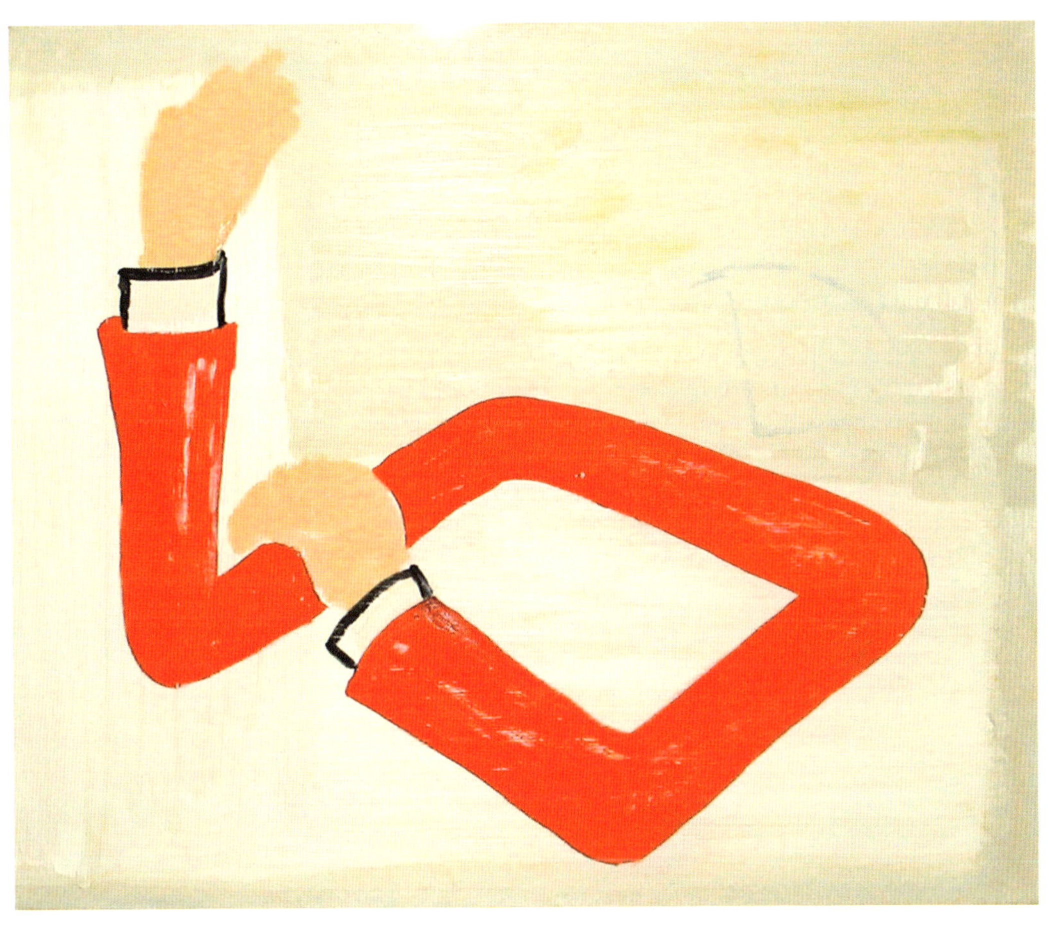

100. **Walter Swennen,**
***Bras d'honneur*, 2003,**
oil on canvas

Mooning

Mooning is one of the more unusual forms of human insult. A fully clothed person turns their back on their victim, adjusts their costume to expose their naked buttocks, and bends forward to protrude their rear end in the direction of the person they are insulting. Superficially it may look like a crude sexual invitation, but its true meaning is either a symbolic defecation on the onlooker, or an unspoken invitation to 'kiss my arse'.

Although it only acquired the name of 'mooning' in modern times, the action itself has a long history. A description of an incident that occurred in the Holy Land in the first century AD records how it once caused many deaths. During Passover in Jerusalem, when Jewish crowds flocked to the city, Roman soldiers stood guard on the battlements to watch for any signs of a disturbance. One of these soldiers jokingly decided to show his contempt for the people below by exposing his buttocks to them, as if to say 'I will defecate on you'. The victims of this insult were so angry that they began throwing stones at the soldiers. As a result, reinforcements were sent to control the situation, but this only panicked the crowd. A mass stampede followed and it is said that 10,000 Jews were crushed to death – all because of a single insult.

There have been many notable incidents of the use of this insult in the centuries that followed. A case of massed mooning occurred at the Battle of Crécy in 1346, when several hundred Norman soldiers exposed their backsides to the English archers, with the inevitable response that is too painful to contemplate.

In the 19th century, another mass mooning took place, this time in a women's forced labour camp in Australia. The female convicts who had been sent there suffered such humiliating punishments that they eventually rebelled. When the governor of the region visited to inspect the camp and attend a service in the chapel in 1838, the women saw their chance. According to an eyewitness, once the governor had finished his speech, 'The three hundred women turned right around and at one impulse pulled up their clothes showing their naked posteriors which they simultaneously smacked with their hands making a loud and not very musical noise.' The governor was so horrified that he never returned.

Of all the modern cases of mooning reported in the press, perhaps the most remarkable was the one performed – again in Australia – by a protester during a visit by Queen Elizabeth II and Prince Philip in 2011. The protester somehow managed to run alongside the royal car for 50 metres (164 ft) with an Australian flag clenched between his exposed buttocks, before being arrested.

The humiliating invitation to 'kiss my arse' also has an ancient origin, and was originally employed as a protection against the evil eye. Because the human species is the only one to possess a pair of rounded buttocks, it was believed that the Devil was deeply envious of this quality. Since he himself lacked buttocks, it was thought that he would become enraged if you reminded him of this fact. So, showing your naked buttocks was one of the worst insults you could offer him. And because Satan, in place of buttocks, had on his rump a second face, it became a familiar taunt to shout out 'Kiss my arse!' when the buttock display was aimed at human companions. This intensified the insult because it implied that the victims of the display were no better than loathsome satanists. All this is now forgotten, but the insult lives on.

Today the exposure of the buttocks is an illegal act in some regions, but is treated simply as a rude joke in others. Its illegality usually rests on whether or not it accidentally exposes the genitalia. In 2006, a United States court ruled that the exposure of the buttocks, when mooning, was not illegal because, if it were, the police would have to arrest every woman wearing a thong or a skimpy bikini on American beaches.

A more modest version of this insult is the 'buttocks slap'. The person bends over, aiming the buttocks towards the victim, but without adjusting the clothing to expose naked flesh. The buttocks are then slapped with the flat of the hand. This version is popular in Eastern Europe and the Middle East. In southern Italy, there is an even simpler action, the 'buttocks thrust', in which the insulter simply turns his back to the victim and thrusts his buttocks in their direction.

Perhaps not surprisingly, images of mooning are virtually non-existent in major works of art. They can, however, occasionally be found in the small marginalia of illuminated medieval manuscripts [101]. One notable exception can be seen high up on the ceiling of the Sistine Chapel in the Vatican, where Michelangelo has depicted God bearing his buttocks to Moses [102]. This refers to a passage in Exodus, where God explains to Moses that he must not see his face as he walks by and is only permitted to see his rear end (Exodus 33:20–23): 'And the Lord said, Thou canst not see my face... I will put thee in a cleft of the rock, and will cover thee with my hand while I pass by. And I will take away mine hand, and thou shalt see my back parts: but my face shall not be seen.' This is not, of course, a true example of mooning, but has nevertheless been cheerfully labelled as one by irreligious observers.

Among more recent works of art, as an act of aesthetic desecration, street artist Nick Walker's *Moona Lisa* [103] puts to shame Marcel Duchamp's quaintly moustachioed version of Leonardo da Vinci's great masterpiece.

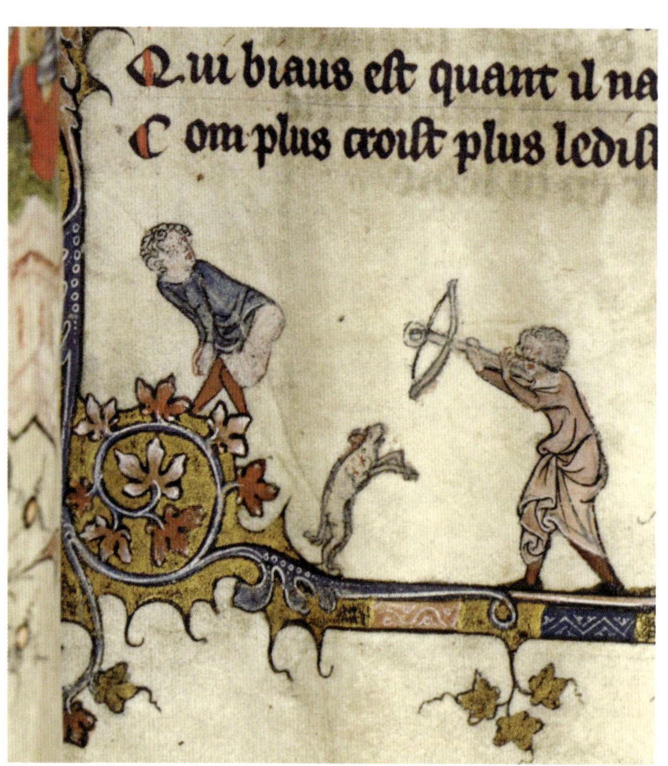

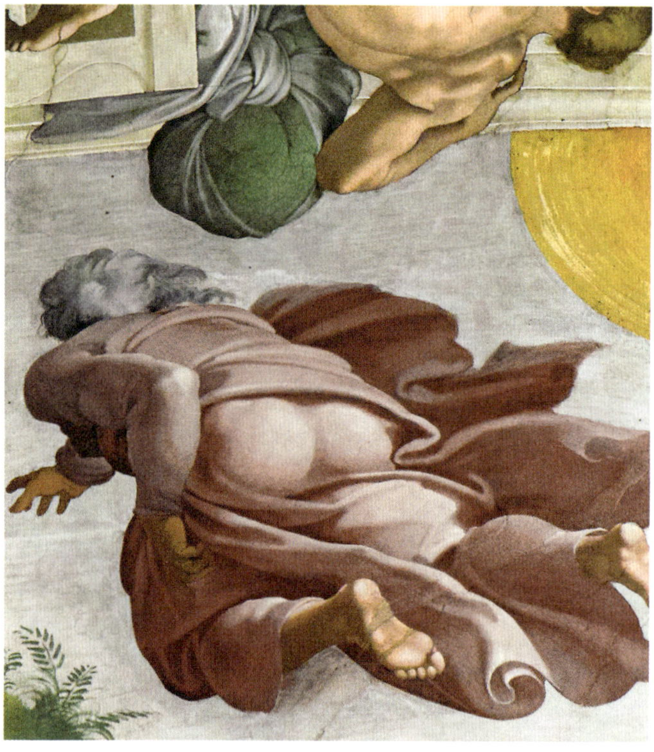

101. above **Jehan de Grise, miniature from** *The Romance of Alexander*, **1338–44**

102. left **Michelangelo,** *The Creation of the Sun and the Moon*, **ceiling fresco (detail), 1508–12, Sistine Chapel, Rome**

103. opposite **Nick Walker,** *Moona Lisa*, **2008, spray paint on wall, London**

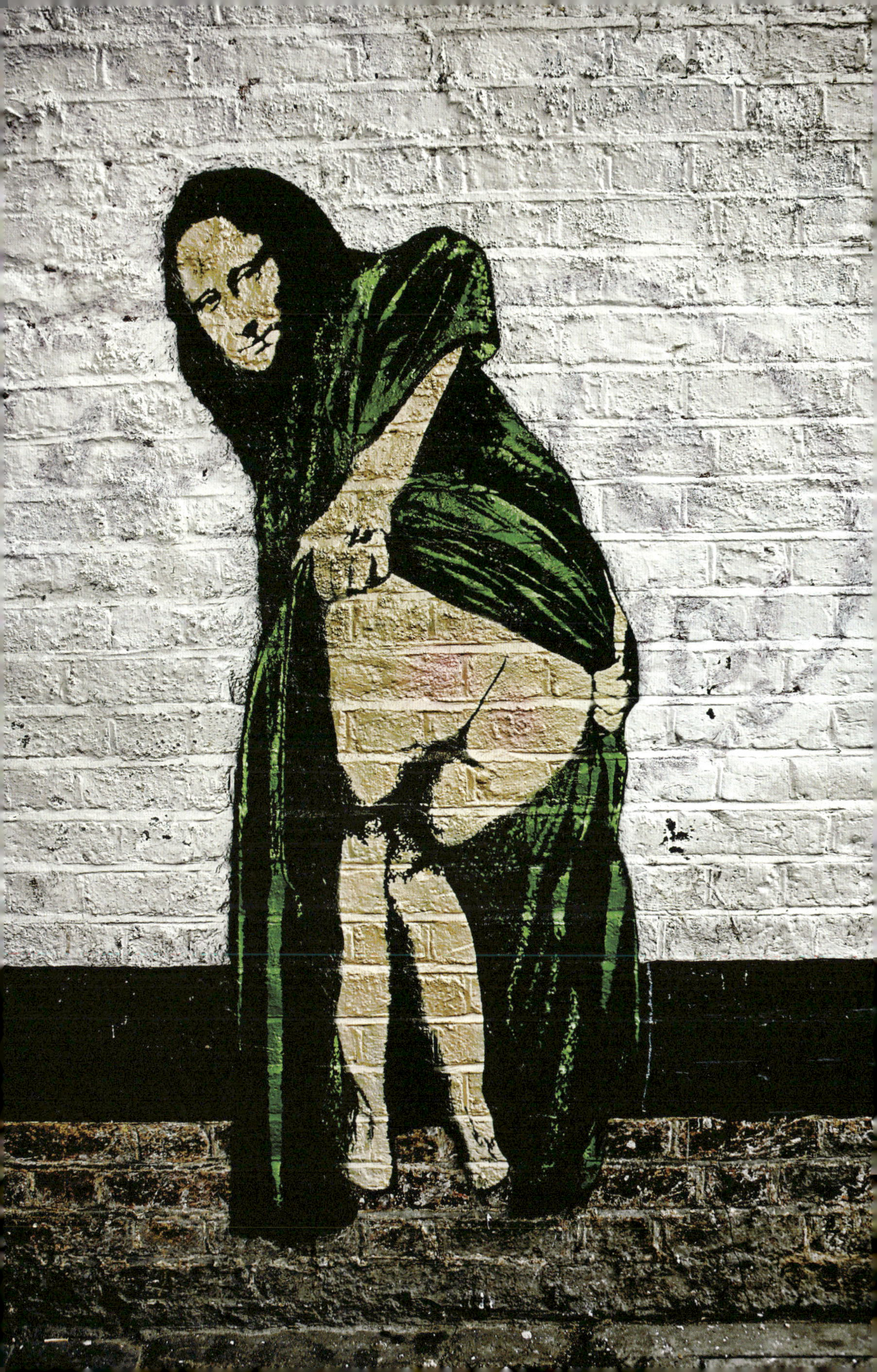

Threats

In the animal world, threat displays are important because they can
be used to settle disputes between rivals and avoid actual conflict.
Serious, out-and-out fighting is rare because an injury can be so costly:
a limping lion cannot hunt, and a wounded antelope cannot flee. Sadly,
in the human world, threat displays are frequently inadequate and real
fighting breaks out far more often. This is, in part, because most of us
no longer live in small tribes, where all threats would be at a personal
level. In the densely populated cities of the 21st century, individuals face
an impersonal existence in which simple, one-to-one body language
is often lost in a sea of strangers.

Nevertheless, where personal antagonisms do still occur, threat
signals can play an important role in social life. There are two distinct
kinds of threat. The first is the kind we do not have to learn to interpret,
such as a raised fist, grasping hands or an angry facial expression. These
are so basic that they are universally understood as threat displays.
The second type of threat is highly stylized or symbolic, and develops
only in particular cultures. While the gestures that fall into this second
category may be interpreted as a serious threat in some parts of the
world, they are not widely known elsewhere. Historic examples include
the glove-slap, in which one man would take off his glove and use it to
lightly slap an adversary on the face. Although this action may seem
trivial by today's standards, in 17th-century Europe it was considered
a serious challenge to a duel and often led to the death of one – or,
sometimes, both – of the men involved. In art, the global actions are,
understandably, much more common than the more localized ones.

The Raised Fist

When a painting or a sculpture depicts a threatening figure, the most popular posture is the raised fist. This is an 'intention movement' (an action that indicates what the person threatens to do next) – in this case, an overarm blow, the most ancient, basic form of attack used by the human species. Observations in nurseries reveal that when there is a dispute between two small children, the use of the overarm blow is automatic and unthinking, as if it is an inborn reaction. Horizontal, forward punches are more sophisticated and appear much later. While professional fighters tend to use forward punches and other specialized techniques, in the rough-and-tumble of street fighting the primitive overarm blow often reasserts itself.

In art, the majority of threatening figures are depicted with the right arm raised, as if to bring it down on the head of a victim. This is also true when they are holding a knife in their raised fist, despite the fact that a forward stabbing movement would be much more effective. Some of the earliest examples of this raised-fist posture can be found in the art of ancient Egypt, in which the dwarf god Bes is often shown with his right arm held high and his fist clasping a knife or small sword [104]. Bes was notorious for his ferocity and his ability to fight off chaotic beings, demons and evil spirits. Originally his role was to protect the pharaoh, but over time he became popular as a protector of ordinary Egyptian people, and he was often depicted on household items or the walls of homes to threaten the enemies of the occupants, whether supernatural or living. He was thought to offer protection from dangerous animals in particular, which is why he is shown clutching a snake in his left hand.

A thousand years later, in the Himalayas, another protective deity was depicted in a similar posture, with his right arm raised threateningly above his head. This intimidating figure was known as Canda Vajrapani, meaning 'fierce holder of the thunderbolt', and his role as a Buddhist deity was to remove all internal and external obstacles to Buddhism and its followers. In keeping with Buddhist philosophy, his wrathful nature is not meant to be malign or in any way demonic, but rather expresses 'the invincible power of compassion'. While he brandishes the thunderbolt as a deadly weapon in his right hand, he makes a gesture of exorcism (Karana mudra) with his left. It is interesting to note that in his warrior pose, he has similar features to the earlier Bes, with a disproportionately large head, rounded belly and bulging limbs.

Associated with both Hinduism and Buddhism, Kali is another ferocious deity who is depicted in a threatening posture, holding a weapon in her raised arm. In Tibetan Buddhism, she is sometimes shown riding on a mule that is covered with the skin of her son. When she failed to convert her son to Buddhism, she flayed him alive and then ate his heart. In paintings, she is shown wearing a garland of severed heads, and sometimes severed arms. In one hand, she holds a drinking cup made from the skull of a child. Occasionally, she is seen chewing a corpse or striding through a pool of blood.

In the 17th century, one of Rembrandt's portrayals of Samson [106] shows him angrily shaking his fist at his Philistine father-in-law. The painting refers to an incident that occurred when Samson came to visit his wife, bringing a young goat as a gift. Samson said, 'Let me go into the chamber to my wife.' But her father would not let him go in. 'I was sure', said her father, 'that you had taken a dislike to her, so I gave her to your wedding companion. But her younger sister is more beautiful than she; let her become your wife instead.' This made Samson so angry that he shook his fist threateningly at the old man, and then left to perpetrate a savage revenge.

In the following century, the threat of a raised fist took on a highly characteristic new form. This was the carefully posed stance of the professional boxer, who stood with his legs placed firmly apart and his clenched fists raised before him – both threatening and defensive. It was a posture invented by Daniel Mendoza, a Jewish prizefighter who revolutionized boxing, turning what was little more than a punch-up into the modern sport we know today. In particular, it was Mendoza who introduced the fighting techniques of feinting and dodging that transformed crude fights into skilful contests. A late 18th-century etching by James Gillray [105] depicts Mendoza in his famously stylized posture, a work that would spawn a whole genre of boxing images.

It is clear that the raised fist is a basic human threat posture that can act as a prelude to various kinds of assault, from a beating with a clenched fist to the use of weapons. In the early 20th century, it was adopted by the Communist Party in Russia, where iconic posters of the new leader, Lenin, showed him with a raised, closed fist held rigidly aloft, as an expression of strength and unity. This posture soon became a popular emblem of the communists and was seen frequently in various forms of propaganda [107], often with the raised fist clutching a hammer and sickle, symbolizing the revolution, respectively, of industrial and rural workers.

In 1937, when the Catalan artist Joan Miró was asked to produce a poster in support of the Republicans, who were engaged in the Spanish Civil War against Franco's fascists, he borrowed the communist salute, showing a Spanish peasant with an exaggerated forearm, raising a clenched fist high into the air [108].

In the 21st century, the raised fist lives on in modern street art. Wherever there is social protest, one invariably finds the fist – often shown in isolation from the rest of the body.

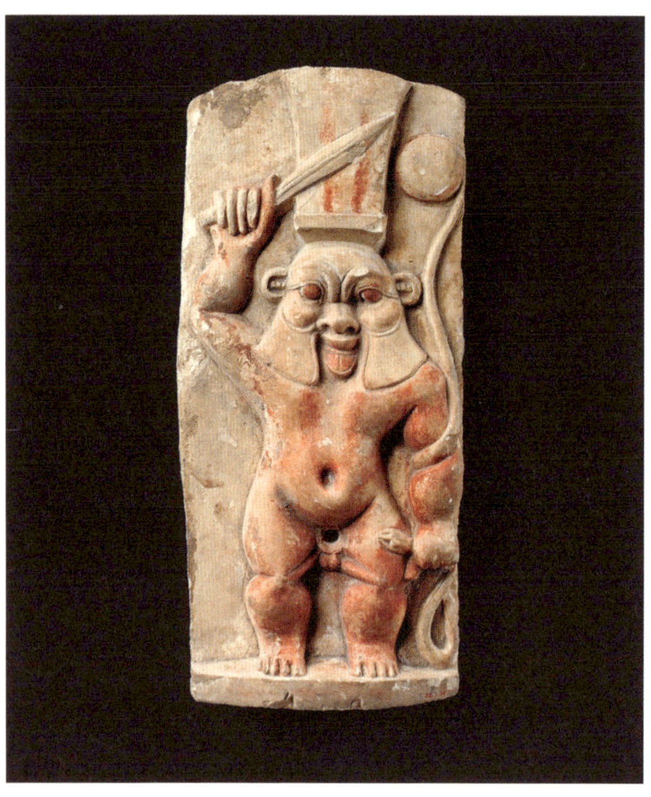

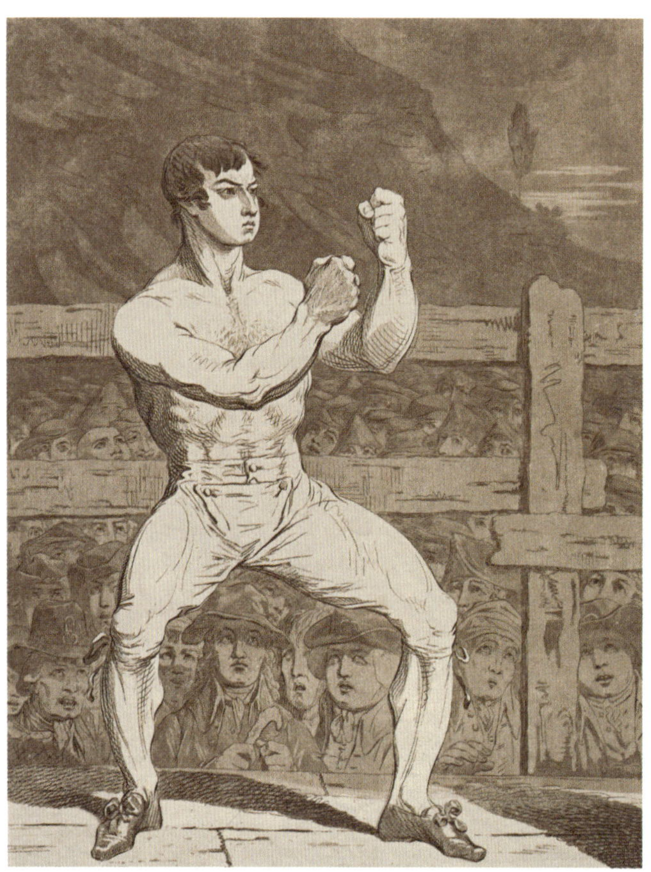

104. above **Stela of the god Bes, Ptolemaic or Roman Period, 4th century BC–1st century AD, paint on limestone, Egypt**

105. left **James Gillray, *Daniel Mendoza*, 1788, etching and aquatint**

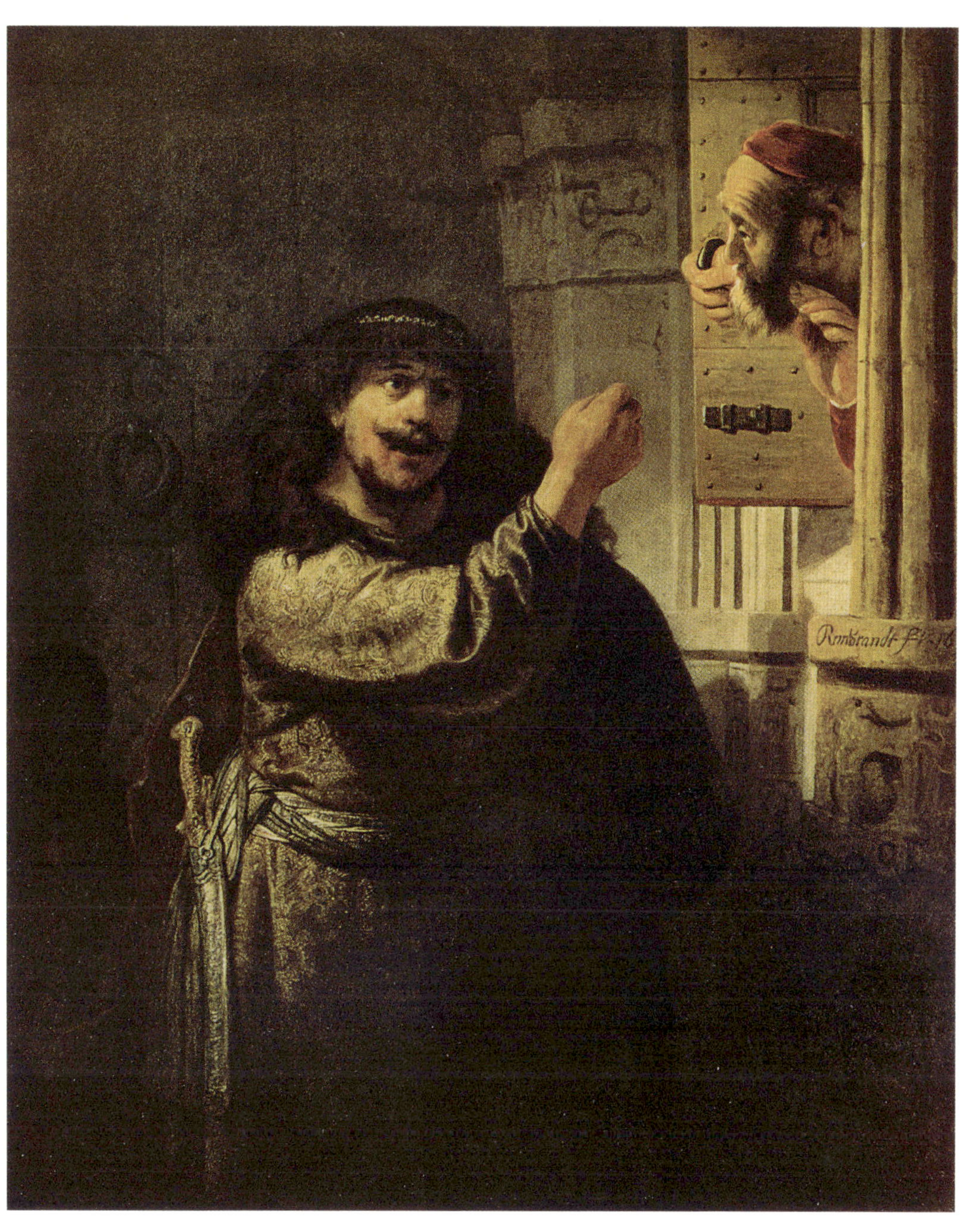

106. Rembrandt, *Samson
Accusing his Father-in-law*,
1635, oil on canvas

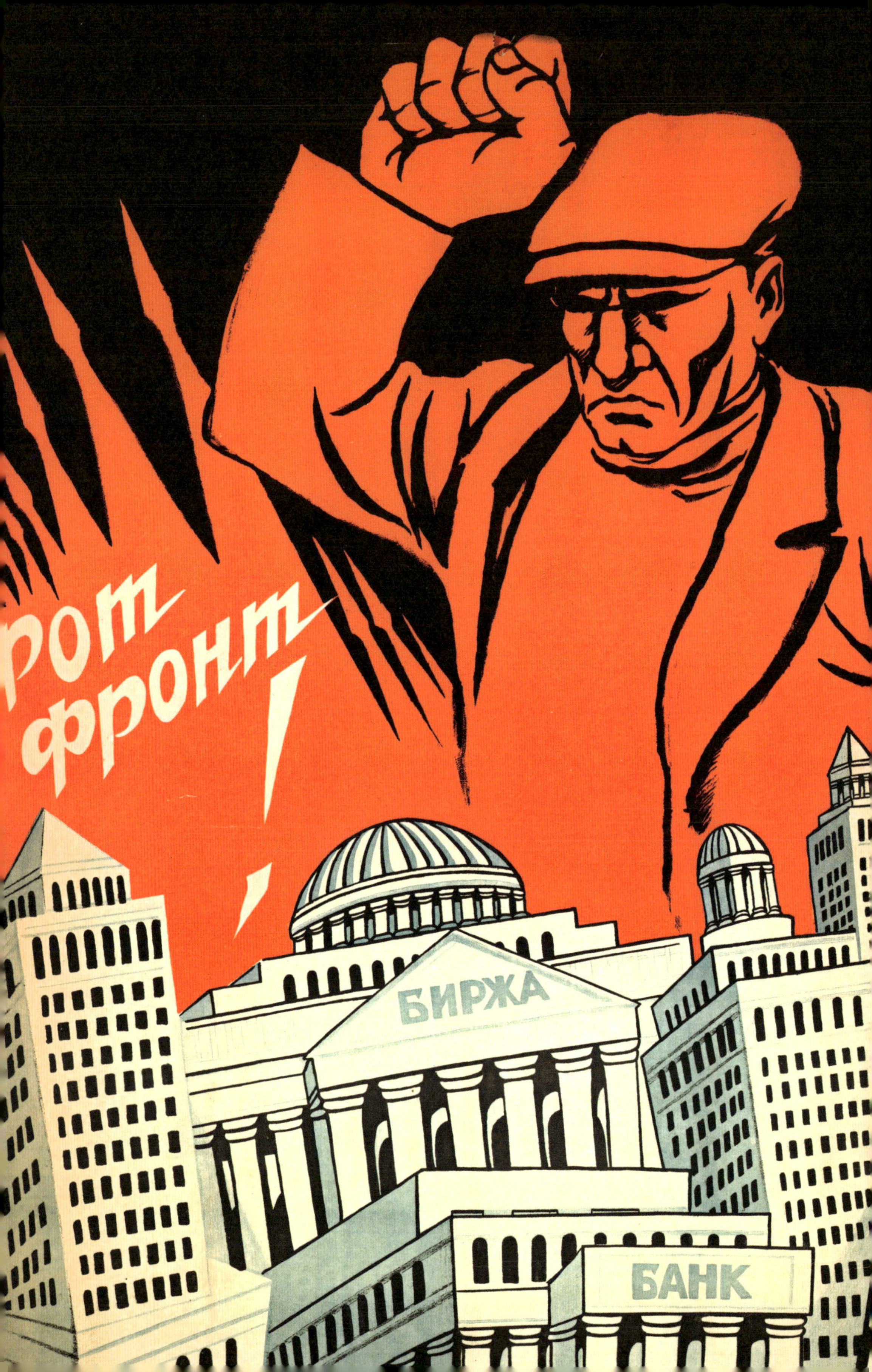
рот
фронт!
БИРЖА
БАНК

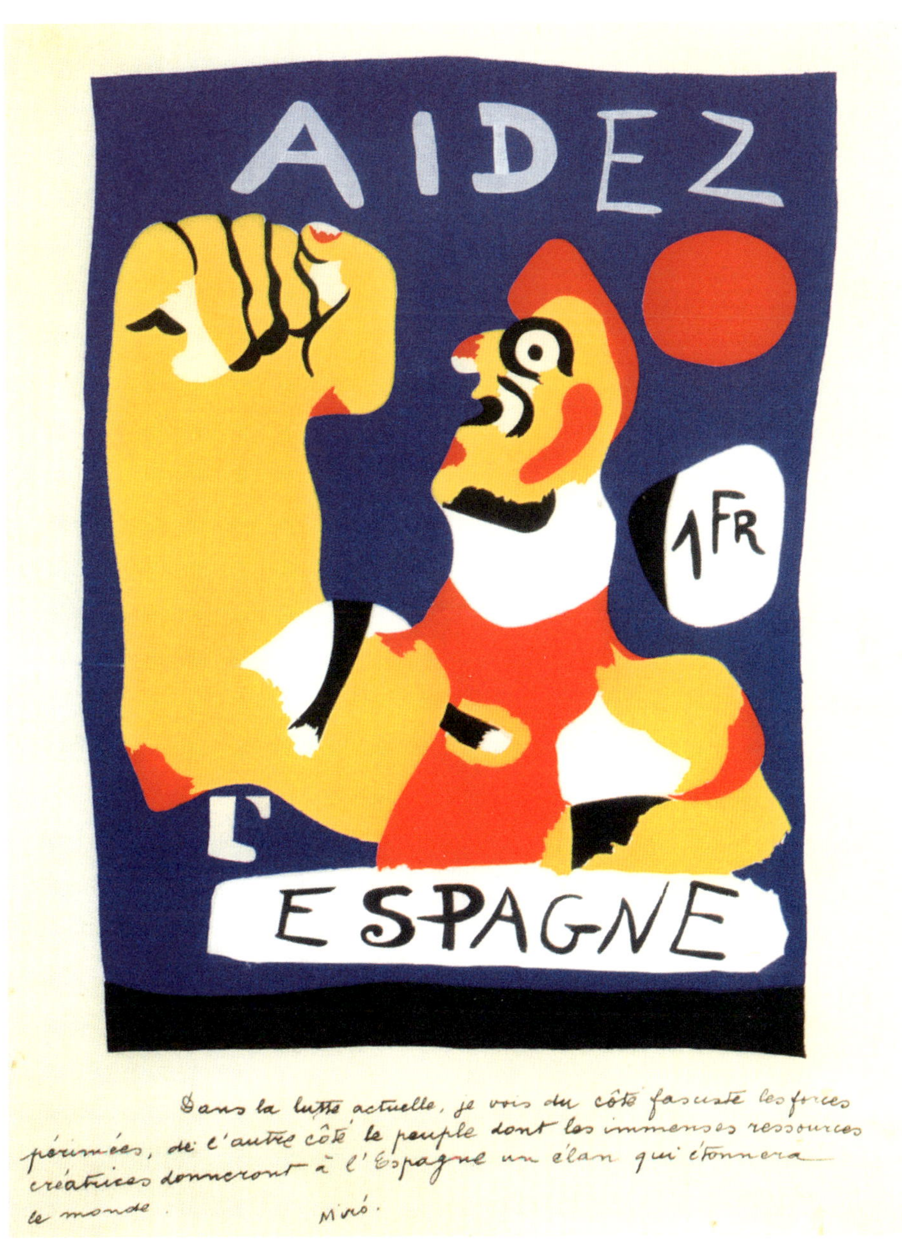

107. opposite **Soviet propaganda
poster (detail), 1930s**

108. above **Joan Miró, *Aidez L'Espagne*,
1937, pochoir with lithographic
inscription on paper**

The Air-grasp

Just as the raised fist can threaten a blow on the head, so the air-grasp can threaten the throttling of the victim. The hands reach out with the fingers stiffly bent and splayed wide apart in anticipation of grasping the victim's throat. This action is often performed playfully by an adult towards a child, when pretending to be a monster. It also appears in Japanese paintings of highly stylized performances by kabuki actors [110, 111].

In scientific terms, this action is referred to as an 'intention movement', with the hands taking up a position that indicates what they threaten to do next. Actions of this kind are often depicted in modern street art, where the grasping hand is employed to reflect a state of anger or revenge-seeking. One famous example, which originated in skateboard art, combines the air-grasping hand with an aggressive, open mouth apparently shouting abuse [109]. Designed by Jim Phillips for the brand Santa Cruz, this amalgamation of two powerful threats creates a forceful, intimidating image.

109. **Street art recreating the 'Santa Cruz screaming hand' by Jim Phillips, date unknown, spray paint on wall, Duisburg, Germany**

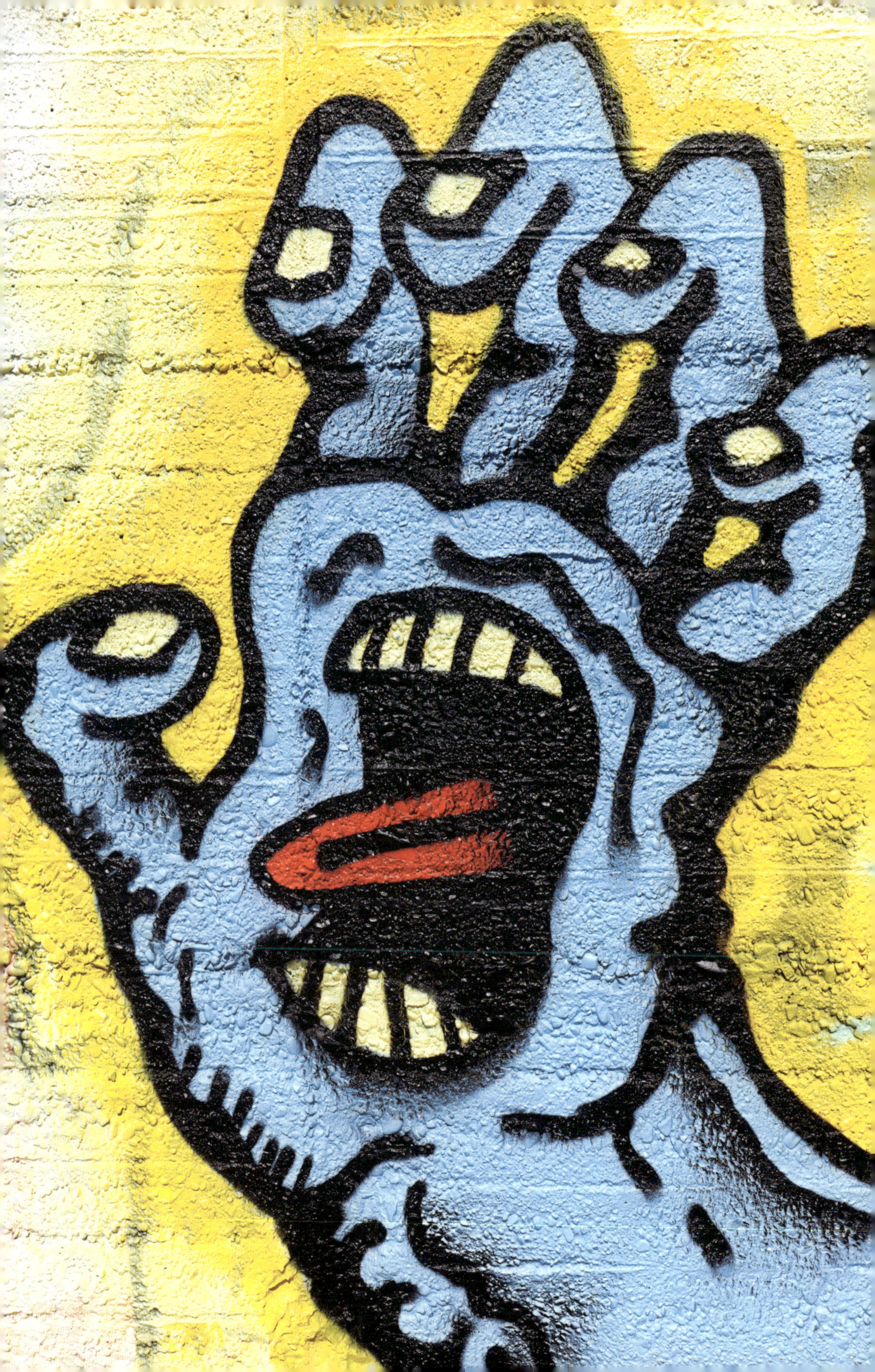

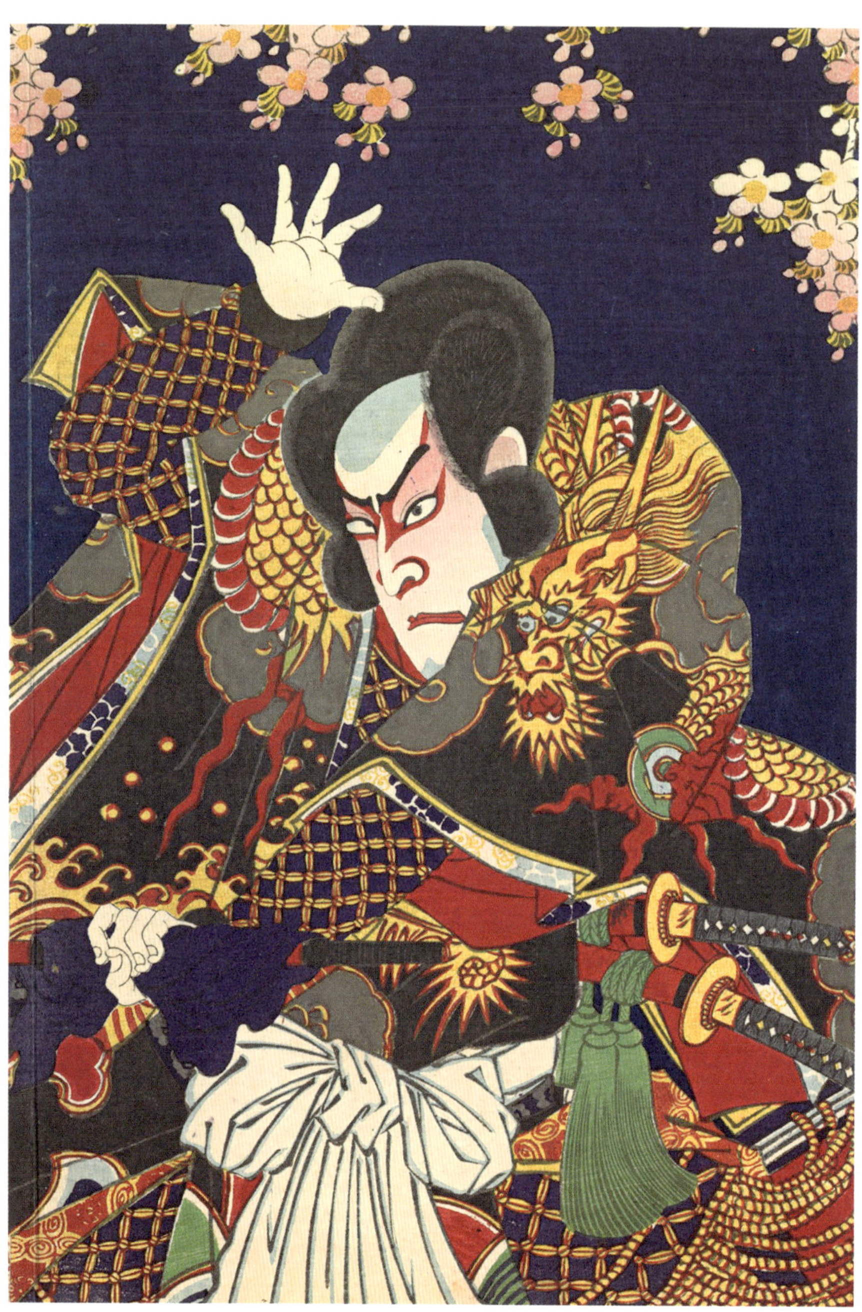

110. above **Toyohara Kunichika,
depiction of a Japanese kabuki actor
(detail), 1883–86, woodblock print**

111. opposite **Toshusai Sharaku,**
***Kabuki Actor Otani Oniji III as Yakko
Edobei* (detail), 1794, woodblock print**

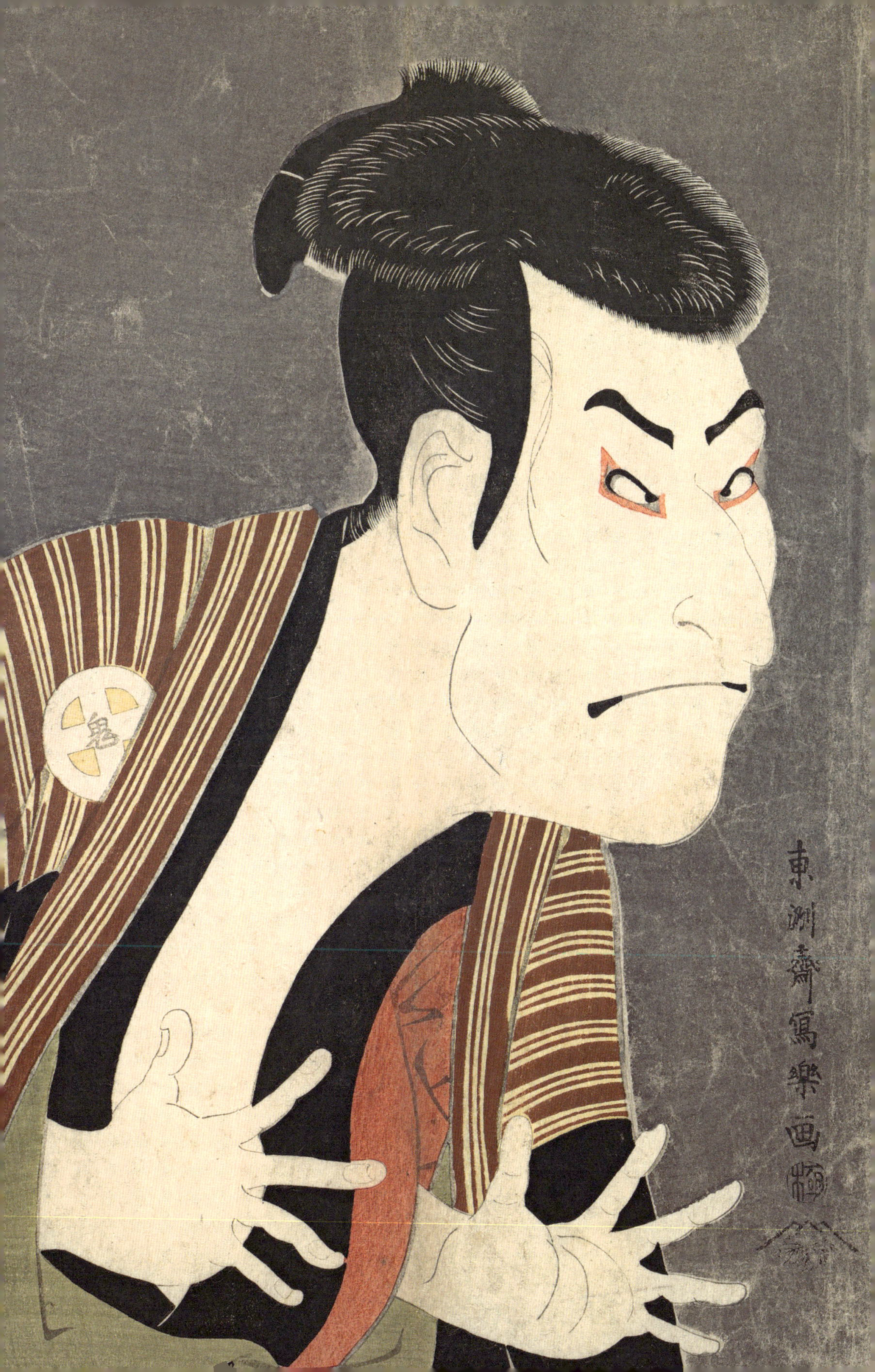

東洲齋寫樂畫

The Threat-face

The facial expression that signals a threat is complicated. There are, in fact, several versions of the human threat-face. This is because the emotional state of the threatening individual is made up of two conflicting elements: aggression and fear. If there were pure aggression without fear, the individual would likely attack. If there were pure fear without aggression, the individual would flee or capitulate. When aggression and fear are both present, the state of conflict that exists produces the threatening display. However, the balance between these conflicting urges varies from case to case, and this is what makes the human threat-face so complex. A further complication arises when the angry face is accompanied by verbal abuse – the silent versus the noisy threat – making for additional variations in the facial expression.

With these variations in mind, it is interesting to see how different artists have portrayed a threat-face. In 2017, the Nigerian artist Kalejaye O. T. (KOT) chose the notoriously abrasive Swedish footballer Zlatan Ibrahimović as his subject [112], capturing the strong muscular contractions that occur in the face at the moment of maximum threat; the mouth is stretched vertically and the brow is lowered into a heavy frown. In modern times, the football match is a rich source of extreme forms of facial expression, and Ibrahimović has perfected a threat-face intense enough to intimidate most rival players. Another skilful portrayal of this form of facial expression was produced by the New York-based street artist WK Interact in a suite of works called *12 Angry Men* [113]. Exhibited at a Manhattan gallery in 2009, the portraits depict expressions of intense – even frenzied – anger and threat.

In New Zealand, the indigenous Maori people challenge visitors with the elaborate *pōwhiri* ceremony. This begins with a ferocious display called the *wero,* in which the Maori warriors shout out battle cries while adopting an extreme form of facial threat. Historically, this was done to test the steadfastness of the visitors. If they stood firm and did not retaliate, the warriors would present them with a symbolic peace offering. The threats displayed during the ceremony might not be taken as seriously as they once were, but the *pōwhiri* remains a central part of Maori protocol, and the wildly exaggerated threat-face survives in all its glory [114].

112. **Kalejaye O. T. (KOT),**
Dare to Zlatan, **2017,**
graphite and charcoal
pencil on paper

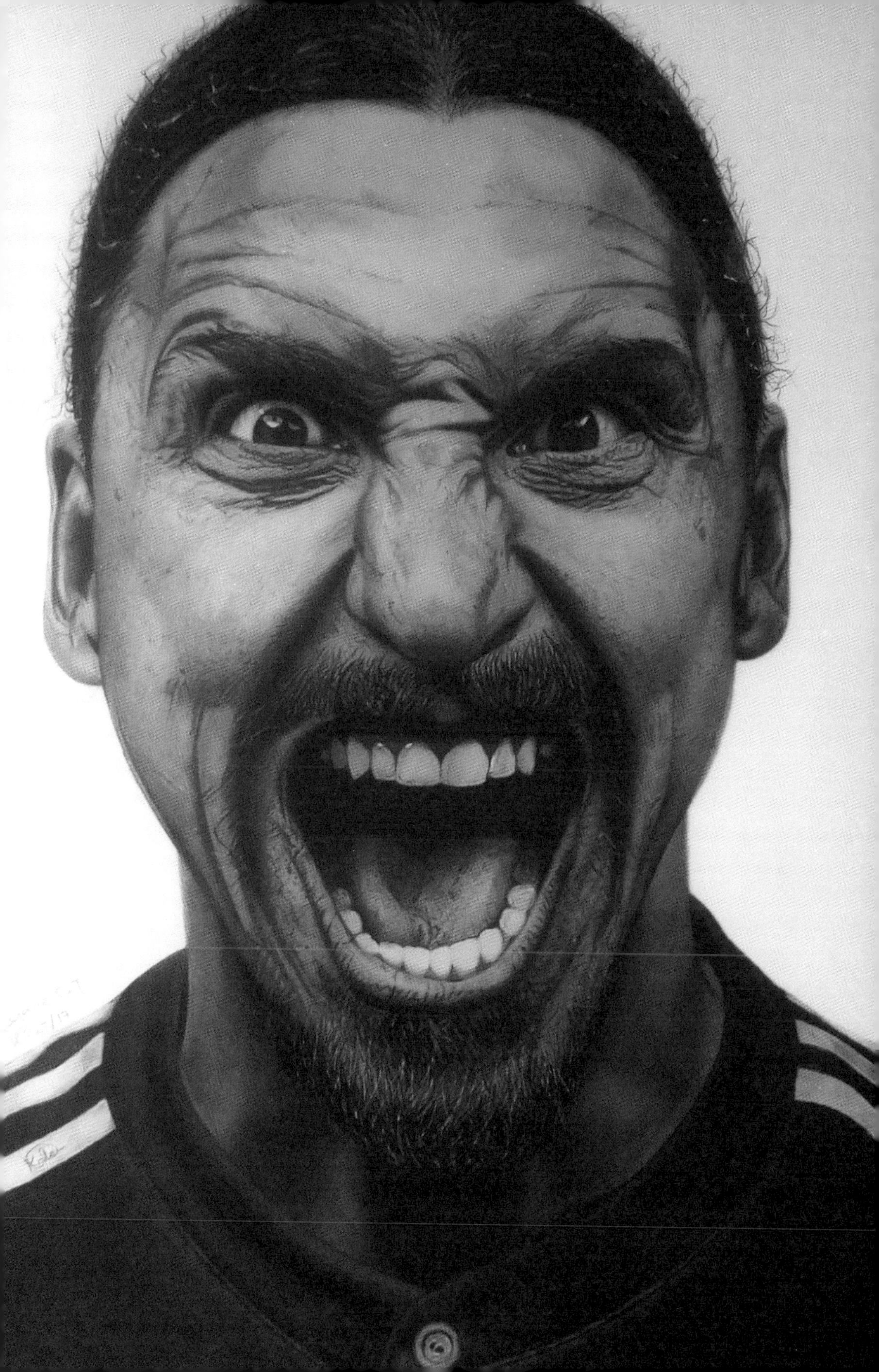

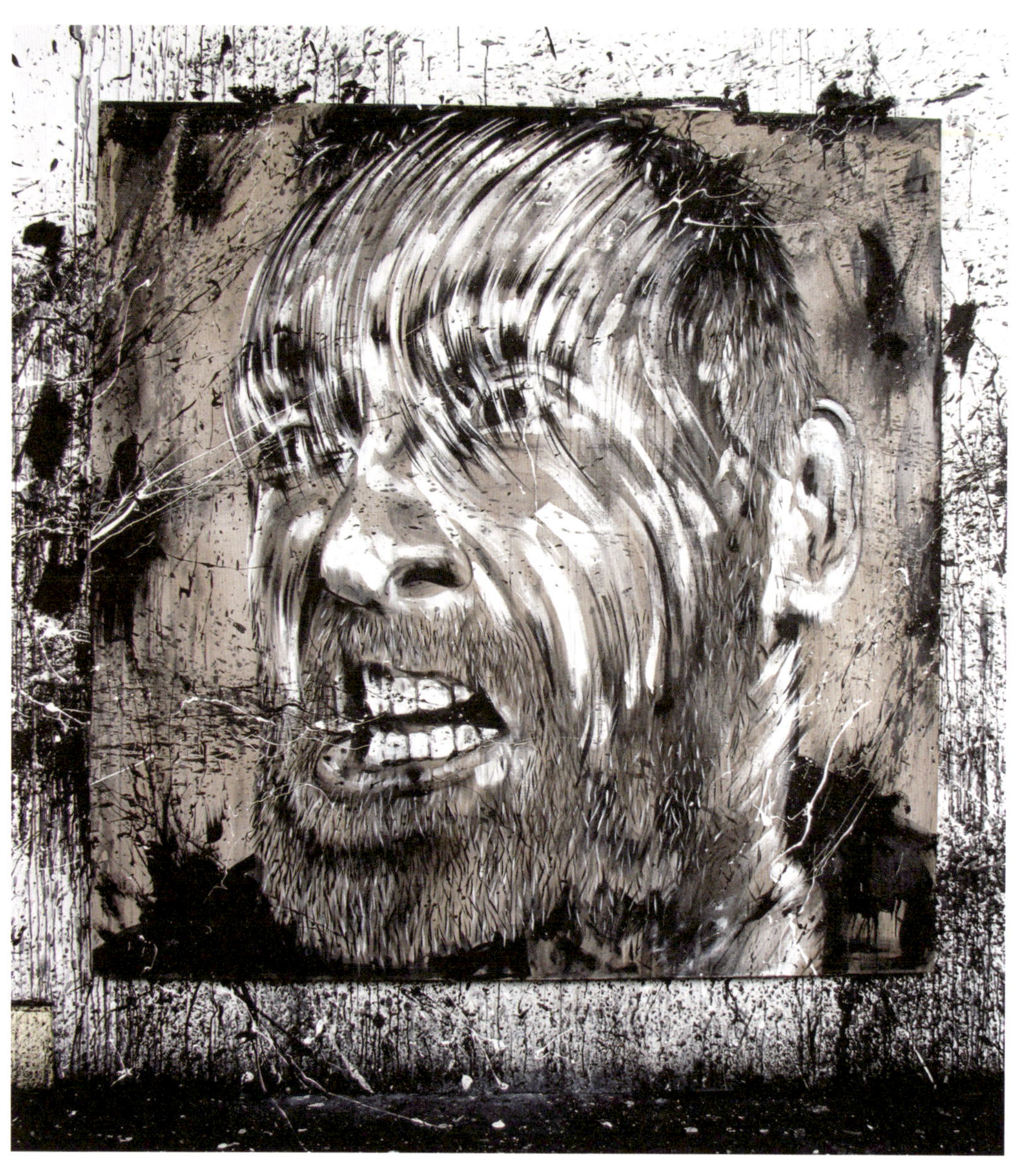

113. **WK Interact,** *Portrait: Patrick* (*12 Angry Men*), **2009, acrylic on canvas**

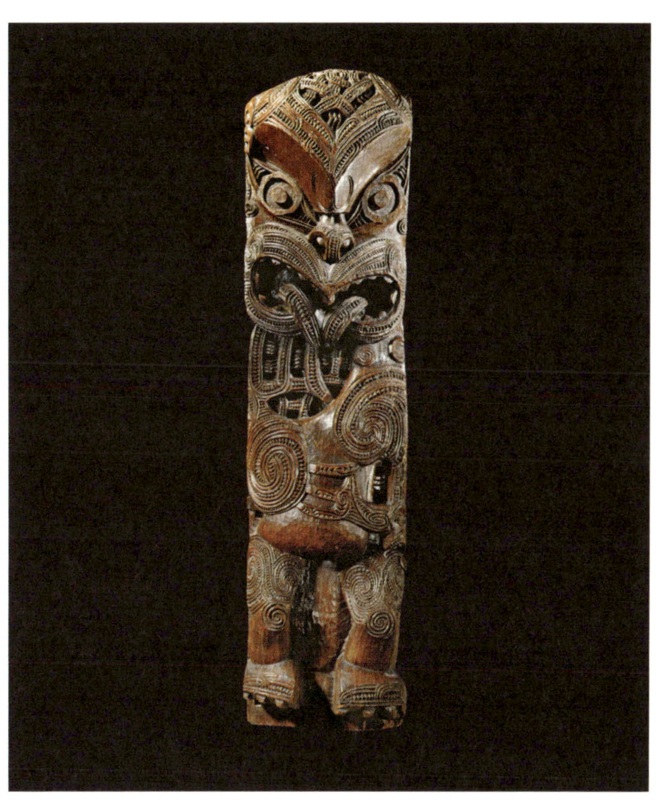

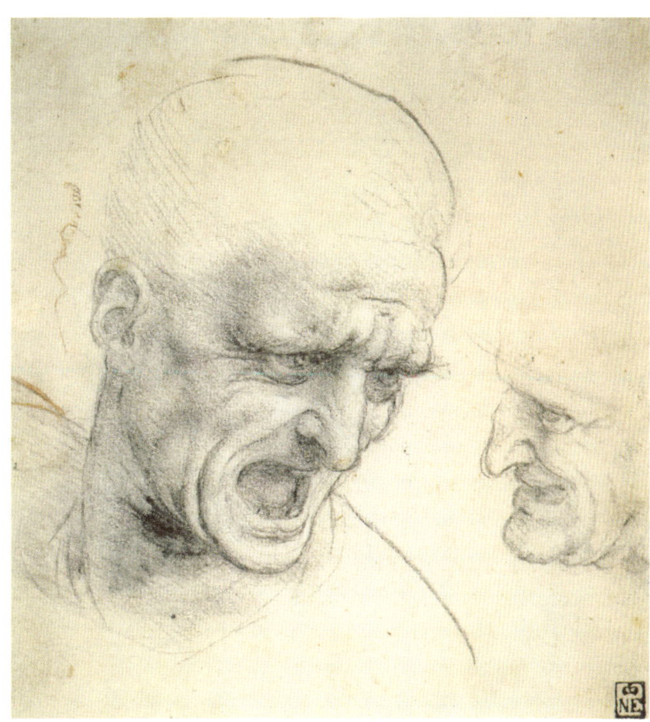

114. above **Carved *amo* (Maori house post)**, *c.* 1800, wood, New Zealand

115. right **Leonardo da Vinci, *Studies for the Heads of Two Soldiers in the 'Battle of Anghiari'*, *c.* 1505, charcoal on paper

The Glove-slap

One of the strangest and most stylized threats is the glove-slap, or *soufflet* – an action that evolved from the medieval practice of 'throwing down the gauntlet', by which a knight would challenge an adversary to a duel. Although the glove-slap has long been abandoned, for hundreds of years it was the formal threat display of an insulted gentlemen or nobleman whose honour demanded that he challenge the offender to a duel. This was a ritual that was forbidden to the lower orders of society, such as servants or peasants, but if a high-status male felt that his honour – or that of his lady – had been questioned, he had no choice but to take off his glove, approach the offender and strike him across the face with it; in the absence of a glove, the palm of the hand would do. As part of the ritual, the challenger might then present the offender with his personal card. Among aristocratic German university students there was a slight variation: the card was torn a little before being presented. If the card was accepted, the duel was on. Any gentleman or nobleman who refused to accept a formal challenge to a duel would be considered a snivelling coward; if his refusal became widely known, he would find himself scorned by society. On the island of Malta, a refusal to fight could even lead to imprisonment.

The duel would be arranged for the following morning in a secluded spot, and the offender would be offered a choice of swords or pistols. The night before the duel, the contestants would put their affairs in order and compose a letter to their loved ones. On the morning of the duel, usually at dawn, the contestants would arrive, aided by seconds, and would be elegantly dressed, restrained in their conduct and courteous to their rival. As soon as a fatal thrust or shot had been delivered, it was usual for the winner of the duel to cast aside his weapon and hasten to the side of his injured adversary in the hope of being forgiven with the man's dying words.

Duelling began in medieval times and lasted until the end of the 19th century, when public opinion turned against it. It reached its peak at the end of the 17th century, and in the thirty years between 1685 and 1715 it is said that, in France alone, 10,000 duels were fought, leading to hundreds of deaths. Deaths and injuries were so frequent, and at one point were taking such a toll on society, that duelling was outlawed in France by Louis XIII and again by Louis XIV, although the practice continued unabated. In 19th-century America, cowboys in the Old West would sometimes enact their own version of the duel, but there would be no choice of weapons: they would use their own trusty pistols, and would meet not in woodland at dawn but in a showdown at high noon on a dusty main street. These brave confrontations were probably more frequent in the cinema than in reality, but they were not entirely fictitious.

Paintings depicting the glove-slap are rare because most artists found
the duel itself a more attractive subject. The slapping action was also
so swift that it was difficult to capture on canvas. The ritual of throwing
down the gauntlet was much easier to portray, particularly the moment
of the challenge itself, with the glove having been tossed to the ground,
and is seen in a number of 19th-century illustrations [117,118].

One of the most unusual stories in the history of the slap-threat
concerns the Italian nobleman Sciarra Colonna – an ally of Philip IV
of France – whose target was none other than Pope Boniface VIII [116].
It is unlikely that his Holiness would have responded by participating
in a duel, so this assault was probably less risky than it appeared. The
incident occurred in 1303, when Colonna had confronted the Pope
in Anagni, to arrest him and take him to trial in France. The attempt
failed, but in the process the angry Colonna managed to deliver what
would become one of the most famous slap-threats, widely known
as 'The Outrage of Anagni'.

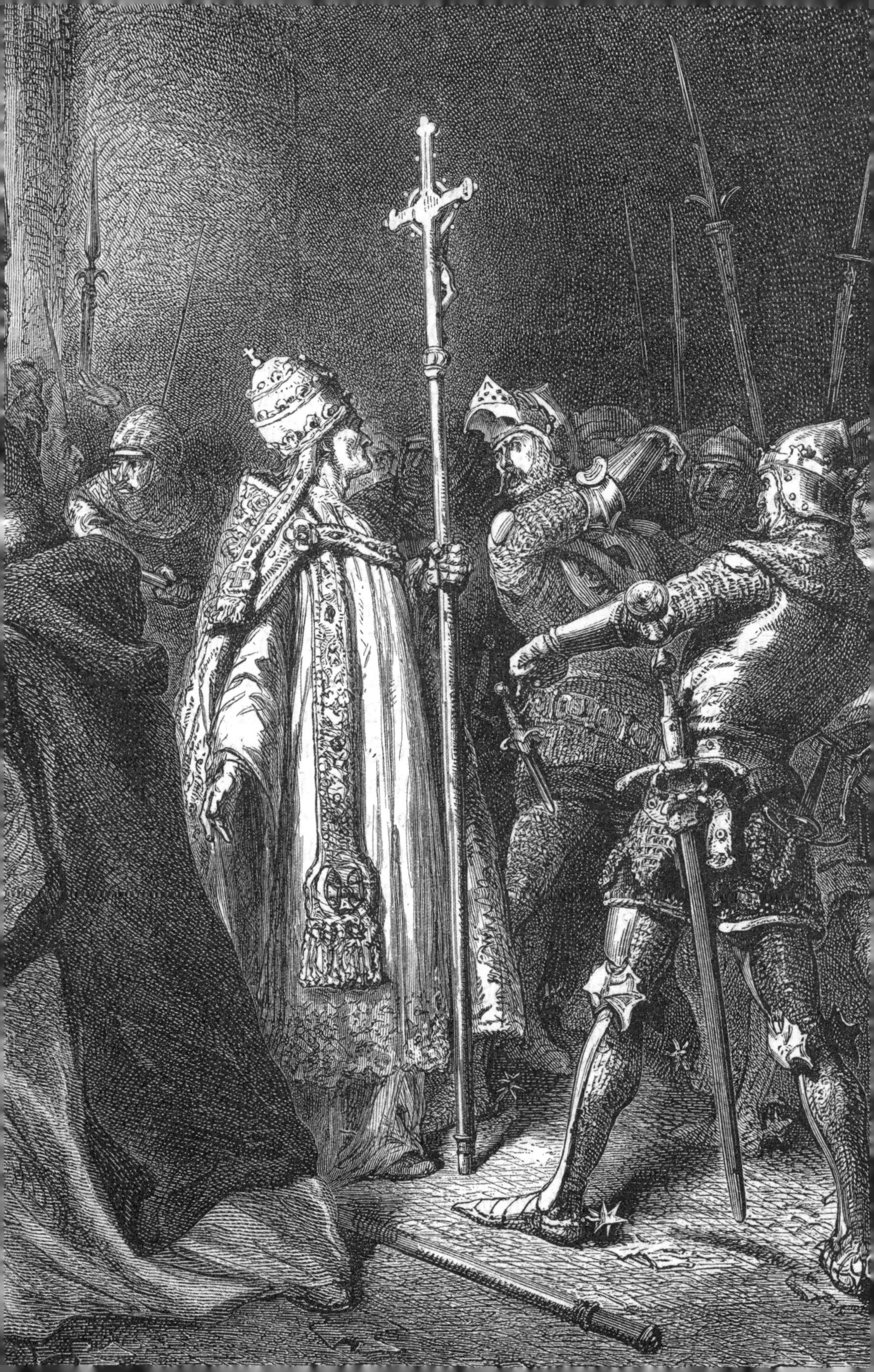

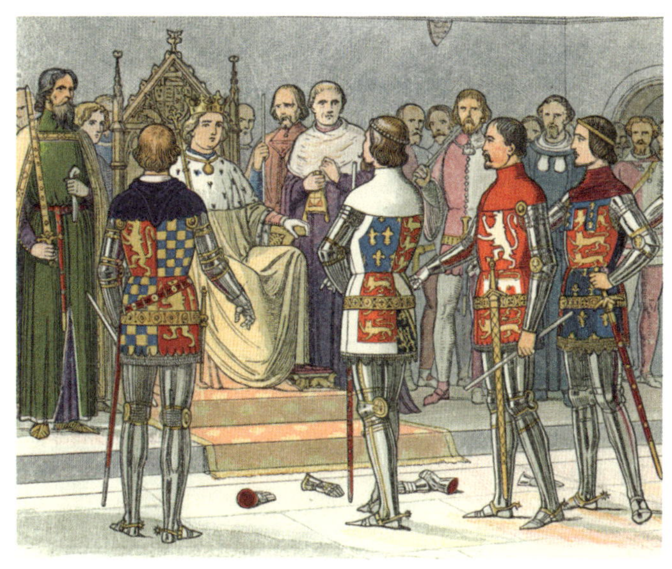

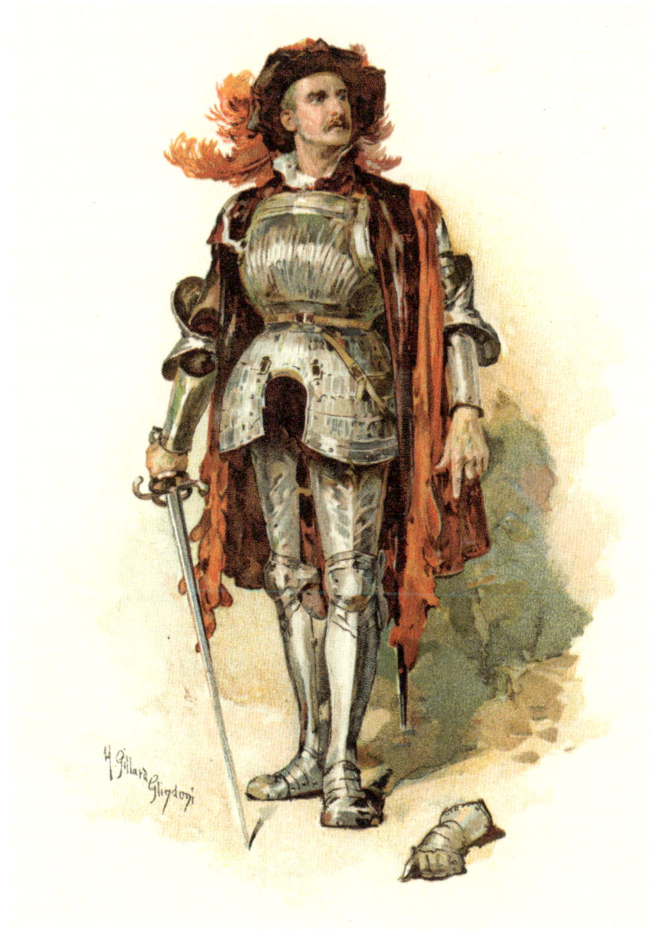

116. opposite **A book illustration by Alphonse-Marie-Adolphe de Neuville, showing Sciarra Colonna slapping Pope Boniface VIII across the face, 1883**

117. above **The Lords Appellant throw down their gauntlets in front of King Richard II, illustration dating from 1864**

118. right **After Henry Gillard Glindoni,** *The Challenge,* **illustration for** *The Boy's Own Annual,* **1898**

Symbolic Threat Gestures

In addition to such basic, universal threat gestures as the clenched fist, there are also a number of stylized, local gestures that employ some kind of symbolism. Usually, they mimic an aggressive act. Drawing a hand across the throat says, 'I am going to slit your throat'. Holding out the hand in the shape of a gun – with the forefinger forming the barrel – says, 'I am going to shoot you'. In Italy, there are several Mafia-related threat gestures, including the 'cheek cut', in which the thumbnail is dragged down one cheek as if inflicting a scar on the face of the victim.

Few of these gestures appear in paintings or sculptures, although there are exceptions. One is a strange, primitive painting by the American surrealist Gertrude Abercrombie called *The Courtship* (1949) [119], in which a man, wearing a burglar's black eye mask, threatens a woman by holding his hand in the shape of a gun, with the forefinger extended, and pointing it at her. She responds by adopting the traditional 'hands up' posture of capitulation.

In another work, *Talking* (1979) [120] by the abstract expressionist Philip Guston, painted during his later figurative phase, an arm juts into the frame as if severed from its body. The first and second fingers of the hand are clasping two cigarettes (one of which is alight) and pointing like a gun in the opposite direction to the hands on the unseen person's watch, suggesting perhaps an act of violence in the past.

119. opposite, above **Gertrude Abercrombie, *The Courtship*, 1949, oil on Masonite**

120. opposite, below **Philip Guston, *Talking*, 1979, oil on canvas**

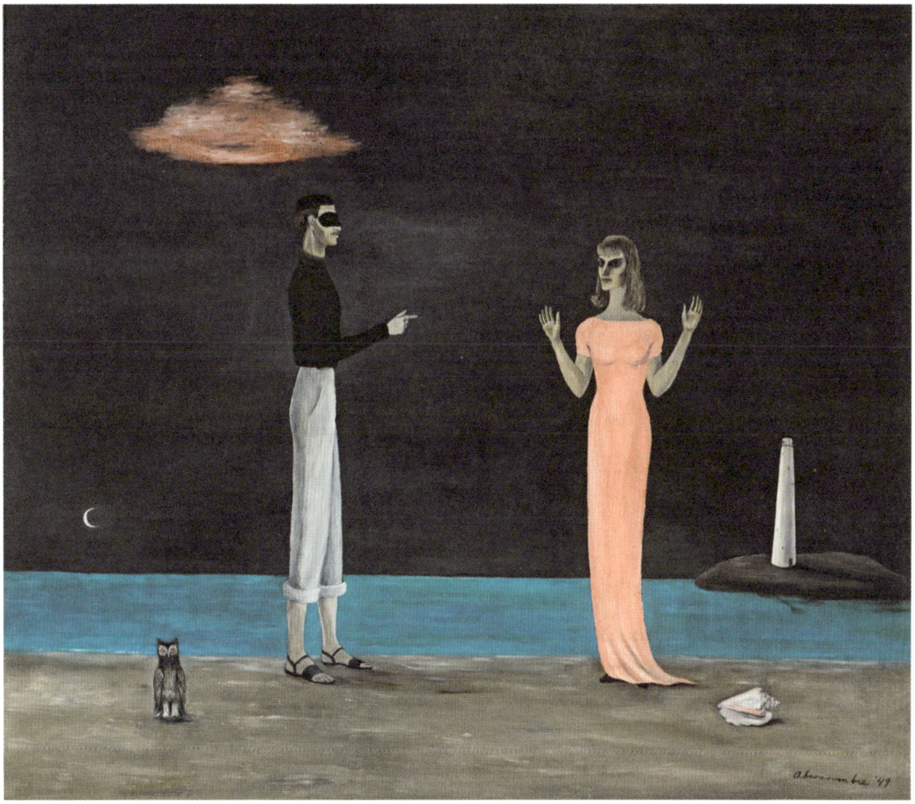

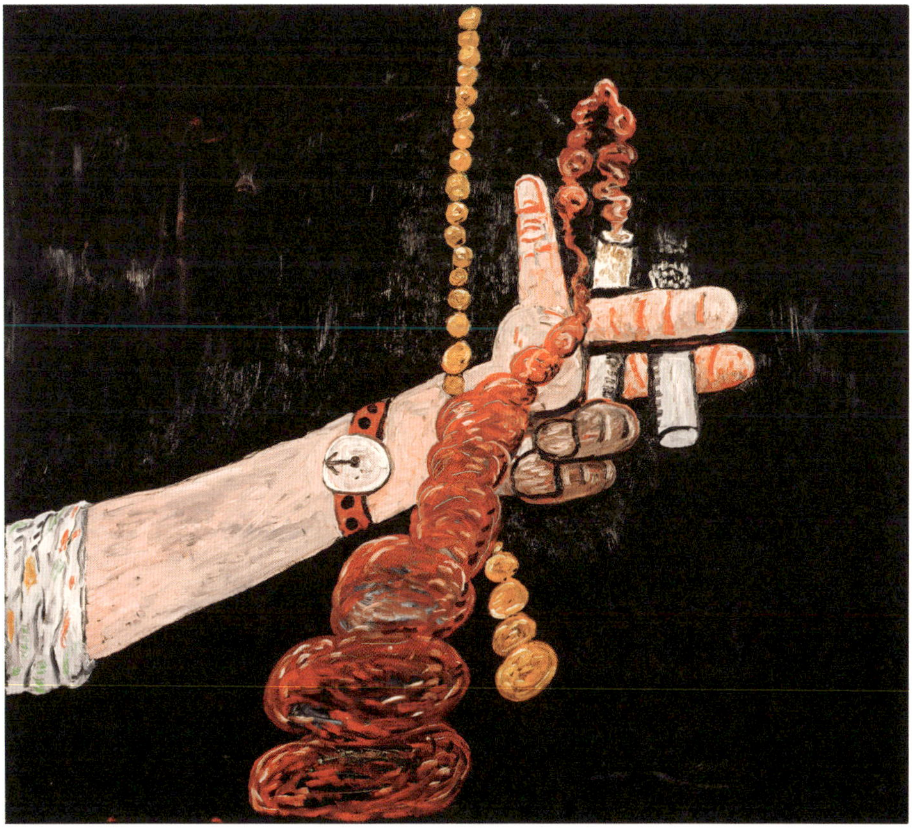

Distress

The portrayal of human beings in a distressed state presents professional artists with a dilemma. On the one hand, they may feel that certain subjects of historical or personal significance require their attention. On the other, they know that scenes of torture, terror or agony will undoubtedly put off some potential collectors; modern portrayals of distress may also be seen as more problematic than historical ones. Such scenes have tended to find wider acceptance in museums, public art galleries and churches, providing, of course, that they carry a worthy message or some kind of historical authenticity. To give an obvious example, the crucifixion of Christ is a scene that no Christian establishment would reject simply because it portrays one of the most brutal forms of torture known to man. The subject may be gruesome, but the message of Christ sacrificing himself for mankind is redemptive.

Early artists seem to have been so wrapped up in the great moral messages of their religious works that they neglected the emotions of those involved. Whether it was Christ being tortured on the cross, or his mother seeing her son slowly dying in such a hideous way, they portrayed their subjects with blank, expressionless faces that told us nothing about their inner feelings. It would take hundreds of years for this to change. Only with greater consideration of human emotion could art finally begin to take up the challenge of portraying distress in all its many forms.

Weeping

Although we tend to take it for granted that an acutely distressed person will at some point begin to cry, this is an unusual response among mammals. Among primates, human beings are the only species that sheds tears; monkeys and apes simply do not display this behaviour. Two explanations have been offered for this anomaly. The first suggests that human tears contain excess stress chemicals, and that weeping helps to wash them out of the system. However, if this is the case, why is it that stressed chimpanzees, for example, do not cry? The second explanation draws on the highly controversial 'aquatic ape' theory: the idea that our early ancestors passed through an aquatic phase, during which they developed a number of adaptations that made them more efficient in the water. Proponents of this theory point to the fact that the production of salty tears is common among marine animals – as a mechanism for disposing of excess salt – but is extremely rare among land animals. One argument against this idea is that we cry when we are intensely emotional or in pain, rather than when we have been swimming.

One of the special features of the human body is that we have a lot of bare skin on our faces compared with our closest animal relatives, so it is very obvious when we are crying. Tears run down our cheeks and act as a powerful social signal, telling others of our state of mind. Furthermore, weeping is an involuntary action that is difficult to fake. Only the greatest actors can weep to order, often by conjuring up memories of acute personal sadness. The rest of us cannot cry on cue, no matter how hard we try, so, in everyday life, weeping is perceived as a truthful response and a social signal that we can trust – unlike smiling, for example, which we can perform even when we are unhappy.

When the subject of a painting has tears running down their cheeks, we immediately recognize their distress, even if they have no other facial expression. Early artists tended to neglect human emotion, portraying their subjects with blank expressions. Gradually, as painters paid more attention to the changing moods of the human face, deeply moving works of art began to emerge. A perfect example is Rogier van der Weyden's painting of Christ being lowered from the cross, entitled *The Descent from the Cross* (before 1443) [122], in which the Flemish artist has skilfully painted glistening tears of misery on the faces of the surrounding mourners.

While it is possible to shed tears with an impassive expression, crying is usually accompanied by a number of other facial details that indicate distress, such as knitted eyebrows, half-closed eyes and pulled-back mouth-corners. In Andrea Mantegna's *Lamentation over the Dead Christ* [123], of about 1483, the Virgin Mary's tears are concealed by her handkerchief, but her eyes are half-closed and her mouth-corners are fully retracted. Pablo Picasso's 'Weeping Woman' series (1937) [121], although highly stylized, also incorporates many of these facial details, including tears, knitted eyebrows, squeezed eyes and tightly pulled-back mouth-corners. The series is based on a figure from Picasso's anti-war mural, *Guernica*, of the same year – a woman holding her dead child.

In Mexico, the mysterious Olmec civilization produced highly emotive depictions of human distress in the form of ceramic figurines of crying babies [125]. With their arms stretched wide, their eyes nearly shut and their mouth-corners fully retracted, these pottery figures are so expressive that you almost feel the urge to pick up the babies and comfort them.

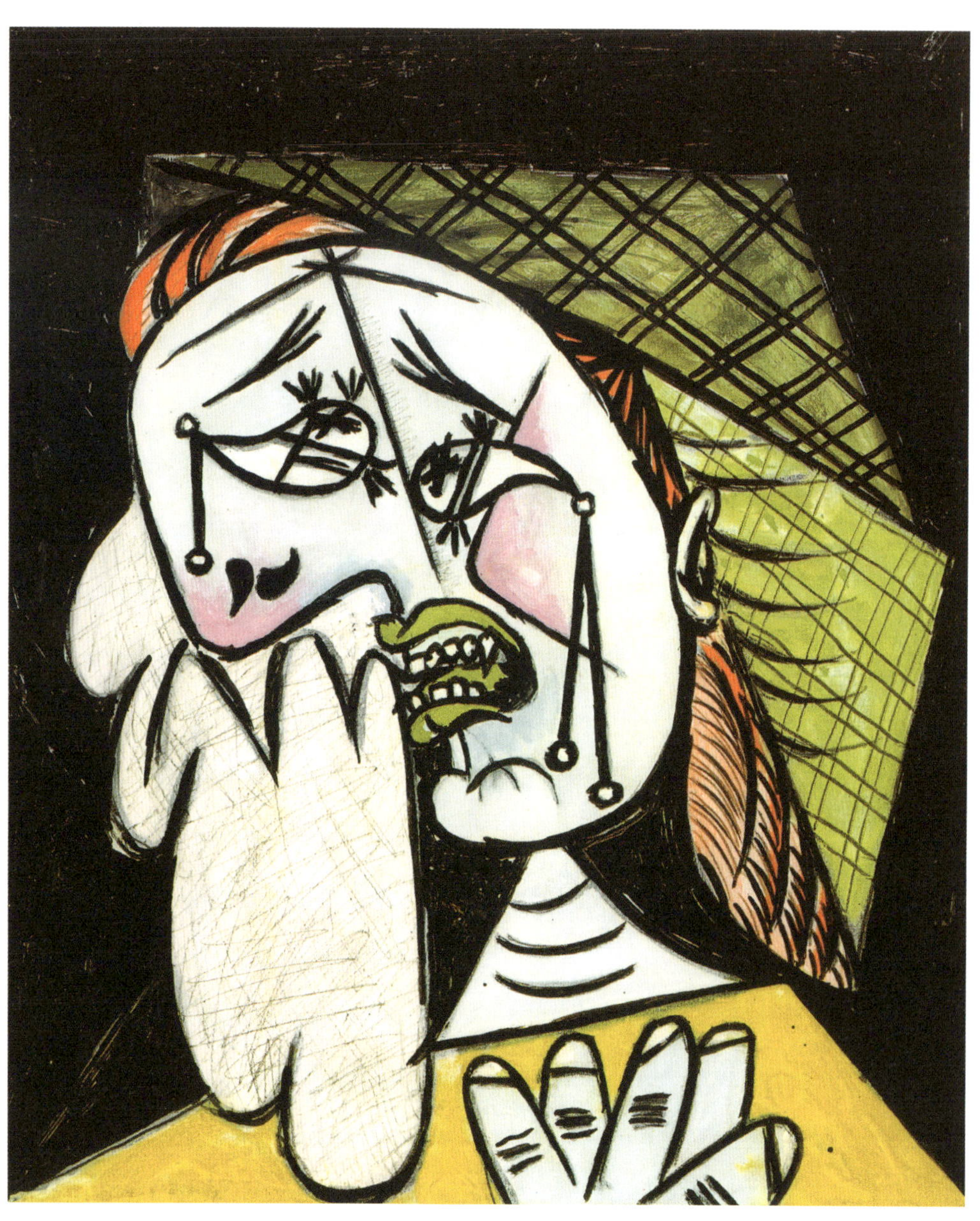

121. **Pablo Picasso, *Weeping Woman with Handkerchief*, 1937, oil on canvas**

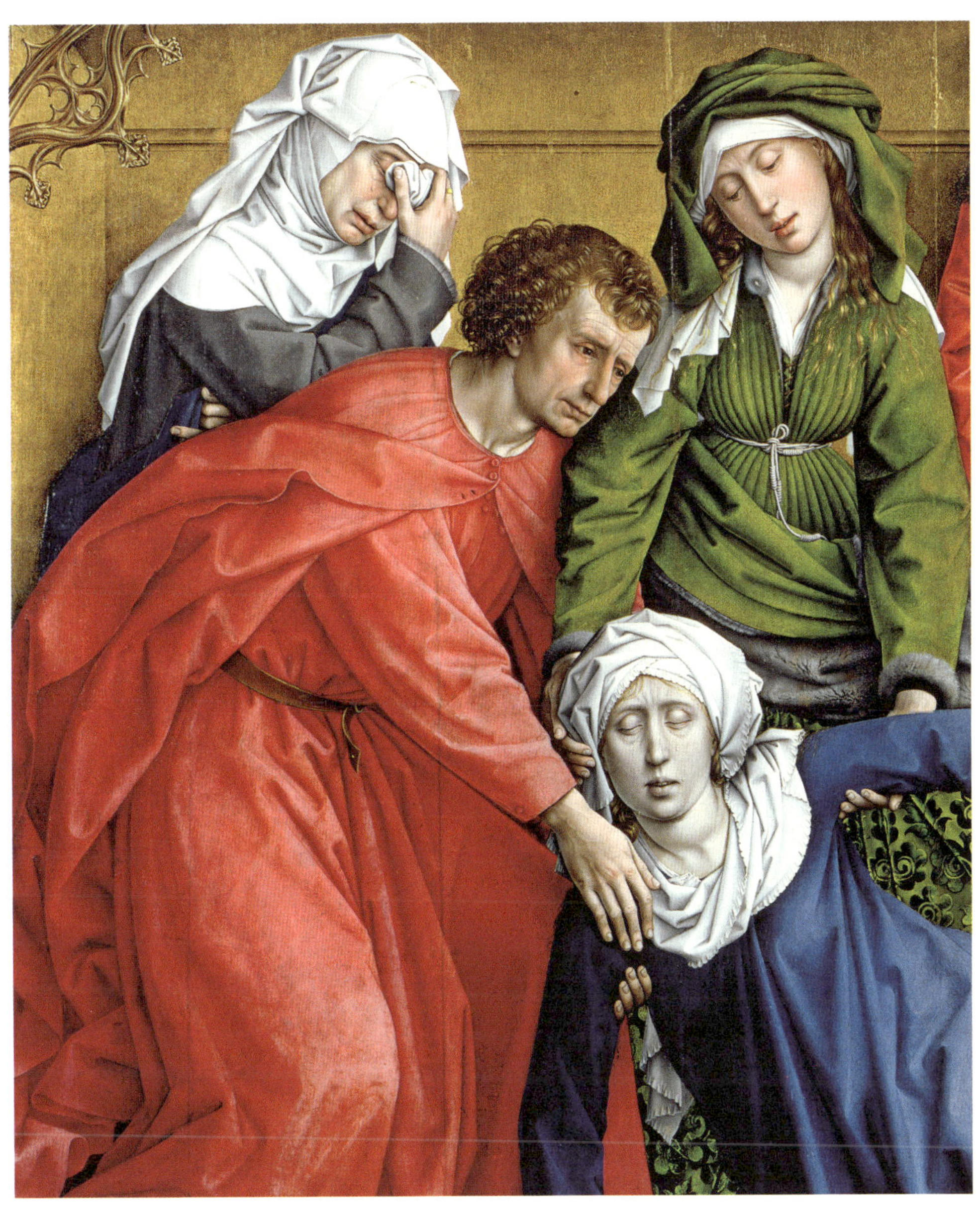

122. **Rogier van der Weyden,**
The Descent from the Cross (detail),
before 1443, oil on panel

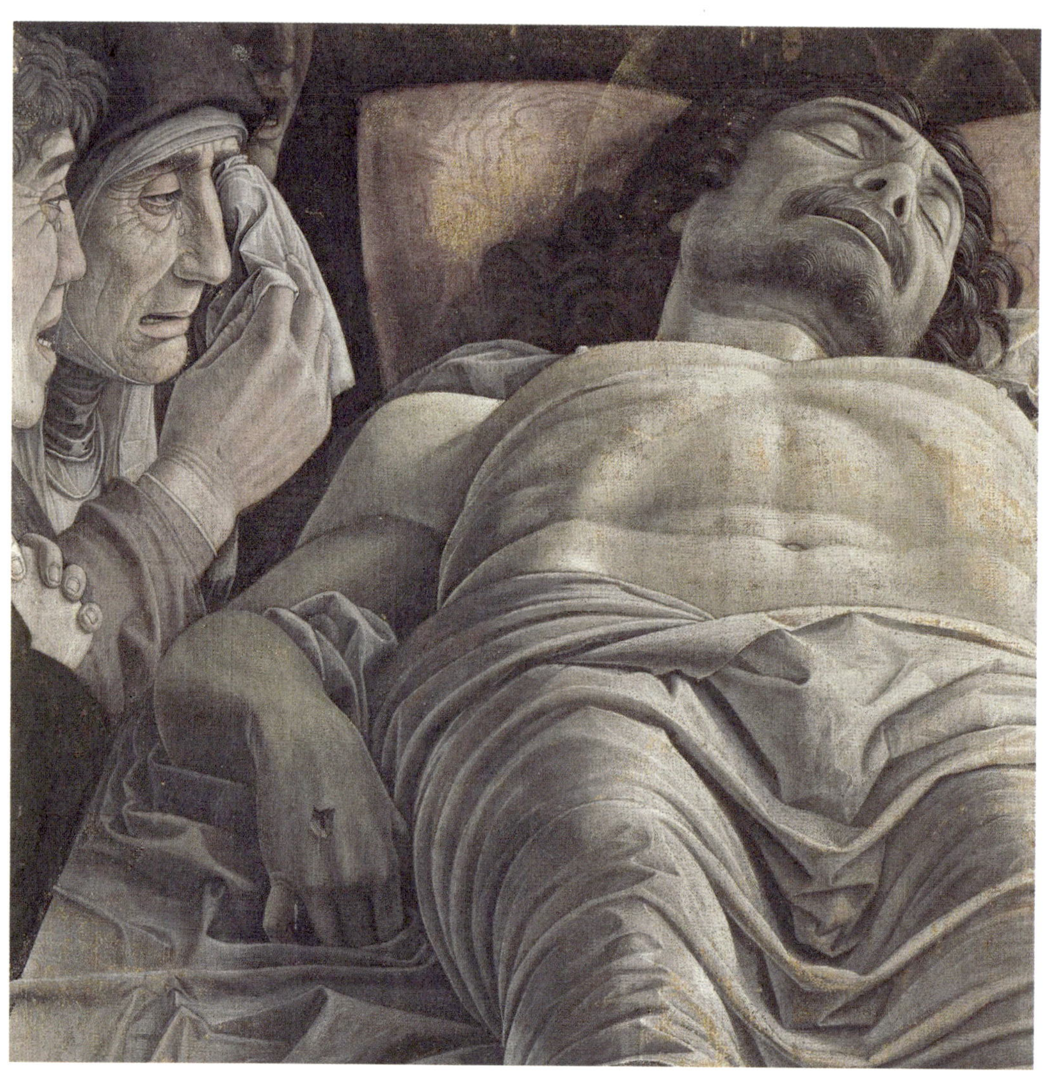

123. above **Andrea Mantegna,**
Lamentation over the Dead Christ
(detail), *c.* 1483, tempera on canvas

124. opposite, above **Qiao Bin,**
Par nirvana (Death and Transcendence
of the Buddha) and Attendant Arhats,
1503, earthenware with polychrome
glaze, China

125. opposite, below **Olmec 'crying baby'**
figure, 1100–900 BC, ceramic, Mexico

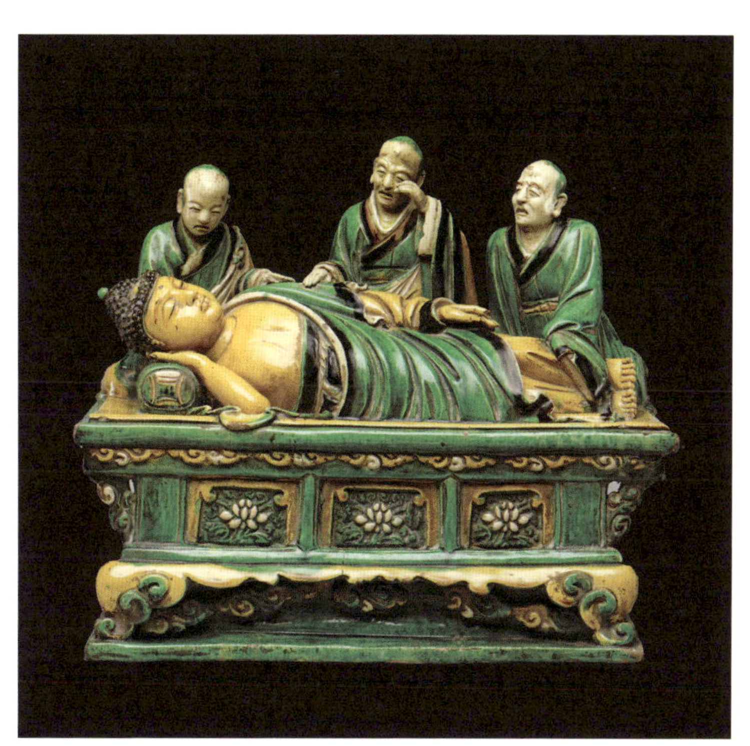

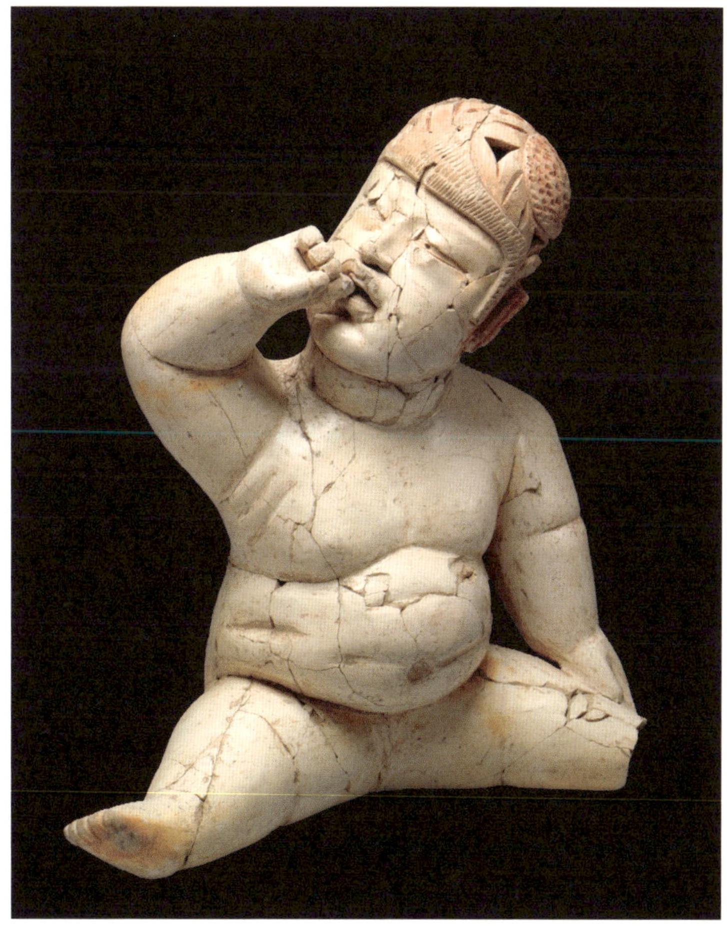

Mourning

The distress felt at the loss of a loved one has given rise to many intense and often elaborate funeral practices involving special kinds of body language. The ancient ceremonies in Egypt and Greece in particular were highly stylized, but they had to be performed in an impressive manner in order to ensure that the deceased would enjoy a successful passage into the afterlife.

In ancient Egypt, female mourners performed set rituals that included tearing out their hair. Paintings on tomb walls show a stylized version of this action, with mourning female figures holding their hands raised above their heads, as if to grab at their hair [129]. During an Egyptian funeral procession, women would not only tear out their hair, but also weep, raise and wave their arms, beat themselves, rip their clothing, and shake their hair and cover their faces with it.

In ancient Greece, women also played a major role in funerary rituals. Once the body of the deceased had been prepared, it was laid out for viewing; female relatives would then gather around it, chanting dirges, tearing at their clothing, striking their chests and pulling at their hair. Images of this event, which was called a *prothesis*, usually show the women with their hands on top of their heads, in the act of grabbing their hair [128]. During funeral processions, while men were subdued and walked in an orderly fashion, women were expected to cry and scream, scratching at their cheeks to make them bleed.

These funerary customs became more and more extreme – to the point where men started hiring extra women to make their funerals more impressive than those of their rivals. This was too much for the authorities, and a restriction was introduced outlawing wailing or crying during processions. Intriguingly, a similar law was introduced in Tajikistan as recently as 2017, when it was decreed that, at funerals, loud wailing, the tearing out of hair, the scratching of one's face and the hiring of professional mourners would no longer be allowed. It is amazing that, in some regions, these ancient practices have managed to survive into the 21st century.

126. **Frederic, Lord Leighton,**
Lachrymae, **1894–95,**
oil on canvas

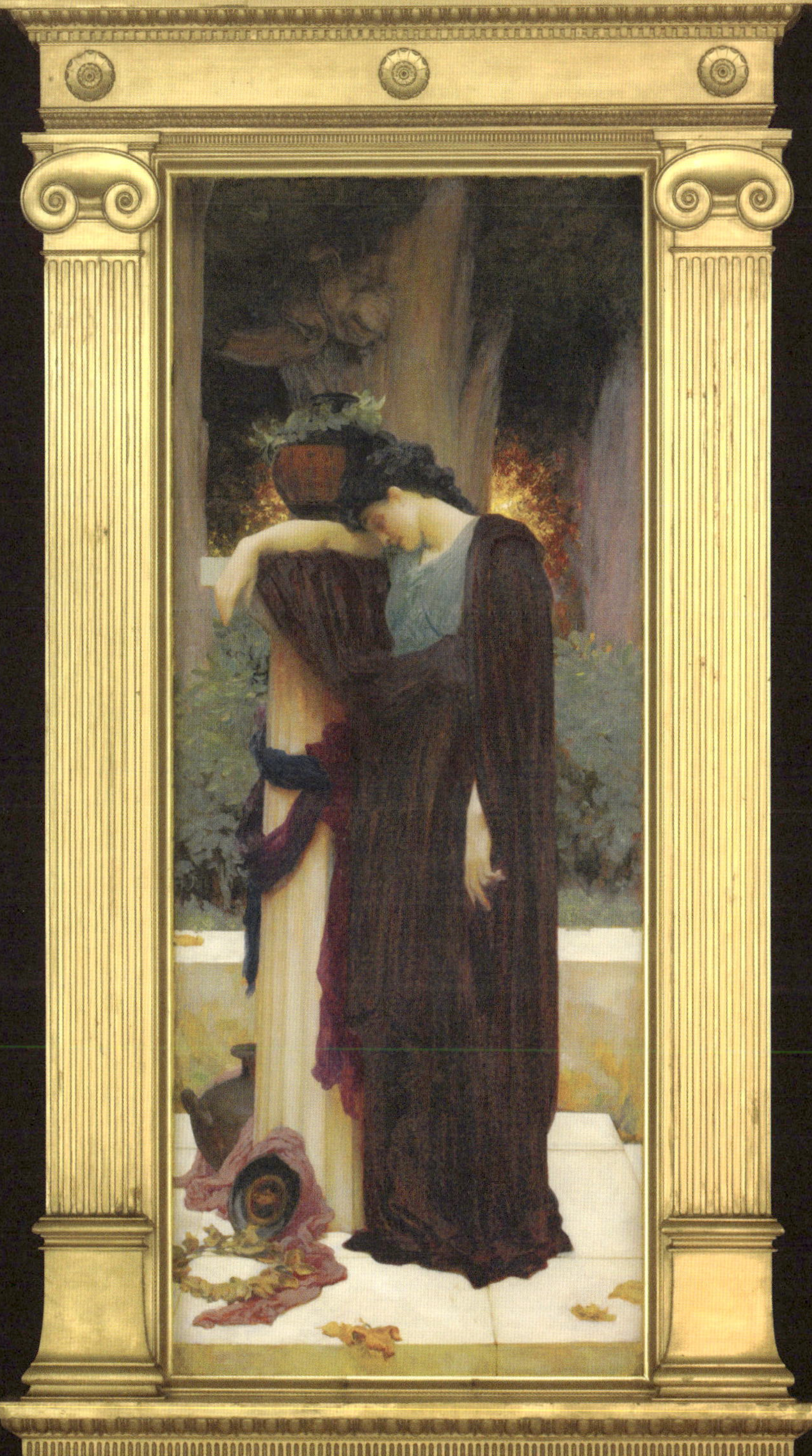

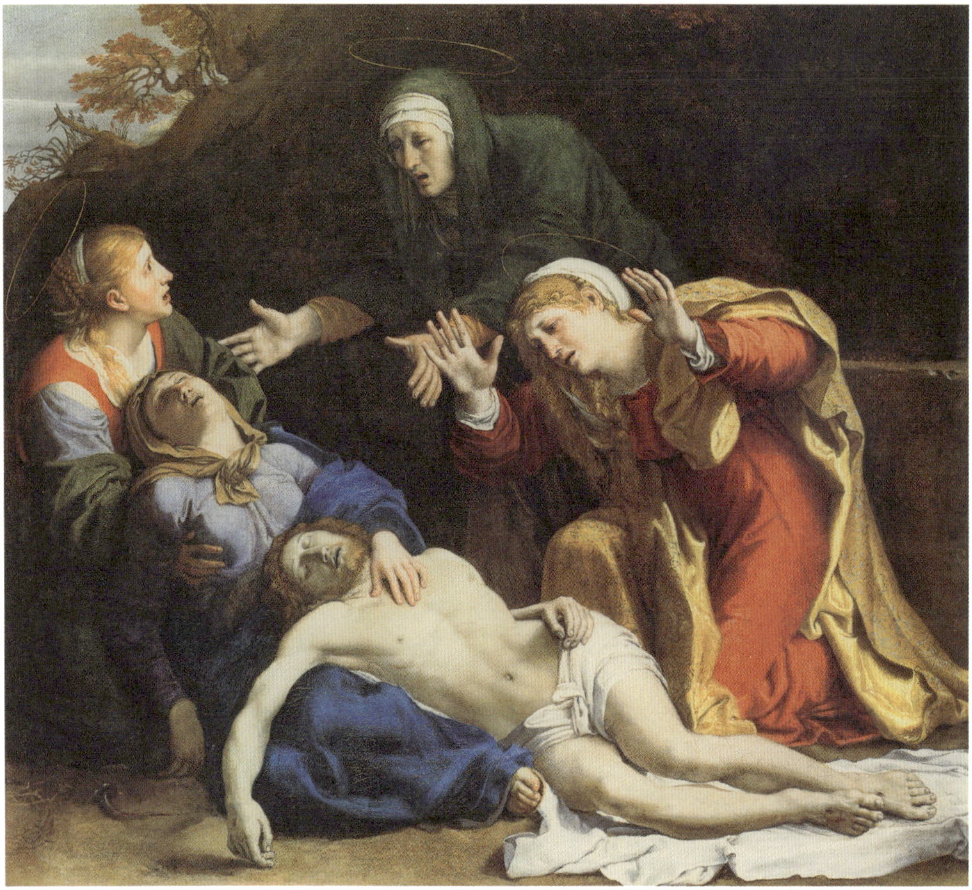

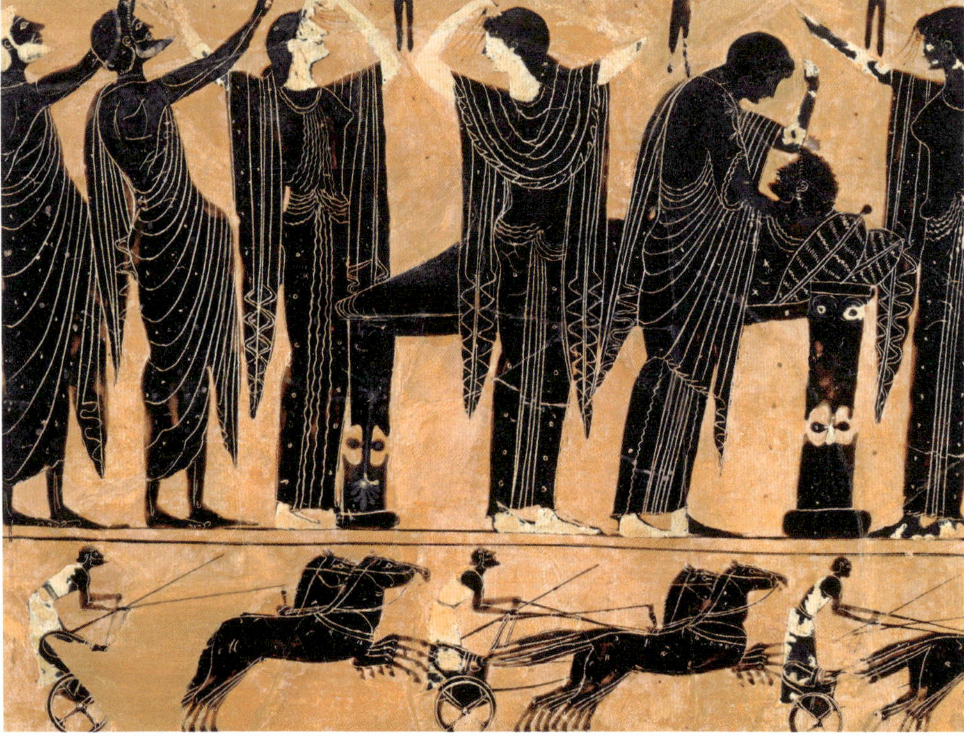

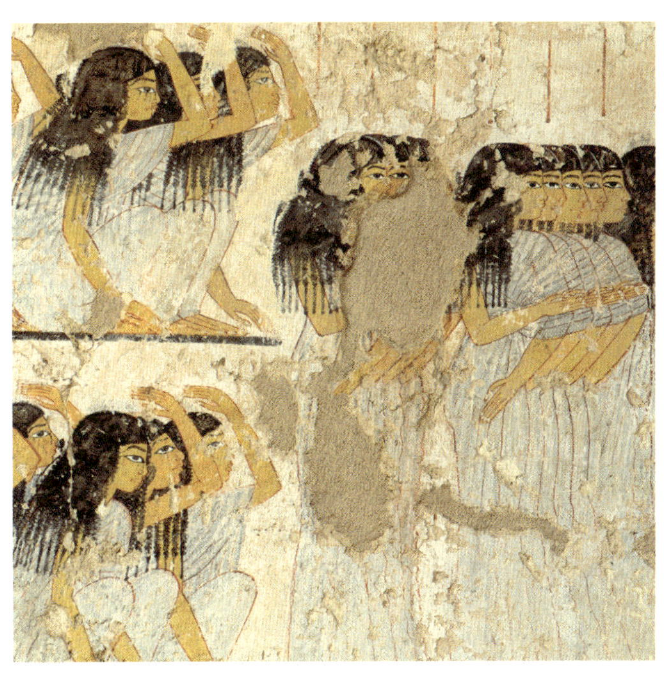

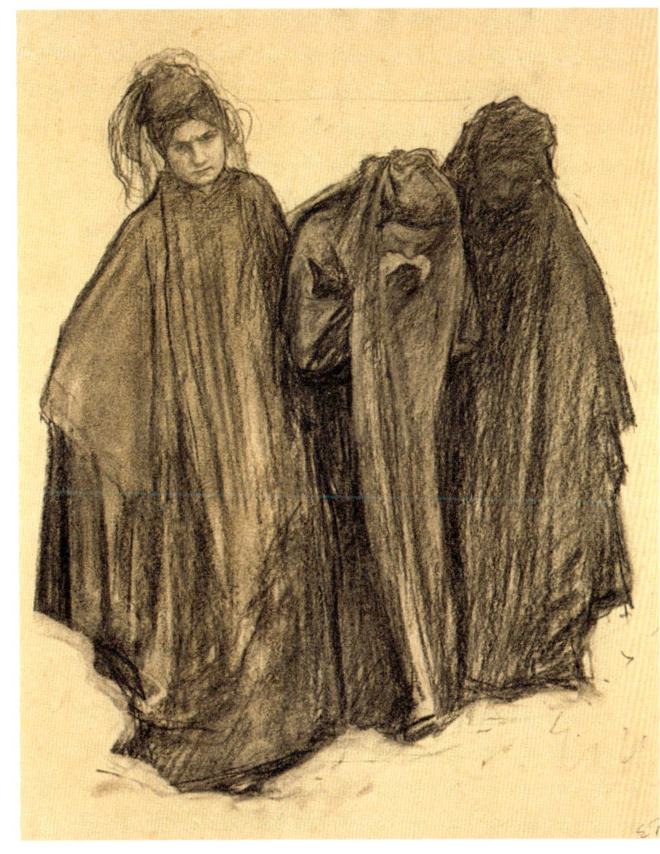

127. opposite, above **Annibale Carracci**, *The Dead Christ Mourned ('The Three Maries')*, c. 1604, oil on canvas

128. opposite, below **Attic black-figure funerary plaque**, c. 520–510 BC, terracotta, Greece

129. above **Funerary scene with mourning women, tomb of Ramose**, XVIII Dynasty, c. 1550–1292 BC, Thebes, Egypt

130. right **Émile Friant**, *Study for 'La Douleur'*, c. 1898–99, charcoal on paper

Distress / Mourning

Agony

It was common for medieval artists to depict scenes of great suffering and pain – from crucifixion to being skinned alive, burned at the stake or stretched on the rack – but they nearly always failed to give their victims a realistically tortured expression. A shift towards depicting such subjects with appropriately expressive, contorted faces began to gain momentum only in the 17th century.

The Flemish artist Adriaen Brouwer masterfully tackled the subject of pain in a number of his paintings. In *Peasants Brawling over Cards* (1630) [133], a fight has broken out between three card-players; one angry player holds another man by the hair as he prepares to strike him with a heavy bowl. The victim has his eyes shut and his mouth open in anticipation of the blow – and the pain that is to come. In another of Brouwer's scenes of everyday life, *The Back Pain* (1635–36), a young man winces as another male figure performs a surgical operation in what appears to be the back room of a tavern. The agony of the procedure – without the benefit of anaesthetic – is etched on his contorted face.

Balthasar Permoser's marble sculpture *Marsyas* [131], completed in the 1680s, shows the tortured expression of a satyr who is being skinned alive. Marsyas had made the mistake of challenging the god Apollo to a music contest. He is portrayed with his mouth open in a prolonged scream; his eyes are squeezed shut, as he tries to cut himself off from the outside world. He appears to have bitten his tongue as the torture progresses, his brow is deeply furrowed, and his head is twisted awkwardly on his shoulders as he squirms in pain. In the satyr's intense expression, *Marsyas* is reminiscent of a number of modern works, including Francis Bacon's writhing, screaming figures of the 1950s [134].

131. **Balthasar Permoser,**
Marsyas, c. **1680–85, marble**

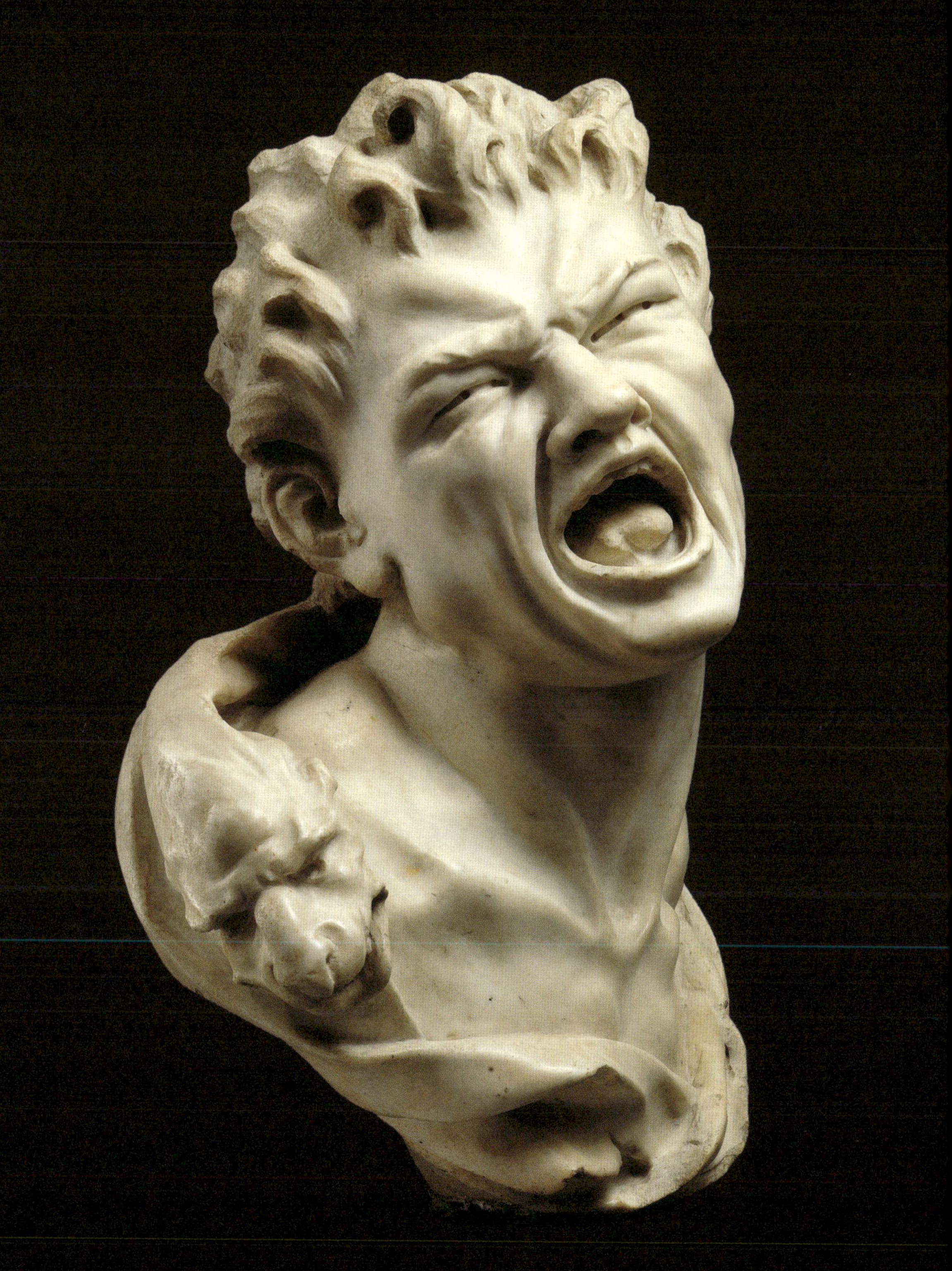

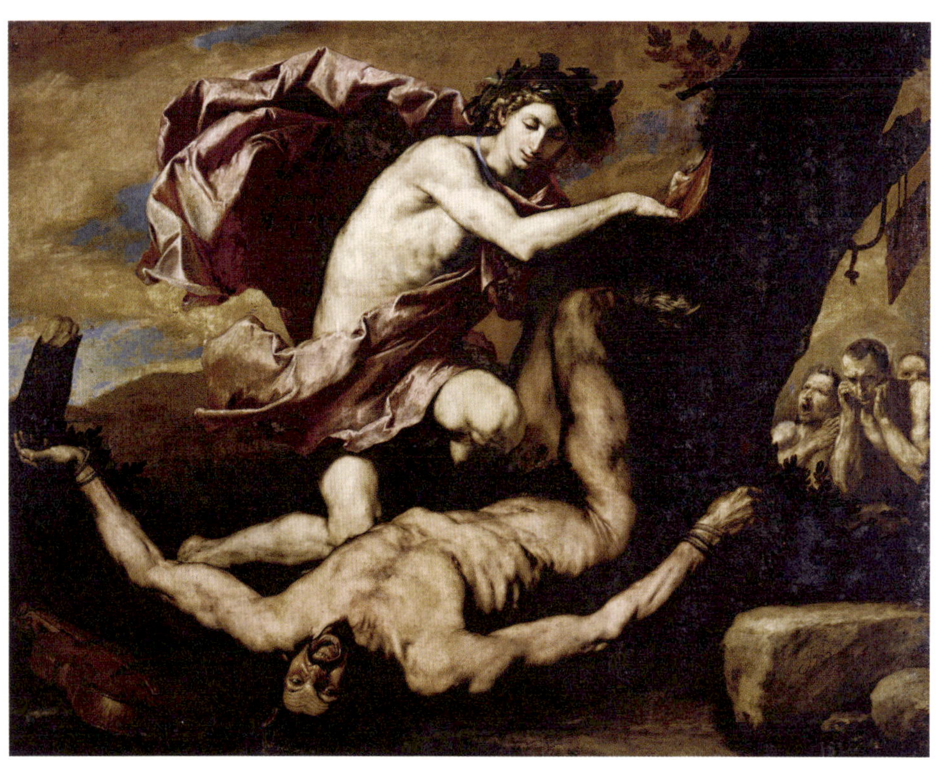

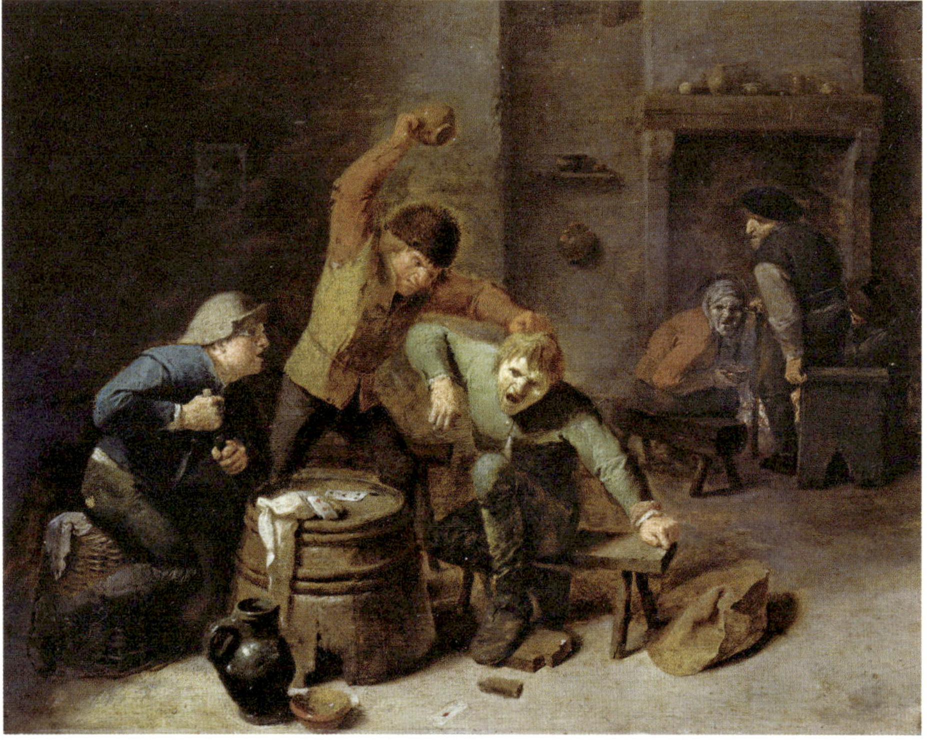

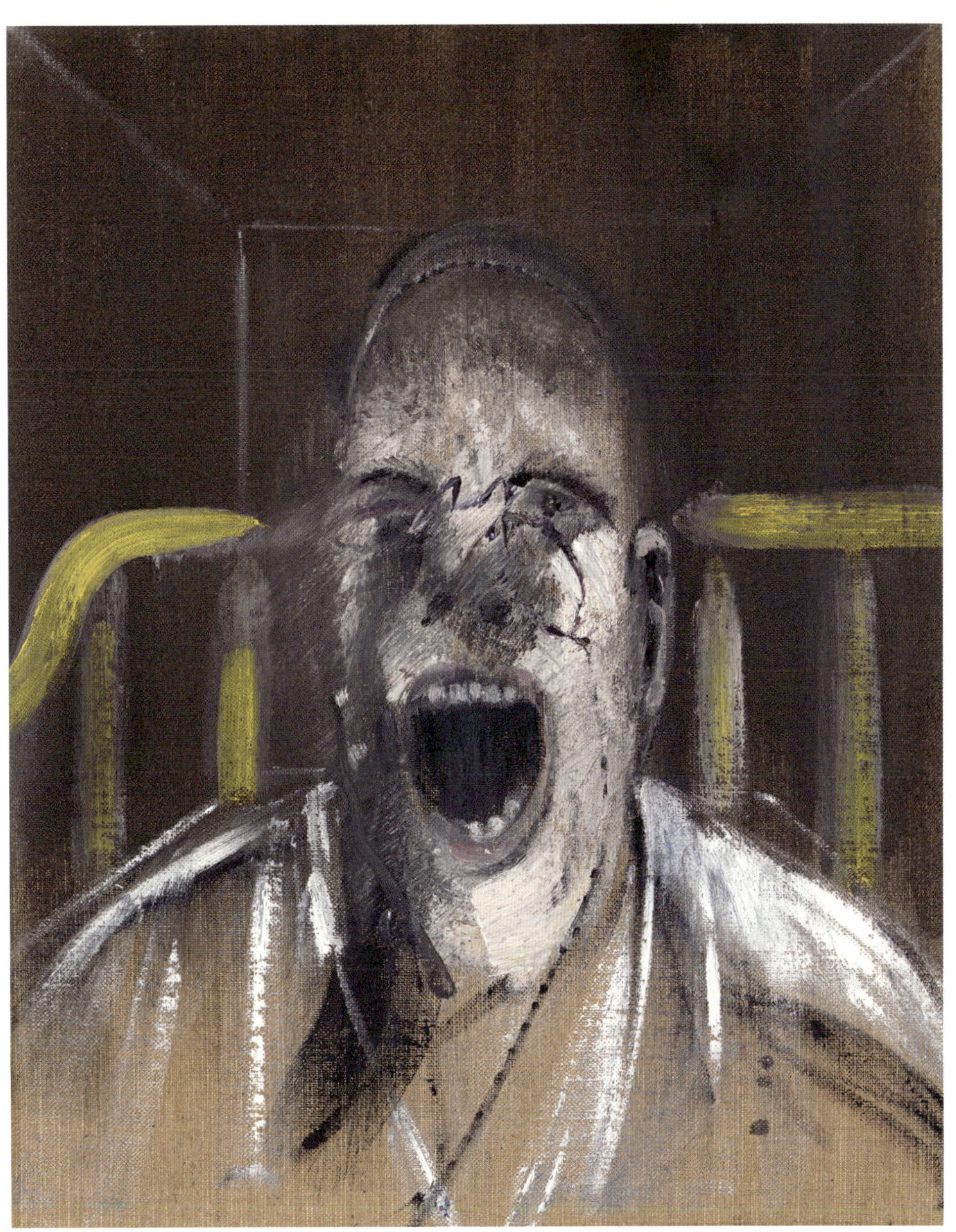

132. opposite, above **Jusepe de Ribera,**
Apollo and Marsyas, **1637, oil on canvas**

133. opposite, below **Adriaen Brouwer,**
Peasants Brawling over Cards, **1630,**
oil on wood

134. above **Francis Bacon,** *Study of a Head*,
1952, oil on canvas

Terror

An expression of terror is characterized by wide, staring eyes and raised eyebrows. This is because we unconsciously broaden our range of vision when we are frightened, making us more alert to possible dangers – from whichever direction they might come. In religious paintings of sinners descending into hell, the damned are invariably portrayed with this facial detail; many of them also have their mouth-corners drawn back. In one of the best examples, Rogier van der Weyden's great 15th-century polyptych *The Last Judgment* [137], groups of naked sinners are depicted with expressions of abject fear as they face the prospect of being thrown down into the pit of hell. This ambitious work was commissioned in 1443 for the Hospices de Beaune, a former charitable hospital in Beaune, France, where it remains to this day.

The French artist Gustave Courbet attempted to portray a state of heightened anxiety in a self-portrait entitled *The Desperate Man* (1844–45) [136]. The painting contains all the elements of a terrified expression – the staring, bulging eyes, the raised eyebrows, the slightly open mouth, even the pulling of hair – yet it comes across as artificial; the artist was clearly acting the part. This work, although masterfully painted, shows just how difficult it is to portray the extremes of emotion. Before the advent of documentary photography, which has captured human beings in all manner of terrifying scenarios, and which allows us to study a certain expression in minute detail, artists had to rely on their imagination. As a result, the portrayal of extreme emotions – and terror in particular – in older works is not always convincing.

135. **Nicolas Poussin,**
The Massacre of the Innocents
(detail), c. 1625–29, oil on canvas

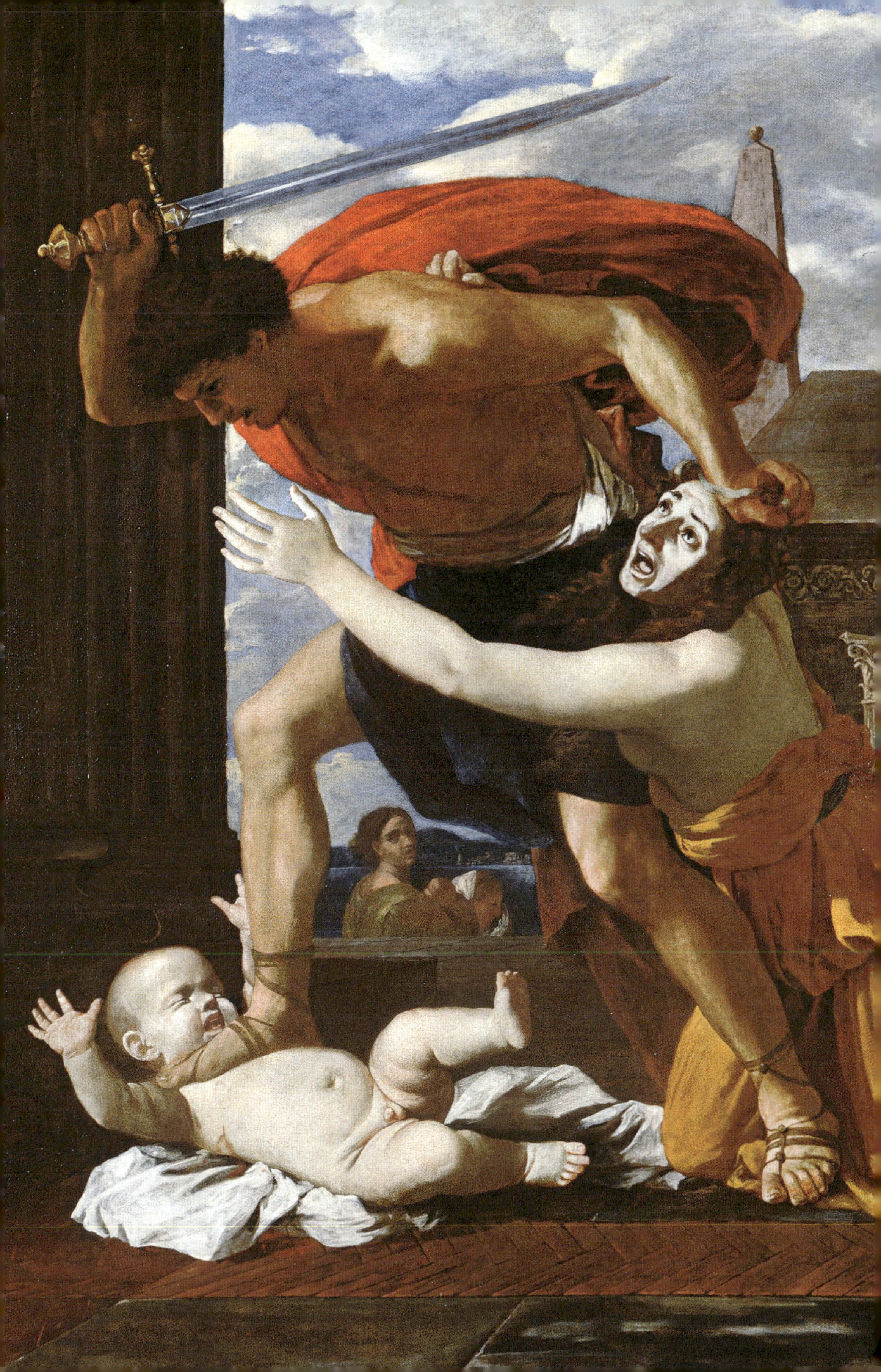

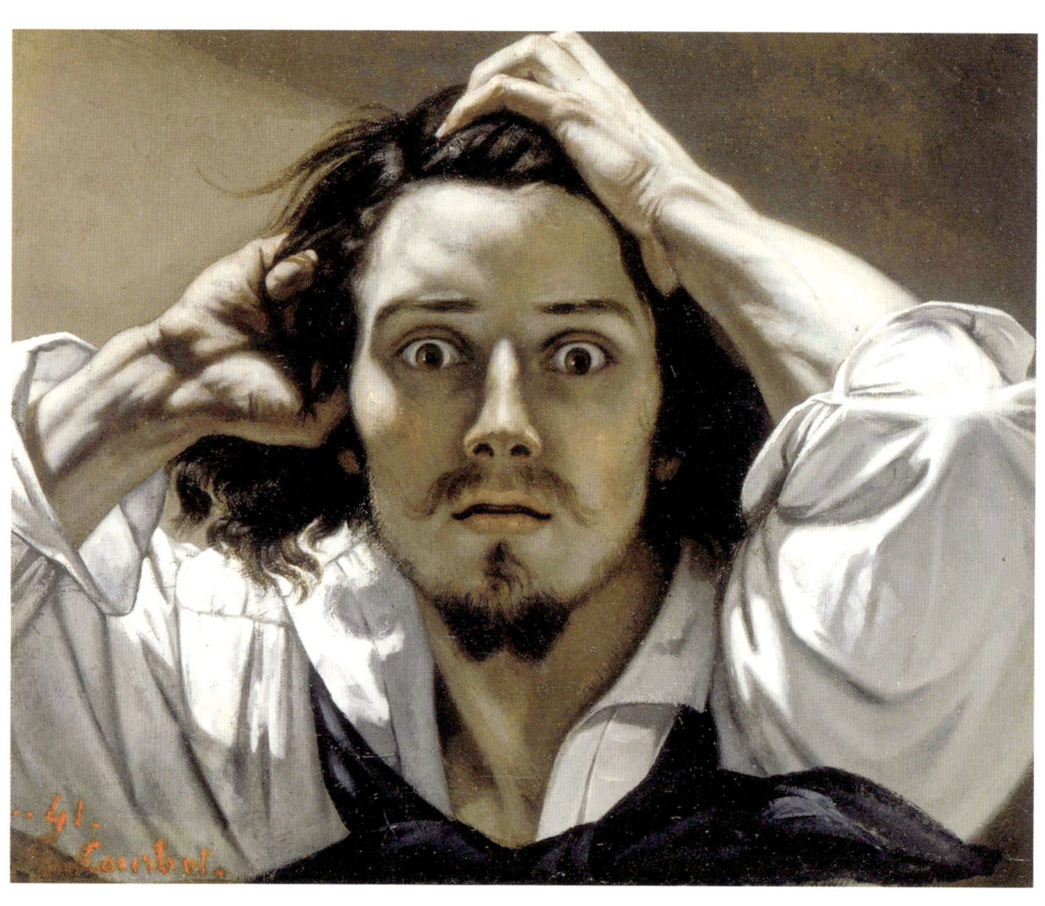

136. above **Gustave Courbet, *The Desperate Man*, 1844–45, oil on canvas**

137. opposite, above **Rogier van der Weyden, *The Last Judgment* (detail), 1445–48, oil on wood**

138. opposite, below **Detail from the *Dionysiac Frieze*, Villa dei Misteri, Pompeii**

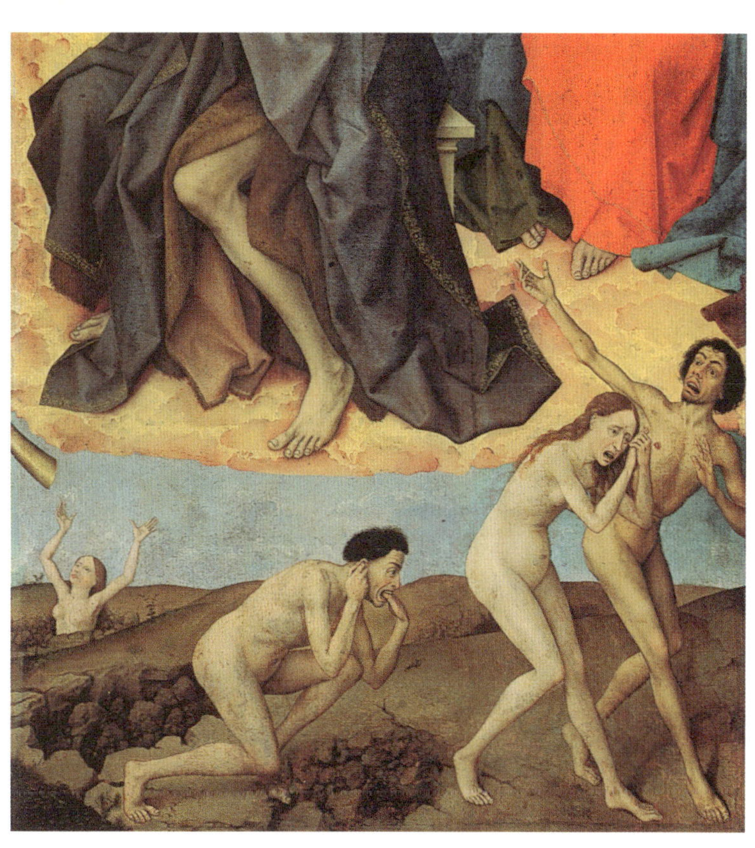

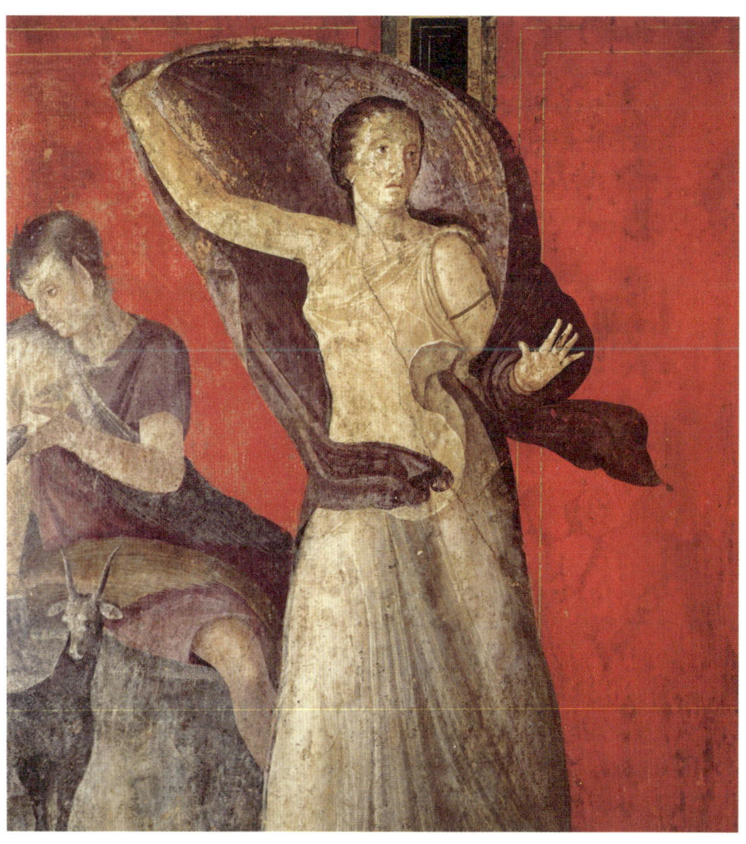

Disgust

Historically, disgust has rarely been made the subject of paintings or sculpture, presumably because it lacks visual appeal. There are, however, a few notable exceptions – artists who have ignored the inclinations of their patrons and have gone all out to record this particular human emotion.

Adriaen Brouwer is one such artist. In *The Bitter Potion* (c. 1636–38) [139], which is believed to be a self-portrait, the Flemish artist captures a man's reaction to a foul-tasting liquid. Grasping a bottle in one hand and a shallow bowl in the other, the subject stands with his mouth open wide and his face scrunched up in a typical display of disgust. The bottle in the subject's right hand suggests that the liquid is a bitter tonic or health potion; it may have been – as some have argued – a herbal concoction made from the cinchona tree, a popular cure for malaria at the time. The extreme distortion of facial features in this work was a pioneering experiment in exaggerated expressions.

In another work, *Smell* (1631) [140], Brouwer depicts expressions of disgust that are equally convincing, albeit less extreme. The painting centres on a man – presumably the father – wiping a baby's bottom, while another figure looks on. Although the man seems to make an attempt to suppress his disgust as he goes about his task, the way he holds his head away from the infant and the subtle grimace give him away. His companion shows no such restraint, displaying a wide, gaping mouth.

In the 18th century, a German-Austrian sculptor called Franz Xaver Messerschmidt suffered a period of mental ill health, during which he became obsessed with portraying the extremes of emotion. He is believed to have created sixty-nine busts of wildly grimacing heads at this time (forty-nine of which survive) – a marked departure from the sedate, neoclassical sculptures for which he was known previously. It has been suggested that the heads represented his own, agonizing fight with his inner demons. To aid him in his work, he would make himself grimace in pain by pinching himself with great force. He would then look at himself in the mirror every half-minute, and recreate what he saw. Of all his faces, the one that comes closest to showing an expression of disgust is *The Vexed Man* (1771–83) [141] – a poor title that was given to it after the artist's death. The down-turned corners of the pursed mouth, the wrinkled nose, the closed eyes and the creased forehead together create a strong sense of revulsion.

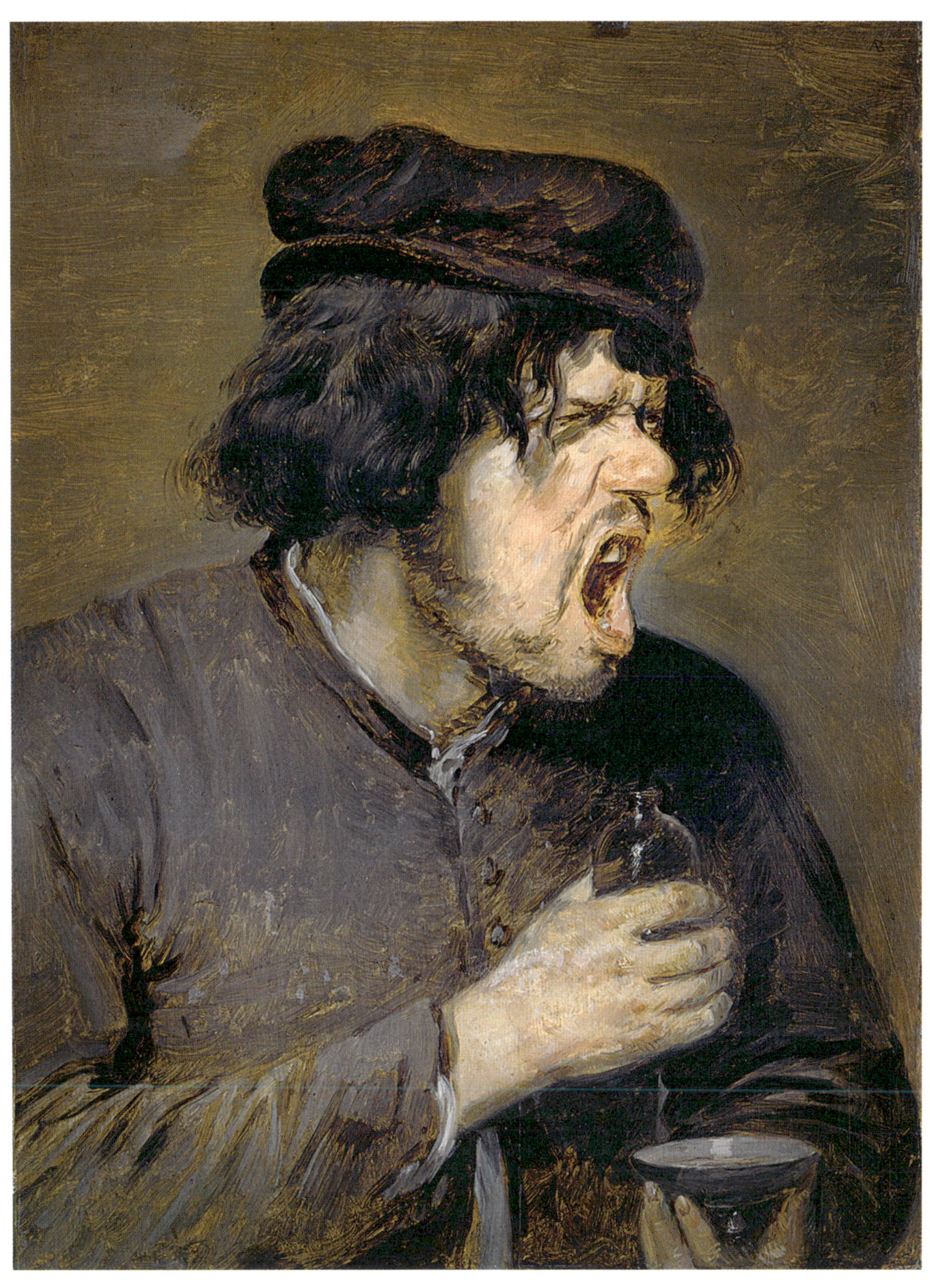

139. **Adriaen Brouwer,**
The Bitter Potion,
c. 1636–38, oil on oak

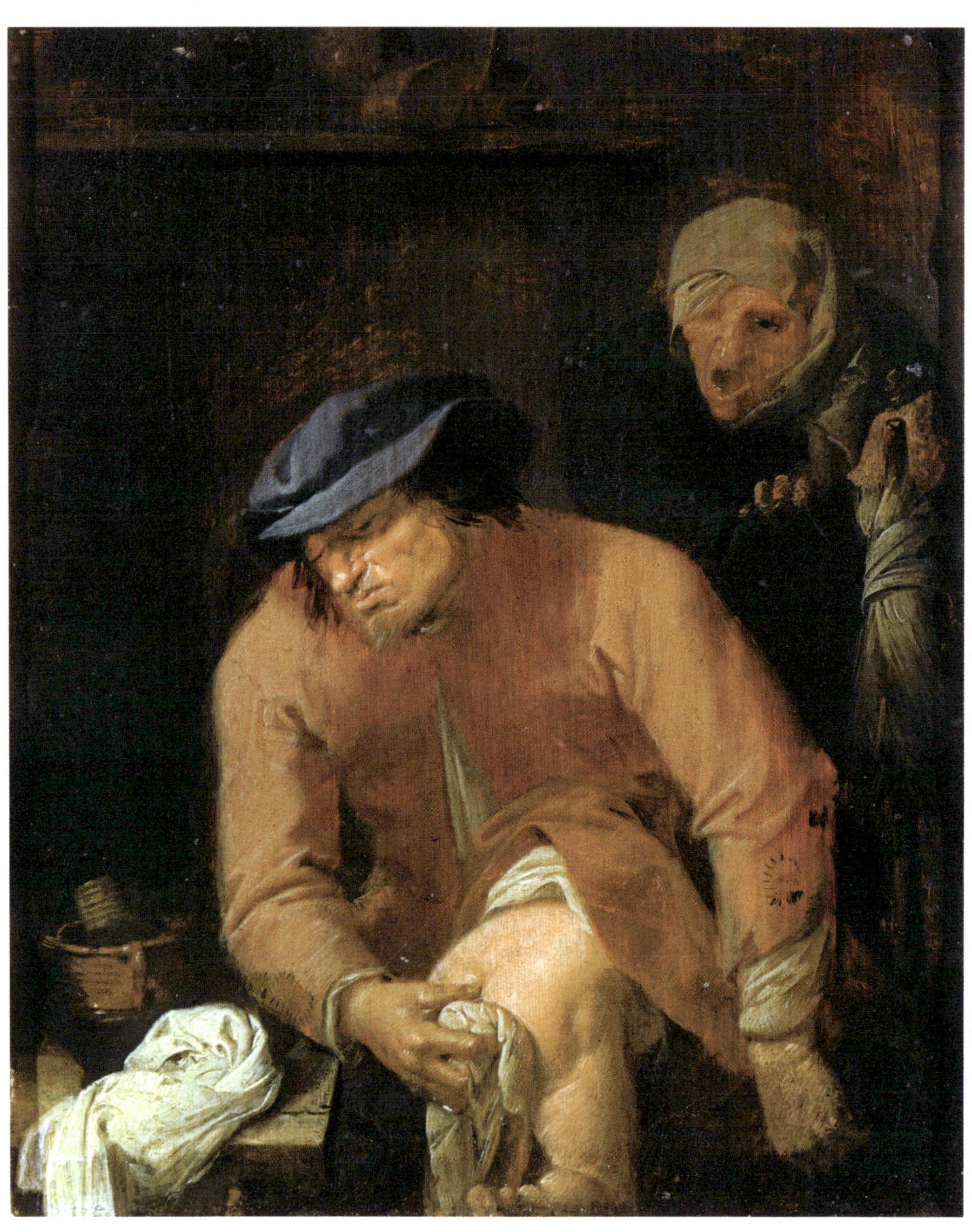

140. above **Adriaen Brouwer,**
Smell (detail), 1631, oil on panel

141. opposite **Franz Xaver
Messerschmidt,** *The Vexed Man*,
1771–83, alabaster

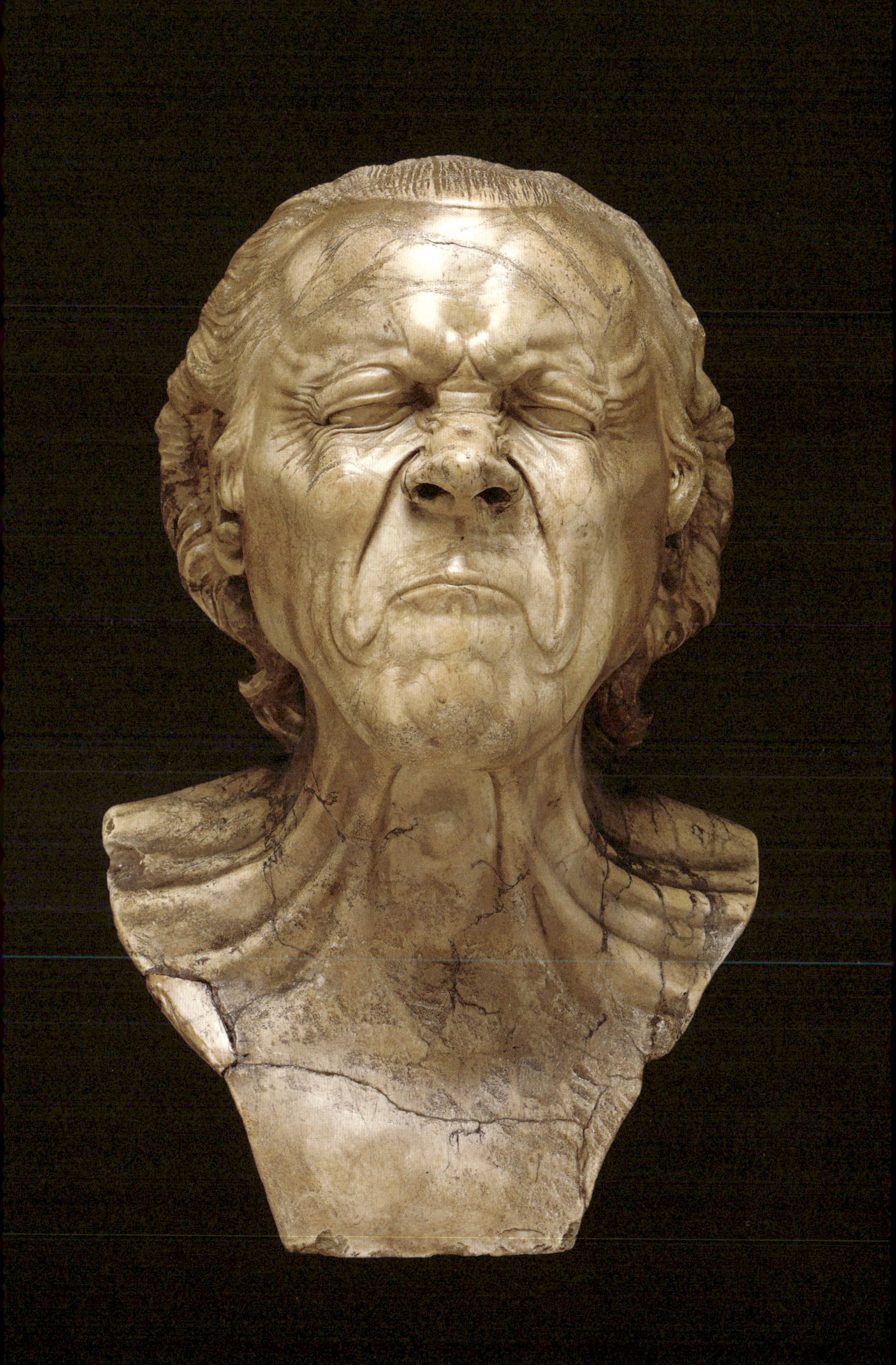

Symbolic Distress

As previously mentioned, human figures in medieval art tend to be portrayed with little emotion; even sinners being boiled alive in the pit of hell are depicted with calmly indifferent facial expressions. This approach to the human face in works of the period appears to have been so widespread that, when the intensity of feeling was impossible to ignore, artists resorted to a symbolic representation. This is seen to great effect in the various depictions of Our Lady of Sorrows [142], which represent the Virgin Mary's suffering from the seven great sorrows in her life. How could a medieval artist convey her agony over such events as witnessing the appalling torture of her son on the cross, yet still follow the artistic conventions of the time? The answer was to ignore her facial expression and instead portray her with seven swords piercing her heart. This extraordinarily contrived solution did not appear as an isolated case: it was repeated over and over again, in both paintings and statues. The convention became so stylized that the number of swords piercing the Virgin's heart sometimes varies. In a 15th-century example of the genre, entitled *Virgin of Seven Sorrows*, only five swords are depicted because that happens to suit the composition a little better.

Icons depicting Our Lady of Sorrows were believed to have magical properties. One of them, a Russian icon known as *Theotokos of Seven Swords*, sometimes called *Symeon's Prophesy*, is said to have had healing powers. It was discovered by a peasant, who had been suffering from a limb-related ailment. He claimed that, one night, he heard a voice telling him to go to the belfry of the local church, where he would find an icon of the Mother of God. He did this and discovered a dirt-covered board, which, when cleaned, proved indeed to be an icon of the Virgin Mary. A service was held to celebrate this discovery, and he found that his infirmity had vanished and he was completely healed.

Many historians believe that there is a simple explanation for this strangely artificial, symbolic approach to visual imagery in early art forms: platonic idealism was the norm in art at the time, and individual emotional expression was not an important element. As society became less focused on 'the eternal, ideal divine world' and focused more on the material world, this began to change. One of the first published treatments of this shift was Charles Le Brun's *Expressions of the Passions of the Soul*, which appeared in 1688.

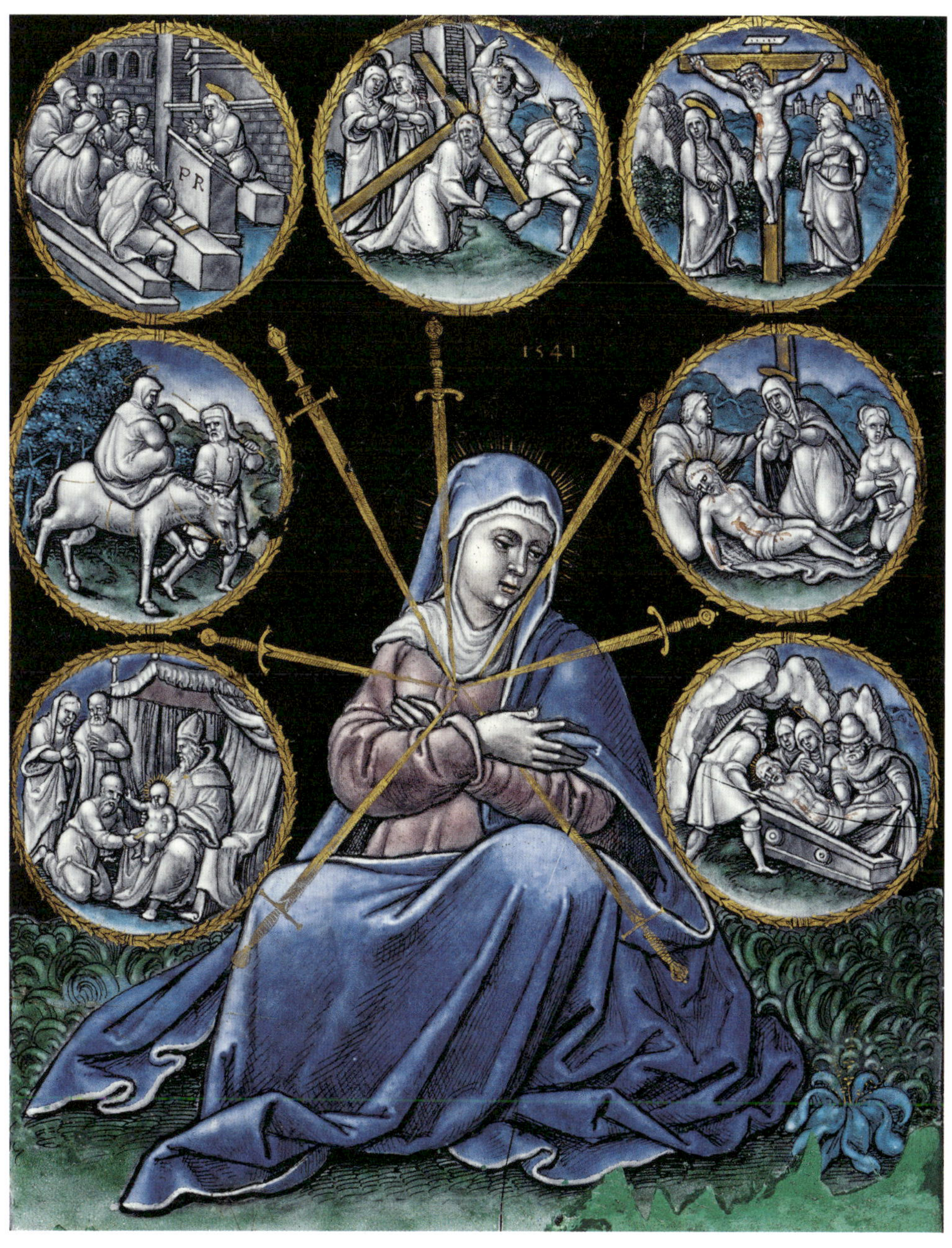

142. **Pierre Reymond,**
Plaque with Seven Sorrows of Mary,
1541, enamel on copper

Self-protection

From the cradle to the grave, life is a hazardous business. All animals have evolved ways of protecting themselves, and human beings are no different. One of our primary responses when threatened with danger is to flee as fast as we can. Artists have occasionally portrayed headlong flight, but they have generally preferred to show the hero or underdog standing his ground. Because we are soft-bodied and lack a hard protective shell, we have had to devise ways of avoiding injury when engaged in hostilities. This has meant shielding ourselves in some way or wearing protective clothing, which has provided a rich source of visual imagery for artists. When all is lost, surrender may be our only option. A formal capitulation may be given, signalling the desire to surrender. In the worst-case scenario, the gesture of surrender is ignored – an outcome that has inspired some artists to make a visual statement with a powerful political message.

The portrayal of self-protection in art does not always centre on conflict, however, and is often far less dramatic. Many of us feel moments of apprehension as we go about our daily lives. Certain social situations, such as interviews, business meetings or family quarrels, may make us feel particularly unsure of ourselves and in need of a little protection. Since most of us don't want to admit to being nervous, we do our best to conceal our insecurities and, instead, pretend that we are perfectly at ease. Unfortunately, our body language can give us away, often through subtle movements that we are not consciously aware of. These include small protective gestures, such as body-cross and arms akimbo postures.

There are also special gestures that we openly perform to make ourselves feel safe, such as keeping our fingers crossed. Wearing a veil or having a tattoo may not be widely thought of in this context, but both began as a form of protection; they were believed to protect the wearer from evil spirits.

Fleeing

Flight is one of the primary responses of an animal faced with danger. However, for human beings, living in fixed settlements, it is not always straightforward. Many of us would be reluctant to leave our home and possessions, and only a major disaster or threat to life would see us abandon them.

The English artist Henry Gibbs imagines such a scene in *Aeneas and his Family Fleeing Burning Troy* (1654) [144]. He emphasizes the family's predicament by depicting their bodies leaning forwards, mid-flight. This sense of urgency is heightened by additional details, such as the way in which the young boy tugs at his father's tunic, and the fact that Aeneas is carrying his elderly father on his shoulders. Aeneas's wife, who doesn't manage to escape with the rest of her family, is seen lagging behind, trying to escape the clutches of a Greek soldier.

In a poignant work entitled *Jews Fleeing War* (1939) [143], the American artist Bernece Berkman tackles the Nazi persecution of Jews in the 1930s. She presents a nightmarish scene in which four people move through a strange, distorted landscape, clearly fleeing in panic. In the foreground, the artist uses the same device as Henry Gibbs to emphasize urgency: a child clinging to its parent. The inhospitable landscape in which Berkman sets the painting symbolizes the dangers and fears experienced by those who have been uprooted and forced to leave their homeland.

143. **Bernece Berkman,**
Jews Fleeing War, **1939,**
oil on canvas

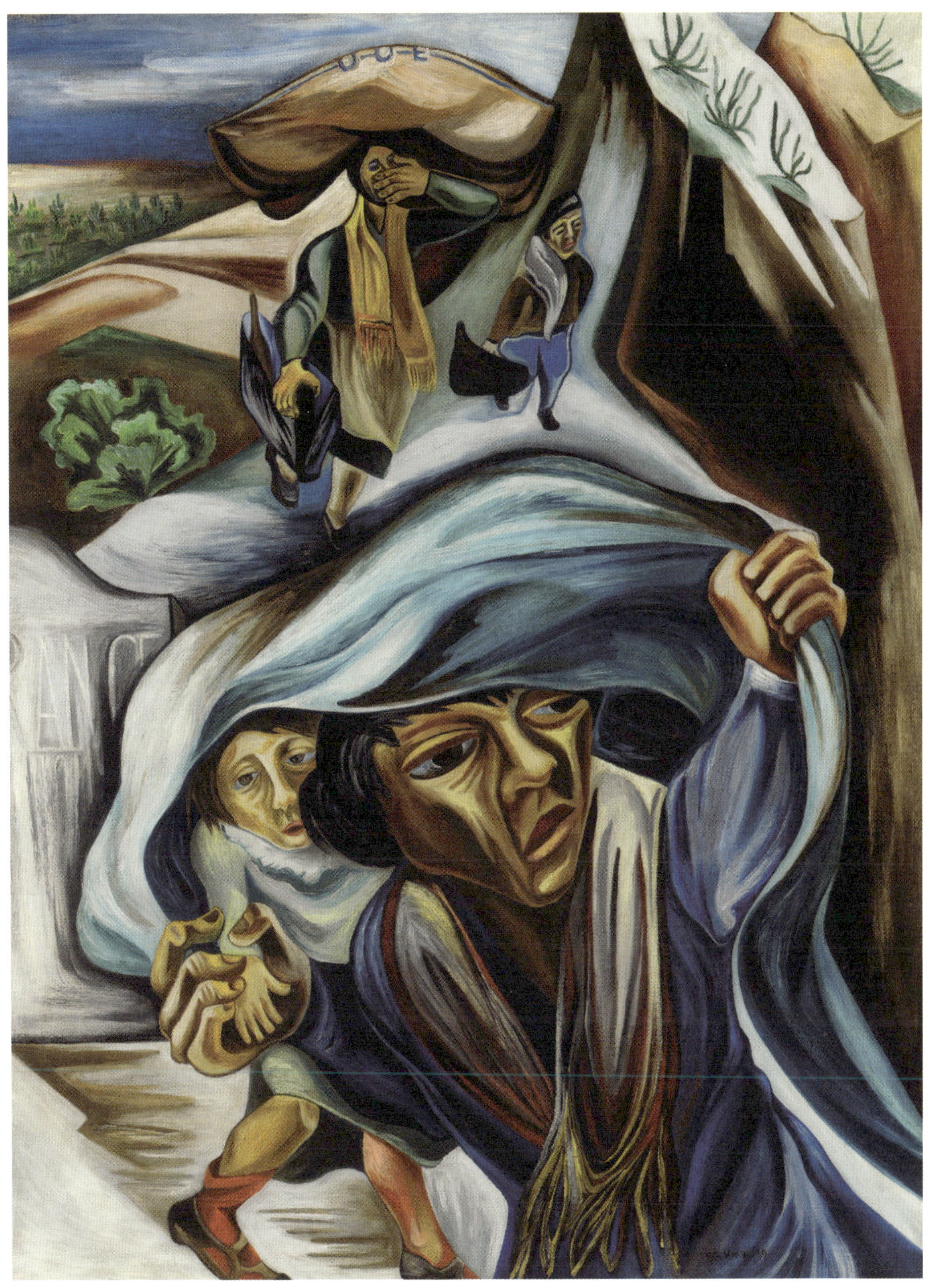
U.O.E

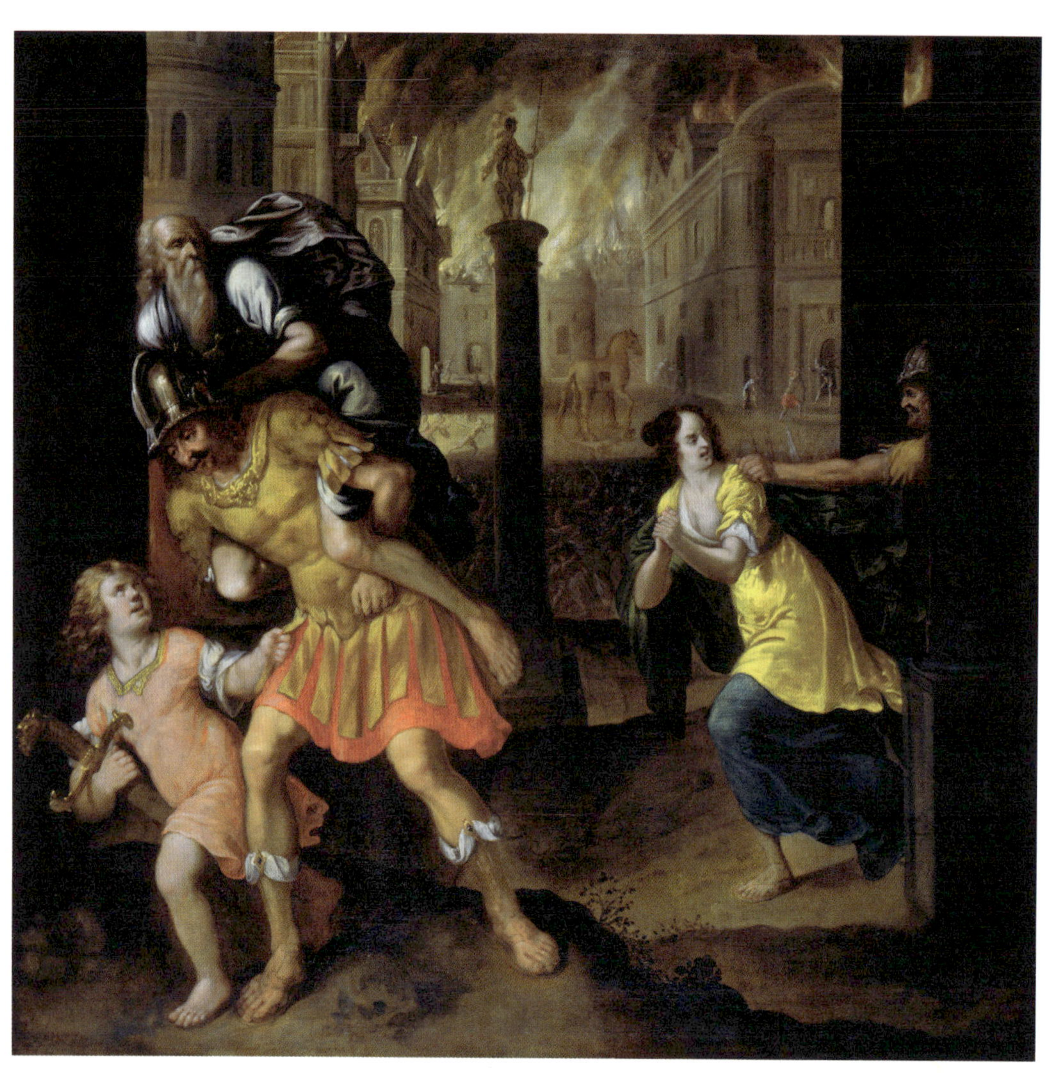

144. above **Henry Gibbs**, *Aeneas and his Family Fleeing Burning Troy*, 1654, oil on canvas

145. opposite **Jacopo Tintoretto**, *Saint George and the Dragon*, c. 1555, oil on canvas

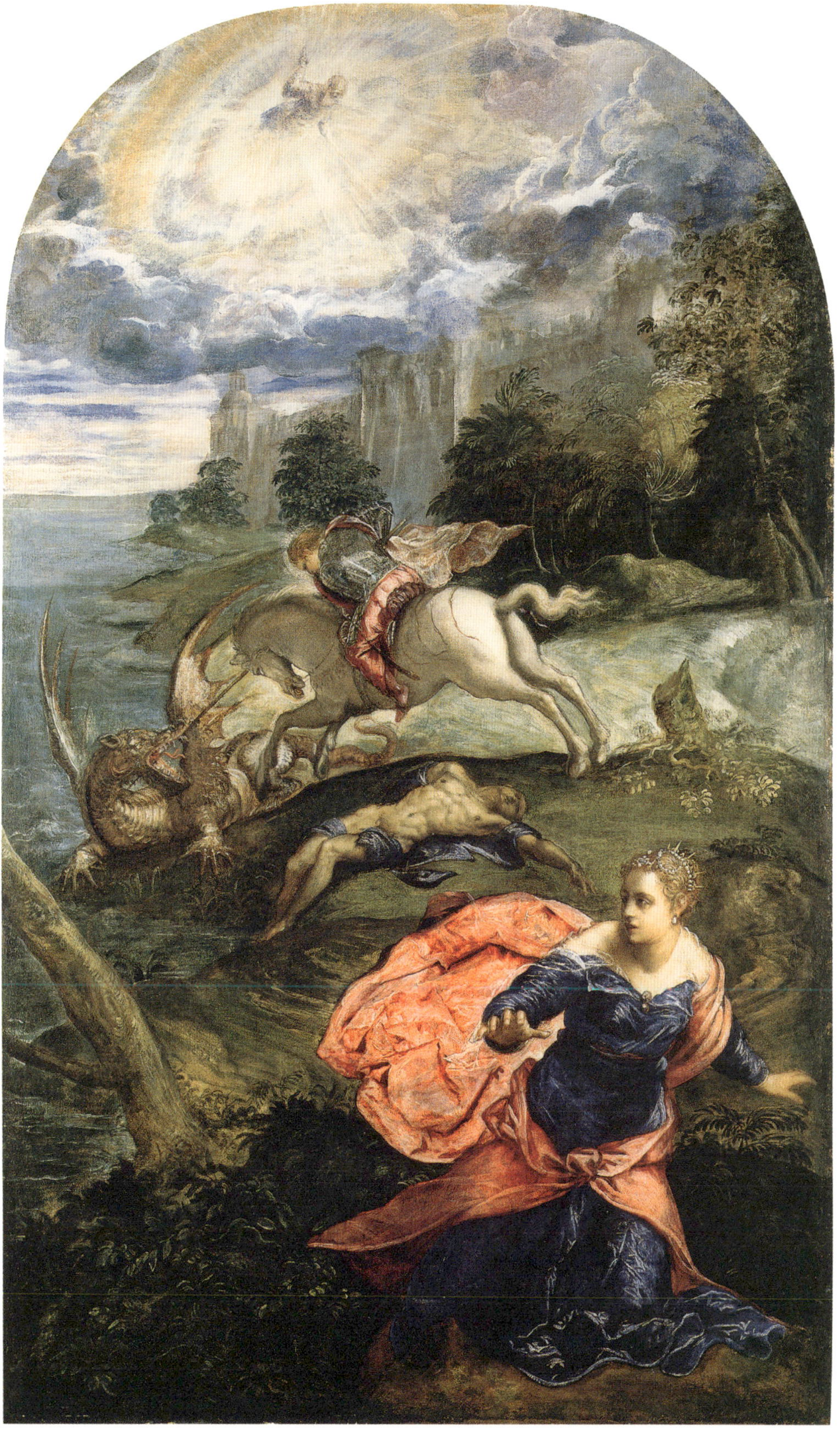

Surrender

The 'hands up' posture is widely recognized as a sign of submission, the simple message being: 'Don't shoot, I surrender'. Like the waving of a white flag, it is generally used only in extreme circumstances as a final, desperate plea for mercy – one that doesn't always pay off.

One painting that shows the jeopardy of adopting such a posture is Francisco Goya's masterpiece *The 3rd of May 1808* (1814) [147], which commemorates Spanish resistance to Napoleon's armies during the Peninsular War. The focal point of this painting is a man in a white shirt, with his hands raised high in the air. At first glance, his body language sends a clear message of surrender to the firing squad in front of him: 'I give up!' However, there is also a sense of defiance and futility in this action because most of his companions lie slaughtered at his feet, and he knows that he will be next.

In 2014, a white American artist, Wesley James Lock, was moved – like Goya two hundred years before him – to portray another unsuccessful 'hands up' surrender to make a political point. He was angry after a jury decided that the white officer responsible for killing an unarmed black teenager, Michael Brown, would not face trial. His response was to create an emotive image, showing a young black man with his hands raised and several bullet holes in his chest. Wesley James Lock called the work *Scars and Stripes* [149], with the bullet holes representing the stars of the American flag, and the lines of blood forming the stripes.

146. **Henri Rousseau,**
Unpleasant Surprise (detail),
1901, oil on canvas

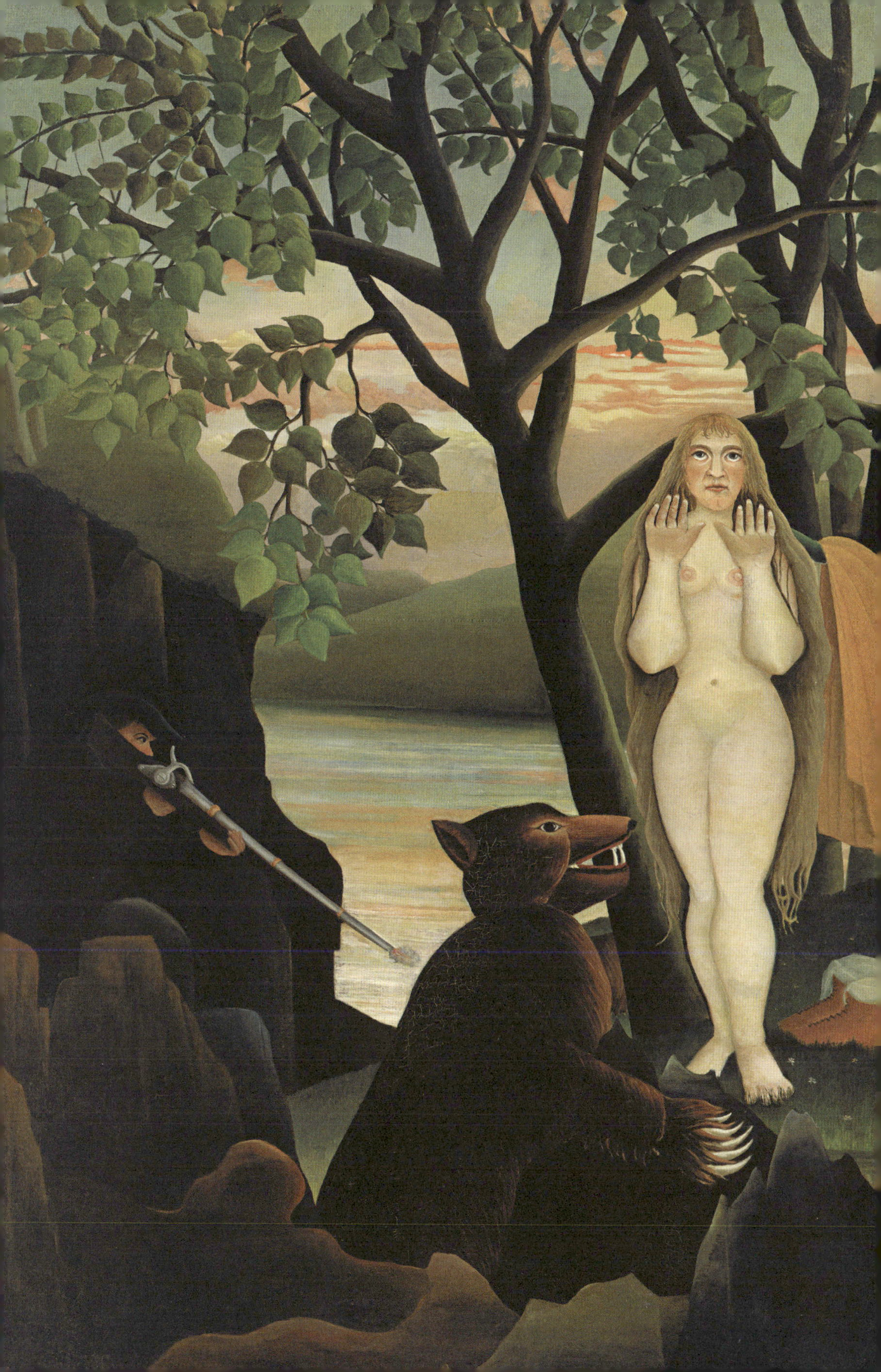

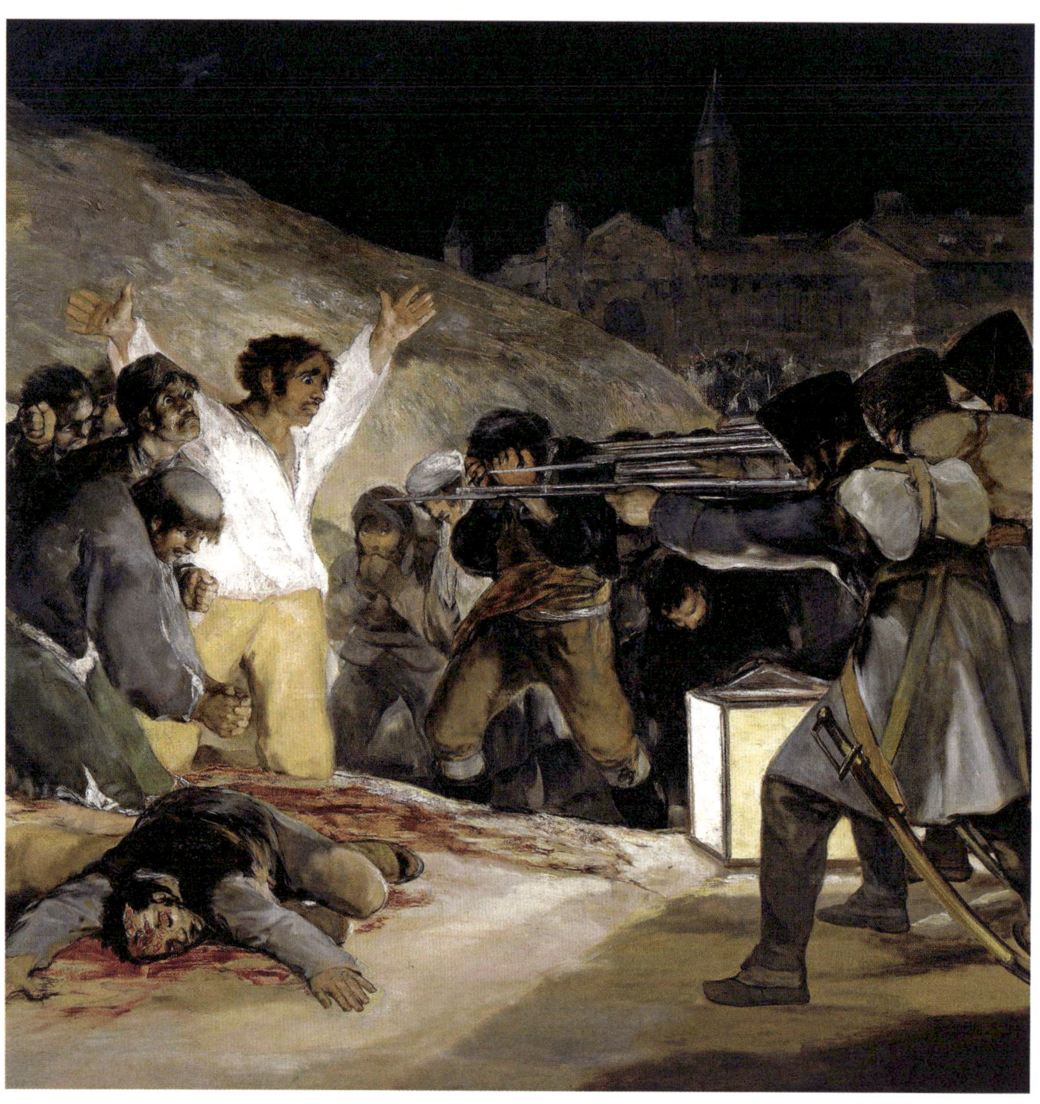

147. above **Francisco Goya,**
The 3rd of May 1808 **(detail),
1814, oil on canvas**

148. opposite, above **Jean-Michel
Basquiat,** ***Untitled,*** **1981, acrylic,
oilstick and spray paint on canvas**

149. opposite, below **Wesley James
Lock,** ***Scars and Stripes,*** **2014,
ink on paper**

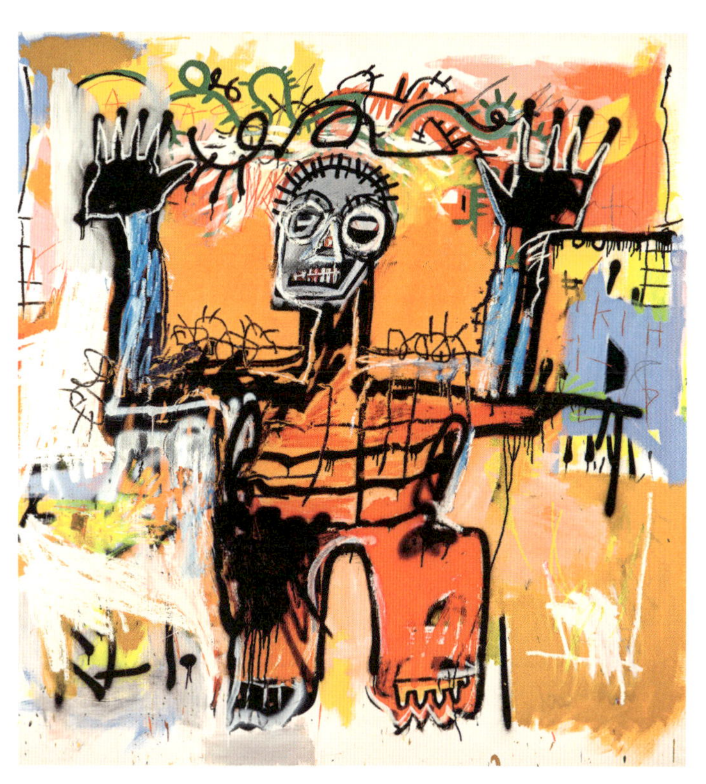

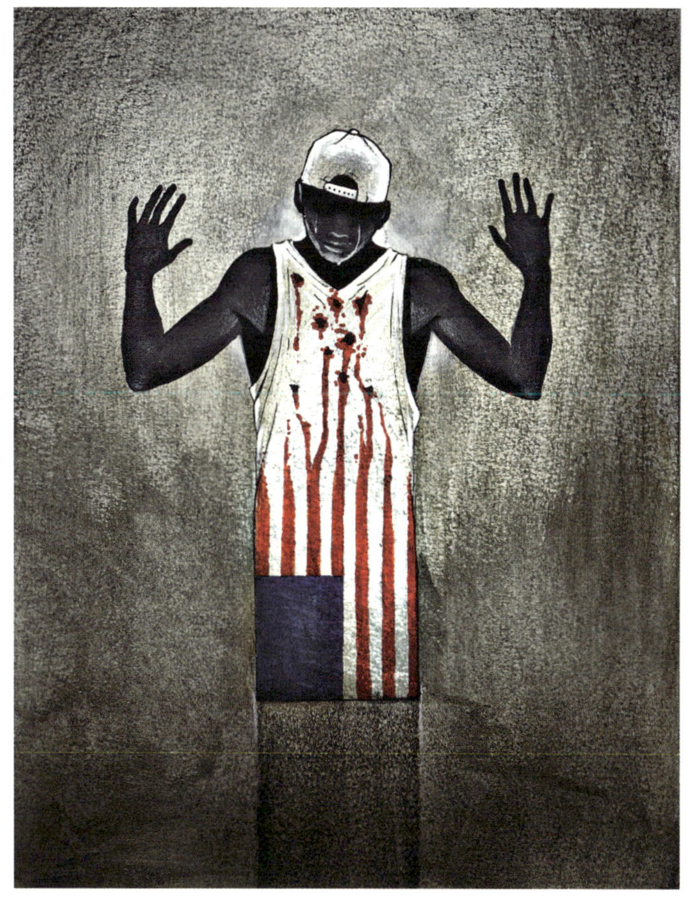

Armour

There are several ways in which animals protect themselves from attack. Some use camouflage, have a hard shell or sharp spines, or are poisonous. Others are so fast that they are able to outpace their predators; a hard shell would only weigh them down. Although humans can run fast, our soft bodies offer little protection if we are cornered.

Our natural instinct is to protect the face and head above all else, because this is where the specialized sense organs are located. The simplest response to physical attack is to bring the hands up in front of the face in order to shield it – a protective device famously employed by Muhammad Ali in the 'Rumble in the Jungle', his iconic 1974 boxing match with George Foreman. Ali held his fists together in front of his face and allowed his opponent to punch him again and again, until he had worn himself out – at which point Ali landed the killer blow. In the world of art, a black-and-white mural by WK Interact [156], painted in New York in 1992, perfectly captures the dramatic moment when a man under threat must resort to protecting himself with only his hands.

Man has used shields as an additional form of protection for millennia, as evidenced by ancient indigenous rock art discovered in the USA [150]. Early shields were made of such materials as animal hides, wood or, less commonly, metal. Before the invention of firearms, most of the great armies would have carried shields. The Romans used shields in a special way by holding them together above their heads (apart from the front row, who held their shields in front of them), forming what was called a *testudo*, or tortoise, formation. Under normal circumstances, a Roman soldier carried his cylindrical leather shield on his left arm; in a *testudo*, in which a group of men crouched beneath their locked-together shields, it became a siege weapon. Acting as a single unit, the soldiers could then approach a besieged wall without any fear of the missiles being dropped from above, as depicted in a scene on Trajan's Column in Rome [154]. More recently, Henry Moore was fascinated by the sculptural possibilities of the circular, hand-held shield, and incorporated it into a number of works in the 1950s and 1970s [155].

Early man had no other option but to try to protect himself with a shield of some kind. With the development of more sophisticated technology, it became possible to improve physical safety by wearing an armoured covering. Although this would be too cumbersome for daily use, it could be worn at moments of acute danger. The earliest forms of armour consisted of hardened leather. By the 4th century BC, linothorax – a type of body armour made by laminating together layers of linen – was being used in ancient Greece. It was strong enough to withstand arrows, and had the advantage of being light and flexible. Alexander

the Great sometimes rode into battle wearing linothorax, protected
by a breastplate bearing the image of the gorgon Medusa, as can be seen
in a famous Pompeian mosaic [152], now in the National Archaeological
Museum in Naples. Other early forms of protection included scale
armour (consisting of small plates of metal or organic material, arranged
in overlapping rows) and chain mail (small metal rings linked together
to form a mesh).

Later, these types of armour were mostly replaced by plate mail
(made of larger sheets of iron or steel), culminating in the heavy suits
of armour that we associate with knights of the medieval period.
Historically, a suit of armour offered more than mere physical protection;
it also said something about the person wearing it. If you could afford
such an expensive item, it meant that you were more likely to be captured
for ransom than killed on the spot. Elaborate examples of plate armour
acted not only as a form of defence, but also as an intimidating visual
display; an armoured warrior on an armoured horse must have been
a terrifying spectacle for an ordinary foot-soldier. By the 17th century,
elegantly decorated suits of armour had become a form of high-status
display for aristocratic males, as in the case of the principal figure in
Caravaggio's *Portrait of Alof de Wignacourt and his Page* (*c.* 1608) [151].

One man's use of armour in the late 19th century has become
legendary. In 1880, having robbed a number of banks and killed two
policemen, the Australian outlaw Ned Kelly engaged in his final shootout
with the authorities. Kelly had made a makeshift suit of armour from
reworked metal plough blades but had left his legs uncovered, which
proved his downfall. Having suffered serious injuries to his lower body,
he fell to the ground and was captured. He was later hanged, at the age
of twenty-five, reportedly uttering the famous last words: 'Such is life.'
In the 1940s, Kelly's escapades were commemorated in a series of
paintings by fellow Australian Sidney Nolan [153].

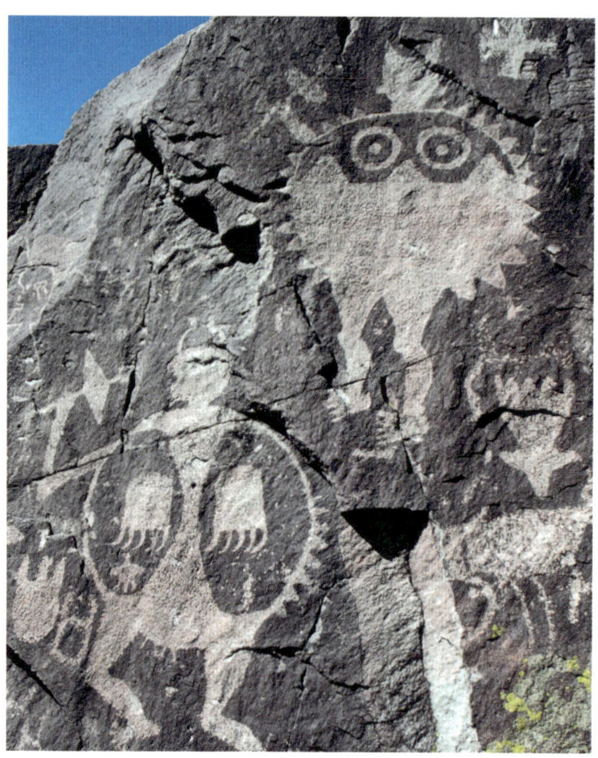

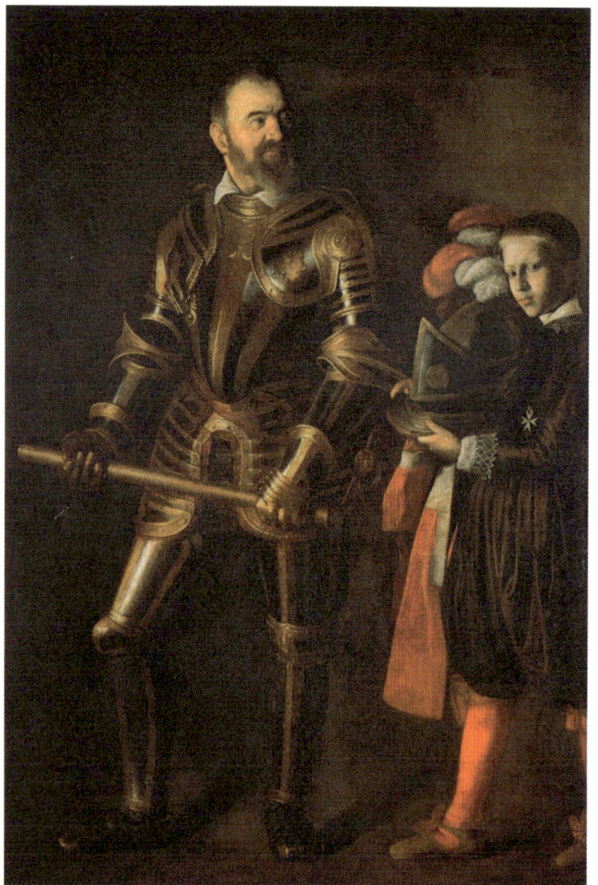

150. above **Ancient Pueblo (Anasazi) rock art, showing a warrior with a bear-claw shield, *c.* 500 BC–AD 500, New Mexico, USA**

151. left **Caravaggio, *Portrait of Alof de Wignacourt and his Page*, *c.* 1608, oil on canvas**

152. opposite, above **Detail from the *Alexander Mosaic*, *c.* 100 BC, originally from the House of the Faun, Pompeii**

153. opposite, below **Sidney Nolan, *Kelly and Horse*, 1946, enamel on composition board**

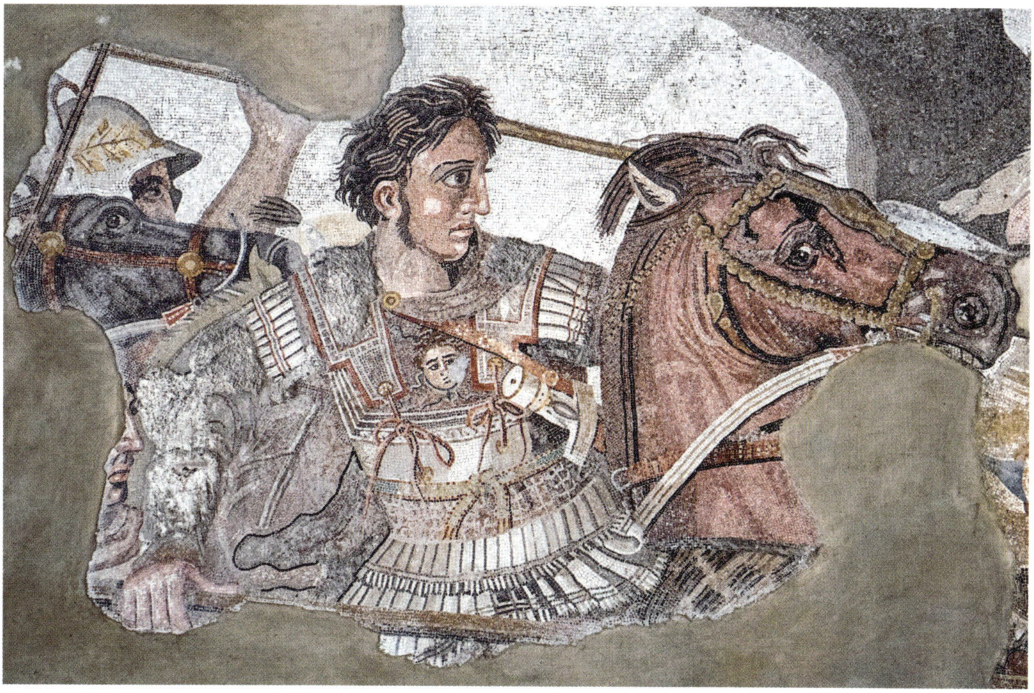

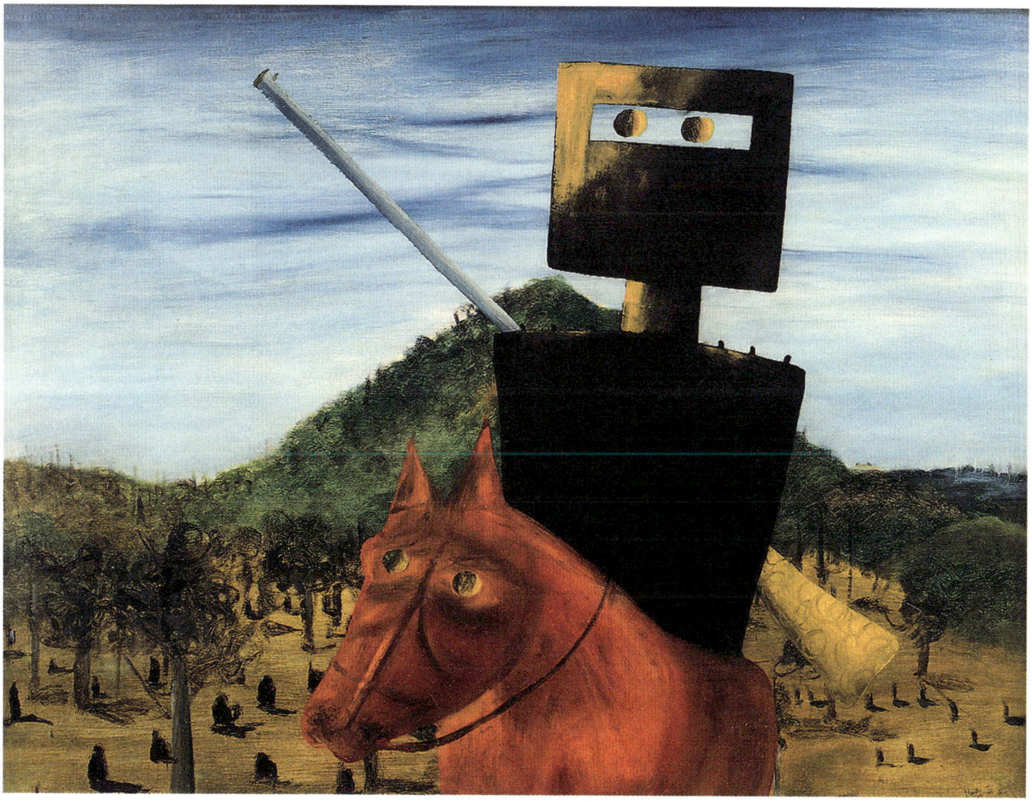

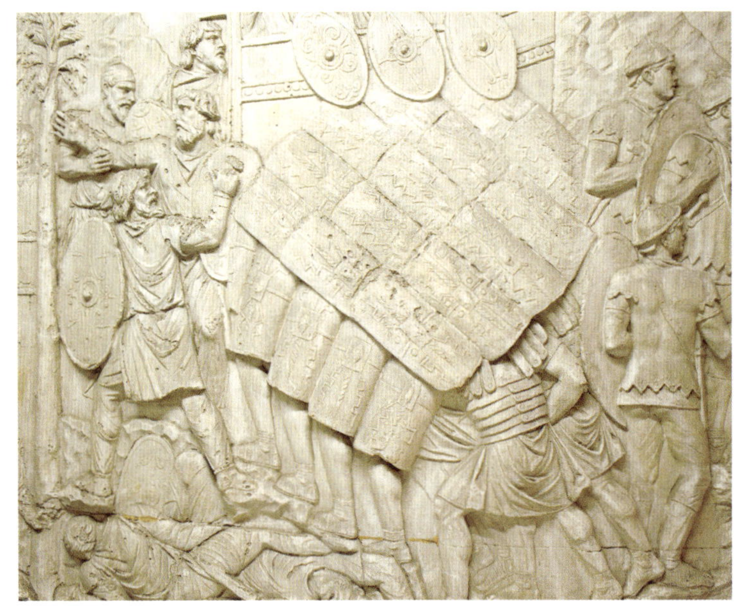

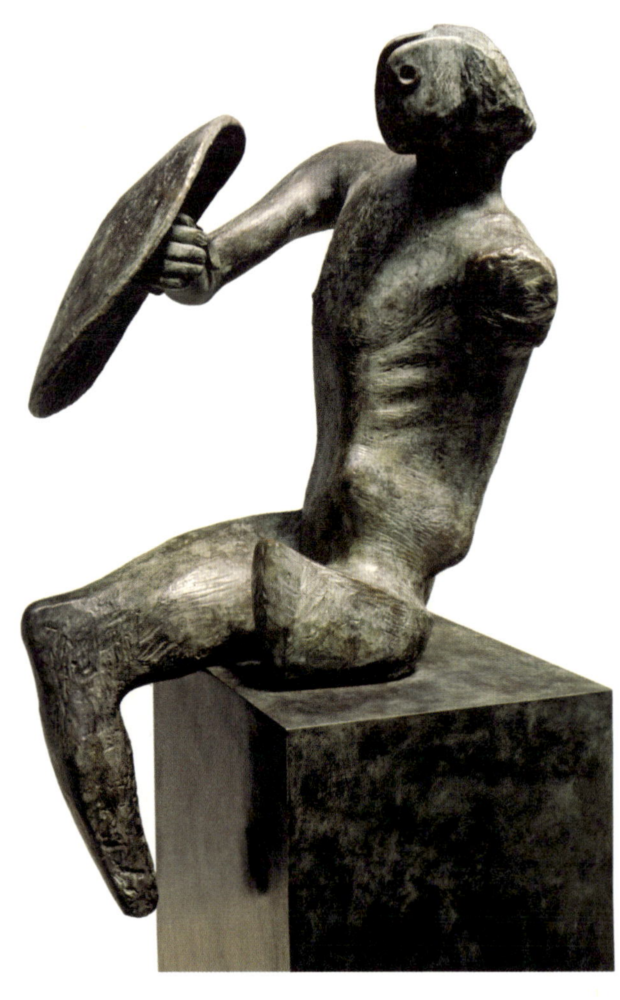

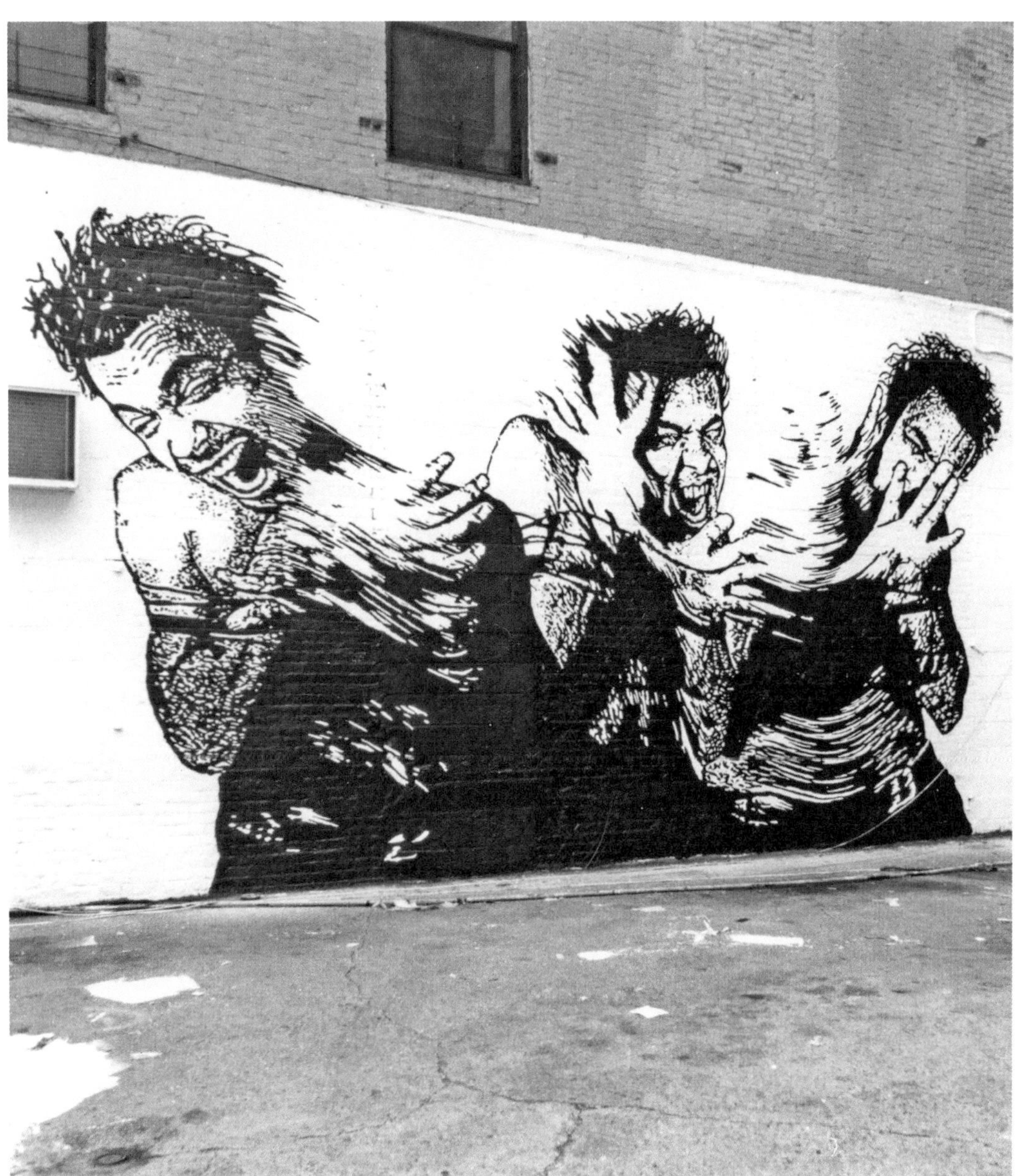

154. opposite, above **Scene from Trajan's Column (AD 113), showing Romans in *testudo* formation, 19th-century plaster cast of marble original in Rome**

155. opposite, below **Henry Moore, *Warrior with Shield*, 1953–54, bronze on wooden plinth**

156. above **WK Interact, *Struggle*, 1992, mural, New York**

Self-protection / Armour

Cut-off

Sometimes, when we are under stress, we feel unable to cope with everything that is going on around us. We find a way of shutting it out, so that we don't have to deal with it. The actions we perform in order to block out the world have been given the name 'cut-off'.

If we're suffering from too much social input, we do our best to damp down the over-stimulation, and this usually means covering our major sense organs – our eyes or our ears. The most basic solution is to remove ourselves from the social scene altogether until we have recovered sufficiently to return to the fray. However, this is a drastic solution that goes far beyond the normal day-to-day cut-off devices that we all employ in our social encounters. The much more frequent moments of minor stress are handled by fleeting actions of a far less dramatic kind.

The most common and obvious of these actions is briefly to close the eyes. We simply lower the shutters on the incoming visual information. A man at a noisy party who has been asked about something he can't remember might shut his eyes tightly as he searches his memory. In more extreme circumstances, we go a step further, not only closing our eyes but also covering them with one or both hands; we might even bury our head in a soft object, such as a cushion or pillow, or perhaps the clothing of a close companion. If it is too much noise that is causing us stress, we may clamp our hands over our ears.

These are honest, undisguised cases of cut-off, and are readily accepted as such, but there is another, special category that is more interesting because it includes four unconscious actions – subtle cut-offs of which the performer is hardly aware. The first is the 'evasive eye', in which a person with whom we are conversing looks away from us for unusually long periods; they can barely meet our eye, and spend considerable time staring at some imaginary object to one side of us, or at the ground. The second is the 'shifty eye', in which the person keeps glancing away and then back again, rapidly repeating these movements while continuing to talk with us. The third is the 'stuttering eye', in which our interlocutor faces us, as if to look us in the eye, but their eyelids flicker up and down. The fourth and final action in this category is the 'stammering eye', in which our companion also faces us squarely, but every so often closes the eyes for several seconds at a time.

All four of these forms of cut-off are rather disconcerting, and we may find ourselves growing irritated by them without understanding why this should be. The explanation is that, intuitively, we know the person with us wants to withdraw from our company for some reason. Perhaps they fear us, dislike us or are bored by us, and would rather be elsewhere, although in every other way they may seem friendly and fully involved in our social encounter; they may just be painfully shy. The cut-off signals are made unconsciously, and we receive them in the same way – with the non-verbal communication taking place just beneath the surface of the encounter, and acting as an unspoken irritant. When an individual is suffering from acute stress, these cut-off actions can become almost unavoidable 'tics', providing tiny but vital moments of relief for the person in question. Each split-second of cut-off is, in a sense, a minuscule, symbolic escape from the tyranny of the moment, lessening – if only for a few seconds – the sensory overload.

For the artist, the unconscious forms of cut-off are usually too subtle or fleeting to capture on canvas, but the deliberate actions of covering the eyes or the ears in intolerable situations have often been recorded. In works of art, the most common form of cut-off is the covering of the face with the hands. There are examples of this action from ancient Egypt right through to modern times. In ancient Egypt, a highly stylized form of cut-off was employed by professional mourners. Statuettes of these mourners, found in a Greco-Roman cemetery, show this very clearly. Two of them are holding their hands over their eyes, and a third has her hands on top of her head. It was the custom, at the time, to hire women to follow the corpse to its burial, who would ostentatiously wave their hands in the air, strike their chest in grief, weep copious tears and cover their face (see p. 174). Statuettes of paid mourners have been found with mummies of only the wealthiest individuals, suggesting that the rich alone could afford such a display.

In an illustration from a 15th-century Book of Hours [159], showing the Agony in the Garden of Gethsemane, Christ is depicted with his hands covering his face. In most portrayals of this scene, he is kneeling in prayer with his hands together in front of him; in this instance, however, the artist has allowed him, in his misery, to employ a cut-off to blot out the world. This illustration – like most works of art that incorporate the face-palm gesture, as this form of cut-off is known – shows the two-handed version, but in the Tuileries Garden in Paris there is a famous statue of Cain (1896), by Henri Vidal, making a one-handed cut-off as he hides his face in shame after killing his brother.

Perhaps the most poignant example of a cut-off in art is a work by the great Florentine Renaissance artist Sandro Botticelli. Entitled *La Derelitta* (1495) [158], which translates as 'The Abandoned One', the painting shows a young woman alone on the steps outside a forbidding building with a sealed door. Some of her clothing has been scattered on the steps beside her, suggesting that she has just been cast out and left to fend for herself. Clearly devastated, she sits with her face buried in her hands, cutting off the outside world in a moment of desperate isolation.

Van Gogh captures a similar mood in his portrait of an elderly man sitting by a fireplace with his head in his hands, entitled *Sorrowing Old Man ('At Eternity's Gate')* (1890) [157]. Consumed with the reality that he will soon be dead, the man tries, for a few moments, to comfort himself by shutting out the world that he knows he will soon be leaving. Significantly, Van Gogh painted this picture in May 1890, some two months before his own death, on 29 July, from a self-inflicted gunshot wound.

Typically, cut-off is performed to reduce stress, but there are other motivations for covering the face – not least the concealment of identity. A celebrity may cover their face with their hands or an item of clothing to avoid being photographed by paparazzi. The creation of an alter ego or pseudonym by artists such as Banksy may be seen as an extension of this type of cut-off. Many graffiti and street artists choose to conceal their identity because of the illegal nature of their work, such that anonymity has become a recurring theme in this art form as a whole. The Irish artist Conor Harrington, whose work blends fine art with graffiti and street art elements, has explored anonymity in a number of paintings, including *Hide and Seek* (2016) [160] – one of a series of works that the artist describes as 'a nod to political deceit, the lies and half truths told to assume a role and gain power, the prevalence of social media selves at the expense of the real self and the graffiti alter ego, acquiring a pseudonym and hiding your true identity'.

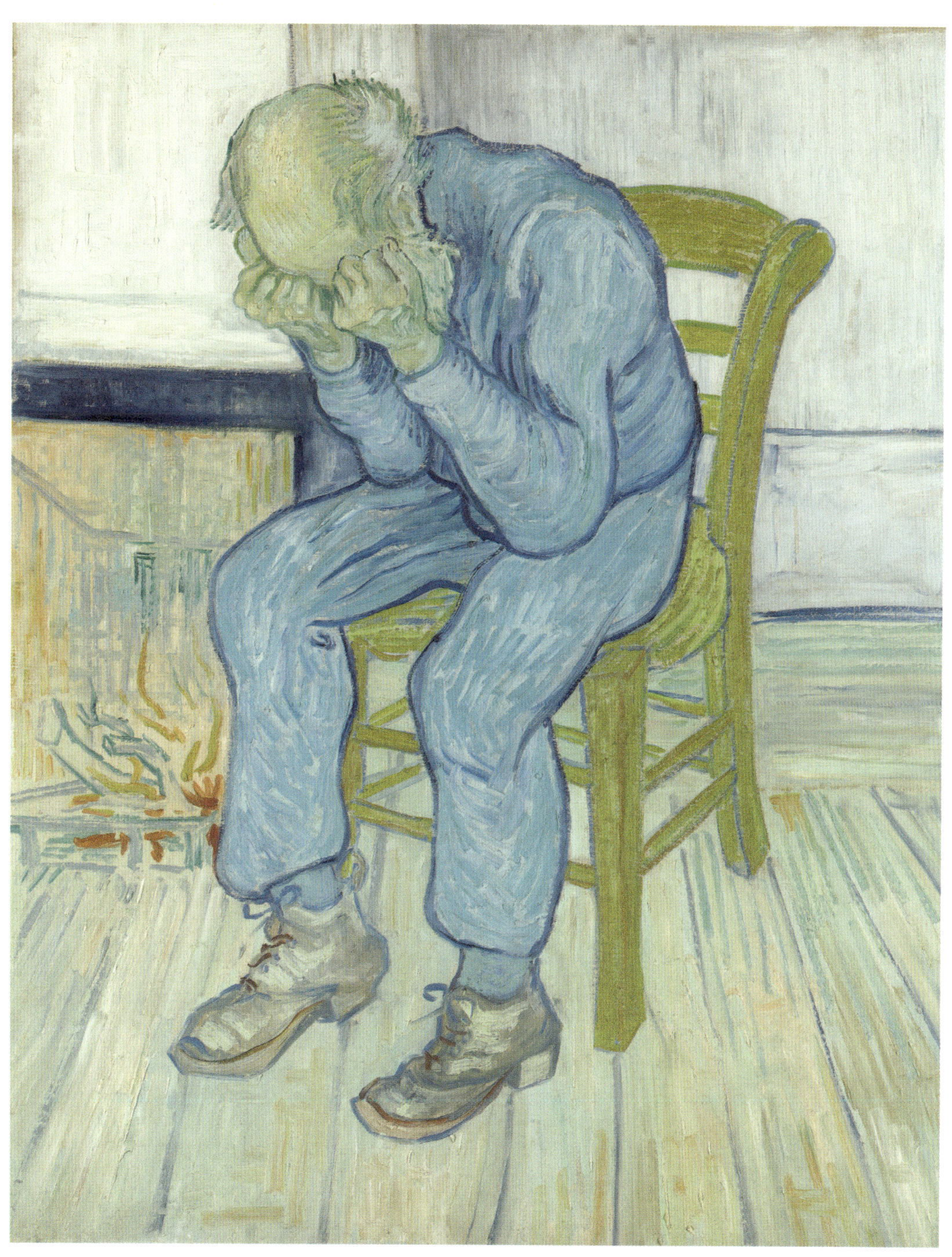

157. **Vincent van Gogh,**
Sorrowing Old Man
('At Eternity's Gate'),
1890, oil on canvas

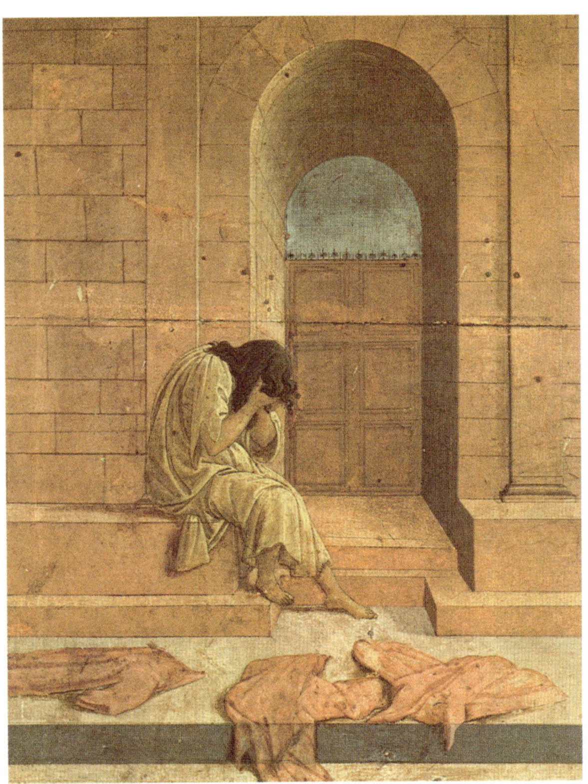

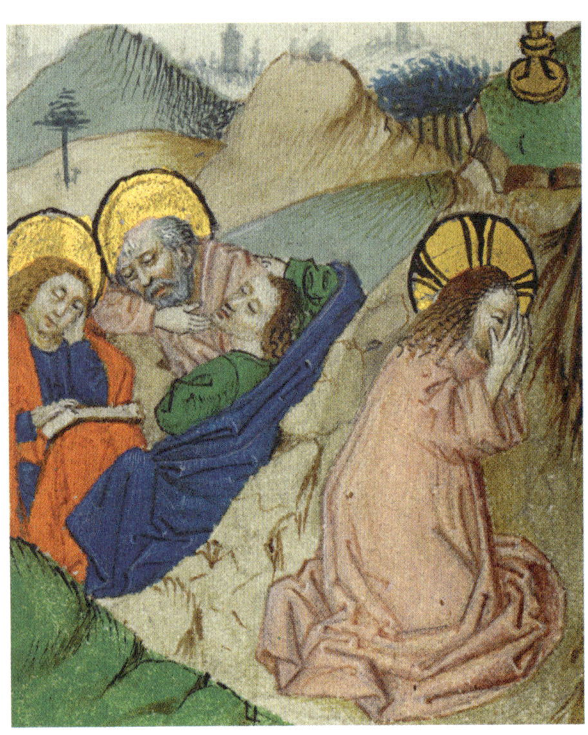

158. above **Sandro Botticelli,**
La Derelitta (detail), 1495, tempera
on wood

159. left **Agony in the Garden
of Gethsemane** (detail), 1470,
Book of Hours, Netherlands

160. opposite **Conor Harrington,**
Hide and Seek, 2016, oil on linen

    Self-protection / Cut-off

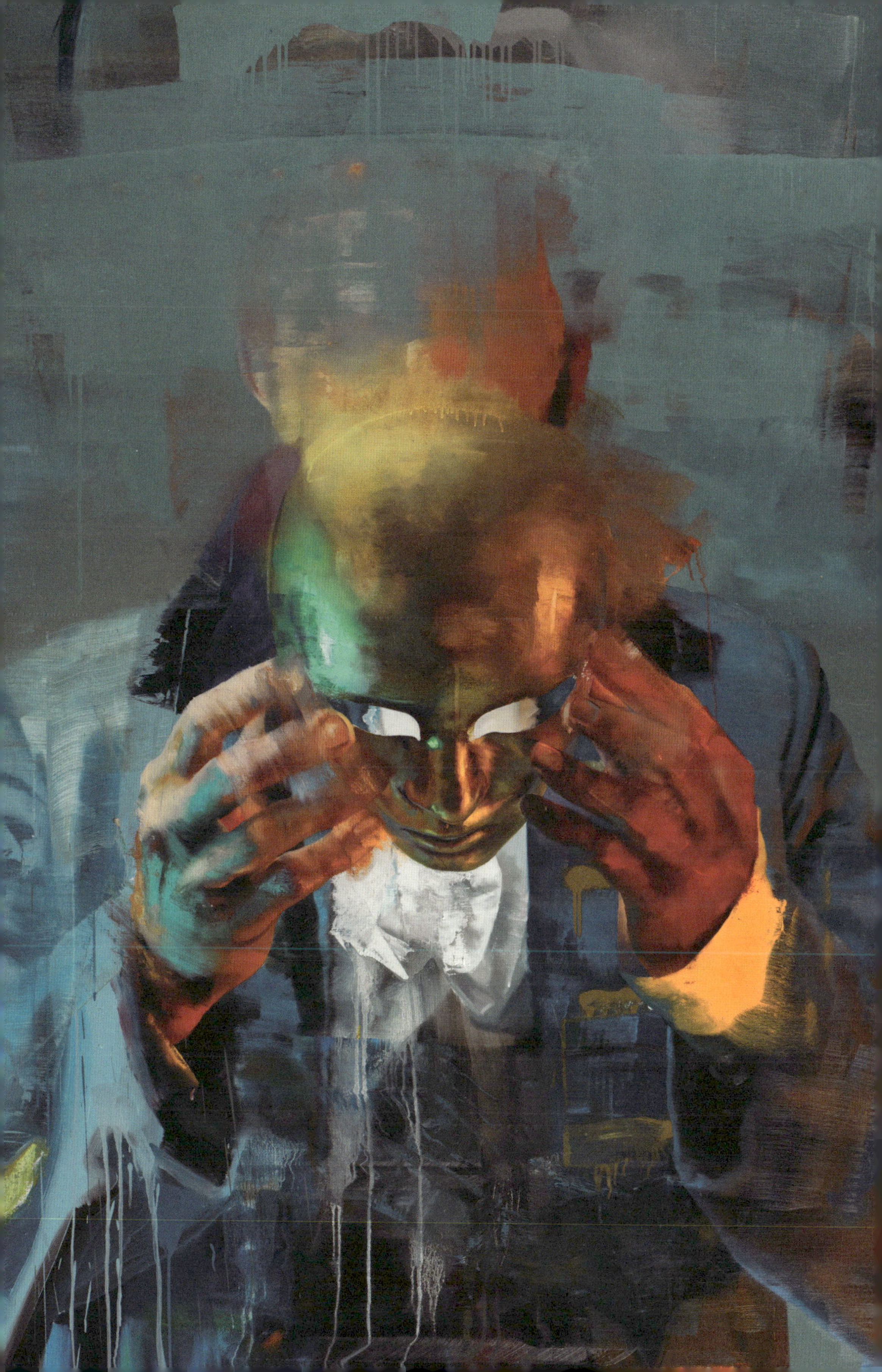

Body-cross

When the police wish to protect a particular area, they set up a barrier. When human beings feel the need for a little protection, they may also set up a barrier by bringing one arm into contact with the other – a posture that is called a body-cross. There is nothing dramatic about it, and we are usually unaware that we are doing it. However, its high frequency, and the fact that it is done by people from all walks of life, suggests that it plays a valuable, if minor, role in social interactions.

There are many versions of the body-cross in art. In the context of portraiture, this posture can offer a degree of comfort to the sitter when posing for long periods of time. In Pablo Picasso's *Seated Harlequin* (1923), the subject sits with his hands clasped, palm-to-palm. He holds his left hand with his right, creating a protective barrier across the front of his body that is designed to make him feel more at ease. In other paintings, one hand is placed on top of the other, palm-to-knuckle. This is seen in Wyndham Lewis's portrait of the English poet and novelist Stephen Spender (1938) [163], as well as in *Portrait of a Man in a Turban* (1440s) [162] by an unknown Netherlandish artist. In another variant, one hand clasps the forearm or wrist of the other arm – a pose that is adopted, albeit loosely, in Leonardo da Vinci's *Mona Lisa* (*c.* 1503–6).

Other versions of the body-cross are centred on the position of the fingers. The fingers may be tightly interlaced, for example, or the fingertips may touch lightly in a posture known as steepling (because the upward-pointing shape is reminiscent of a church steeple). There is also an upside-down version of the latter, which is known as the inverted steeple – a gesture that, incidentally, is employed by President Trump whenever he meets a fellow head of state.

Another version of the body-cross involves the arms being held against the chest in an X-shape [161], with one wrist resting on top of the other. This posture is perhaps most commonly associated with religious figures in art, giving them a saintly air. It is also a sign of modesty, and is particularly evident in paintings of female nudes, as a means of covering the breasts. There is a straight-armed variation of this posture, in which the arms are crossed just below the waist, to leave the hands resting against the legs.

161. **Paula Modersohn-Becker,**
Old Peasant Woman (detail),
c. **1905, oil on canvas**

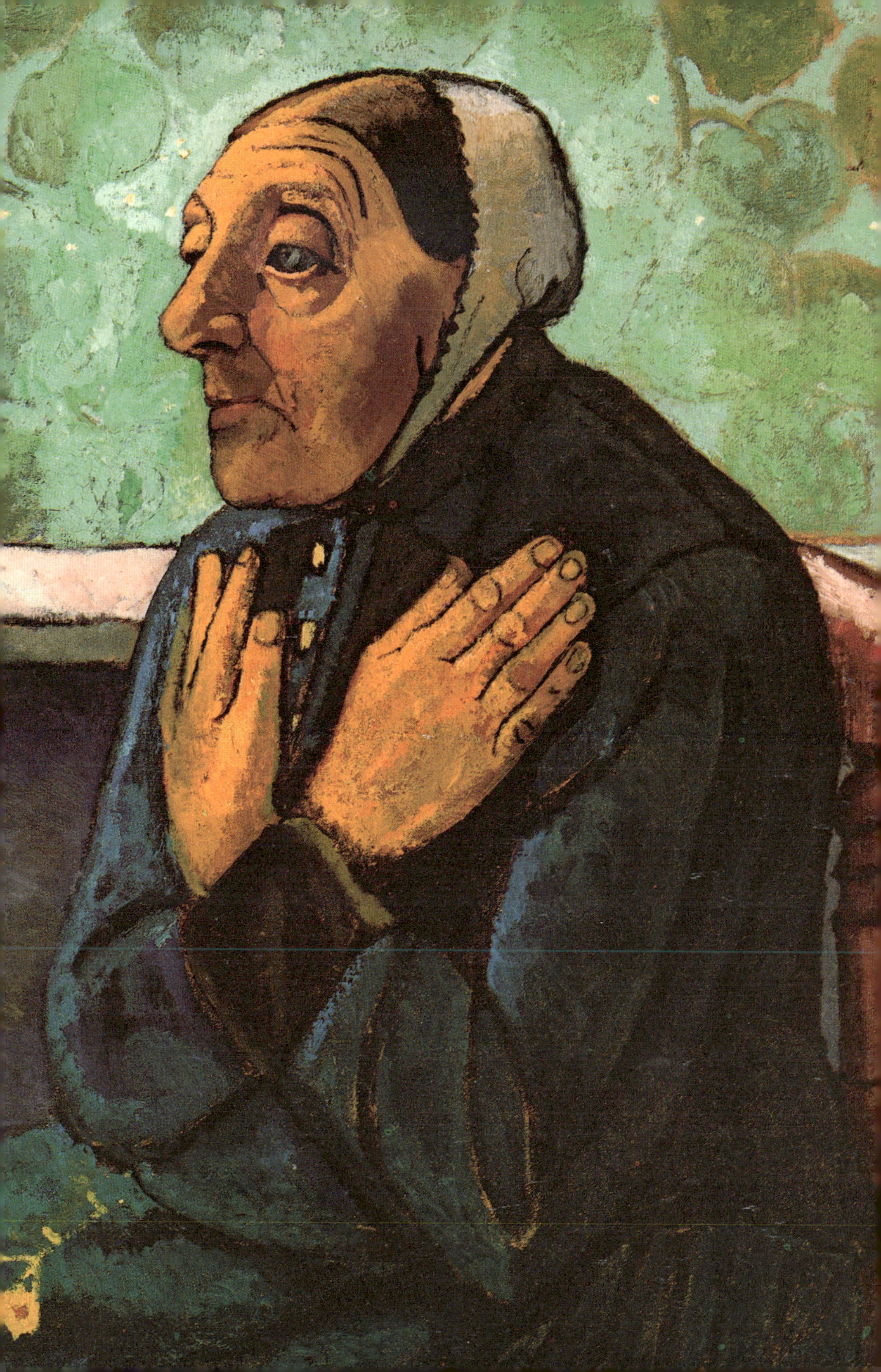

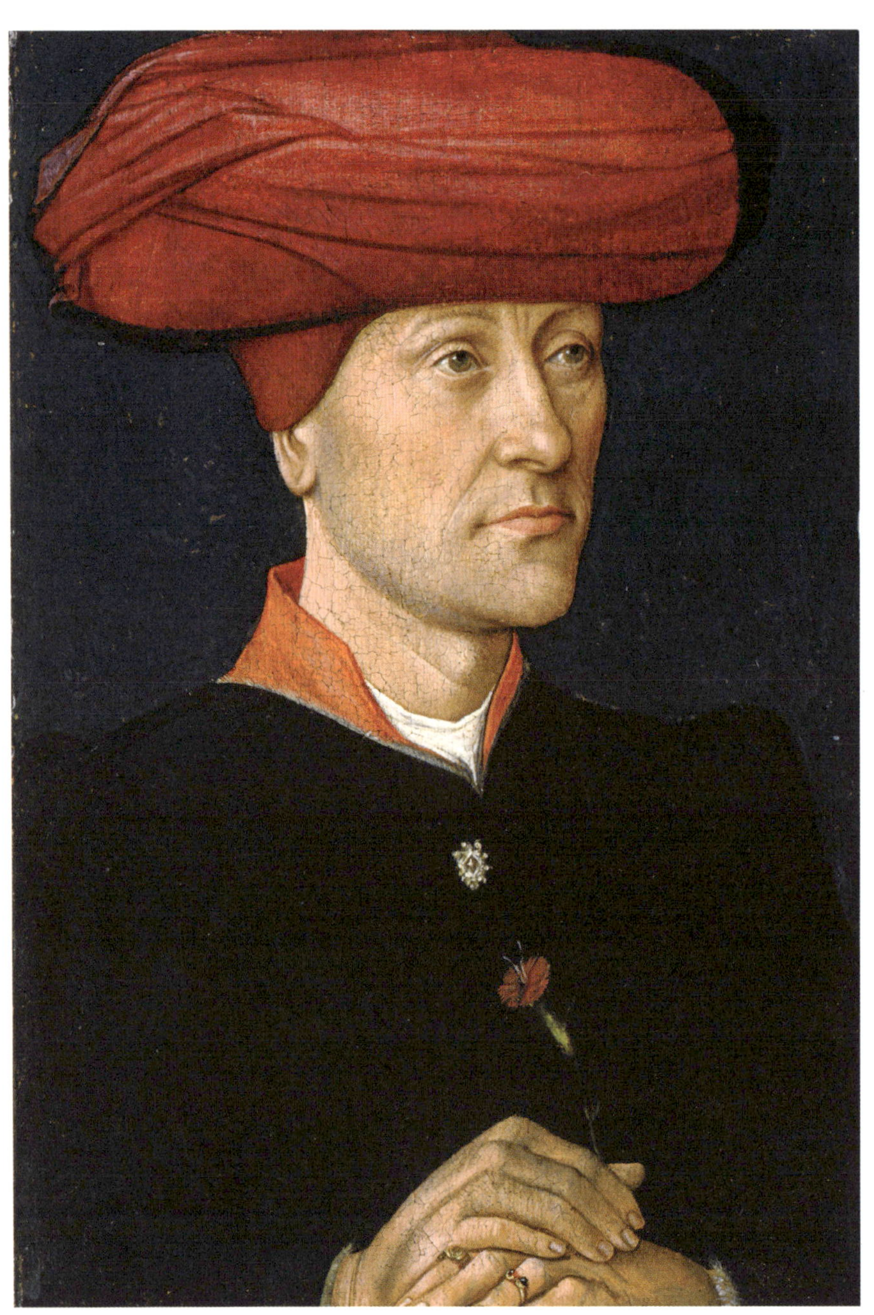

162. above **Netherlandish painter,**
Portrait of a Man in a Turban,
1440s, oil on wood

163. opposite **Wyndham Lewis,**
Stephen Spender, **1938,**
oil on canvas

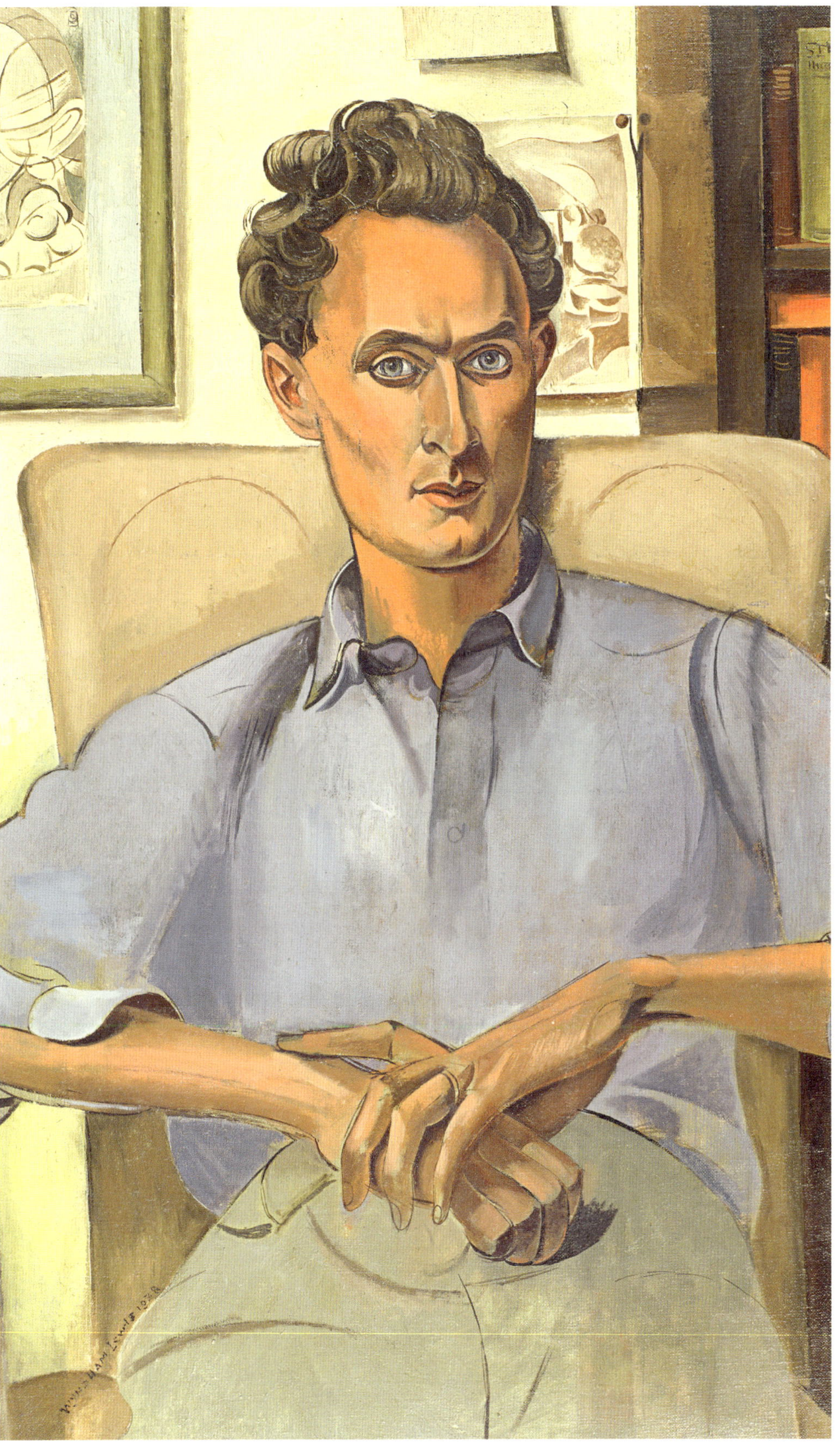

Arms Folded

There are two distinct kinds of arm-folding, and both are protective actions. The first is highly deliberate, and has an air of defiance about it; it is the 'power pose' typically adopted by bouncers at nightclubs when they want to make themselves look bigger. The second occurs unconsciously during social encounters in which we feel slightly uncomfortable or mildly threatened; the conversation may have taken a turn for the worse or touched on a sensitive issue, or we may feel anxious – when we are being interviewed, for example, or speaking in front of a large audience. Our feeling of unease is so slight that usually we are unaware that we have adopted the folded-arms posture, but subconsciously we have recognized the need for self-comfort. The roots of this action are believed to lie in childhood, and specifically the reassuring moment when we are given a hug by a parent; as adults, we mimic that hug by folding our arms tightly across the chest – essentially hugging ourselves.

Sitting for a portrait can also be an intimidating experience, and can sometimes cause anxiety and insecurity. While an artist often influences the choice of pose, if we are invited to adopt a position in which we feel comfortable, we are likely to sit or stand with folded arms. For this reason, many portraits show sitters adopting this protective posture, from Francisco Goya's painting of an architect, Tiburcio Pérez y Cuervo (1820) [164], to Paul Cézanne's *Peasant Standing with Arms Crossed* (*c.* 1895) [165].

164. **Francisco Goya,**
Tiburcio Pérez y Cuervo,
the Architect (detail),
1820, oil on canvas

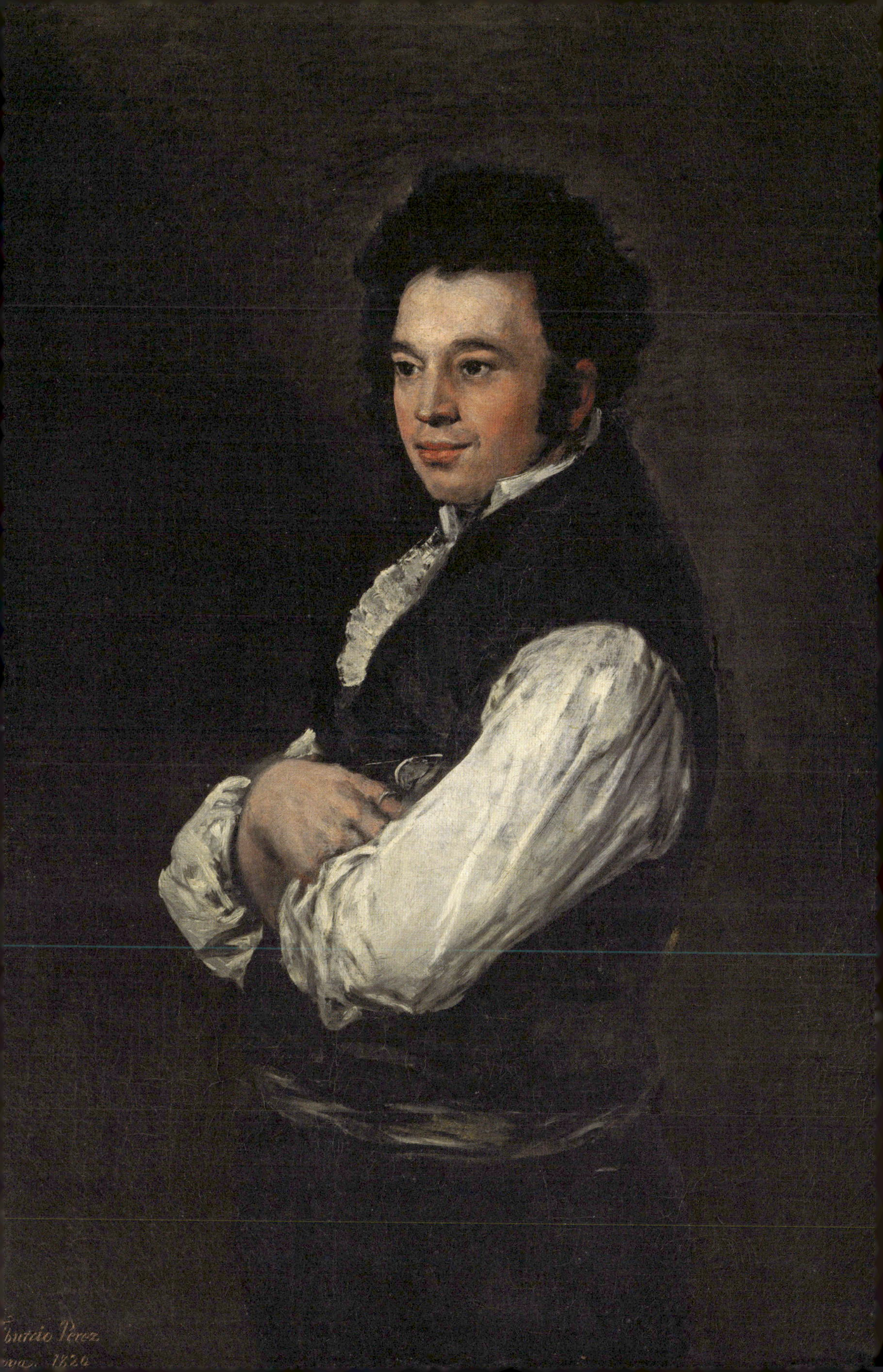
Tiburcio Perez
...a. 1820

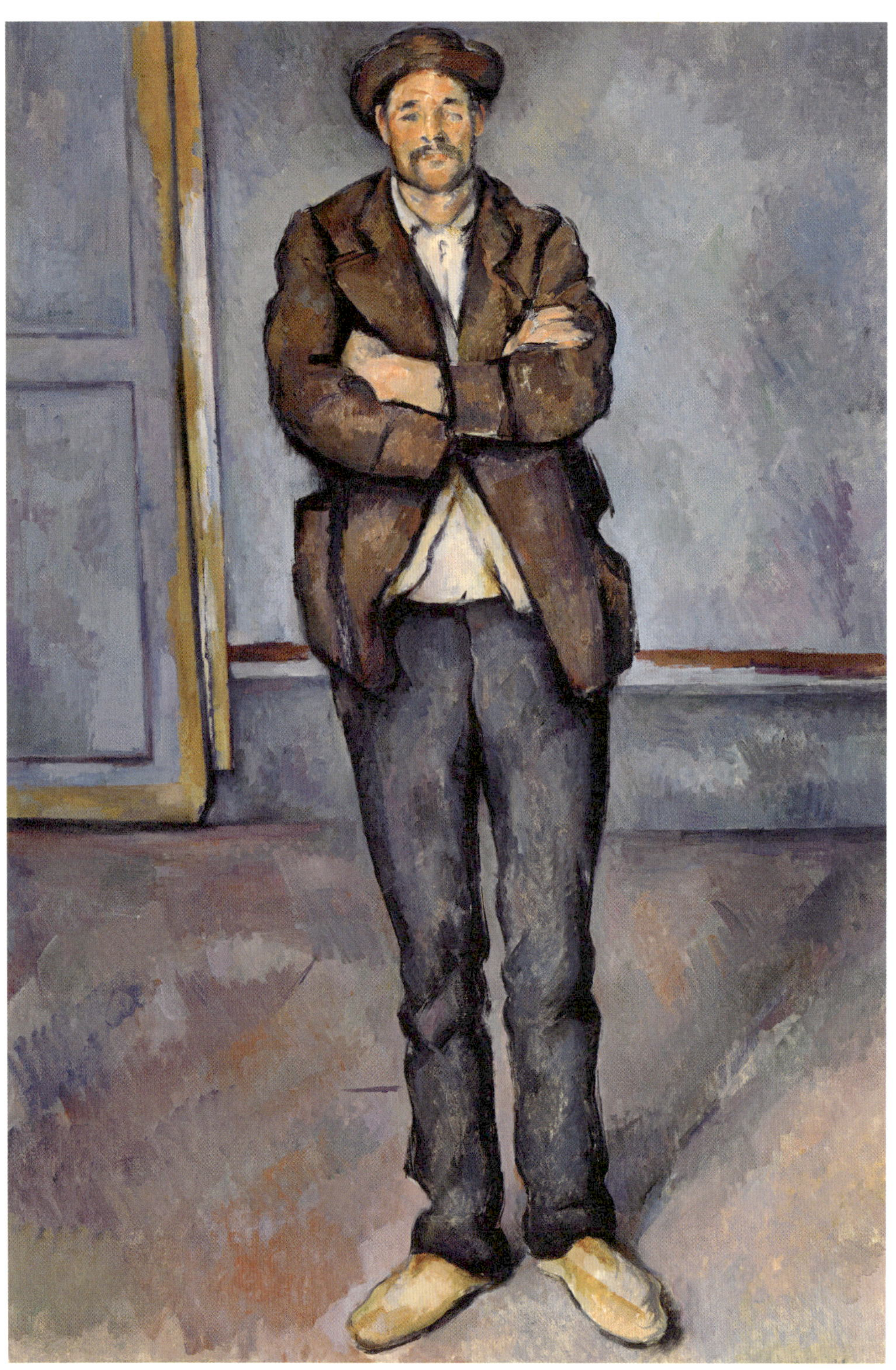

   Self-protection / Arms Folded

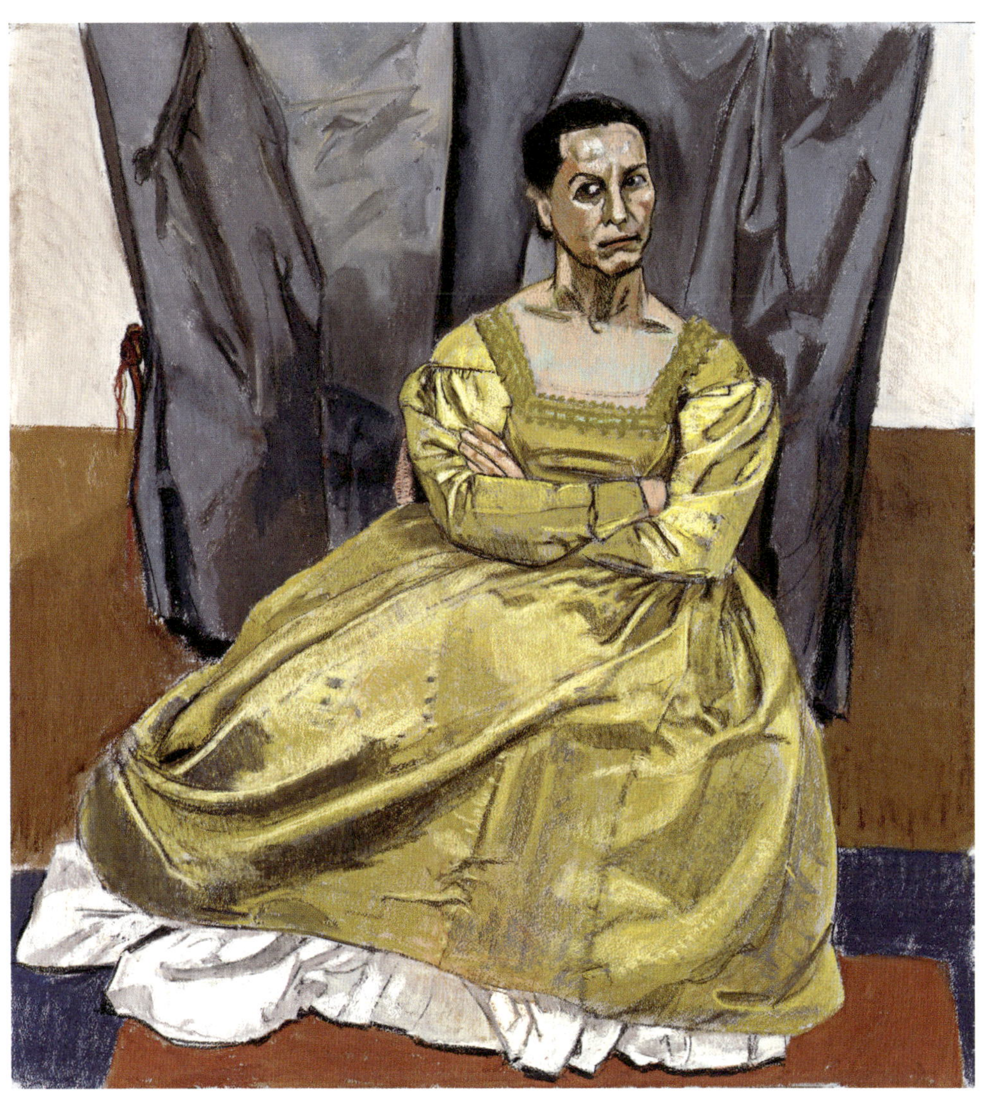

165. opposite **Paul Cézanne,**
Peasant Standing with Arms
***Crossed**, c. 1895, oil on canvas*

166. above **Paula Rego,**
central panel of the triptych
***Vanitas**, 2006, pastel on paper*

Arms Akimbo

The posture known as 'arms akimbo', which involves standing with the
hands on the hips and the elbows protruding sideways, appears in two
very different social contexts. On the one hand, it is often seen in early
portraits, in which it forms part of a pompous display of power by a high-
status individual (see p. 86); on the other, it can be a sign of embarrassed
dejection by someone who has just publicly lost face. But what do these
two seemingly contrasting scenarios have in common? The answer is
that, in both cases, the individuals involved are behaving in an anti-social
manner. In essence, the akimbo posture is a way of unconsciously saying,
'keep away from me, do not embrace me, do not hug me'. The protrusion
of the elbows at the side of the body forms an arrow shape pointing away
from the trunk, effectively telling everyone to keep back. Indeed, if one
did attempt to embrace someone with their arms akimbo, it would be
difficult to do so. When we adopt this posture, we may be unaware of the
visual statement that we are making, but the pointed elbows symbolically
issue a warning: don't come any closer.

The two examples shown here, *Portrait of a Man with Arms Akimbo*
(1658) [167] by Rembrandt, and *The Bellboy* (1925) [168] by the Russian-
French painter Chaïm Soutine, clearly demonstrate that these individuals,
by adopting the arms akimbo posture, are unconsciously protecting
themselves from any form of physical contact, albeit for very different
reasons. Rembrandt's figure is aloof, while Soutine's bellboy is dejectedly
lost in thought.

167. opposite, above **Rembrandt,**
Portrait of a Man with Arms Akimbo,
1658, oil on canvas

168. opposite, below **Chaïm Soutine,**
The Bellboy, **1925, oil on canvas**

     Self-protection / Arms Akimbo

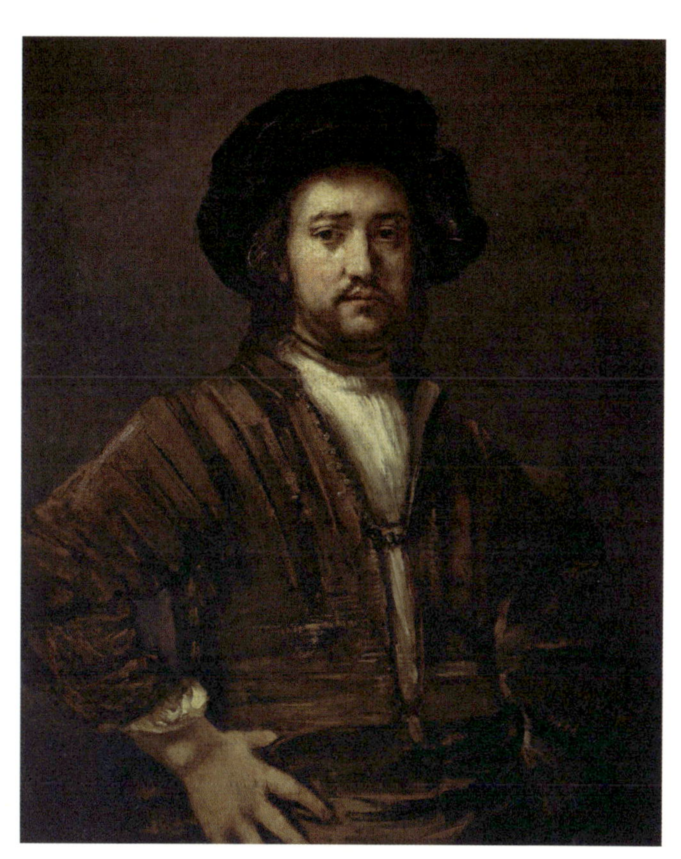

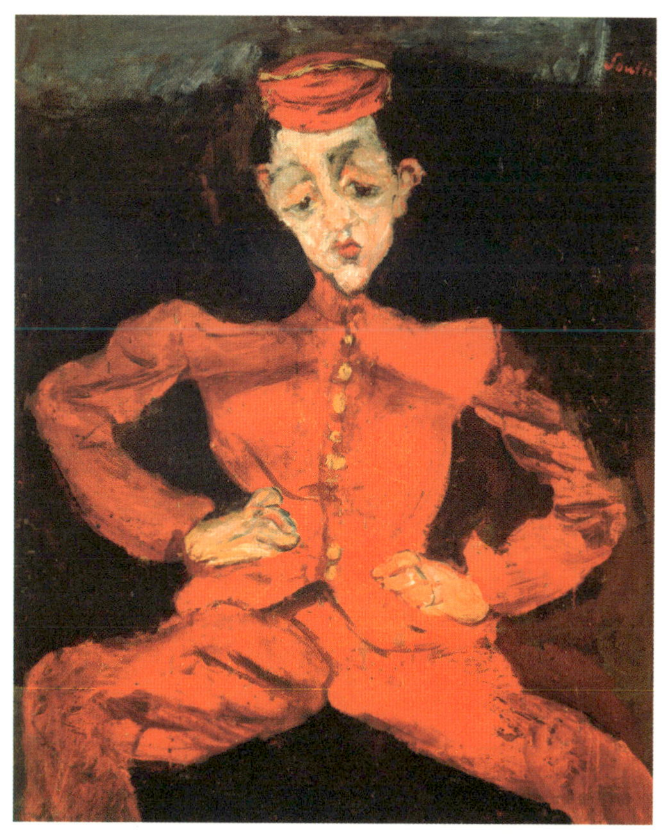

Fingers Crossed

'I am keeping my fingers crossed' is a popular expression in English-speaking countries. We say it when we are hoping for a good outcome; sometimes, we physically cross our fingers at the same time. This gesture – which consists of twisting the middle finger over the forefinger, while the other fingers are bent back and held under the thumb – is generally considered a sign of luck. It is performed in one of three ways. If the gesture is being made openly, the hand is held up for others to see. If it is being done secretly, the hand is kept in a pocket, or hidden in some other way. Lastly, in a special version of the 'secret' gesture, the hand is held behind the back. This particular version is performed when someone is telling a lie to the person standing in front of them, in the hope that it will protect them from retribution. It is usually done to let the person behind them know that what they are saying is false.

There have been several explanations of the origin of the 'fingers crossed' gesture, but arguably the most convincing is that it began as a secret way of making the sign of the cross. For early Christians, particularly those facing persecution, the gesture was a way to summon up the protection of the Holy Cross without disclosing their faith. As Christianity became more widely accepted, the gesture survived as a means of protection against ill fortune. Many people who use the gesture in a light-hearted way, to wish for good luck, are likely unaware of its possible origin as a symbol of the Christian cross.

An odd feature of the 'fingers crossed' gesture is that it appears to have been absent from Western art before the 20th century, despite the fact that it is widely recognized as a good luck sign across Europe. Today, the gesture remains popular in the world of street art. In 2014, a Baltimore street artist called Nether set out with a group of friends to decorate abandoned buildings in the city with murals that carried a social message. In several cases, he showed disadvantaged people making the 'fingers crossed' gesture [169], as a way of saying that they needed some luck in their lives.

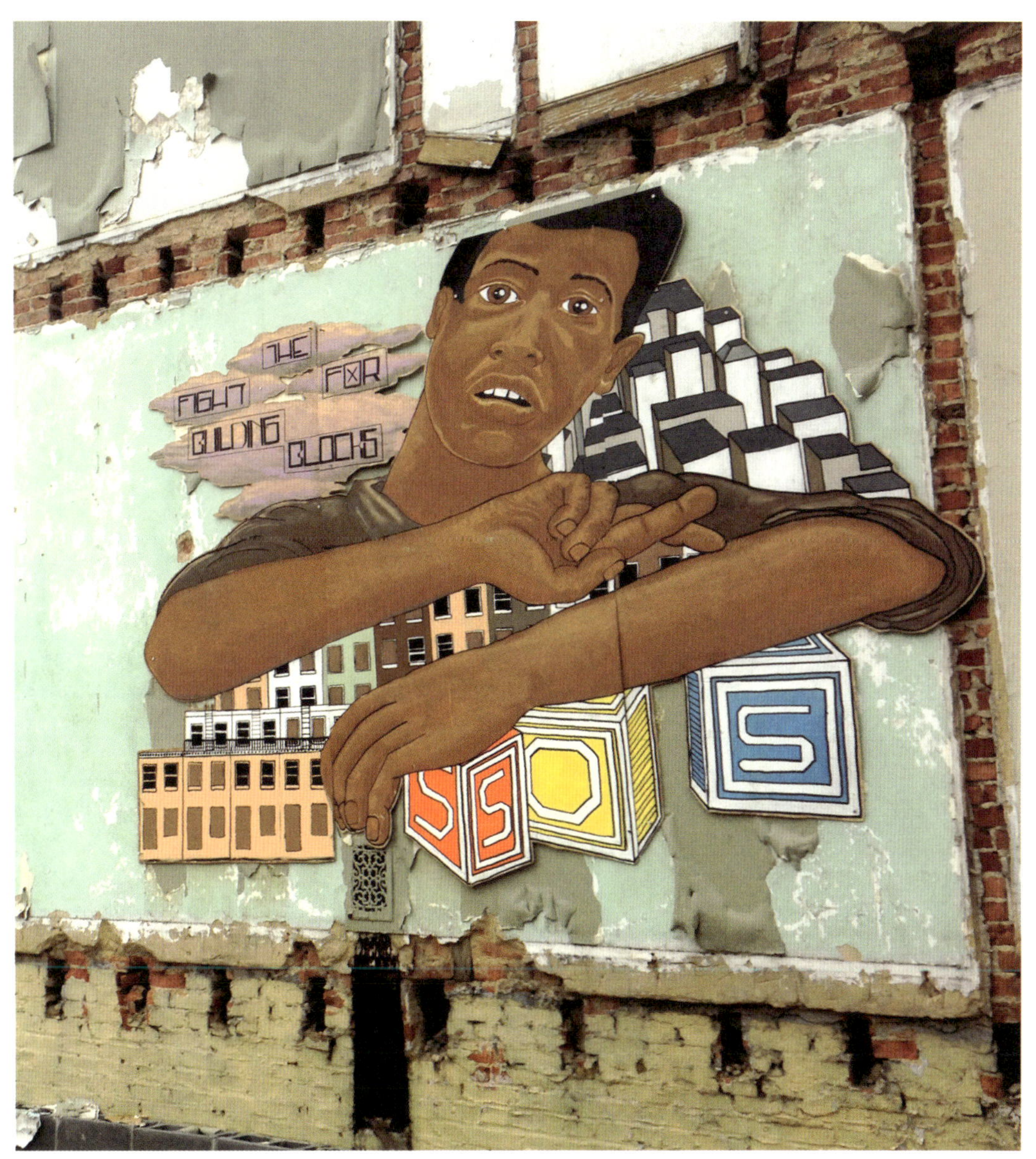

169. Nether, *The Fight for Building Blocks*, 2014, Baltimore, USA

Protective *Cornuta*

The gesture known as the *mano cornuta*, or 'horned hand', is made by extending the forefinger and little finger, while using the thumb to bend back the other two fingers. It is widely recognized in the Mediterranean, where it has two distinct uses: as a sexual insult (see p. 132), and as a protection against the evil eye. When the hand is held vertically, the gesture is nearly always intended as an insult. However, when the horned-hand sign is made horizontally, it has a protective function designed to shield the person making the gesture from a potential threat. In this context, it is similar to Catholics crossing themselves when they sense danger.

The protective form of the *cornuta* dates back hundreds of years. It originates from ancient bull worship, the finger-horns of the hand, as it is jabbed forward, symbolizing the charging of the great beast. It has been identified in wall paintings in ancient Etruscan tombs, and in early pottery of the Daunian culture that flourished in Italy around 500 BC. Early Christians also adopted it, and it appears as the hand of God, pointing down from the sky, in a mosaic in the Basilica of San Vitale in Ravenna [171], dating from the mid-6th century AD.

As mentioned, the *cornuta* gesture has been used to protect against the evil eye, a malevolent force that is thought to do you great harm if it fixes its gaze on you. This widely held superstition, which persists in many cultures to this day, was sometimes taken very seriously – as an incident described by the Italian antiquarian Andrea De Jorio, writing in 1832, reveals:

> Observing that a lady whom she believed to be a *jettatrice* [a woman who possessed the evil eye] was highly praising the beauty of her husband, and especially of his well formed thighs...she pretended to have need of a handkerchief. She therefore put her hand into her husband's pocket, and there made the *mano cornuta*. Then, with the points of her index and little fingers well extended, began to stab the thigh bone of her husband with such force as if she wanted to pierce through it... Nor did she leave off her preventative operation until the believed *jettatrice* turned her talk in another direction.

Belief in the evil eye was also present in the Romany culture in the 19th century. In a self-portrait by John Phillip [170], the travelling Scottish artist portrays himself making a field-sketch of a young female gypsy, who directs a horned hand at him to protect herself.

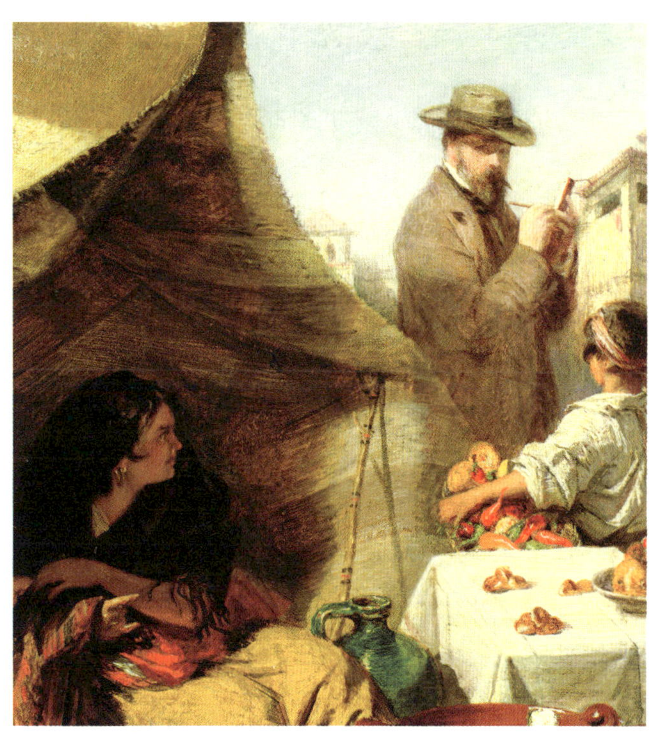

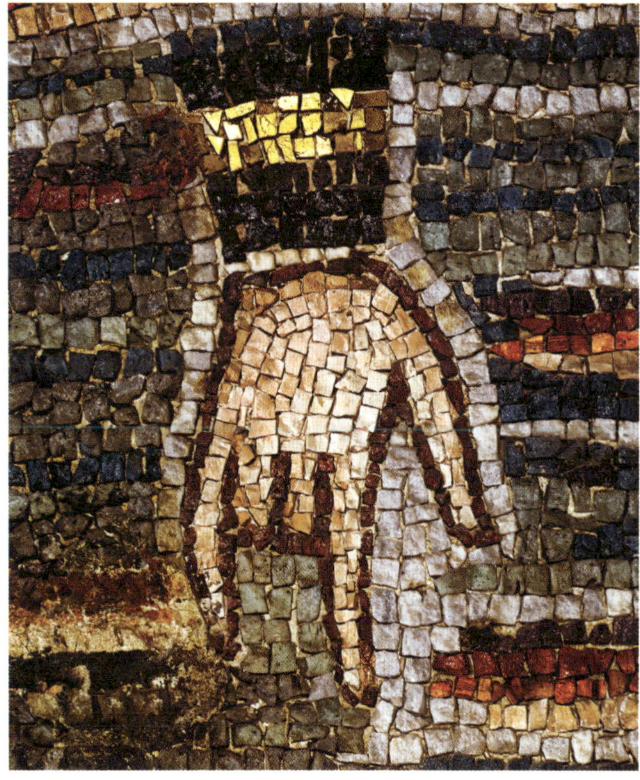

170. above **John Phillip,
The Evil Eye (detail), 1859,
oil on canvas**

171. right **Detail from *Sacrifices
of Abel and Melchizedek*, mid-6th
century AD, mosaic, Basilica of
San Vitale, Ravenna, Italy**

Tattoos

Today, tattoos are generally viewed in three different ways: as a sign of endurance (because their application is painful), as a form of body art, and as a symbol of social rebellion. To be tattooed is to belong to a select minority, and can therefore make an otherwise conventional person seem more interesting. In some cases, tattoos are displays of allegiance to a particular element or member of society – an organization, a club, a celebrity or a loved one.

All these modern considerations ignore one of the ancient functions of tattooing: to protect the bearer against ill fortune or evil spirits. Instead of wearing a lucky charm, a talisman or an amulet, which could be broken, lost or stolen, our ancient ancestors may have had their good luck emblems permanently inscribed on their skin. This is now largely forgotten in the West, but in certain parts of the world the protective role of tattooing – as opposed to its decorative appeal – remains its primary function. In Cambodia, for example, a protective tradition going back hundreds of years is still being practised. *Sak yant* are sacred, magical tattoos that are believed to ward off evil spirits and keep danger at bay. Each intricate pattern has its own unique significance, passed down from generation to generation. The tattooists are monks, who create the sacred patterns using a bamboo needle and carefully choose the appropriate protection for each person. One pattern may protect you from a hostile relative, another from being shot, and so on. The monks explain to their subjects that, if the magic of the tattoos is going to work, they must follow strict rules, such as avoiding alcohol and restricting their diet to certain foods. Once completed, the tattoo has to be blessed in a pagoda.

In the West, the mysticism of Eastern tattoos holds wide appeal, although the significance of such tattoos is often misunderstood. The Western fashion for traditional tattoos has been attributed, in part, to the Hollywood film star Angelina Jolie, who asked a master monk to inscribe an ancient Khmer script on her left shoulder when she visited Cambodia in 2003. Many young Westerners today, whether they realize it or not, have ancient protective tattoos, in addition to the purely decorative ones.

Among the most ancient tattoo traditions are those of certain North American indigenous peoples, the Samoans and other islanders in the South Pacific (who gave us the word 'tattoo'), and the Maori of New Zealand, where the designs are perhaps the most elaborate and complex of all. Nineteenth-century drawings and paintings bear testament to the dramatic facial tattoos displayed by high-ranking Maori [172].

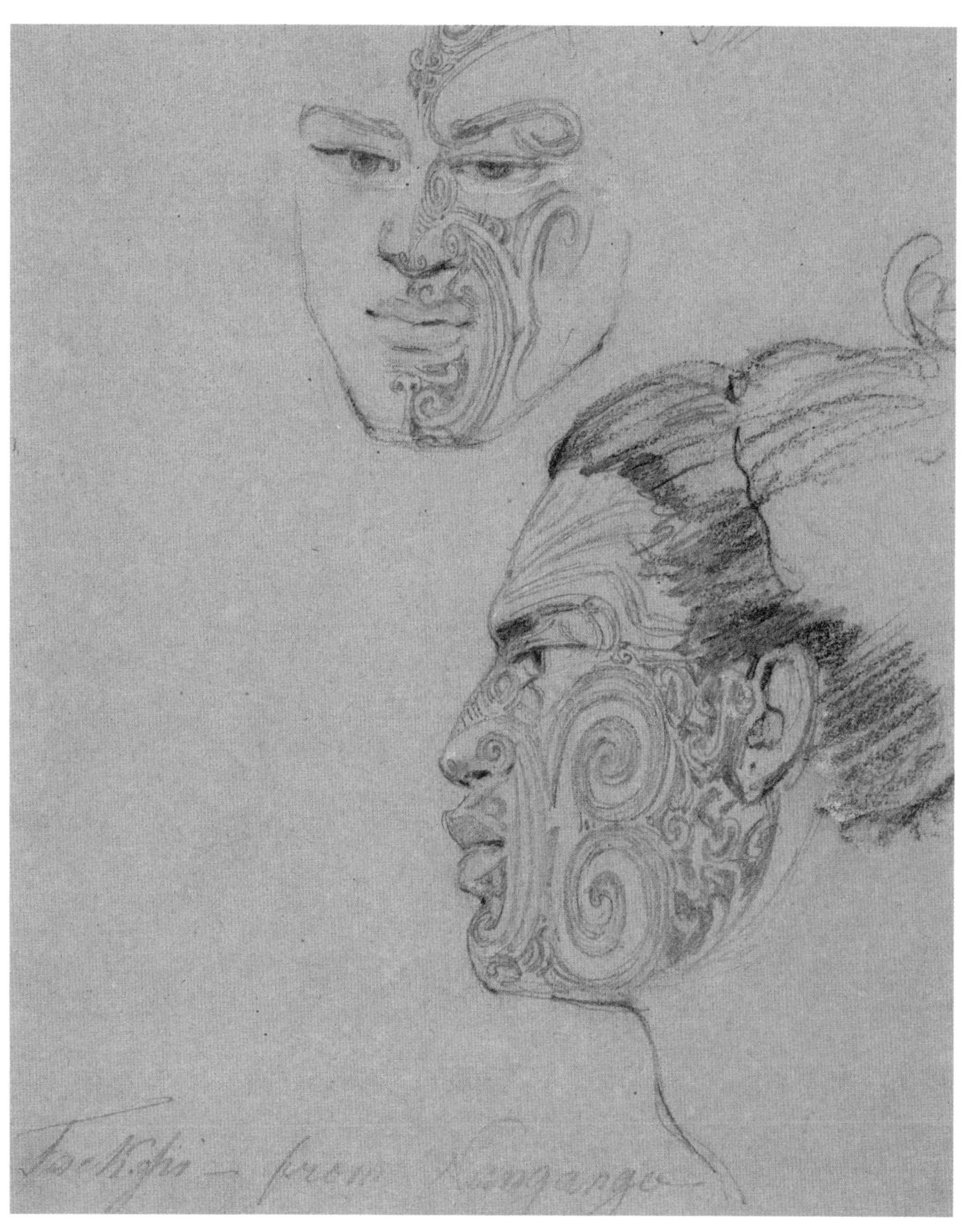

172. **Charles Rodius, two views
of a tattooed Maori man (detail),
1834–35, pencil, black chalk with
stump, heightened with white**

The Veil

A veil has been used as a protective device for thousands of years. Historically, its primary function has been to protect a woman's face from the prying eyes of men when she goes out in public. Three thousand years ago, in ancient Assyria, a woman of high social standing would always wear a veil in public because it was assumed that her elite status would automatically make her the subject of vulgar scrutiny. As a result, the veil became a symbol of high status, and women from the lower classes were forbidden to wear one. The punishment for disobeying this law was horrific, as the following excerpt from the *Middle Assyrian Law Code* demonstrates: 'Whoever sees a veiled prostitute shall seize her, secure witnesses, and bring her to the palace entrance. They shall...strike her 50 blows with rods; they shall pour hot pitch over her head... Slave-women shall not veil themselves, and he who should see a veiled slave-woman shall seize her and bring her to the palace entrance: they shall cut off her ears.'

A thousand years later, in ancient Greece, women of high status were expected to wear a veil in public, although they were supposed to seclude themselves as much as possible. In ancient Rome, young unmarried women were allowed to appear in public without a veil, but once they were married, they were required by their husbands to wear one.

In a sense, this is the opposite of what happens at a traditional Christian wedding ceremony, where the bride-to-be arrives at the church wearing a wedding veil, which is then removed only once the ceremony has been completed. The roots of this practice are deeply embedded in superstitions of the past, when people believed in evil spirits that could cause harm, including the evil eye. All kinds of strange measures were introduced to protect people from such threats. It was thought that evil spirits were especially attracted to life's happier moments, and weddings were an obvious target. So the bride-to-be's face was covered to protect her – not from the prying eyes of lustful men, but from a malevolent supernatural force. The veil could be lifted as soon as the couple had been declared man and wife because it was believed that, once married, a woman had her husband's protection.

Historically, in the West, a wife was expected to wear a veil of some sort on the death of her husband – as a sign of mourning, but also to protect her from inappropriate male attention – although customs differ hugely between cultures and have evolved over time. Today, the veil remains widely used in strict Muslim societies, in which it functions primarily as a display of modesty.

Despite being notoriously difficult to portray, the veil has been widely depicted in art. One of the finest examples is the statue known as *Veiled Truth* (1750) at the Cappella Sansevero in Naples. The statue is made of marble – a medium that seems far too solid to mimic a flimsy material – and shows the incredible skill of the Venetian artist Antonio Corradini, who has masterfully conveyed the sense of a swathed, veiled figure. However, at the time, the statue caused controversy because it was commissioned as a memorial, and the revealing details visible beneath the veil were deemed by some to be inappropriate for a funerary monument.

In the following century, a similar criticism could have been levelled at the French artist Jean-Léon Gérôme's *Veiled Circassian Woman* (1876) [174]. The elegant lady depicted in the picture wears a black veil, perhaps suggesting that she is in mourning for the death of her spouse, but both her hair and her cleavage are clearly visible. A possible explanation is that the *Circassian Woman* is a fanciful orientalist invention by Gérôme, who loved to portray the Middle East in a highly romanticized manner. He first visited the region in 1856, travelling through Egypt, the Holy Land and Syria, which triggered a whole genre of idealized scenes of Arab life that became popular back in Europe.

In 19th-century England, a young Italian artist, Raffaelle Monti, followed in the footsteps of Corradini, working, like him, in the difficult medium of marble to create a highly skilful veiled figure of a woman – *Veiled Vestal Virgin* (1846–47) [173]. It is said that, when this statue was first exhibited, Victorian audiences refused to believe that the marble veil was not made of some delicate fabric.

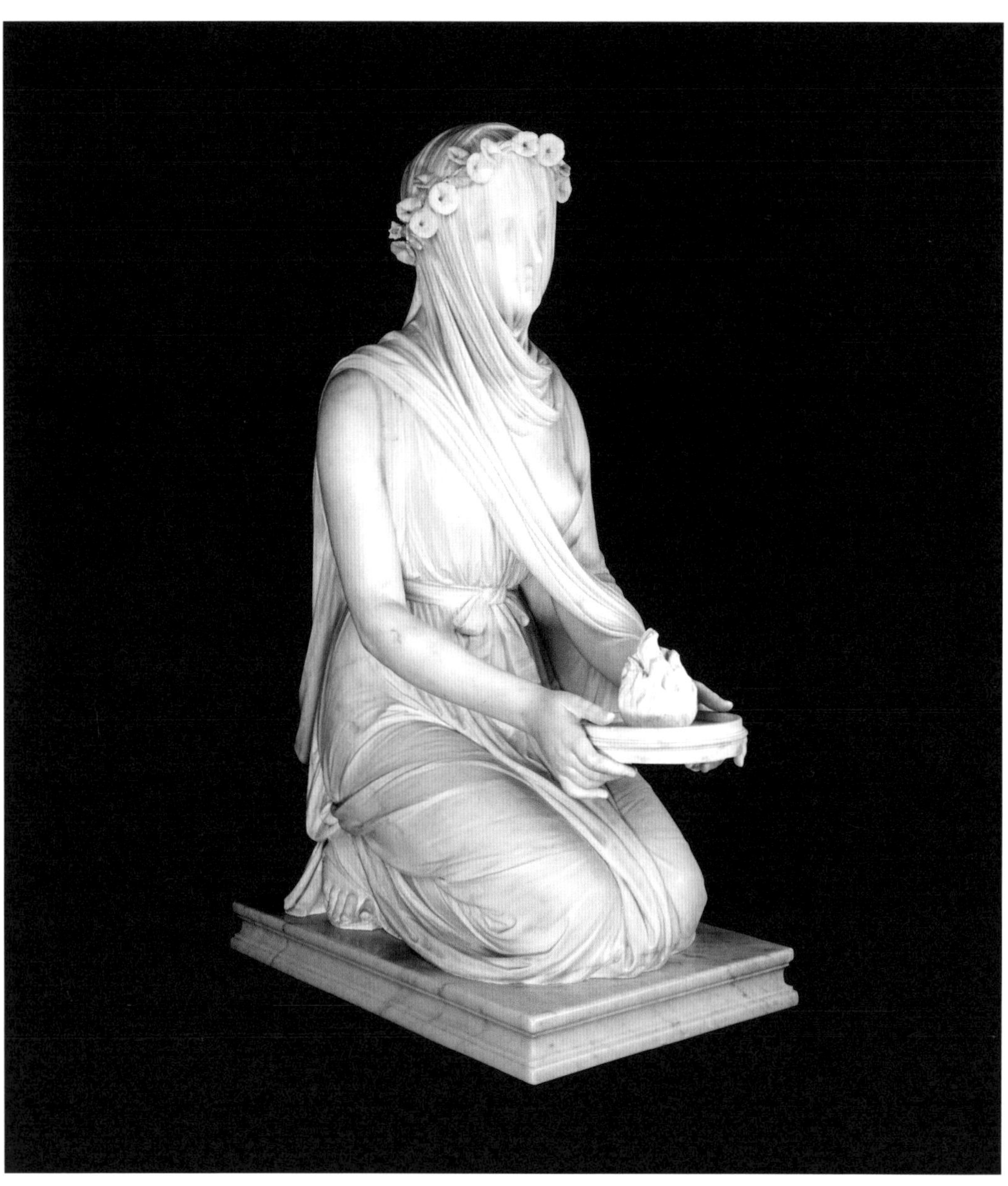

173. above **Raffaelle Monti,**
Veiled Vestal Virgin, 1846–47, marble,
Chatsworth House, England

174. opposite, above **Jean-Léon Gérôme,**
Veiled Circassian Woman, 1876,
oil on canvas

175. opposite, below **Edmund Blair
Leighton,** *Olivia*, 1887, oil on canvas

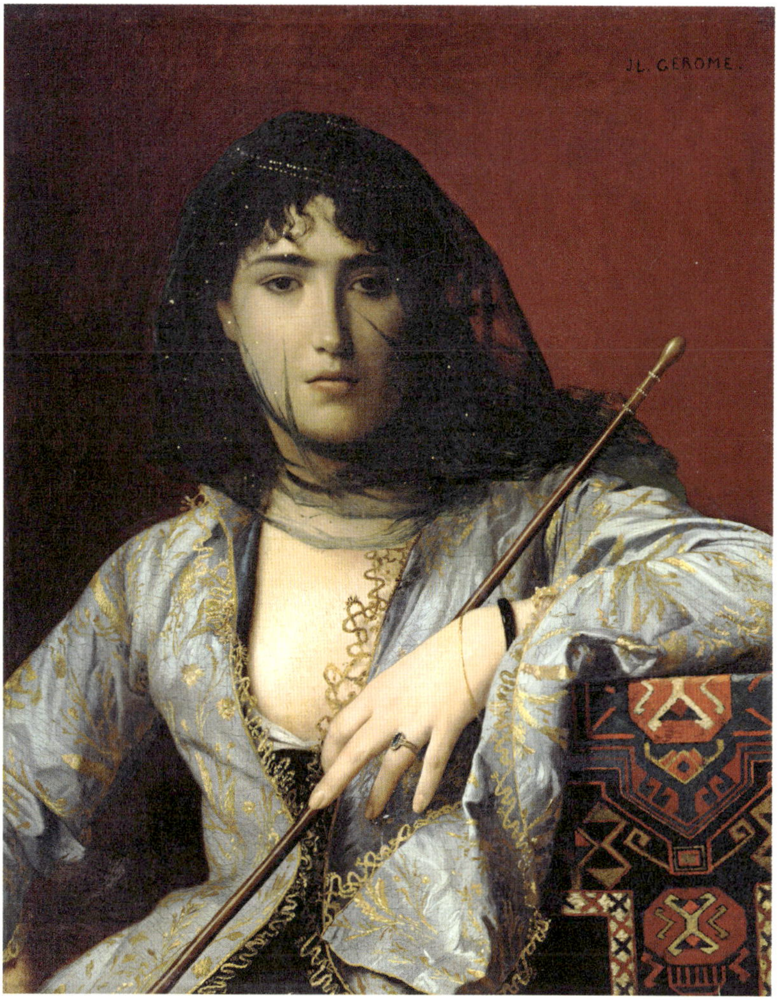

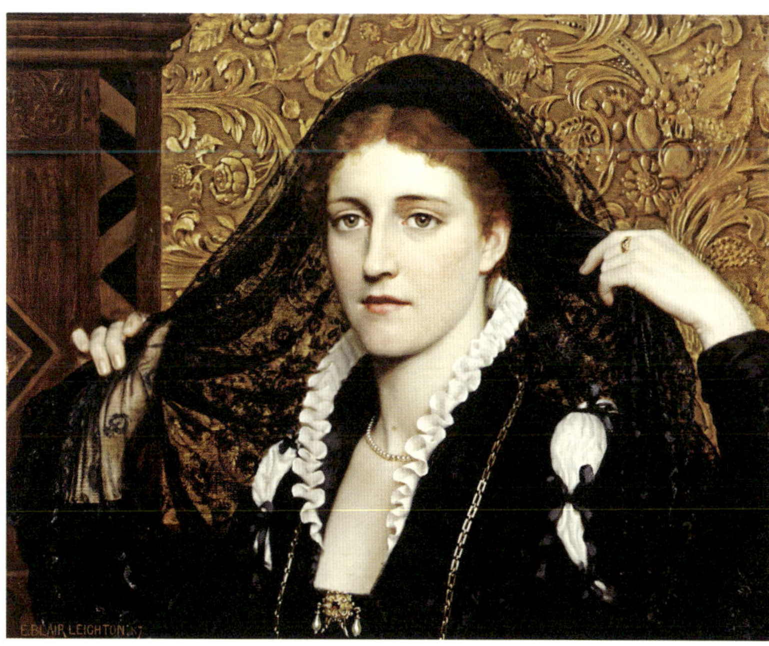

The
Erotic

Works of art that portray sexual body language fall into two distinct groups: the erotic, or sensual, and the explicit, or pornographic. It is surprising just how many major artists have, from time to time, reverted to the latter, portraying the anatomical facts of sexual interaction in such salacious detail that the paintings in question have rarely been displayed to the general public. Such artists include Picasso, Dalí, André Masson, Leonor Fini, Roberto Matta, Jean Dubuffet, Hans Bellmer, Balthus, Gilbert & George, Man Ray, Karel Appel, George Grosz, Egon Schiele, Gustav Klimt, Auguste Rodin, J. M. W. Turner, Gustave Courbet, Aubrey Beardsley, Henry Fuseli, Thomas Rowlandson, and even Rembrandt. When an artist chooses to depict the genitals, for example, in deliberately obscene detail, this particular element inevitably overwhelms the rest of the painting, making it almost impossible to view as a work of art in the conventional sense. For this reason, I am not including such depictions in this book.

Where there is, instead, an attempt to convey the sensuality of the human body, the results are often intriguing. Paintings that belong to this group tend to fall into one of several, often overlapping categories. The most obvious example is the female nude, which has been a favourite subject of countless artists for generations, and the depiction of the female breast in particular. Less obtrusive are scenes of tender, tentative courtship, which may include an embrace between lovers or a mouth-to-mouth kiss. Finally, there are depictions of bondage with strong erotic undertones, which usually have a mythological or legendary setting that serves as a convenient disguise.

The Nude

Attitudes towards nudity vary enormously depending on culture and context, and have evolved over time. Historically, people in Western societies were expected to cover up, and the baring of flesh would have caused shock and disgust. In Victorian England, for example, if a woman lifted her dress a little and showed her ankle, it was seen as improper. Nowadays, while Western attitudes towards nudity are more tolerant than they once were, citizens are still expected to uphold public decency. In 2003–4, a British man called Stephen Gough, who became known as the 'Naked Rambler', put nudity laws to the test by attempting to walk the length of Great Britain – from Land's End in the south to John O'Groats in the north – wearing only his boots and socks, a rucksack, and sometimes a hat. It took him several months to complete the 900-mile (1,450 km) trek, and much of that time was spent in jail.

In many parts of the world, artists have the freedom to exhibit almost any kind of nudity they choose, including sexually explicit activities. One of the last cases of the police closing down an exhibition in the UK occurred in 1970, when a show of John Lennon's drawings in London was cut short on the grounds of obscenity. One year later, a feminist art exhibition by Margaret Harrison was also shut down by the police because it included images of Captain America and Hugh Hefner in drag with their genitals showing (Hefner's were in the shape of a rabbit's head).

In 2014, a female performance artist, Deborah de Robertis, went into the Musée d'Orsay in Paris, walked over to Gustave Courbet's *The Origin of the World* (1866), which offers a close-up view of the female pudendum, and recreated the infamous painting in the flesh by sitting on the floor in front of it with her legs apart. She was applauded by visitors to the gallery, who were soon ushered out by the museum staff. The artist was then arrested. This event sums up the difference in public attitudes towards the nude in art and the nude in real life. Clearly, painted or sculpted nudity has some kind of licence to exist that real nudity lacks.

The history of the nude in Western art is a complex one. Generally speaking, nudity has been freely permitted and accepted in art if it has fallen into one of two categories. The first includes works of art that celebrate human anatomy. This type of nudity has existed in art for millennia, but is particularly associated with ancient Greece. The second category centres on non-sexual activities that require the removal of clothing, such as bathing, washing and swimming, or scenes of punishment, martyrdom or humiliation in which the subject has been stripped naked. In this context, the artist can use the activity as an excuse for exposing naked flesh, while the viewer can claim that their interest in the scene has nothing to do with its erotic undertones. This pretence shared by both the artist and the viewer, which applies equally to studies of human anatomy, has enabled such works to be publicly displayed – often at times when, if similar degrees of nudity were present in daily life, it would have been illegal or socially condemned.

It was in ancient Greece that artists first sought to portray the naked human form in an anatomically correct way, and in naturalistic postures. The Romans followed suit, but, after the fall of Rome in the 5th century AD, the nude virtually disappeared as a subject for major works of art. It resurfaced with the Renaissance, and although the proportions of the naked bodies depicted in paintings at that time were at first rather stylized – as in the work of Lucas Cranach the Elder [176] – they gradually became more accurate and naturalistic.

Perhaps the most famous nude of all time is *The Rokeby Venus* (1647–51) [178] by the Spanish artist Diego Velázquez, which avoided censorship by showing the subject of the painting from behind. By having the small, winged Cupid in the composition, the artist also made it clear that this was not a portrait of a real person, but a mythological scene. This was a device used by many artists to allow them to paint naked figures without being accused of obscenity, although this particular painting clearly did excite male interest. When Velázquez's masterpiece was exhibited at the National Gallery in London in 1914, a suffragette – who became known as 'Slasher Mary' – was so outraged by the sight of men staring at it that she attacked the painting with a meat chopper, making five deep cuts. When asked why she had chosen to attack the painting, she replied that she was angry at 'the way men visitors gawped at it all day long'.

At the beginning of the 19th century, the Spanish master Francisco Goya became involved in a scandal concerning his famous reclining nude, *The Naked Maja* (1795–1800) [177]. The painting had been kept by the Spanish prime minister, Manuel de Godoy, in a private room for several years when it was discovered by investigators for the Spanish Inquisition. It was deemed to be 'indecent and prejudicial to the public good', and the prime minister was forced to name the artist involved. Goya was then summoned before a tribunal and accused of 'moral depravity'. He managed to escape prosecution on the grounds that he was following in a tradition of officially accepted nude paintings. He was lucky, because his painting had taken a liberty that *The Rokeby Venus* and earlier nudes had avoided. Goya had not presented his nude woman as a mythological being, but had taken the bold step of making her a real person, with a face that smiles straight at the viewer of her naked body.

In the mid-19th century, the French artist Jean-Léon Gérôme also found a way of showing erotic nudes without causing a scandal. He had travelled extensively in the Near East, at a time when slavery was still being practised, and the slave market was a recurrent theme in his work.

By depicting a naked female slave being offered for sale, he allowed the viewers of the work to express their moral outrage while at the same time admiring the beauty of the human form. In *The Slave Market* (1866), he shows a prospective buyer examining the teeth of an unclothed female slave in an open-air market, while the slave-trader looks on. Gérôme made the setting and context so distant from the society of 19th-century Europe that he got away with depicting a real woman in the flesh. Similarly, in *Phryne Revealed before the Areopagus* (1861) [179], by using the story of a legendary courtesan in ancient Greece who was put on trial for impiety and disrobed before the jury, the artist was able to avoid a public outcry. In both these paintings, however, Gérôme is careful not to show the female sexual anatomy in any detail, which would have been a step too far for 19th-century sensitivities – at least, in a public context.

At the height of Victorian prudery, while nude paintings did still appear, the women depicted were usually shown in coy postures that obscured their erogenous zones. Even in the few cases in which these were visible, the pubic region – as in the case of Gérôme's paintings – lacked any kind of detail. This doll-like version of the adult female body was so widely known in art at the time that, when the art historian John Ruskin was married and discovered, on his wedding night, that his wife had pubic hair, he is said to have been so horrified that he was unable to make love to her. The marriage was never consummated, and was eventually annulled.

At the other extreme are those works of art that are blatantly sensual. One historic example is a female nude by François Boucher [180], which is thought to depict one of Louis XV's young mistresses, an Irish girl by the name of Louise O'Murphy. She had been seduced at the age of thirteen by Casanova, who had then commissioned a nude portrait of her. When the French king saw that painting, he is said to have been so enamoured that he took her as one of his mistresses, and later asked Boucher to immortalize her. Boucher's painting shows her in a very suggestive pose, lying fully naked on her front, with her legs apart.

In the late 19th century, the French sculptor Auguste Rodin started making a long series of rapid sketches from life. Rodin asked his naked female models not to adopt any formal poses but simply to sit, sprawl, stretch, dance, lie or move about in a completely natural manner while he made what he called 'drawings without looking', keeping his eyes fixed on the models rather than what was emerging on the paper. The result was a set of magically spontaneous drawings that were far ahead of their time. Rodin commented, 'I know why my drawings have this intensity: it's because I do not intervene. Between nature and paper, I eliminated talent. I do not reason. I simply let myself go.' When some of the drawings were exhibited at the Weimar Fine Arts Museum in 1906, they caused so much controversy that Count Harry Kessler, the museum's flamboyant director, was dismissed.

In the 20th century, the nude portraits of two artists stand out above all others in terms of their erotic impact. When the Italian artist Amedeo Modigliani arrived in Paris in 1906, he devoted himself wholeheartedly to his twin passions: drugs and sex. He was at his most productive when he had indulged in his favourite combination of hashish, absinthe and cocaine. The twenty-two nude paintings of his young lovers that he completed before his death, at the age of thirty-five, set a new standard in sexual intensity. When some of them were exhibited in Paris in 1917, they caused a sensation and the police closed the show. The main objection, voiced by one of the police officers, was that the nudes were displaying pubic hair; but the truth was that Modigliani had somehow managed to depict a raw sensuality so powerful that the only question in the viewer's mind when looking at one of the paintings was whether the naked woman and the artist had just made love, or were just about to [181]. Working at around the same time, the Austrian artist Egon Schiele also created a stir with his provocatively erotic portraits of women in a variety of contorted postures. In 1912, Schiele caused such outrage that he was arrested and imprisoned for making pornographic pictures, but this did not stop him from continuing to produce erotic portraits, such as the now famous *Reclining Woman* (1917). In this painting, a woman is depicted with her breasts exposed and her legs wide apart – her sex partly covered by a sheet wrapped around her waist.

Later in the 20th century, the Belgian artist Paul Delvaux also had a great fondness for the female form, and many of his large surrealist canvases show naked women standing around like sleepwalkers in seemingly incongruous urban locations. In these works, the contrast between the nudity and the setting intensifies the impact of the naked figures. Picasso also created a number of famous nudes, but his were more curvaceous and playfully voluptuous than intensely erotic. Likewise, when his compatriot Joan Miró produced nude figures, they were usually so abstracted or distorted that their explicit and often enlarged sexual anatomy became little more than visual symbols.

The most celebrated nudes of recent years – those by the British artist Lucian Freud – are so brutally unflattering that they lack even the smallest hint of eroticism. Since then, the painted nude has been in decline, although nudity has been employed in a number of ways in the sphere of performance art, as well as in other, non-painterly artistic activities.

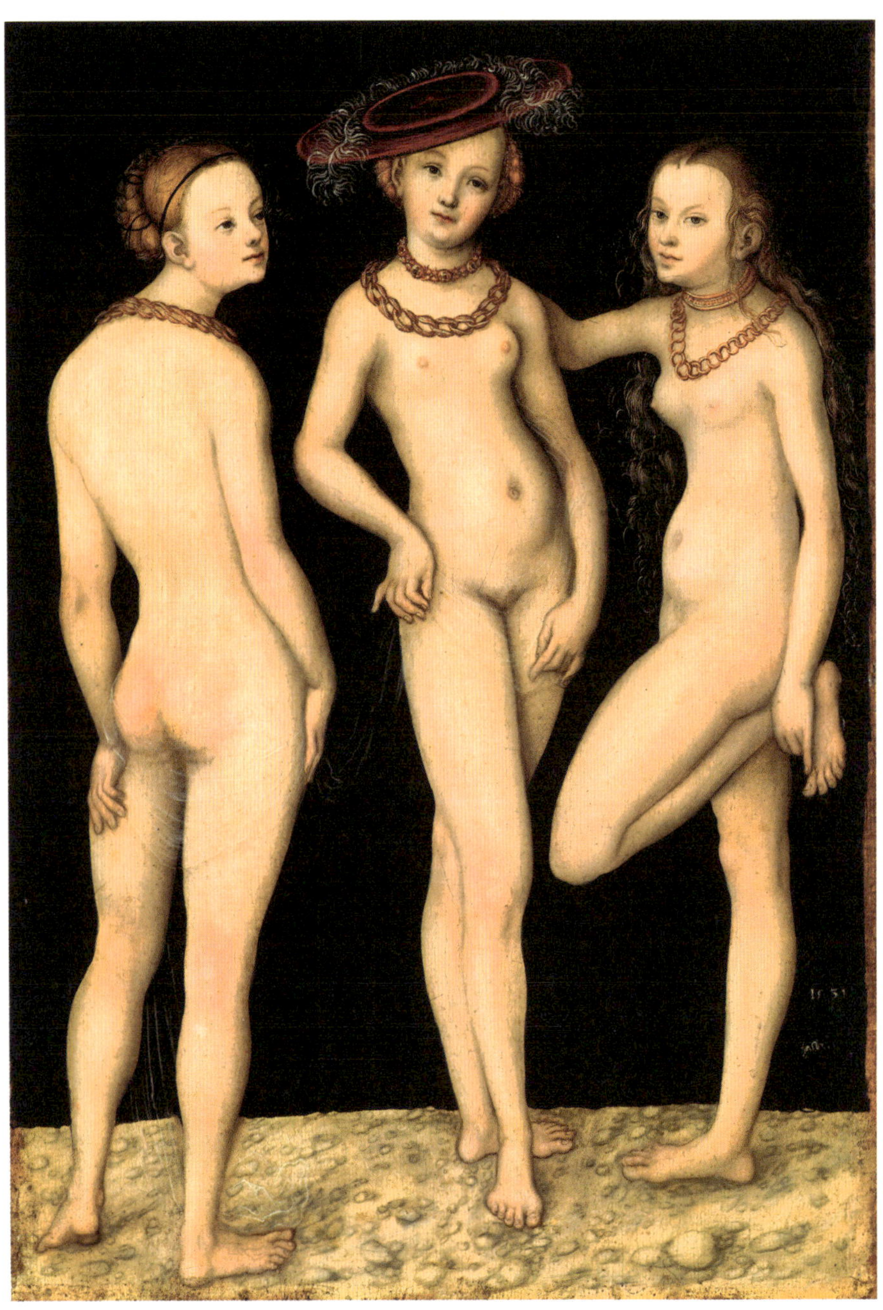

176. **Lucas Cranach
the Elder, *The Three Graces*,
1531, oil on wood**

      The Erotic / The Nude

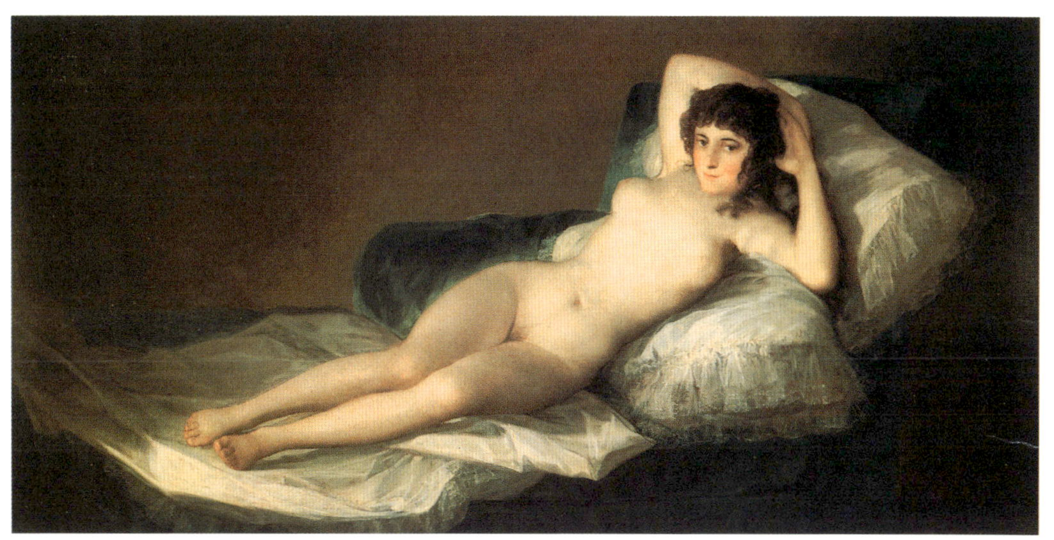

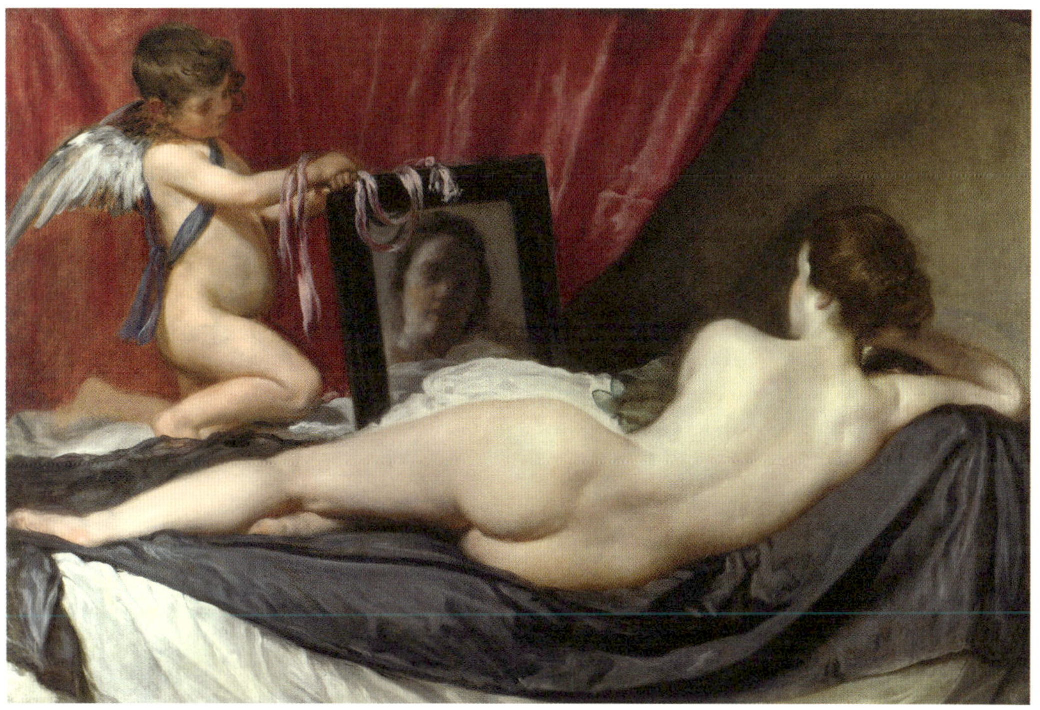

177. top **Francisco Goya,**
The Naked Maja, 1795–1800,
oil on canvas

178. above **Diego Velázquez,**
The Rokeby Venus (detail),
1647–51, oil on canvas

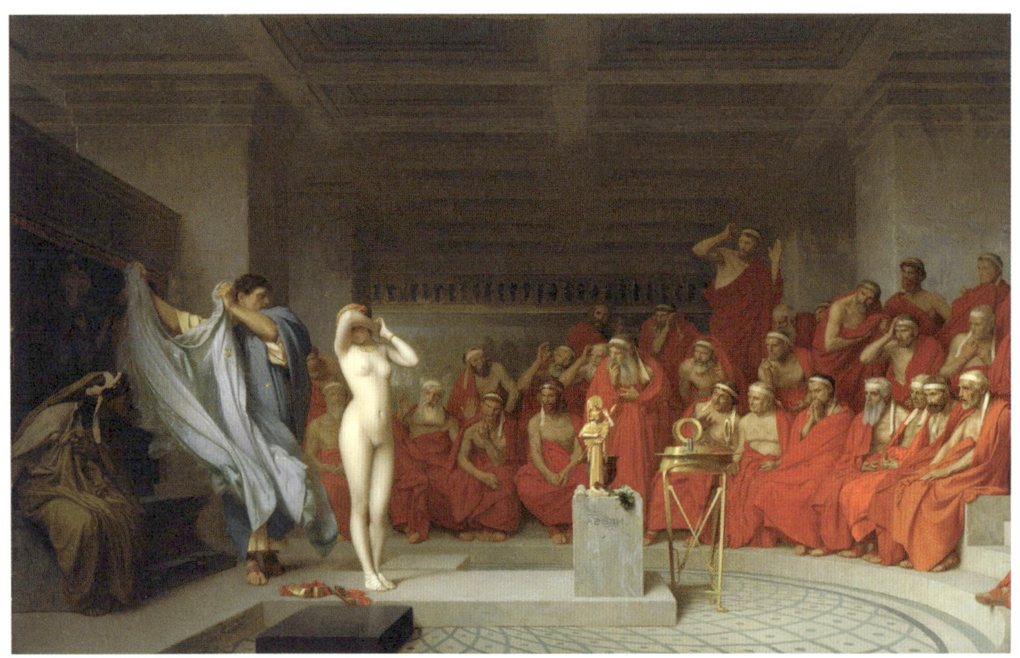

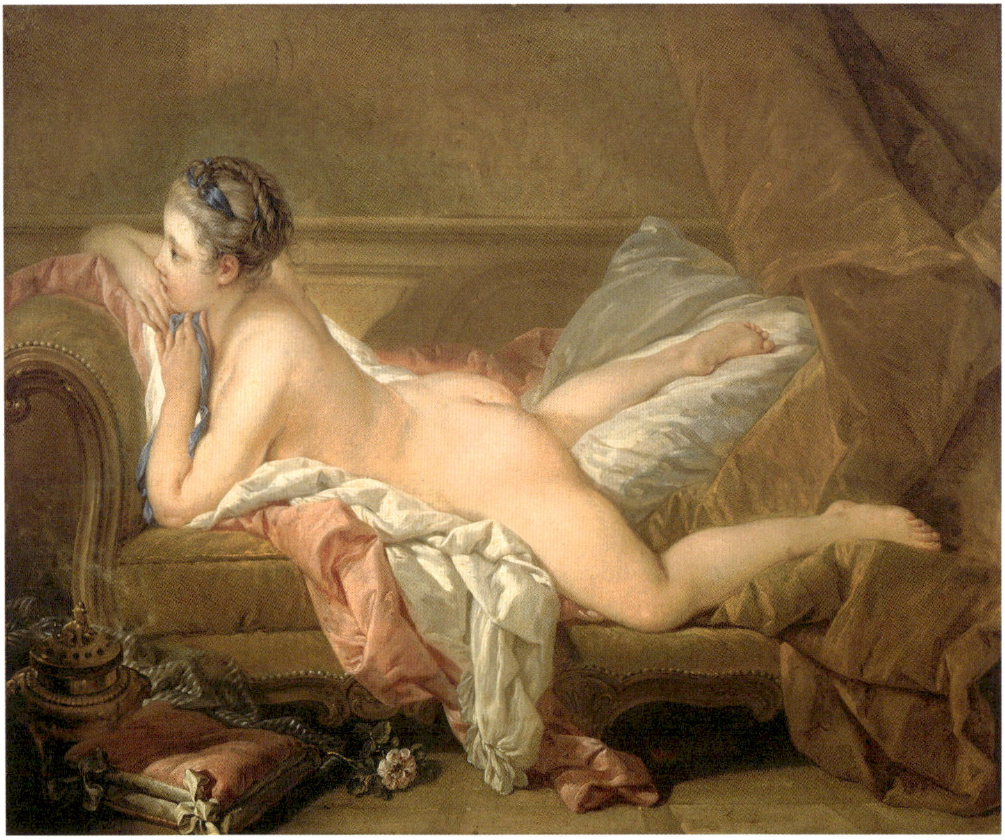

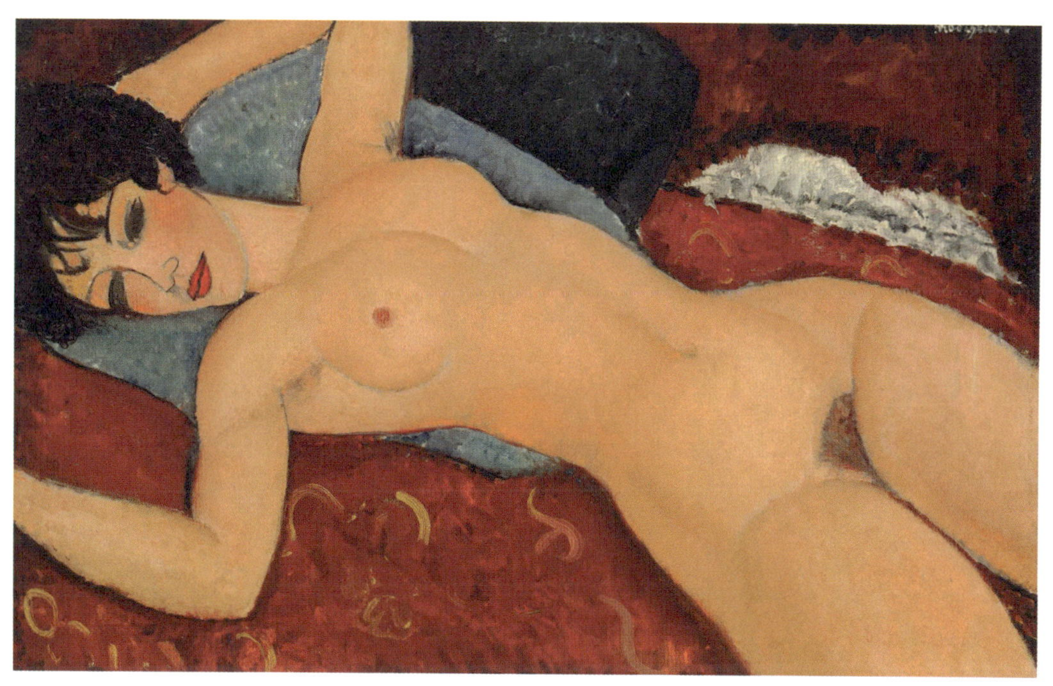

179. opposite, above **Jean-Léon Gérôme,
Phryne Revealed before the Areopagus,
1861, oil on canvas**

180. opposite, below **François Boucher,
Louise O'Murphy, 1752, oil on canvas**

181. above **Amedeo Modigliani,
Reclining Nude, 1917, oil on canvas**

The Female Breast

The female breast plays a special role in erotic art. Although the breast has a practical function in supplying babies with milk, there is strong evidence that its shape is purely sexual. To understand this claim, one has to look at our closest animal relatives. Female monkeys and apes are flat-chested, and it is only when they are lactating that the area around the nipples becomes swollen. Even then, it does not approach the hemispherical shape of the human female breast. Also, when a baby monkey or ape has been weaned, the mother's chest becomes flat again. The female breast in humans is very different, becoming rounded at puberty and remaining hemispherical for the entire reproductive life of the woman, whether she is lactating or not. An examination of the physiology of the breast reveals that most of its bulk is made up of fat tissue, and only a small part is glandular tissue related to milk production. The inevitable conclusion is that the shape of the human female breast acts as a sexual signal. In evolutionary terms, this unique feature of our species is linked to the fact that we stand upright and spend a great deal of time facing one another, so that the appropriate place for such sexual signals is on the front of the body. Historically, artists who wanted to make their works more appealing to a male audience by including the female breast could use its function as a maternal organ as a pretext, to avoid censorship.

In Western art, the female breast has a long history – indeed, a long prehistory. The earliest known Venus figurine, the Venus of Hohle Fels [182], dating from between 35,000 and 40,000 years ago, has an enormous pair of almost spherical breasts that dominate her anatomy, presenting an image of exaggerated sexuality. In the thousands of years that followed, many more Venus figurines displayed conspicuous breasts, which are often cupped by the hands to emphasize their presence. Another remarkable figurine is a Minoan snake goddess, dating from 1600 BC. Found on the island of Crete, the figurine is fully covered except for her prominent white breasts and holds a serpent aloft in each hand, foreshadowing the story of Eve in the Garden of Eden. The dramatic emphasis of her breasts marks her out as a vivid symbol of female sexuality.

In the ancient civilizations of Greece and Rome, the naked female breast is reduced to more naturalistic proportions, but still plays an important role, especially in the case of nude female statues. It also appears in a number of the erotic frescoes found in Pompeii.

The female breast then disappears for about a thousand years, resurfacing in the religious context of the Madonna nursing the infant Christ. It was not until roughly the 16th century that the female breast became 'secularized'. One of the most famous examples from this period is a portrait of a young woman, known as *La Fornarina* (1518–19) [185], by Raphael. 'La Fornarina' is the nickname given to one of the artist's lovers, a baker's daughter, although the identity of the sitter has been questioned. There has been a great deal of academic debate about why her right hand is touching her left breast. It has been suggested that she may have been breastfeeding a baby whom she had had by Raphael, and the sensitivity of that breast was causing her discomfort. Others have argued that she's trying to conceal a medical condition, and point to the fact that the breast seems to have a strange shape; in fact, the apparent indentation in the left breast seems to be the result of the strong light falling on the figure from the left-hand side of the painting, which has caused the forefinger of the right hand to cast a dark shadow across it. A more plausible explanation as to why the figure touches her breast is that she is raising her hand to cover it (or, perhaps, to keep in place the piece of sheer material she is holding) – a gesture of token modesty, to show that she is aware she has been asked to pose in a manner that would have been seen as improper at the time. Its effect on the viewer, of course, is to draw attention to the naked breast and heighten the portrait's erotic appeal.

One of the strangest paintings to focus on the female breast also dates from this period. *Gabrielle d'Estrées and One of her Sisters* (*c.* 1594) [183], by an anonymous artist, shows two young women taking a bath together. With its strongly erotic mood, it has sometimes been used as an icon of lesbian love; in reality, however, it is thought to depict an affectionate scene between two sisters, with the figure on the left teasing the other about being pregnant. The figure on the right is believed to be Gabrielle d'Estrées, mistress to King Henry IV of France, who is pregnant with his child; her sister is depicted playfully tweaking her nipple, as if to say, 'You'll soon be needing this'. The artist likely used this maternal reference to allow him to portray what is, by any standards, a highly erotic work of art.

In the early 17th century, it became popular to have one's portrait painted in fancy dress. One of the most popular themes was the shepherdess, and fashionable young women would pose wearing a highly romanticized costume that was nothing like the rough clothing worn by working women tending their sheep. Dressing up in this way allowed them to be someone else for a moment and, in this other role, to behave in a more uninhibited way than if they were wearing their own clothes.

Late in his life, Rembrandt also painted portraits in which sitters would dress up in historical costumes. A famous example is the work known as *The Jewish Bride*, painted around 1665–69, shortly before Rembrandt's death at the age of sixty-three. The title was not his, but was given to the work in the 19th century. Although uncertainty surrounds the subject, it is widely believed to show an amorous couple in historical dress, enjoying a private moment of physical intimacy. Vincent van Gogh was so impressed by its loving tenderness that he said he would give up ten years of his life just to be able to sit in front of it for two weeks.

In 17th-century England, the return to the throne of the liberally minded King Charles II saw the female breast reassert itself in works of art, following the strict prudery of the Cromwellian period. A well-known portrait of the king's mistress, Nell Gwyn, dating from about 1670 and attributed to Simon Verelst, shows her exposing her breasts in a blatantly erotic manner. It is said that, during this relaxed period, female necklines became so low that a lady's dressing table would routinely display pots of carnelian employed as make-up for nipples.

Perhaps one of the greatest celebrations of the beauty of the female breast is a miniature entitled *Beauty Revealed* (1828) [184], painted on ivory by the American artist Sarah Goodridge. There seems little doubt that this self-portrait – painted using a mirror – was a gift for the man she loved. Although, in fact, he married someone else, he never parted with this special gift. It is difficult to imagine a more delicately erotic depiction of the subject, the impact of which is heightened by the way the artist has framed her breasts with clothing, eliminating all other details of her body.

After the First World War, as Western attitudes towards nudity became more liberal, the female breast began to appear freely in works of art. The surrealists played many strange games with this part of the female anatomy, with the Belgian artist René Magritte arguably producing some of the most striking examples.

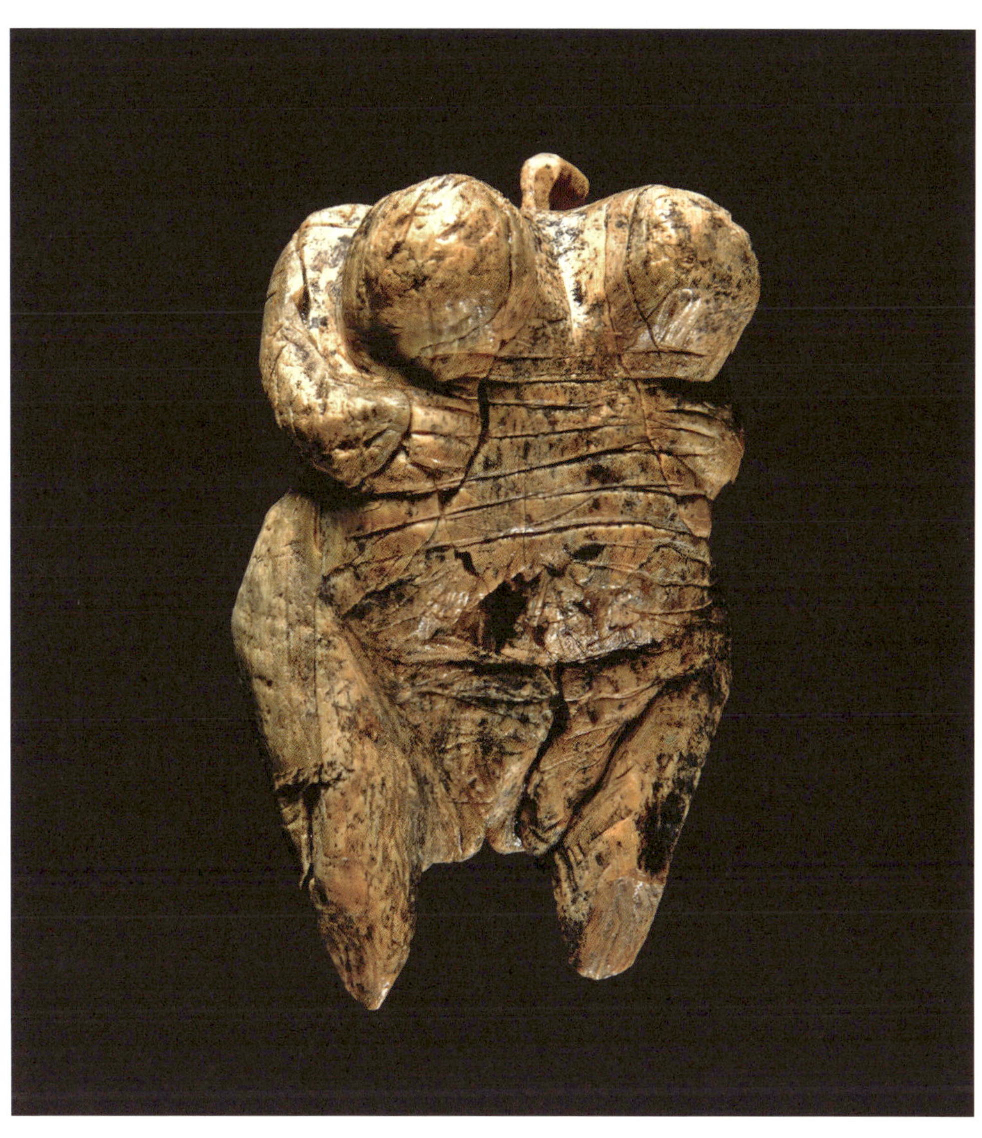

182. **Venus of Hohle Fels,**
38,000–33,000 BC,
mammoth ivory

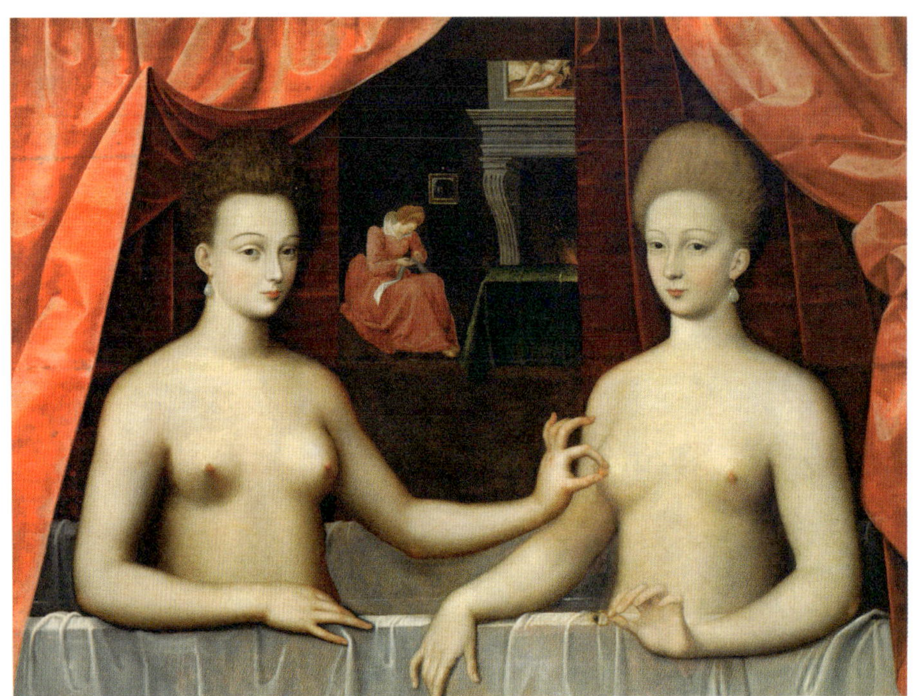

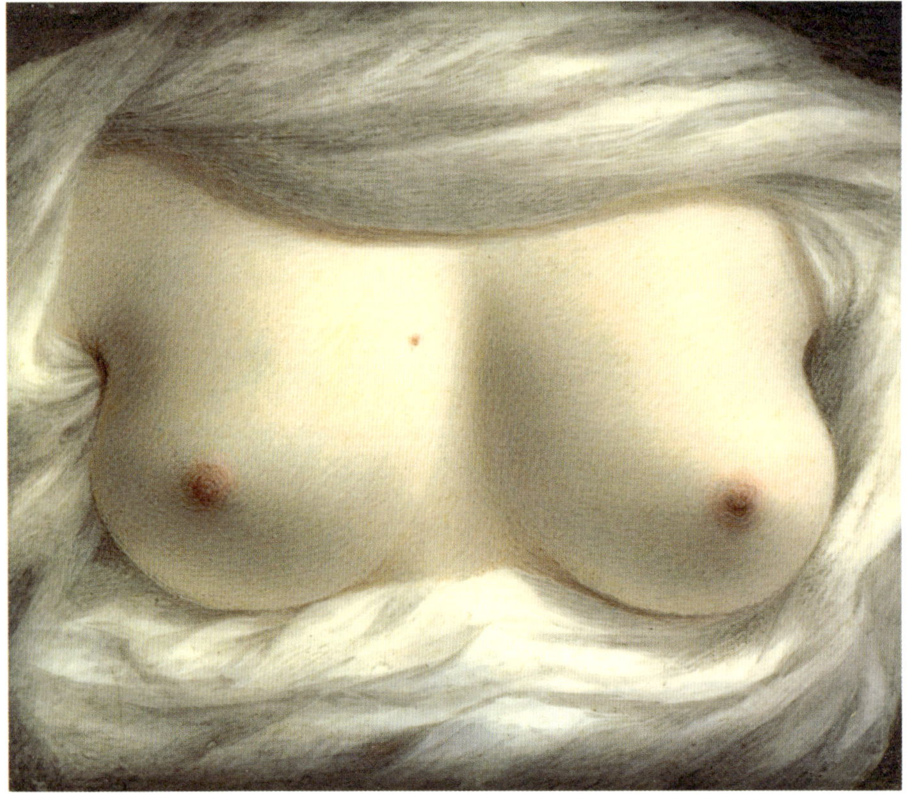

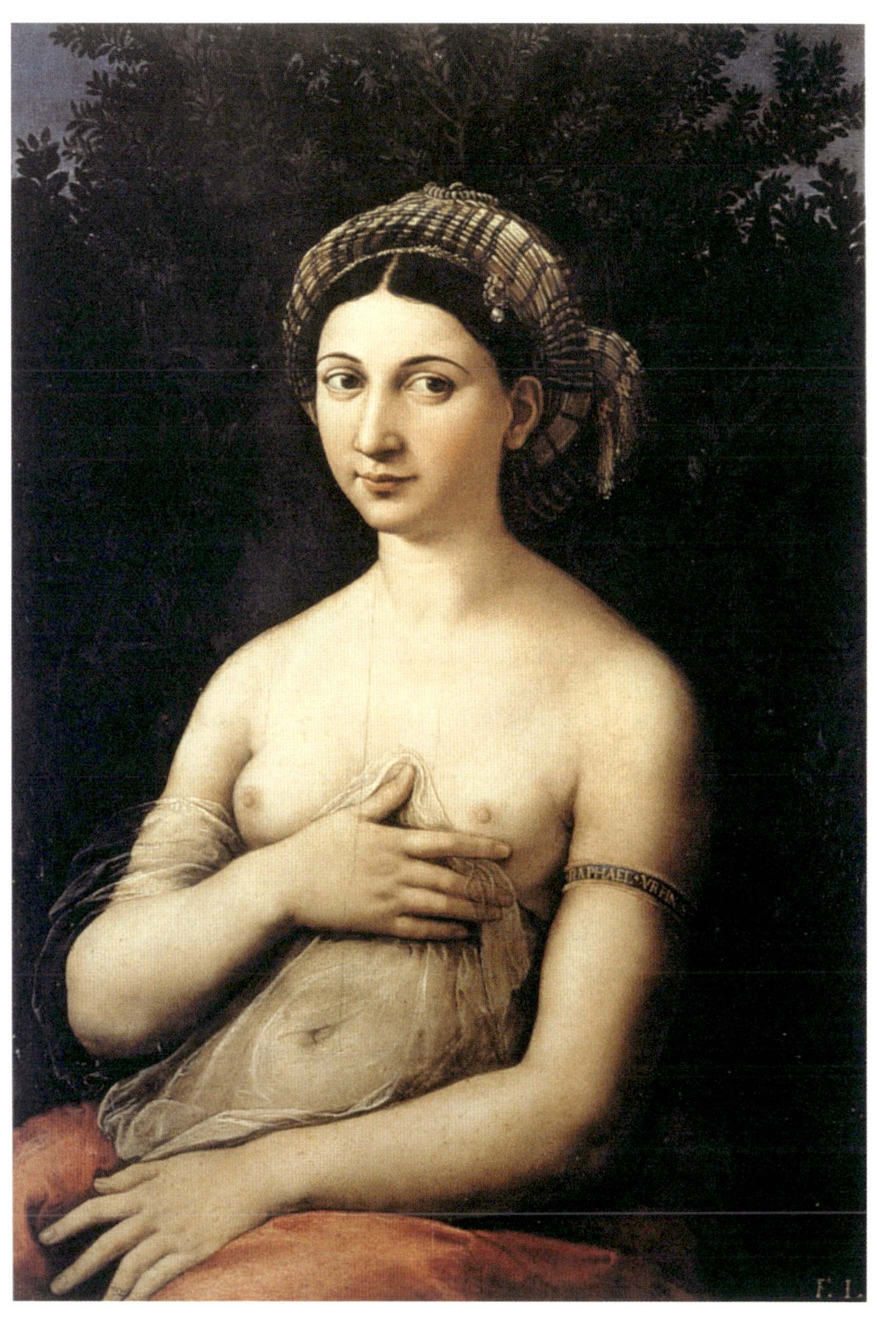

183. opposite, above **Unknown artist,**
Gabrielle d'Estrées and One of her Sisters,
c. 1594, oil on wood

184. opposite, below **Sarah Goodridge,**
Beauty Revealed, **1828, watercolour on ivory**

185. above **Raphael,** *La Fornarina,*
1518–19, oil on wood

The Fig-leaf

It is interesting to note that, at different times, artists have employed various means to prevent their work from being censored. One example is the practice of depicting the female pubic triangle as completely smooth. At other times, the genital region has been covered up. Sometimes, this has been as simple as posing a subject in such a way that the 'offending' parts of the body were naturally concealed. Other artists utilized a more mischievous device, retaining frontal postures for their naked figures but including small details that concealed the erogenous zones. The classic detail – now a cliché – was, of course, the fig-leaf, but this is just one of many contrived devices. A lock of hair, a strap, a hand, a branch of a tree [186], a wisp of clothing – these and a variety of other such details were carefully placed to obscure the private parts. Officially, these small obstructions were there to counter the puritanical rules of the day. In reality, of course, they had the opposite effect: by drawing attention to the sexual anatomy of the subjects, they gave the viewer a chance to enjoy the romantic idea of a forbidden zone.

When Michelangelo's frescoes in the Sistine Chapel were unveiled in the mid-1500s, there was outrage from some quarters about the degree of nudity. The Papal Master of Ceremonies complained that the fresco known as *The Last Judgment* (1536–41), which covers the altar wall, was more suitable for public baths or taverns than a chapel, saying it was 'disgraceful that in so sacred a place there should have been depicted all those nude figures, exposing themselves so shamefully'. He demanded that all of Michelangelo's work be removed. Although the paintings were allowed to remain in place during Michelangelo's lifetime, after his death, in 1564, a pupil of the great master was brought in to cover up some of the body parts.

Michelangelo's huge marble statue of David, complete with its conspicuous genitals, also attracted a scandal. Its public life had started badly when it was pelted with stones on its way to being installed in Florence in 1504, but the scandal surrounding it would occur much later, when a full-sized cast of the statue, 6 metres (20 ft) tall, was presented to Queen Victoria in 1857. The queen was so shocked by its explicit nudity that a large plaster fig-leaf, half a metre high, was quickly manufactured. This was hung between the statue's legs whenever she paid a visit to the Victoria and Albert Museum in London, where the statue was displayed.

186. **Lucas Cranach the Elder,**
Adam and Eve, **1533, oil on wood**

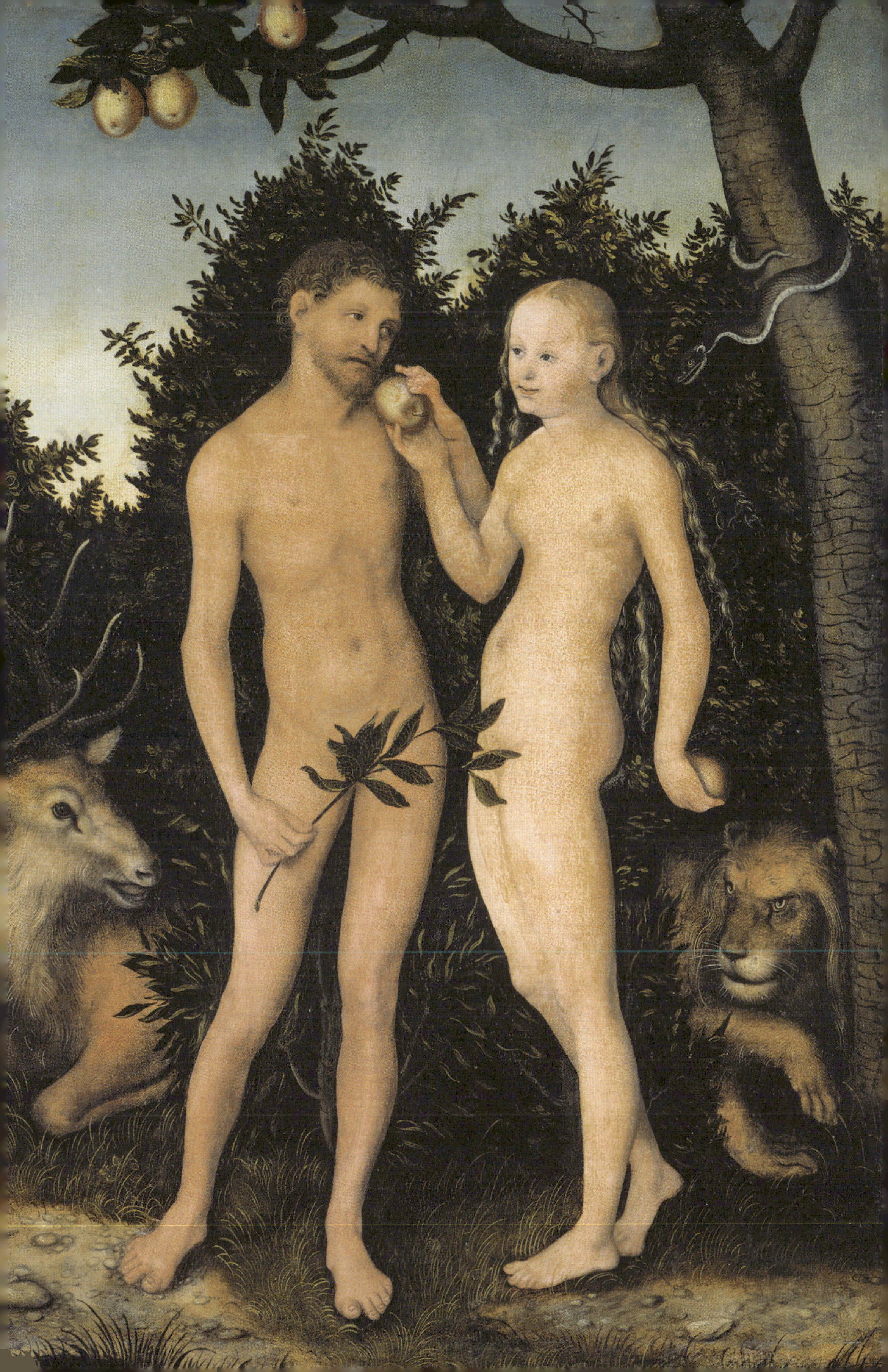

The Sexual Embrace

There are just a handful of social contexts in which adult humans engage in a full embrace: greetings, when emotional bonds are being re-established; farewells, when emotional bonds are being broken; triumphs, when the joy of the moment needs to be shared; disasters, when one person shows great sympathy for another; and in moments of erotic foreplay, when one amorous partner embraces the other as an act of love or lust, or both.

Erotic embraces have been portrayed by many artists over the centuries. Painted in the 16th century, Titian's *Venus and Adonis* [187] was at the time considered rather scandalous because it showed a naked woman taking the initiative with a loving embrace. Adonis is fully clothed and equipped for the hunt, holding a spear in one hand and the leads of two large hunting dogs in the other. Venus clings to him with a seductive embrace that has stopped him in his tracks, uncertain as to which of his two great pleasures he should pursue. The posture of Venus leaves us in no doubt as to what she has in mind.

At first glance, Jean-Honoré Fragonard's clever composition *The Bolt* (*c.* 1777) [190] appears to depict an amorous scene between two lovers. A young man, grasping his companion firmly around the waist, reaches out to bolt the door of what is clearly a bedroom. However, on closer inspection, the portrayal of the young woman in particular – who can be seen pulling away from her companion – is ambiguous. Is she half-heartedly resisting his advances, as is commonly thought, or does the man's action of locking the door point to something more sinister? The erotic symbolism in the painting (most obviously, the forcible thrusting of the bolt into the lock, hinting at the sexual action that is about to occur) and the apparent disarray of the room only make the composition more compelling.

For *The Fisherman and the Syren* (1856–58) [189], Frederic, Lord Leighton took inspiration from a poem by Johann Wolfgang von Goethe, in which a mermaid rises from the water to tell a fisherman that he is enticing her children to death, and to lure him into the depths with her beauty. The painting shows the reluctant young fisherman being seduced by the naked, curvaceous siren in one of the most intensely erotic embraces ever depicted. As with many other works during this period, Leighton managed to avoid censorship by focusing on a mythical scene.

In Frederic William Burton's *Hellelil and Hildebrand, the Meeting on the Turret Stairs* (1864) [188], we witness a tender, tragic moment between two doomed lovers. According to a medieval legend, the young woman's father disapproved of her lover and ordered her brothers to kill him. Burton's watercolour imagines their final, secret meeting:

Hellelil cannot bear to look at her lover and turns away, while the young man is reduced to lovingly cradling no more than her right arm.

In the early 20th century, Egon Schiele produced numerous depictions of lovers holding each other. In perhaps the best-known example, *The Embrace* (1917), the artist portrays a naked couple who are clinging to each other in an almost desperate way. They are angular and nervous, rather than voluptuous and serene. Theirs is an embrace of raw, calculating lust.

In the Far East, there has been a long-standing tradition of colour prints and paintings that show explicit couplings between lovers in an impressive variety of positions, and with even more impressive male anatomical dimensions. Usually depicted in woodblock prints, *shunga* (meaning 'picture of spring') was a popular form of erotic art in Japan, reaching its height in the 17th and 18th centuries.

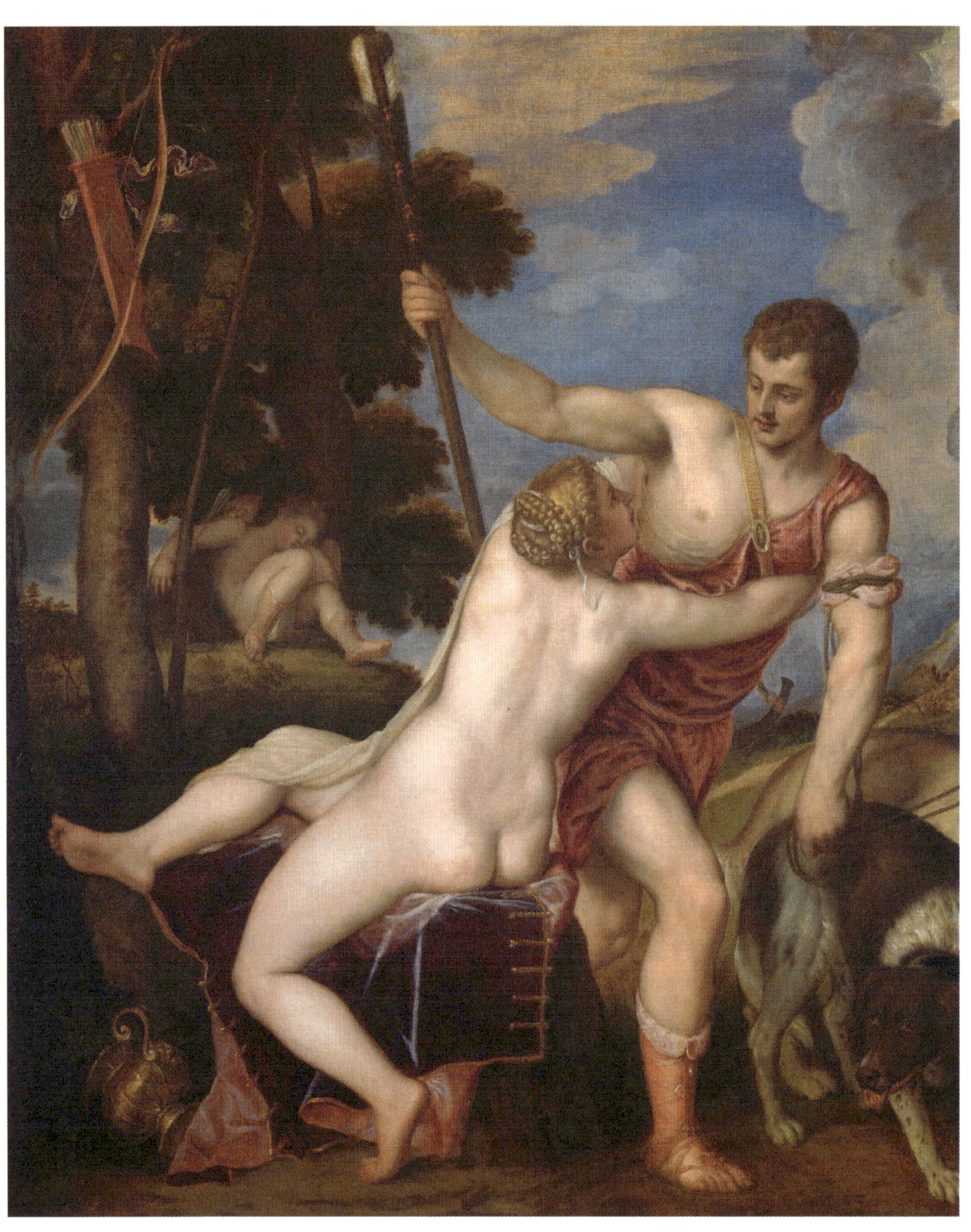

187. above **Titian, *Venus and Adonis*
(detail), 1554, oil on canvas**

188. opposite **Frederic William Burton,
*Hellelil and Hildebrand, the Meeting
on the Turret Stairs*, 1864, watercolour
and gouache on paper**

 The Erotic / The Sexual Embrace

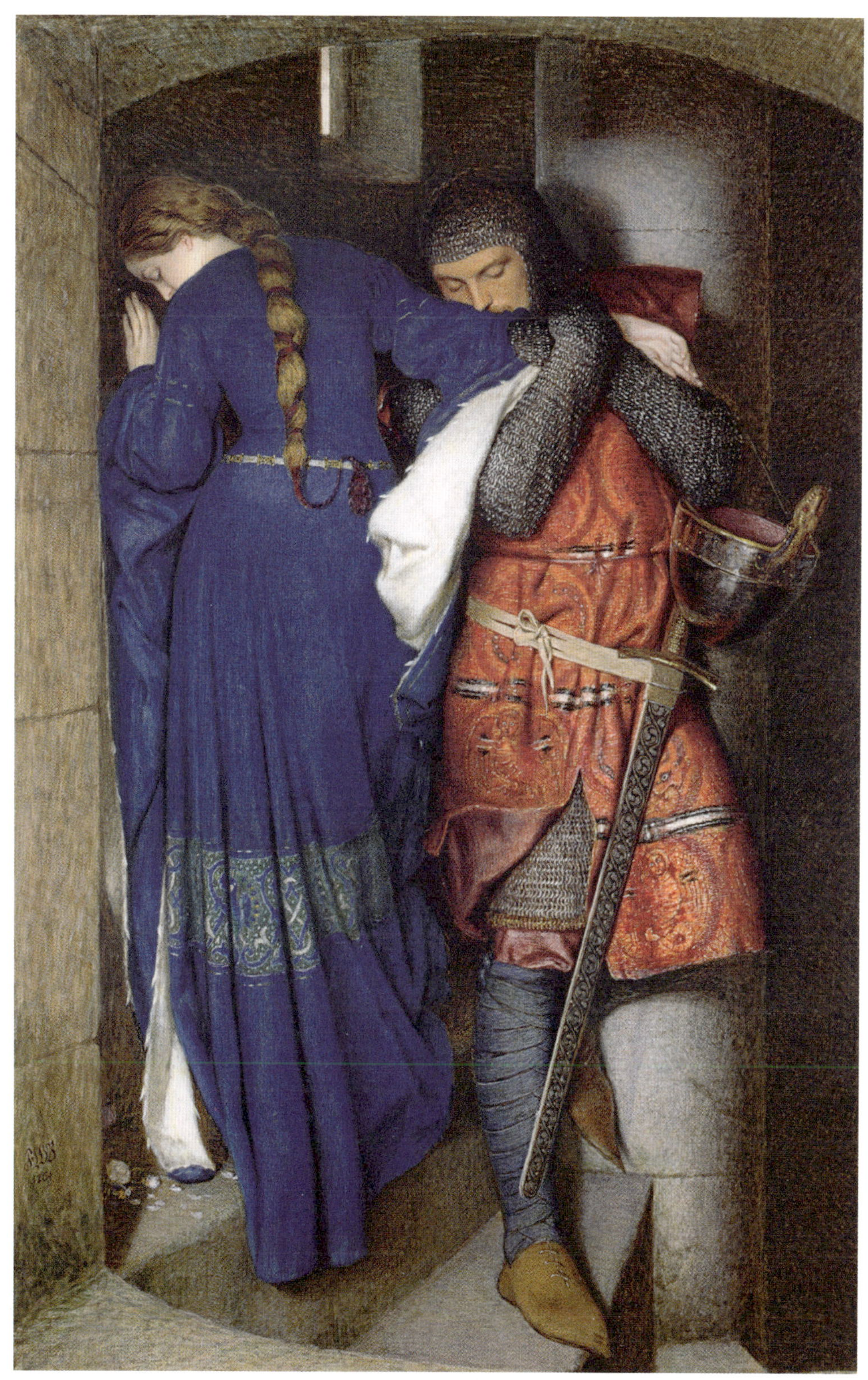

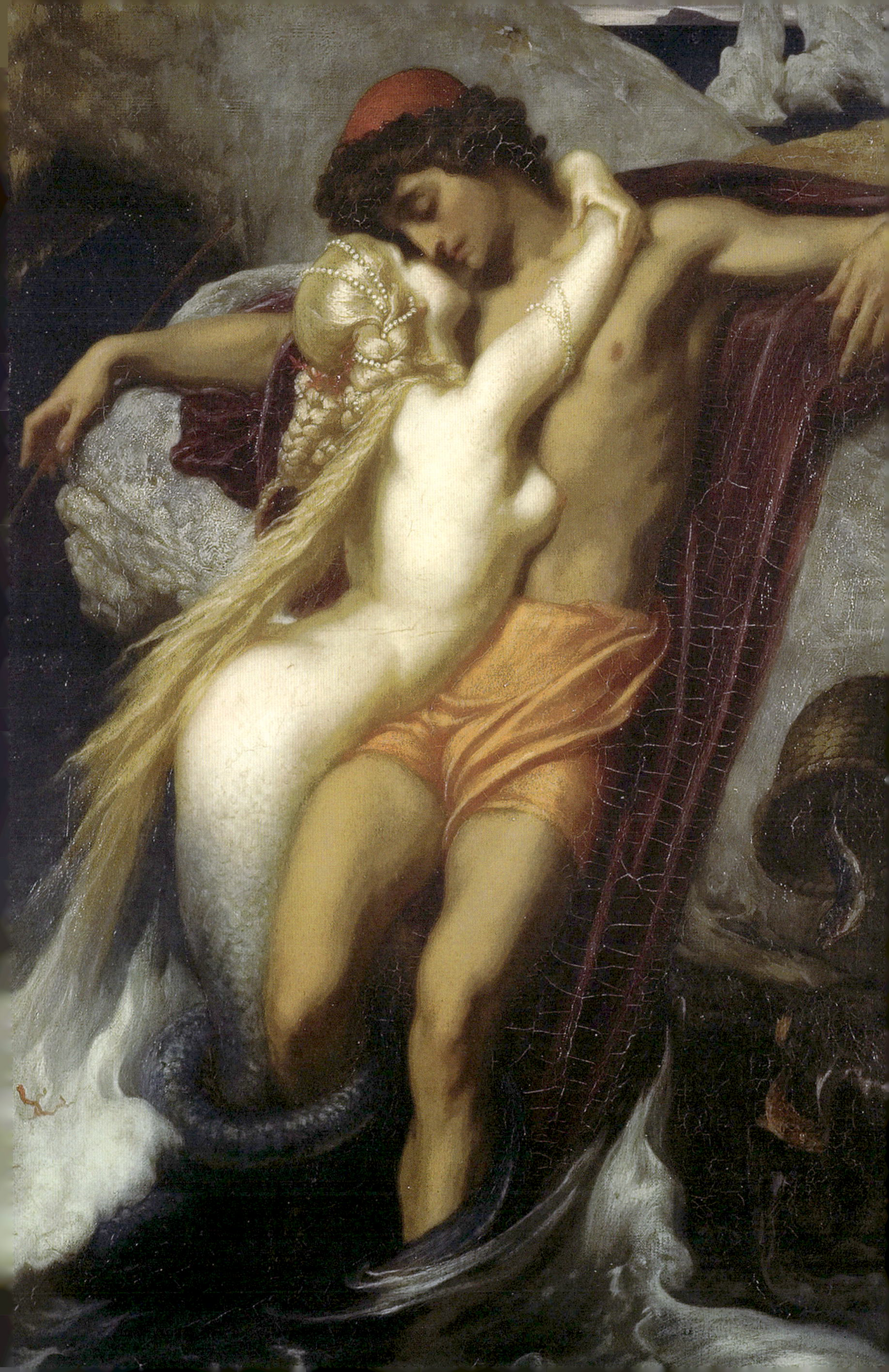

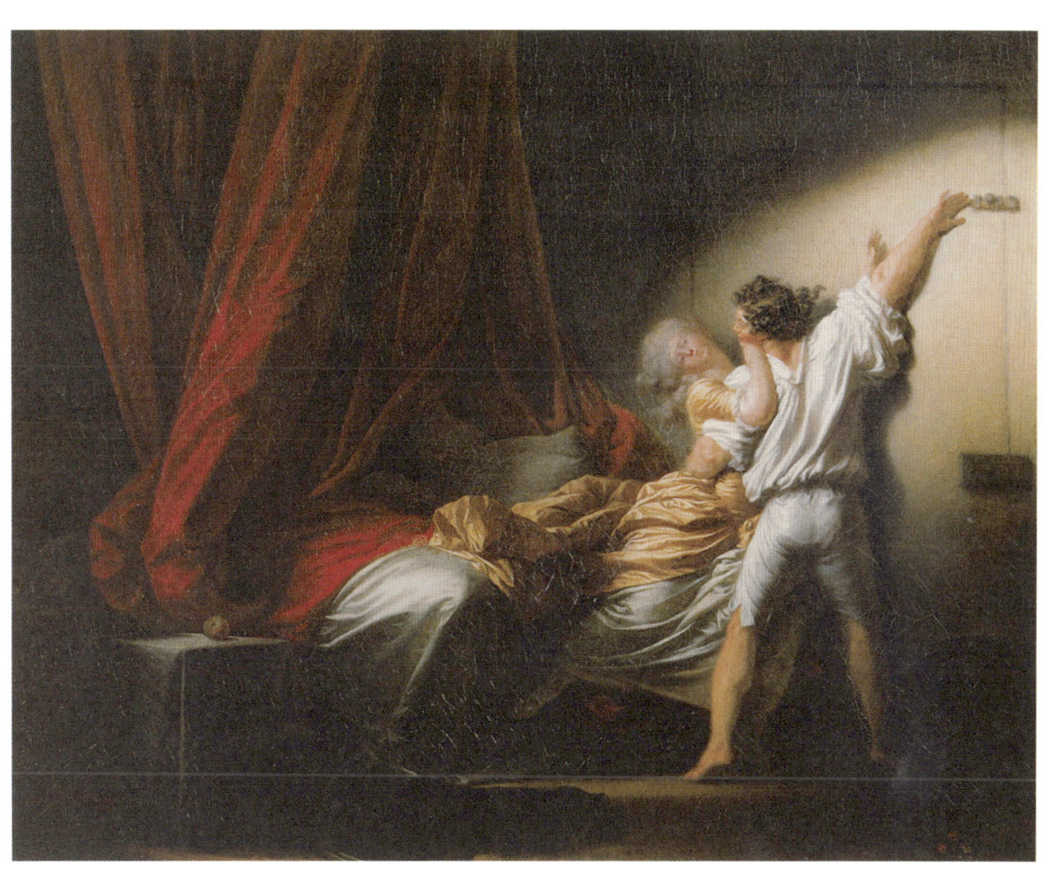

189. opposite **Frederic, Lord Leighton,**
The Fisherman and the Syren, 1856–58,
oil on canvas

190. above **Jean-Honoré Fragonard,**
The Bolt, c. 1777, oil on canvas

The Erotic Kiss

The mouth-to-mouth kiss may have an unusual origin, and it is one that many young lovers are completely unaware of. To understand how kissing began, it is necessary to turn back the clock to primeval times. It is thought that, in early human societies, mothers weaned their children by chewing up their food and then passing it into the infantile mouth by lip-to-lip contact. This almost bird-like system of parental care may seem alien to us today, but our species is likely to have practised it for a million years or more. Evolutionary biologists suggest that the mouth-to-mouth kiss is a relic of our prehistoric past. Whether it has been handed down from generation to generation, or whether we have developed an inborn predisposition towards it, is hard to say.

Today, when we observe a couple kissing in a public place, we tend to react in one of two ways: either we see it as a charming display of affection, or we think it distasteful in a public setting. It is perhaps because of this ambivalence that mouth-to-mouth kissing is comparatively rare in works of art. As long as we are able to enjoy the couple's loving feelings towards each other, we seem happy enough to view the action in an artwork of some kind. At the same time, however, the fact that, at the moment of the kiss, the couple are totally engrossed in one another may make us feel excluded. Indeed, a couple may sometimes deliberately engage in a prolonged kiss in a social situation in order to emphasize our exclusion from their relationship.

Two works of art, both called *The Kiss*, and both of which have divided opinion, have almost become visual clichés. The first, Auguste Rodin's white marble statue of 1888–98 [191], was based on an incident in Dante's *Inferno*, in which an adulterous couple were discovered by the woman's husband, who killed them both. Admirers view the work as the epitome of sensuous, loving contact between a devoted pair, while critics see it as too carefully posed, as if we are attending a life class rather than eavesdropping on a passionate couple. Rodin himself said that he thought it was overly traditional, and considered it overrated, calling it 'a large sculpted knick-knack following the usual formula'. Although the erotic impact of this sculpture may seem tame to us today, when a copy of it was exhibited in Chicago in 1893, it was considered too obscene to be put on public display and was hidden away in a special chamber, where it could be viewed only by personal application.

The second *Kiss* is Gustav Klimt's glittery-gold painting of 1907–8 [193], which is thought to represent the artist embracing his lover. Some people see it as the perfect lovers' kiss, the kiss that 'takes us to a different state of being', but critics have commented that the elaborate gold pattern overwhelms the two figures and reduces them to a corner detail. Also, closer inspection of the woman's expression suggests that she may be merely tolerating her lover's engulfing attention, rather than finding herself lost in a romantic haze.

In terms of sheer tenderness, both works fail to match Henri de Toulouse-Lautrec's painting of a young couple kissing in bed. At first glance, *In Bed: The Kiss* (1892) [192] appears to show a young woman on the left and a young man, with shorter hair, on the right. But in reality this is a depiction of two Parisian female prostitutes relaxing in each other's arms and enjoying the kind of affection that was almost certainly missing from their professional lives. The artist was particularly pleased with this work, reportedly saying: 'This is better than anything else. It is the very epitome of sensual delight.'

Pablo Picasso painted and drew kissing couples on many occasions, usually depicting them engaged in a moment of intense lust, rather than tender love. He often portrayed an elderly man (presumably representing himself) forcibly pressing his face against that of a swooning woman. In one drawing, made when he was in his eighties, he shows a couple with their tongues thrust into one another's mouths, as if searching for food, echoing the primeval origins of the act of mouth-to-mouth kissing.

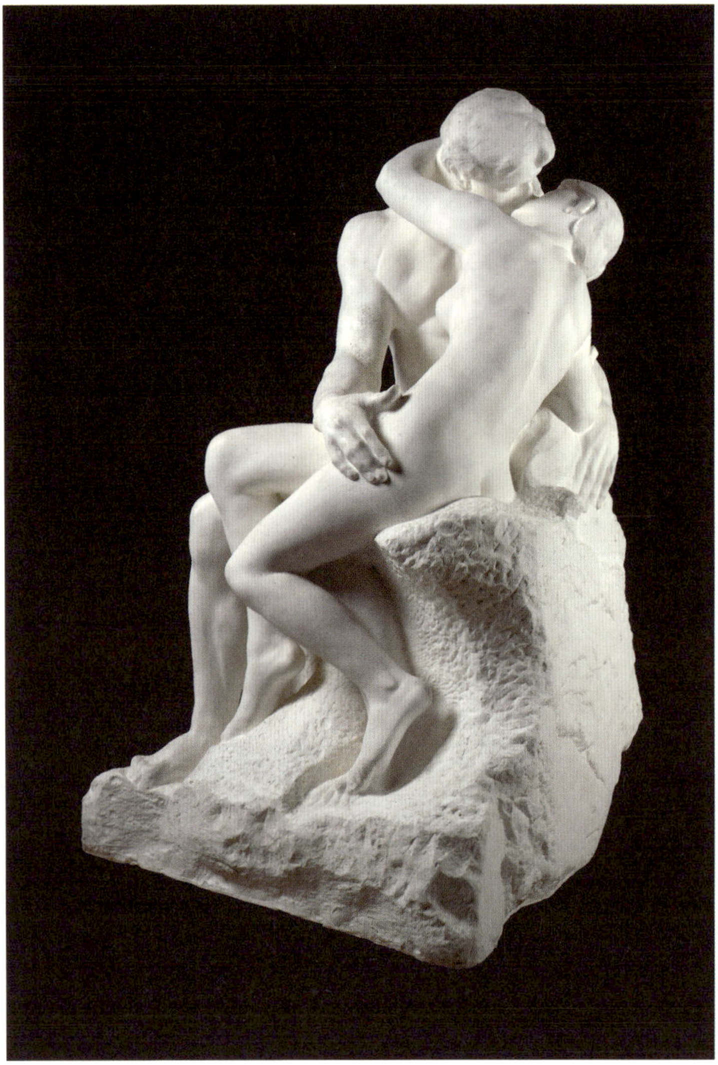

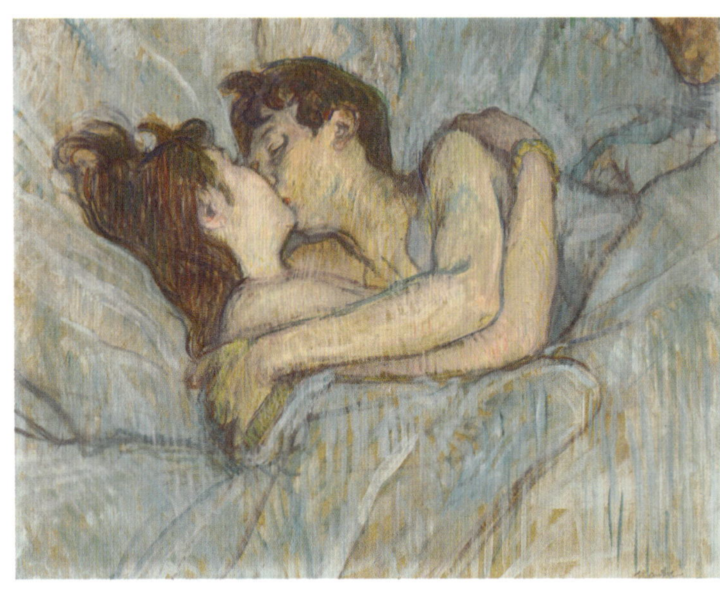

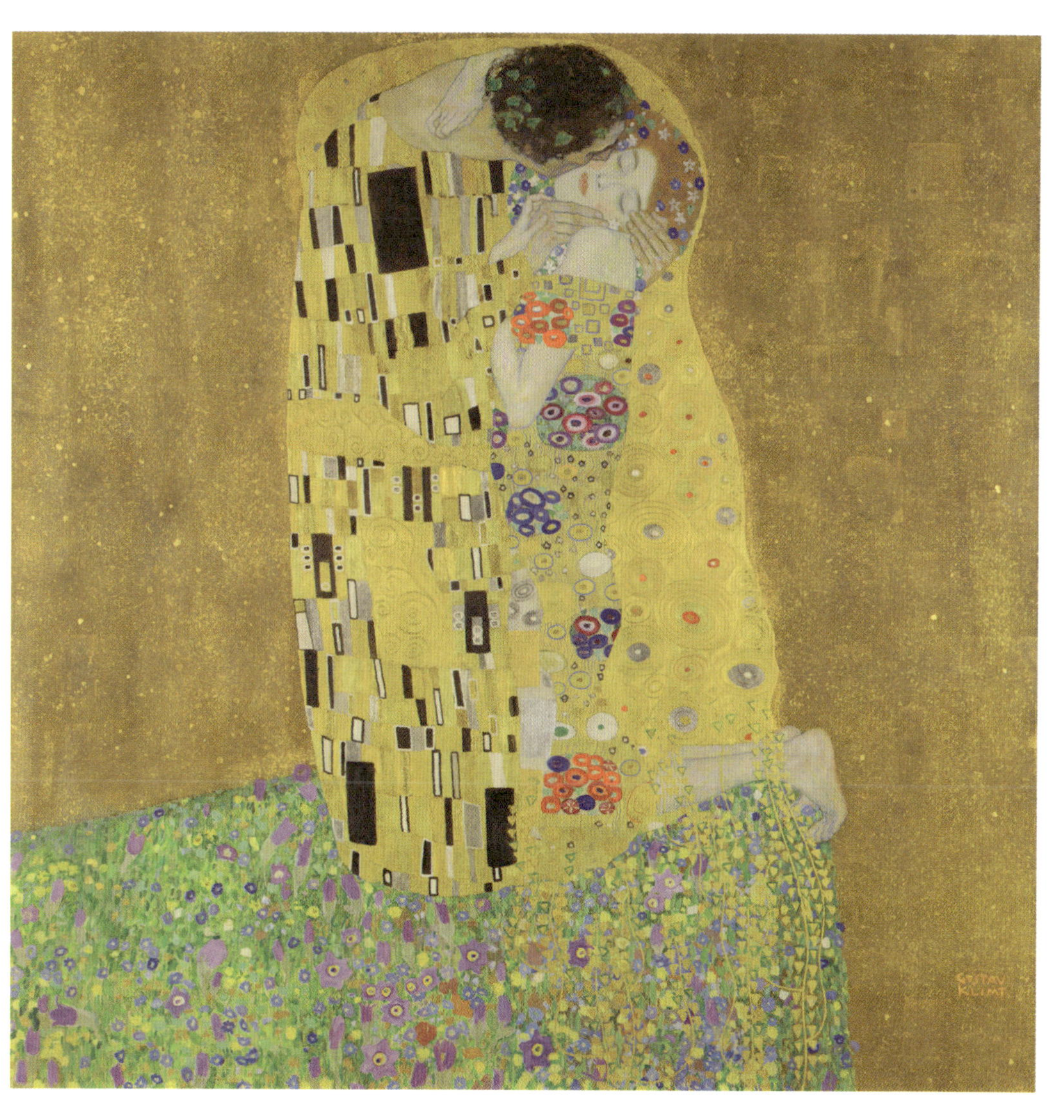

191. opposite, above **Auguste Rodin,** *The Kiss*, **1888–98, plaster cast from marble after 1898**

192. opposite, below **Henri de Toulouse-Lautrec,** *In Bed: The Kiss*, **1892, oil on wood**

193. above **Gustav Klimt,** *The Kiss*, **1907–8, oil and gold leaf on canvas**

The Erotic / The Erotic Kiss

Bondage

Bondage might not be a theme you would immediately associate with historic paintings, but such works have existed for centuries. In general, they centre on a naked female figure in a dire predicament: bound and helpless, she has no choice but to await her fate in scenes that are clearly designed to appeal to the dark side of the male ego. Historically, such paintings have worn a heavy mask of respectability by being firmly rooted in classical mythology. We are supposed to believe that the bound naked beauty is merely part of the story, even though it seems abundantly clear from the way in which these paintings are composed that their main purpose is not the acting out of the traditional legend.

One famous story in particular has provided the perfect excuse for artists to create these works of mild pornography: Perseus and Andromeda. When the Aethiopian queen Cassiopeia bragged that her daughter Andromeda was more beautiful than the sea nymphs, it so enraged the sea god Poseidon that he sent a sea monster to destroy the kingdom. There was only one way to appease the gods, and that was to sacrifice Andromeda. The sacrifice was of a particularly unpleasant kind: Andromeda would be chained to a rock-face on the seashore, where, desperate and terrified, she would have to await the arrival of a notorious sea monster, which would then devour her. As if this were not enough, she would first have to be stripped naked. The sacrifice was offered, but just as the monster was about to attack, Perseus turned up and dispatched the beast, setting Andromeda free. The hero fell in love with Andromeda, and the two were married.

It is amazing just how many major artists – including Titian, Paolo Veronese, Giorgio Vasari, Giuseppe Cesari [194] and Peter Paul Rubens – were drawn to this myth. Even the great Rembrandt had a go at it, although his Andromeda came under criticism for going against the classical conventions of beauty. The earliest portrayals of this story can be found on ancient Greek vases, as well as in later mosaics and wall paintings of ancient Rome. In these examples, Andromeda is usually clothed, and it is Perseus who is naked. When the subject resurfaces in the 15th century, Andromeda is again clothed and appears to be marooned on a small rock, instead of chained to it, while Perseus is portrayed as a knight in armour. It was not until the 16th century that artists had the courage to show their heroine stripped and chained, creating a formula that would be repeated time and again over the centuries.

There is a male equivalent of this depiction of bondage: the martyrdom of St Sebastian. Sebastian was a captain in the Praetorian Guard in the third century AD, at a time when Christians were being persecuted. When it was discovered that Sebastian was a Christian and had converted many others, he was sentenced to death. Despite being shot repeatedly with arrows and left for dead, a widow found him alive and nursed him back to health. Her efforts proved fruitless, however: when he admonished the emperor about the cruel treatment of the Christians, Sebastian was clubbed to death and thrown in the sewers. In art, St Sebastian is typically depicted tied to a tree, with arrows piercing his body.

As with Andromeda, the ways in which different artists have approached the story is revealing. In *The Martyrdom of St Sebastian* (*c.* 1475), the German painter Hans Memling shows Sebastian as a slender young man, far too delicate and boyish to have been a captain in the Praetorian Guard. He stands against a small tree, with one wrist bound high above his head and the other behind his back. His clothes, which have been stripped from his body, lie at his feet, emphasizing his humiliation. In a German altarpiece of the same period, by an artist known simply as the Master of the Holy Kinship, Sebastian is again portrayed as a skinny young man, stripped from the waist up, and with his wrists bound to a tree high above his head. The bizarre feature of this particular portrayal is Sebastian's head, which is clearly that of a young woman. Most of the major Italian Renaissance artists also featured Sebastian in their repertoire, including Piero della Francesca, Giovanni Bellini, Sandro Botticelli, Andrea Mantegna and Pietro Perugino [196].

Modern artists, such as the surrealist Hans Bellmer, have produced more explicit examples of female bondage that are still considered serious works of art, although the past few decades have seen an increase in works that verge on pornography and have little or no artistic merit. One exception is a 2015 painting entitled *A Foot Next to My Leg* [195] by the Australian neo-surrealist William Johns. It shows a naked woman tied to a chair, pulling against her restraints in a tense, semi-aggressive stance, as a faceless man on one knee offers her a neck-tie – recalling, perhaps, Freud's assertion that the neck-tie is a phallic symbol. It is the puzzling ambiguity of the scene that gives it its special quality.

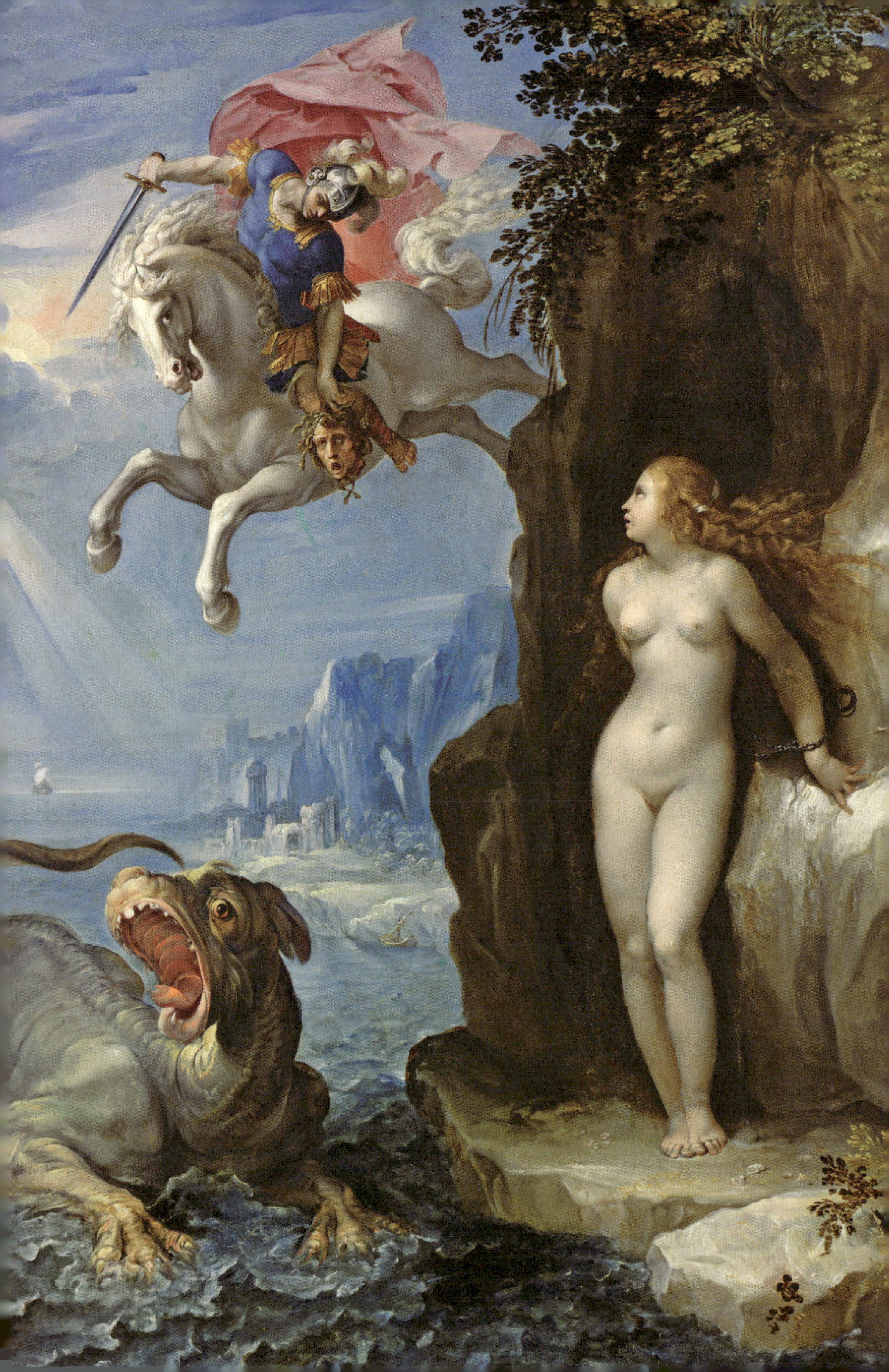

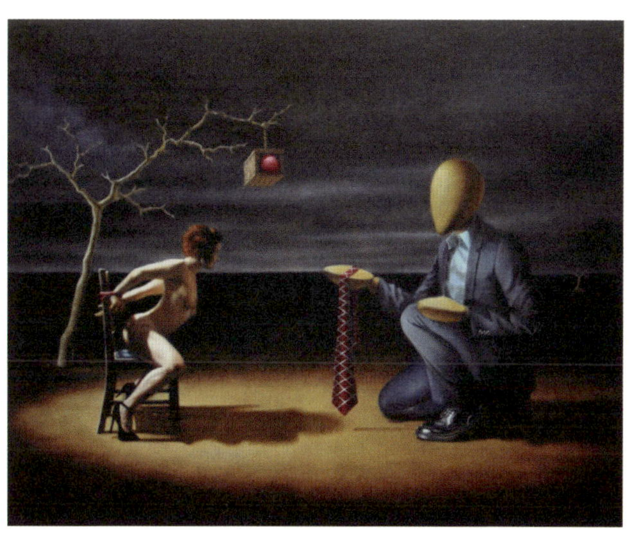

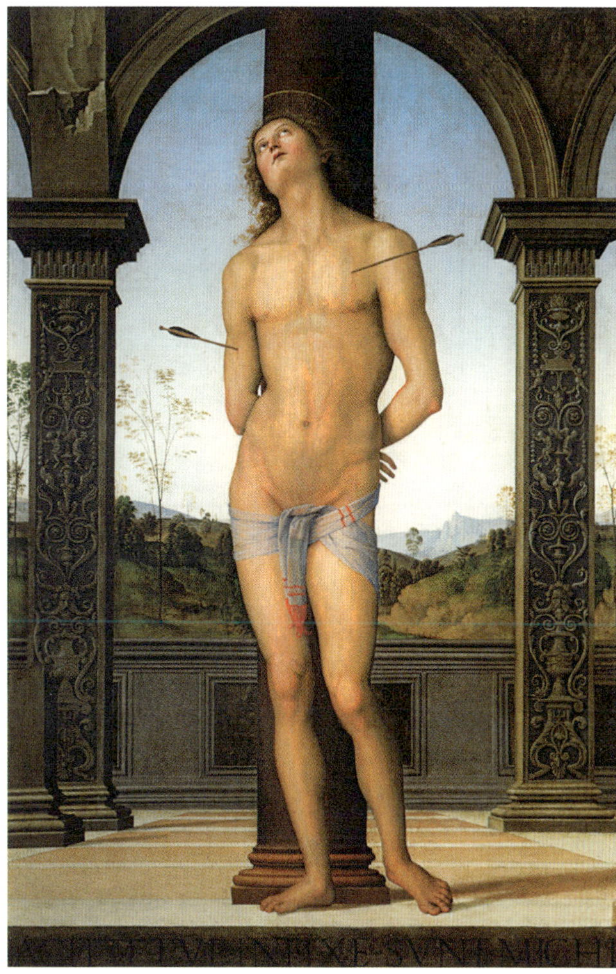

194. opposite **Giuseppe Cesari,**
Perseus and Andromeda (detail),
c. 1592, oil on slate

195. above **William Johns,**
A Foot Next to My Leg, 2015,
oil on canvas

196. right **Pietro Perugino,**
The Martyrdom of St Sebastian,
1495, oil on panel

The Erotic / Bondage

At Rest

For centuries, artists have depicted the human body at rest. The appeal is clear: the more relaxed the sitter is, the easier it is for them to hold a particular pose for long periods of time. Also, human resting postures are wonderfully varied compared with other animals. In bed, we have more than ten different sleeping postures, and when we fall asleep accidentally, there is an even greater range of positions.

When we are sitting down, we can enjoy varying degrees of relaxation depending on how we cross our legs. If we decide to lie down without going to sleep, we may rest on our back, our front or our side. If we choose to squat, again there are several ways of doing this, and if there is a wall or a tree nearby, we are liable to lean up against it to give our back a rest. Sometimes, when we feel drowsy but need to keep awake, we offer ourselves a little help unconsciously by propping the weight of our head on a hand or an arm, or some other surface. When sleep beckons a little harder, we start to yawn – a mysterious action, the function of which nobody quite understands. Finally, there is the comfort to be gained from the to-ing and fro-ing of a rocking chair, a motion that magically recreates the sensation we enjoyed when we were snug inside the womb.

Legs Crossed

Sitting with the legs crossed is so commonplace that we rarely give it a thought. It does, however, act as an important – if somewhat ambiguous – social display. On the one hand, the cross-legged posture can be a form of cut-off, indicating that we are feeling defensive or insecure, and wish to shut out the world. On the other, it can be a sign that we are relaxed in the company of others. This is because it is the very opposite of the pose we adopt when we are deferential or alert, when we would usually sit upright and keep our legs free, in case we need to become active quickly. We are generally unaware of these differences in leg posture. In social situations, our minds are busy with other matters, and our legs have to take care of themselves. As a result, the legs have been described as the most honest part of the body. We may find it easy to mask our true feelings on our face, smiling politely when we would rather be elsewhere, but the position of our legs, or fidgety feet, can give us away.

We might also cross our legs when we are alone – not as a social signal, but as a way of increasing our body-comfort. The crossing action is a form of auto-contact, a term describing a variety of gestures that are performed to mimic physical interaction with another person and soothe the body. An extreme version of this auto-contact can be seen when we hug our legs: the knees are bent and brought up to the chest, and the arms are wrapped around the legs; the head may also rest on the knees.

There are cultural differences in how, and when, we cross our legs, of course. In the West, it is common to cross the legs by positioning one knee on top of the other, as seen in Lucian Freud's 2003–4 portrait of Brigadier Andrew Parker Bowles [198]. Here, the sitter's posture gives him an air of composed relaxation, and stands in stark contrast to the standard military practice of posing for group photographs in a symmetrical sitting position with the palms on the knees. A self-portrait by Shurooq Amin, entitled *A Man of No Importance* (2012) [200], appears to present the Kuwaiti artist in a similarly conventional pose: wearing dark sunglasses and her hair loose, she is seated in an upright position, with her bare legs crossed at the knees. However, on closer inspection it becomes clear that this piece addresses the role of women in Middle Eastern society. When the painting was first exhibited in Kuwait City in 2012, as part of the artist's 'It's a Man's World', the show created such controversy that it was closed down within hours of opening. The painting forms part of a series of works that the artist has called 'Popcornographic', all dealing with subjects that are considered taboo in the Middle East.

There are several variations of the standard leg-cross. The mildest form is the ankle-on-ankle cross – a pose often adopted by female members of the British royal family, who traditionally avoid crossing their legs when seated in public. A Chinese figure, dating from the 5th century AD, shows this posture to great effect [197]. The ankle-on-knee cross is perhaps the opposite of the demure ankle-on-ankle cross, and is often interpreted as a display of self-confidence. Although the posture is predominantly associated with men, Auguste Renoir depicts a little girl in a loose variation of this pose in *Georgette Charpentier Seated* (1876). The leg-twine, meanwhile, in which one leg is wrapped around the other, is performed almost exclusively by women, and is much more ambiguous: depending on the context, it can be seen as a form of cut-off or, at the other extreme, a sexual display. Anthony Brandt's *Nude with Crossed Legs* (1959) [199] depicts a strikingly contorted female figure adopting this posture.

One further variation involves sitting cross-legged on the ground, with the feet tucked under the knees or thighs. The posture is widely associated with meditation in the West, although it is used in a variety of everyday social contexts in many parts of the world. One particularly complex version of this posture is the full lotus position, in which the feet are placed on the opposing thighs, with the soles facing upwards. Originating in India, it is believed to calm the mind, and works by applying pressure to the lower spine, which encourages relaxation.

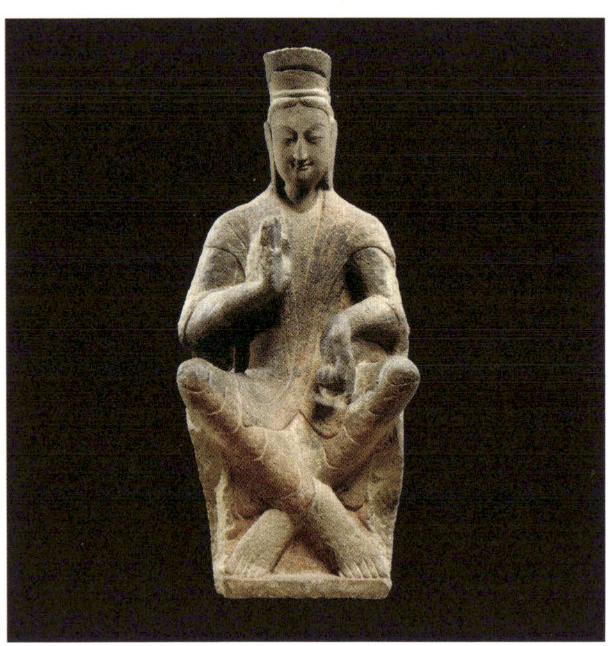

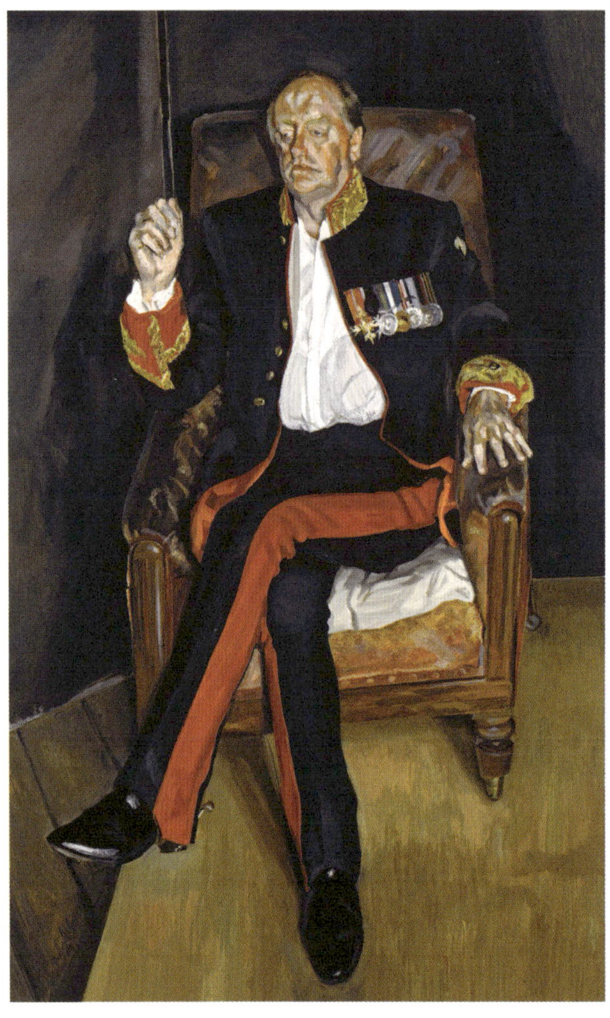

197. above **Chinese bodhisattva, probably Avalokiteshvara, AD c. 470–480, sandstone with pigment**

198. left **Lucian Freud, *The Brigadier*, 2003–4, oil on canvas**

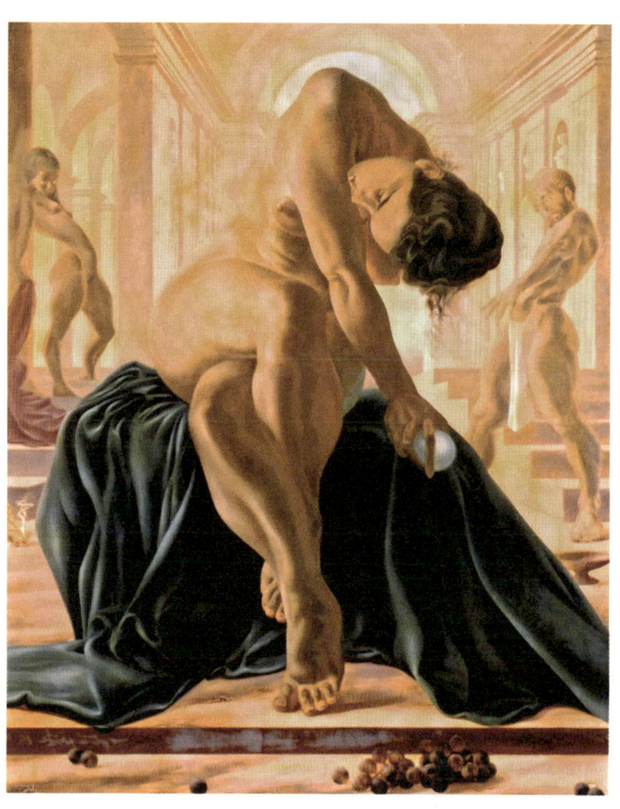

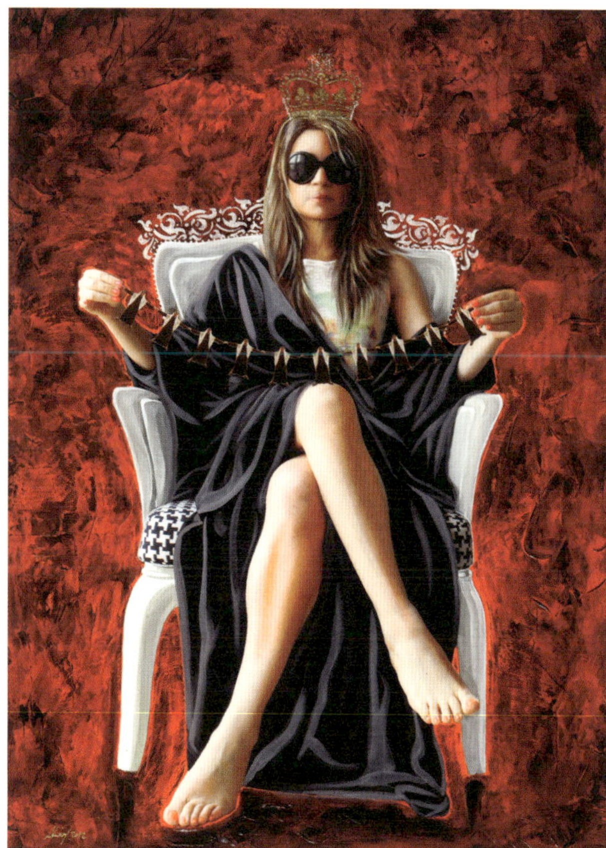

199. above **Anthony Brandt,**
Nude with Crossed Legs, 1959,
oil on canvas

200. right **Shurooq Amin,**
A Man of No Importance, 2012,
**mixed media on canvas mounted
on wood**

Squatting

Squatting is generally understood as a crouching position in which the knees are bent and the heels are close to or touching the buttocks or the back of the thighs. It is less popular as a resting posture in the West than it is in many cultures, particularly in Asia, where squatting is often preferred to sitting or standing.

In works of art, it is not uncommon for crouching figures to be depicted with their buttocks touching the ground; others are shown in a semi-squatting posture, kneeling on one leg and squatting on the other, perhaps using one or both hands as a prop. Further variations in the squatting posture often centre on the position of the hands and the arms. The hands may be held to the chest, clasped together or resting on the knees, for example. A subject may be shown with the elbows propped on the knees, or with the arms folded on the knees or wrapped around the legs. It is interesting that, in many prehistoric squatting figurines, the arms are held tightly to the chest. This was likely for practical reasons: if the arms were outstretched, there was a greater risk that they would be damaged or broken off.

Some ancient Egyptian statues show figures in a crouching position with their arms folded on top of their knees [202]. This squatting posture appears so many times in the art of ancient Egypt that the figurines have acquired a particular name: Egyptian block statues (due to their block-shaped form). In many examples, the details of the limbs are omitted, increasing the block-like quality of the sculpture. Egyptian block statues were placed on the floor of temples, often with their heads tilted back slightly, as if observing the temple rites and processions.

While the majority of figurines in a squatting position are bilaterally symmetrical, in *Crouching Boy* (c. 1530–34) [201] Michelangelo has cleverly introduced an element of asymmetry to create a more interesting composition. He does this by showing the boy with his hands joined together, but with one arm passing between the bent legs and the other going around the outer leg.

Squatting female figures also appear in a number of works by Pablo Picasso. Like Michelangelo, he managed to find ways of slightly disrupting the bilateral symmetry, by twisting a foot or an arm, by viewing the figure at an angle or by showing a semi-squat.

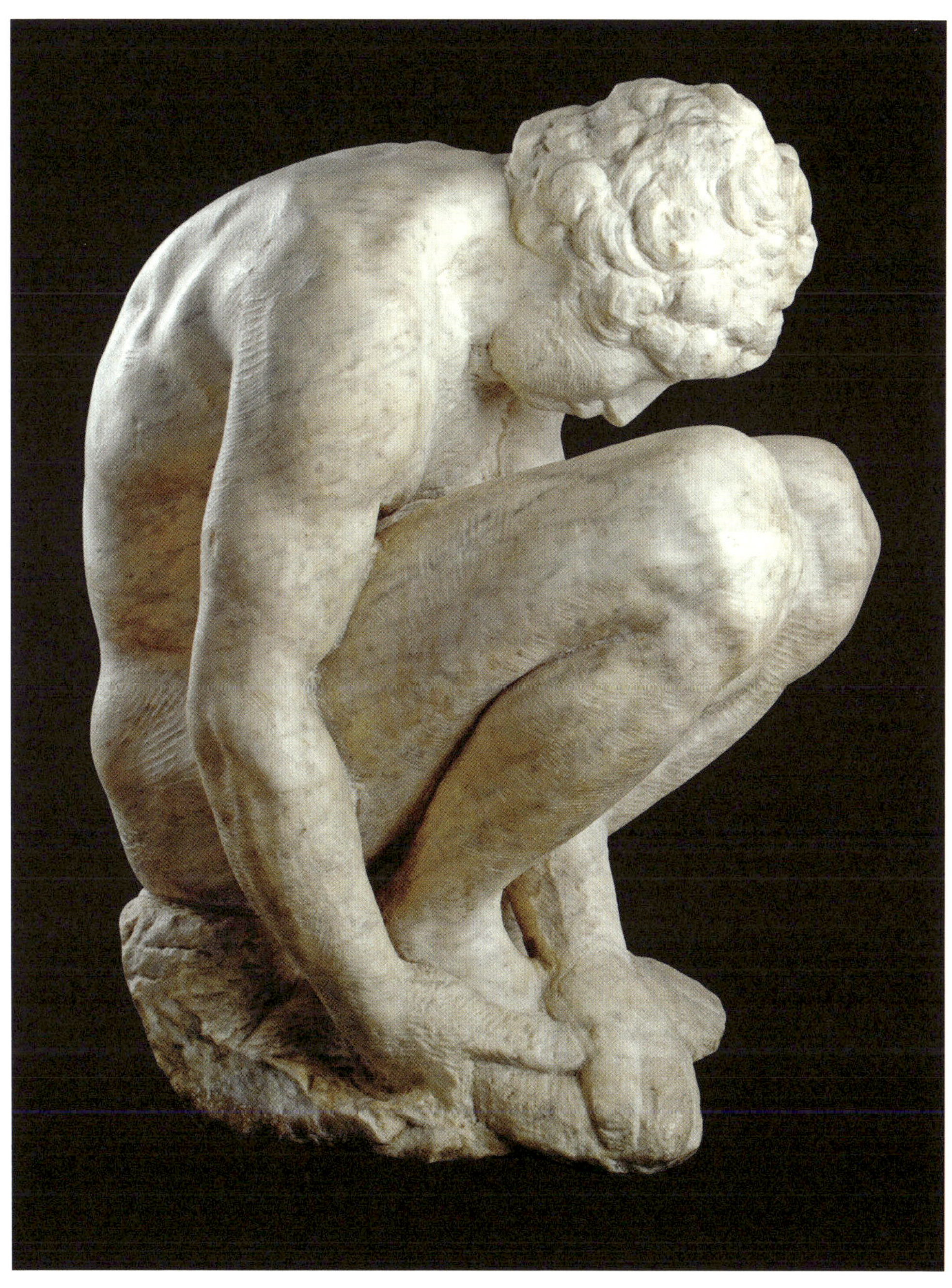

201. Michelangelo,
Crouching Boy,
c. 1530–34, marble

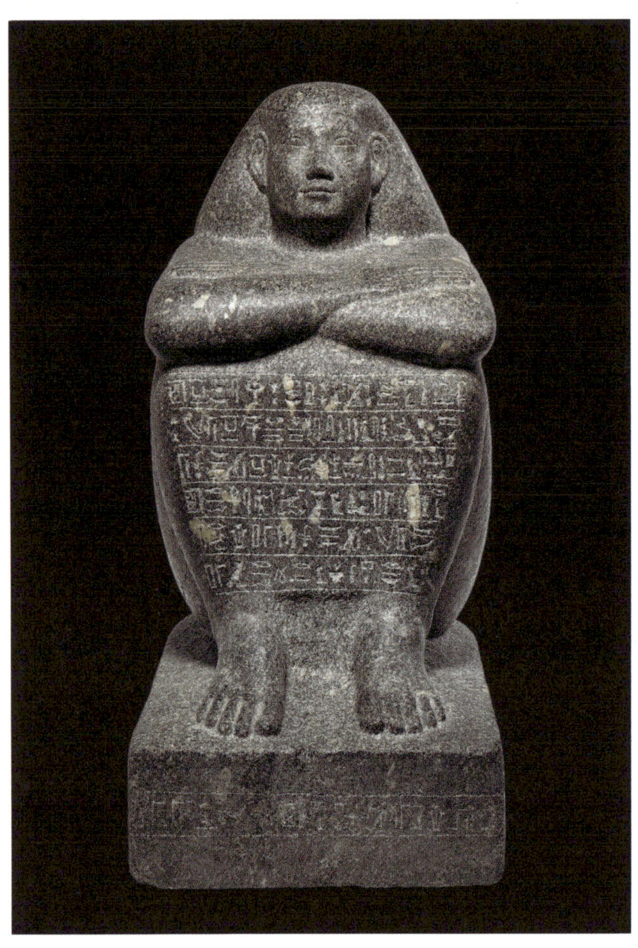

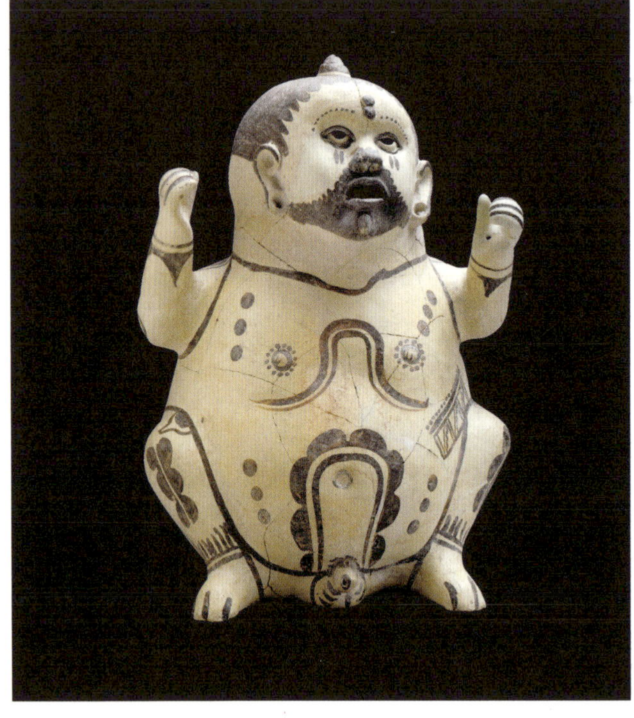

202. above **Egyptian block statue of Padimahes, c. 680–650 BC, granodiorite**

203. left **Huastec figurine, 16th century, Mexico, ceramic**

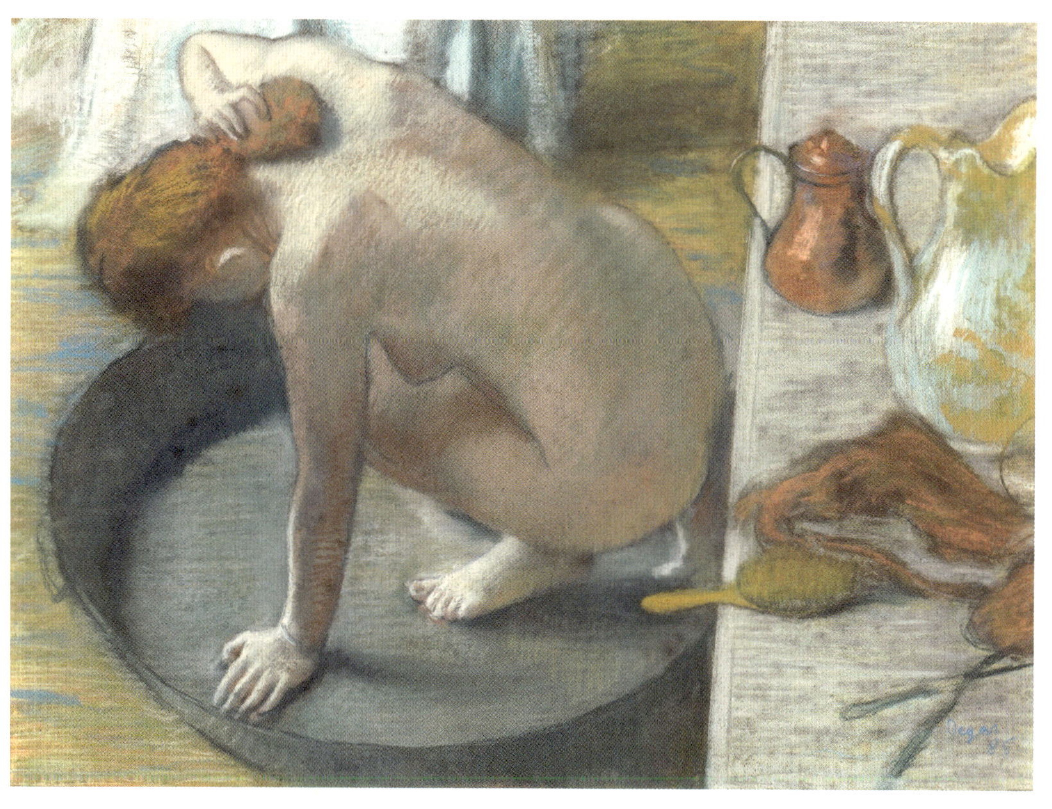

204. **Edgar Degas, *The Tub*,
1886, pastel on card**

Leaning

One of the milder forms of rest consists of leaning the body against a vertical surface, which acts as a prop. There is a charming 16th-century miniature of a young man leaning against a tree in a rose garden by Nicholas Hilliard [207]. Believed to be Queen Elizabeth I's favourite, Robert Devereux, 2nd Earl of Essex, he is portrayed with his hand on his heart, as if daydreaming about his beloved. Devereux was an eloquent poet and a warrior, but his relationship with the queen fluctuated wildly. In the end, he was executed for treason.

In *The Woodman's Daughter* (1851) [205] by the Pre-Raphaelite John Everett Millais, we are presented with a scene of budding friendship as a boy, leaning nonchalantly against a tree, offers strawberries to a girl. However, the picture is not as idyllic as it seems. It was inspired by Coventry Patmore's poem of the same name, which tells the tragic tale of Maud, the woodman's daughter, and the son of a wealthy squire. Divided by class, they can never marry, and Maud ultimately has an illegitimate child by him and suffers a mental breakdown. In Millais's childhood setting, the clothing and postures of the pair are used to reinforce the class divisions.

In an equally emotive painting, *A Martyr: The Violet Vendor* (1885) [206], Fernand Pelez depicts an exhausted young flower-seller propped against a wall. The boy is so tired that he can barely keep his eyes open, but his very survival depends on the few pennies he may earn from selling violets. The painting was designed to move its 19th-century audience to take action against the social conditions that were causing such acute poverty among urban populations at the time.

When we are tired (or, sometimes, bored), we may also rest our head against another part of the body. We tend to do this automatically, without thinking, and the action can take several forms. One of the most common examples is the palm-prop, in which the elbow rests on a solid surface, such as a table, and the vertical forearm is positioned under the head. The palm is usually placed on the chin or the cheek, as shown in a portrait by the British artist Tai-Shan Schierenberg [209]. In a variation of this position, the knuckles of the hand are used to support the chin or the cheek. This is the pose adopted by a lady in a portrait attributed to Peter Lely (late 17th century) [208], giving her a relaxed air. If more support is needed, these actions can be doubled by using both arms. Other variations in posture include resting the side of the head on one knee, as seen in Egon Schiele's *Seated Woman with Bent Knee* (1917) [210]. A reclining person may also support the head by wrapping the arms around it. If sitting at a table, we may slump forward until the side of our head rests on a forearm.

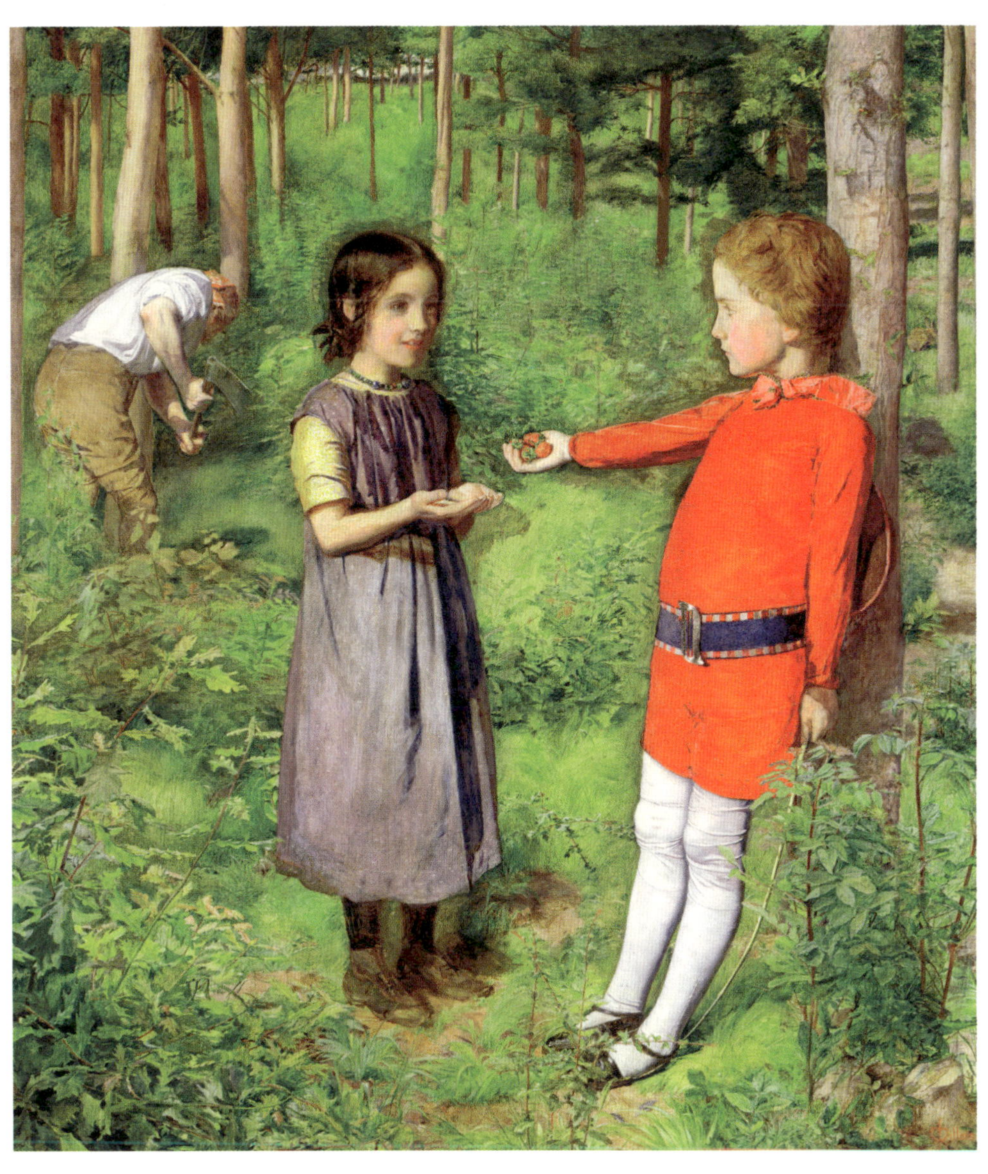

205. **John Everett Millais,**
The Woodman's Daughter
(detail), 1851, oil on canvas

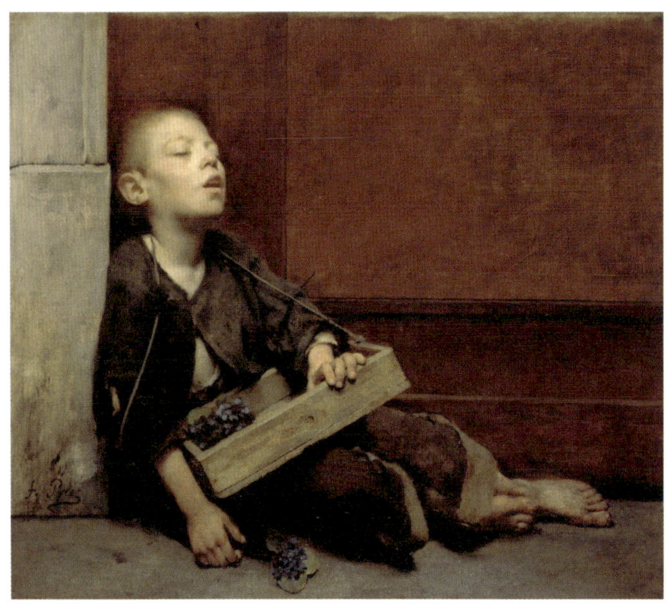

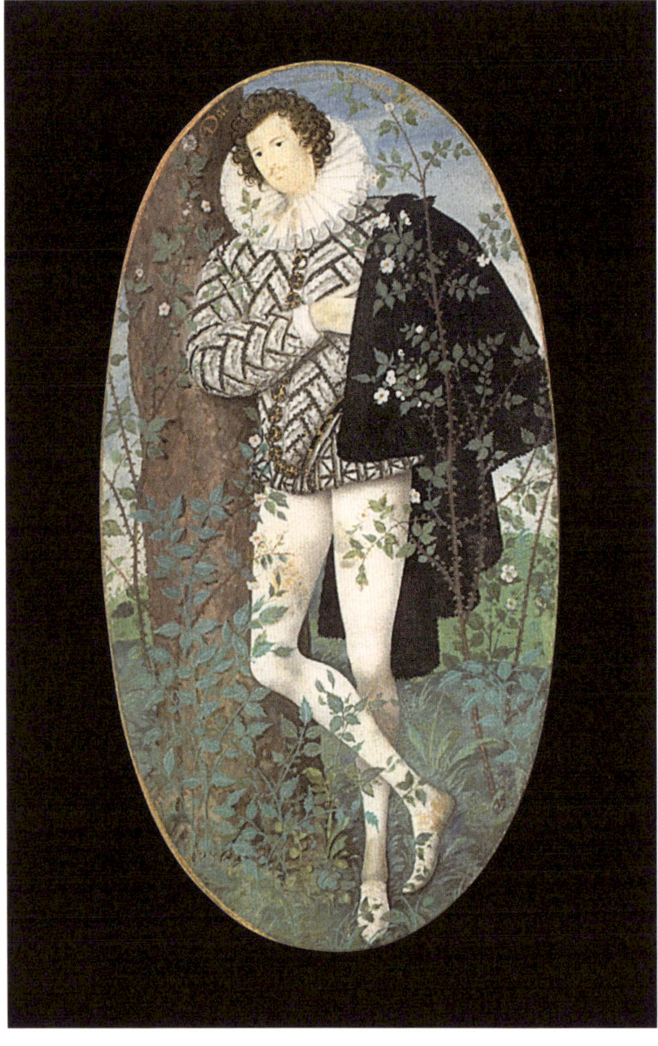

206. above **Fernand Pelez,**
A Martyr: The Violet Vendor,
1885, oil on canvas

207. left **Nicholas Hilliard,**
A Young Man Leaning Against
a Tree Amongst Roses, possibly
Robert Devereux, 2nd Earl of Essex,
1585–95, watercolour

208. opposite **Attributed to Peter Lely,**
Countess of Dorchester (detail),
late 17th century, oil on canvas

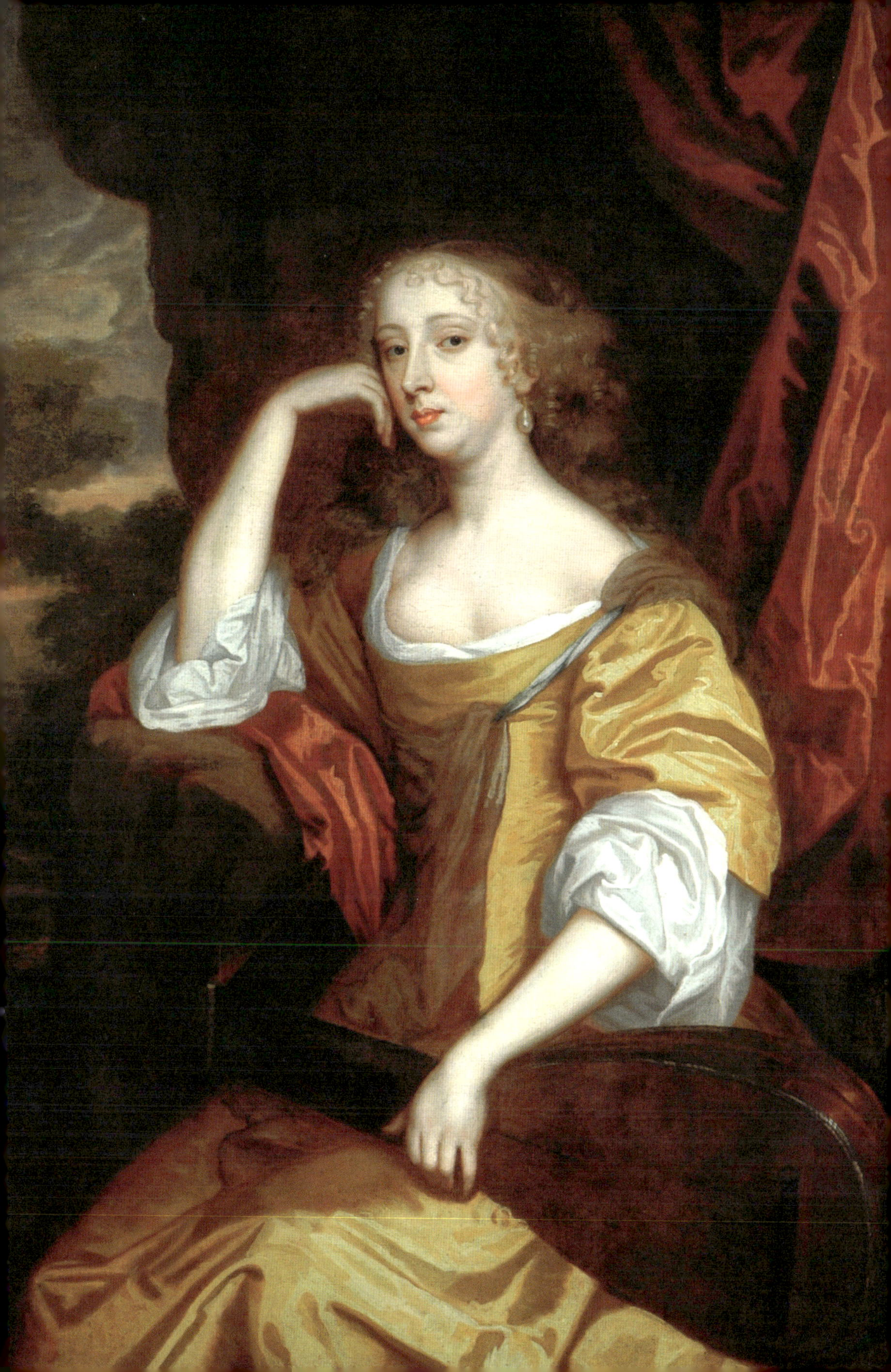

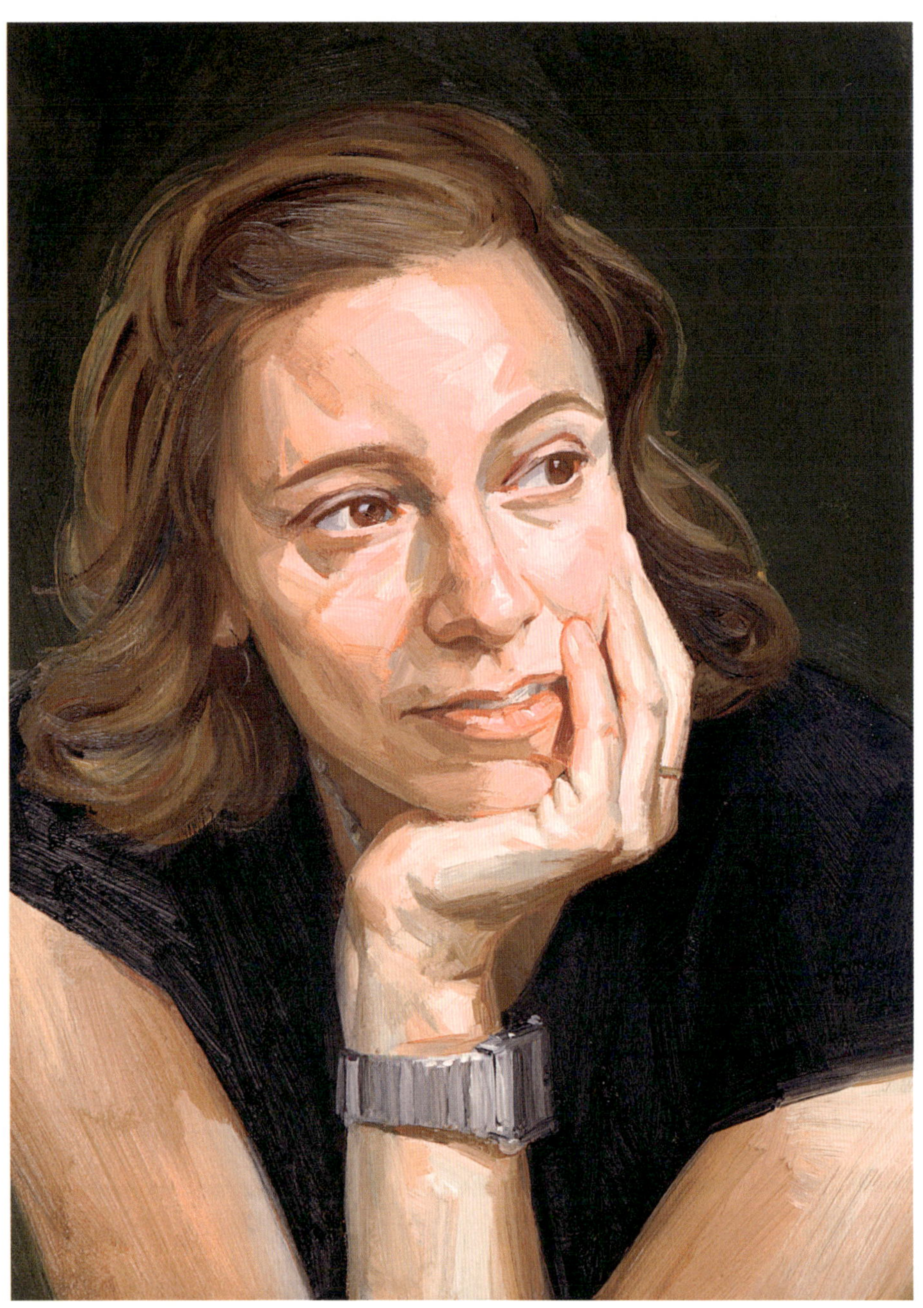

209. above **Tai-Shan Schierenberg,**
Portrait of Nicola Usborne,
2010, oil on canvas

210. opposite **Egon Schiele,**
Seated Woman with Bent Knee,
1917, crayon and gouache

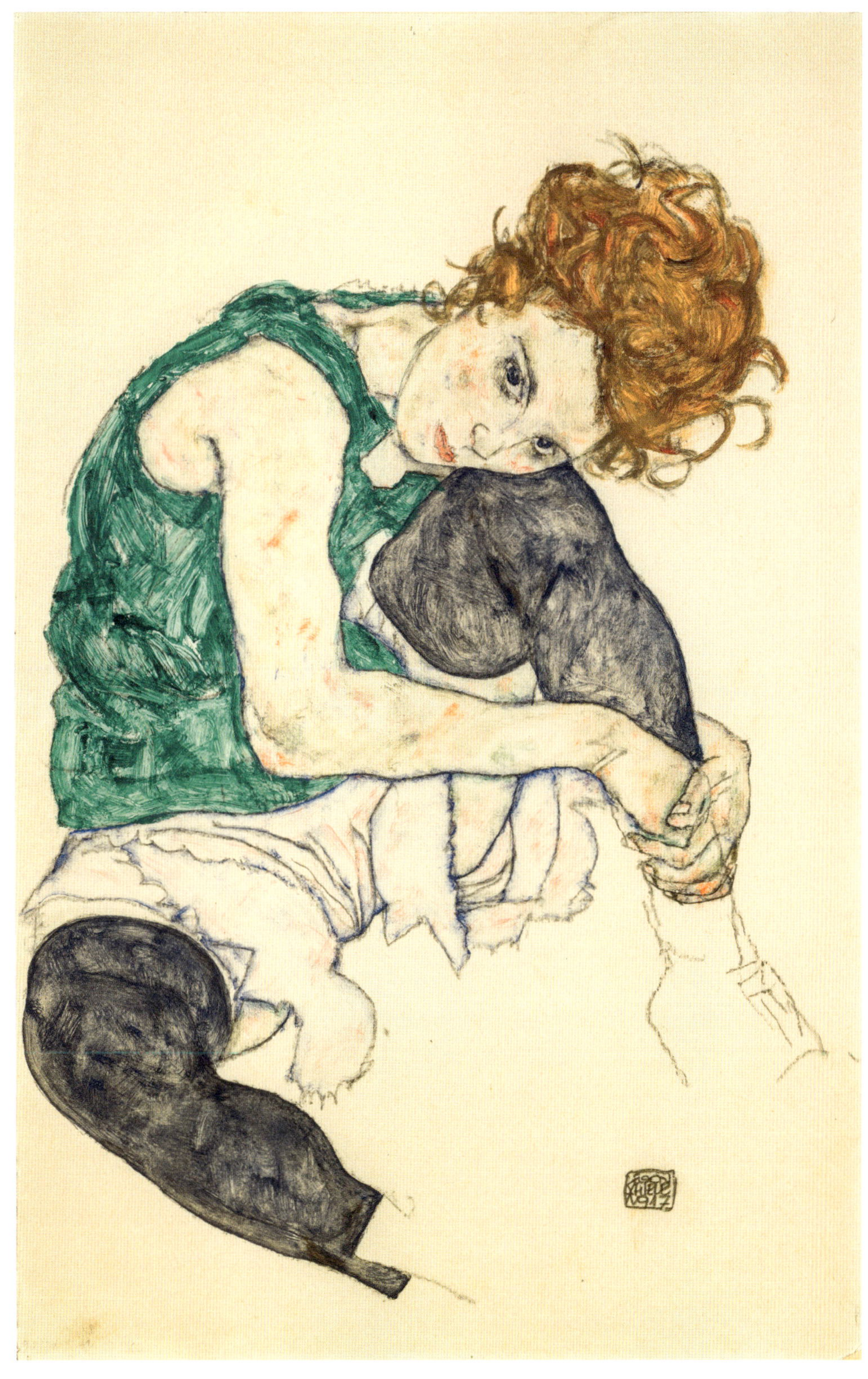

Lying Down

There is a long-standing tradition of the reclining female nude in Western art (see also 'The Nude', p. 236). Historically, artists generally presented their subject in a mythological setting, which effectively legitimized their use of nudity. *Sleeping Venus* (*c.* 1510), attributed to the Italian Renaissance painter Giorgione, is the earliest known example, showing a naked Venus lying on her back against a landscape of rolling hills. As is common with reclining nudes, Venus is depicted with her eyes closed, and with her head resting against her raised arm. In a much more sensual depiction, Titian's *Venus of Urbino* (1538) [211], a nude young woman is shown reclining on a bed or a couch in a sumptuous room, and looks the viewer straight in the eye. Although interpretation of the painting has caused much debate, it is unapologetically erotic.

The flattened line of a reclining figure can create a boring composition, and so artists often introduced vertical elements to make the scene more interesting. In one of the most famous reclining female nudes, *Olympia* (1863) [212] by Édouard Manet – which took inspiration from Titian's *Venus of Urbino* – the artist props up his subject on large pillows, and adds a servant in the background, who is bringing her flowers. In *Large Reclining Nude* (1935) [213], Henri Matisse achieves verticality by the extravagant position of the reclining figure's limbs. The private parts of these supine figures are obscured – by the position of the legs in the case of Matisse, while Manet makes use of Olympia's hand.

Even so, when *Olympia* was first exhibited in 1863, it caused an uproar. This was because the painting includes a number of small clues, lost on us today, that Olympia, instead of being a grand lady, is, in fact, a prostitute. To choose a prostitute as a subject for a major work of this kind was considered scandalous in the mid-19th century. Like Titian's Venus, she looks the viewer straight in the eye, but Olympia's gaze is almost confrontational. Even the position of the left hand, superficially so modest, was interpreted as meaning: if you want to see this part of me, you will have to pay.

The French Impressionist Auguste Renoir had a fascination with the naked female back, and many of his reclining nudes are viewed from behind. His early nudes were sharply defined, but his later ones had softer, fuzzier outlines that many critics heralded as an advanced form of Impressionism. In reality, the aged Renoir suffered from both myopia and acute arthritis in his fingers, which meant that he was no longer able to achieve the same level of precision in his work. It must be said, however, that the softness of his later work did add to its erotic appeal.

The British painter John William Godward was also fond of painting female figures in a variety of reclining positions, although his are fully clothed. Godward was a protégé of Sir Lawrence Alma-Tadema and found inspiration in ancient Rome and Greece. This can be seen clearly in *Dolce Far Niente* (1904) [216], one of his best-known paintings, in which a beautiful young woman in classical dress lies on soft furs by a lily pond with a faraway look in her eyes.

In *Young Ladies on the Banks of the Seine* (1857) [215], Gustave Courbet depicts the central female figure clothed but on her stomach, while her female companion stares dreamily into the distance. When the painting was exhibited at the Paris Salon, it created a stir because it undermined the rather rigid rules that were then applied to the portrayal of women, particularly in its erotic undertones. The principal figure not only reveals her feet and her petticoat, but gazes at the viewer of the painting with sensuously hooded eyes. This made the painting more shocking to mid-19th-century eyes than if she had been depicted as a classical nude. The presence of a man's hat in the nearby boat made the scene even more suggestive.

In *Sunbather* (1966) [214], David Hockney also depicts his male subject on his front, but he is naked. This is one of a series of paintings executed in Los Angeles in the 1960s, a period in which the theme of the swimming pool became increasingly prominent in the artist's work. Indeed, the water is as much the subject of *Sunbather* as the male figure. Hockney draws on another recurring theme in Western art – that of bathers (perhaps most popularly associated with Georges Seurat and his *Bathers at Asnières* of 1884) – but offers a homoerotic take on the popular tradition.

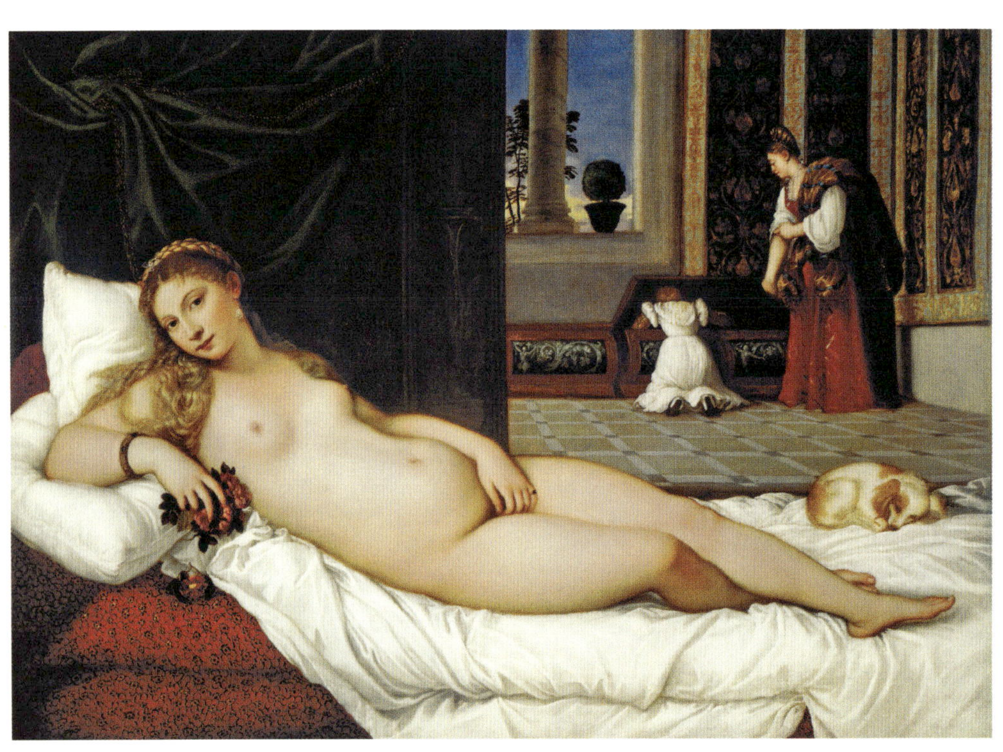

211. **Titian,** *Venus of Urbino,*
1538, oil on canvas

     At Rest / Lying Down

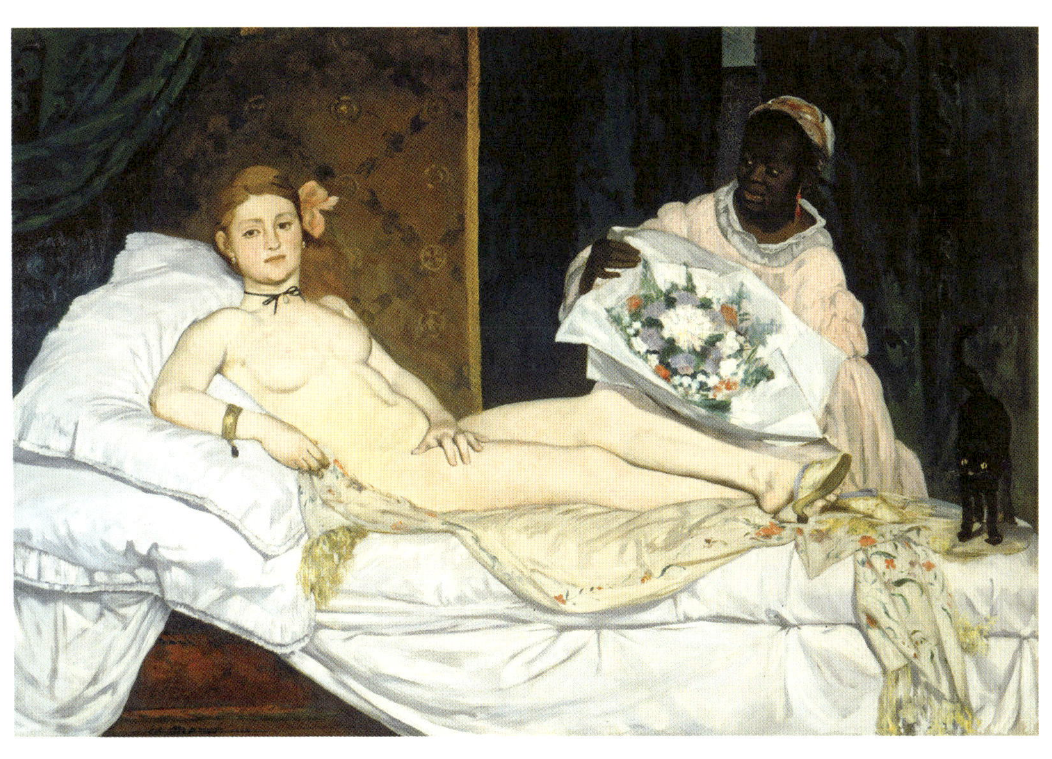

212. **Édouard Manet,**
Olympia, **1863, oil on canvas**

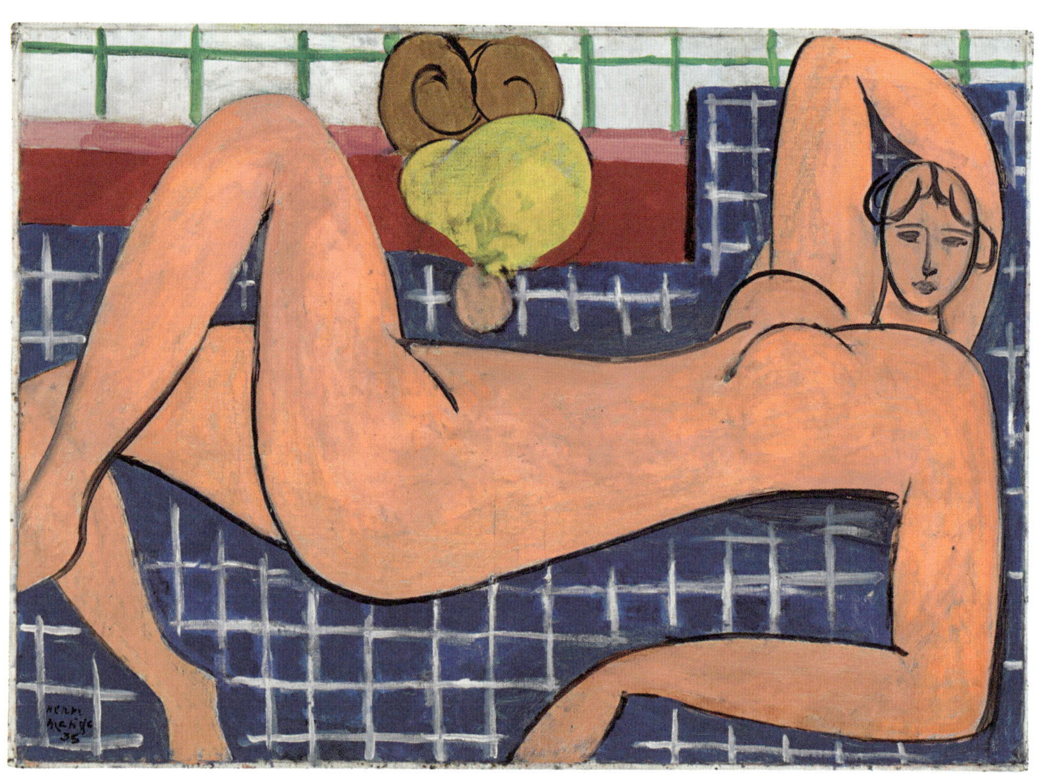

213. **Henri Matisse,**
Large Reclining Nude,
1935, oil on canvas

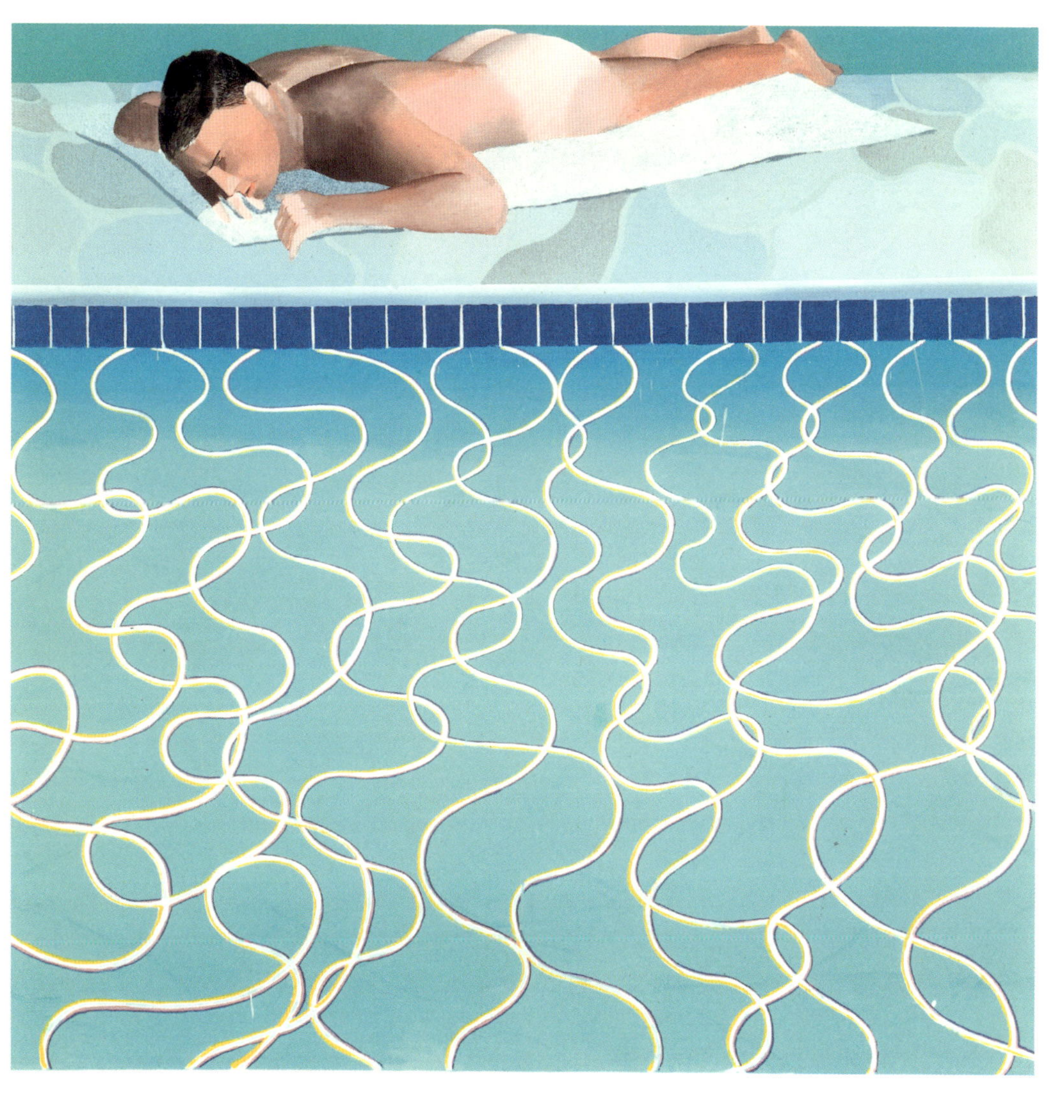

214. **David Hockney,** *Sunbather,*
1966, acrylic on canvas

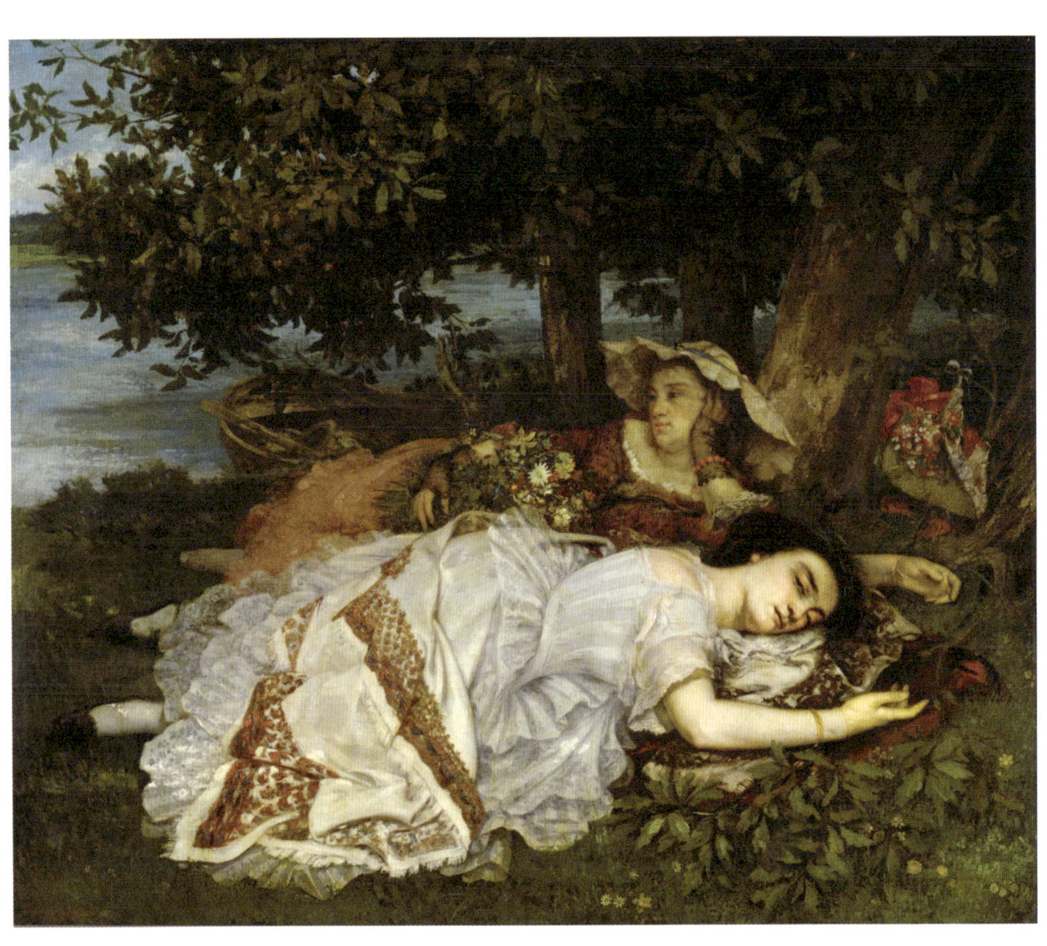

215. **Gustave Courbet,**
***Young Ladies on the Banks of
the Seine***, 1857, oil on canvas

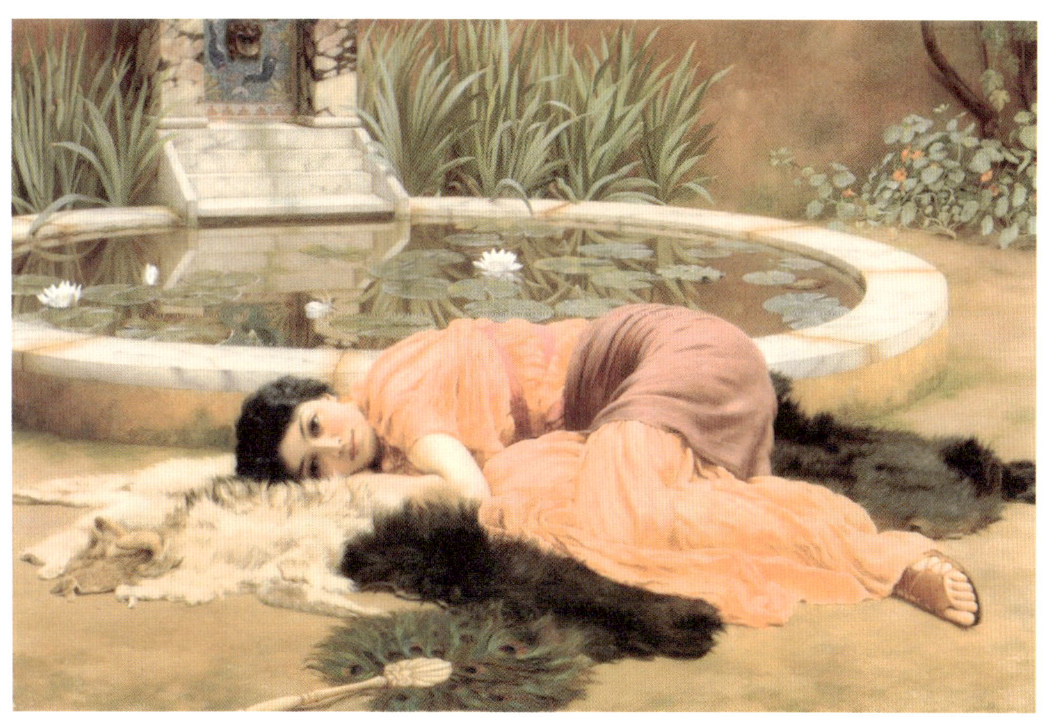

216. **John William Godward,**
Dolce Far Niente, **1904,**
oil on canvas

Rocking

It may seem strange to include rocking as a form of resting, but it does have an important role to play. It can be traced back to life in the womb, when a fetus is exposed to three basic rhythms: the beating of the mother's heart, the breathing of the mother's lungs, and the swaying of the mother's body as she walks. In its later stages of development, the fetus is sensitive to each of these three rhythms, and may continue to associate them with a state of restful tranquillity once born.

Without knowing why she does it, a mother will intuitively rock her baby in her arms when she wishes to calm it. If this rocking action is performed too quickly or too slowly, it is unlikely to have the desired effect. Careful studies have shown that the optimum calming speed for rocking is between 60 and 70 rocks per minute. This closely matches the average heart rate of an adult, and suggests that this is the crucial rhythm that leaves its mark on the baby.

Being rocked by a mother is the first form that this action takes, but it also appears in several other contexts. One is being rocked to sleep in a cradle, which is also believed to be most effective at heart rate speed. If a small child feels miserable, it may console itself by rocking its upper body back and forth in a rhythmic manner. A similar action can be seen in adults if they find themselves in a state of acute distress or grief. It is thought that this kind of response to a stressful situation may be linked to the calming associations of the rocking action in childhood.

A device that exploits the soothing influence of being rocked back and forth is the rocking chair, and artists have, from time to time, portrayed its restful, gently reassuring rhythmic movement. Although rocking cradles have existed since ancient times, rocking chairs for adults were not invented until the early 18th century. Some of the earliest depictions of people seated in rocking chairs appear in American folk art from this period.

In the 19th century, rocking chairs became popular as a subject for portrait painters. In *Young Woman in a Rocking Chair* (c. 1873) [218], a study for *The Last Evening*, the French artist James Tissot depicted a young woman, lost in thought, resting in a rocking chair. An early work by Edvard Munch, entitled *Aunt Karen in the Rocking Chair* (1883) [219], depicts the artist's aunt in a subdued mood. However, the most famous advocate of the rocking chair was arguably President John F. Kennedy [217]. He suffered from back pain throughout his life and owned a series of rocking chairs – including one that he used when he travelled on Air Force One.

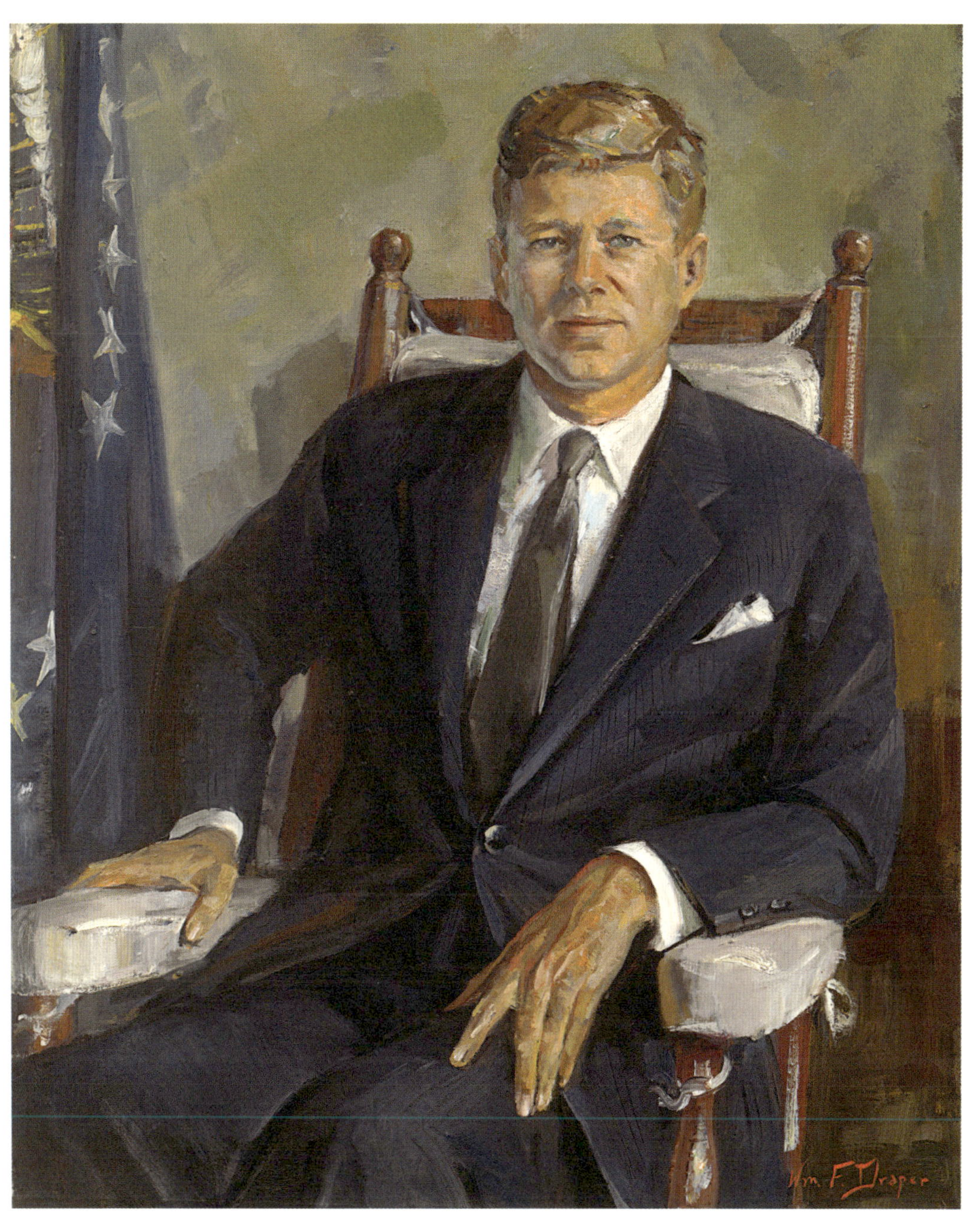

217. **William F. Draper,**
John F. Kennedy,
1966, oil on canvas

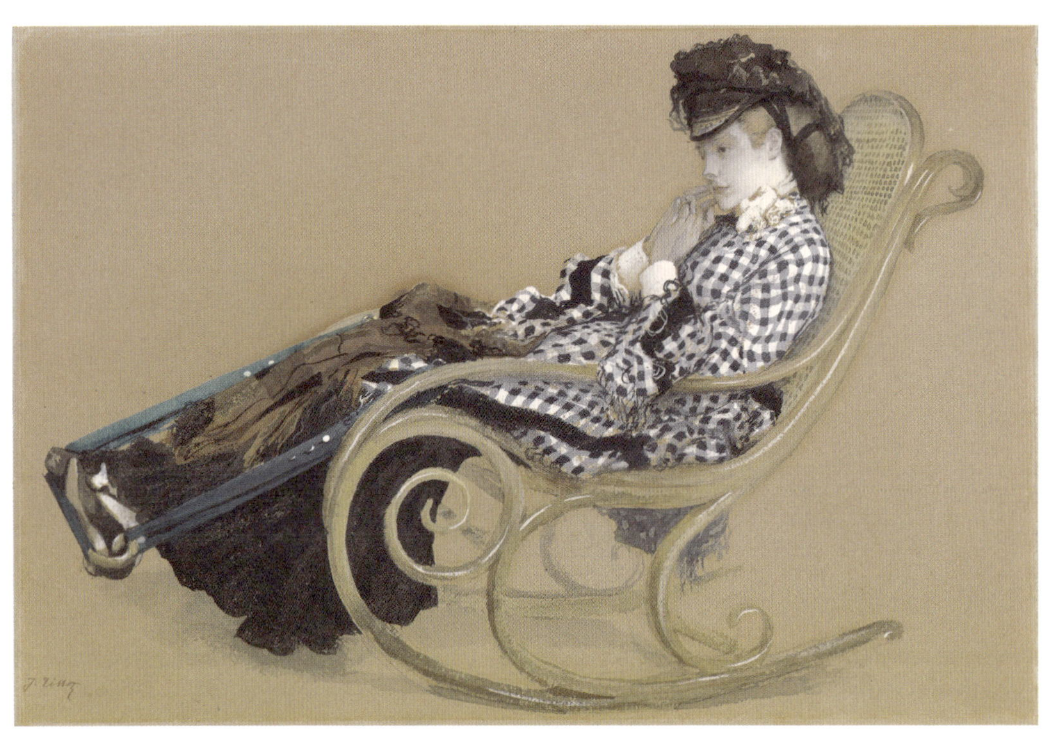

218. **James Tissot,** *Young Woman in a Rocking Chair*, **study for the painting** *The Last Evening*, **c. 1873, brush with gouache and watercolour, over graphite on brown paper**

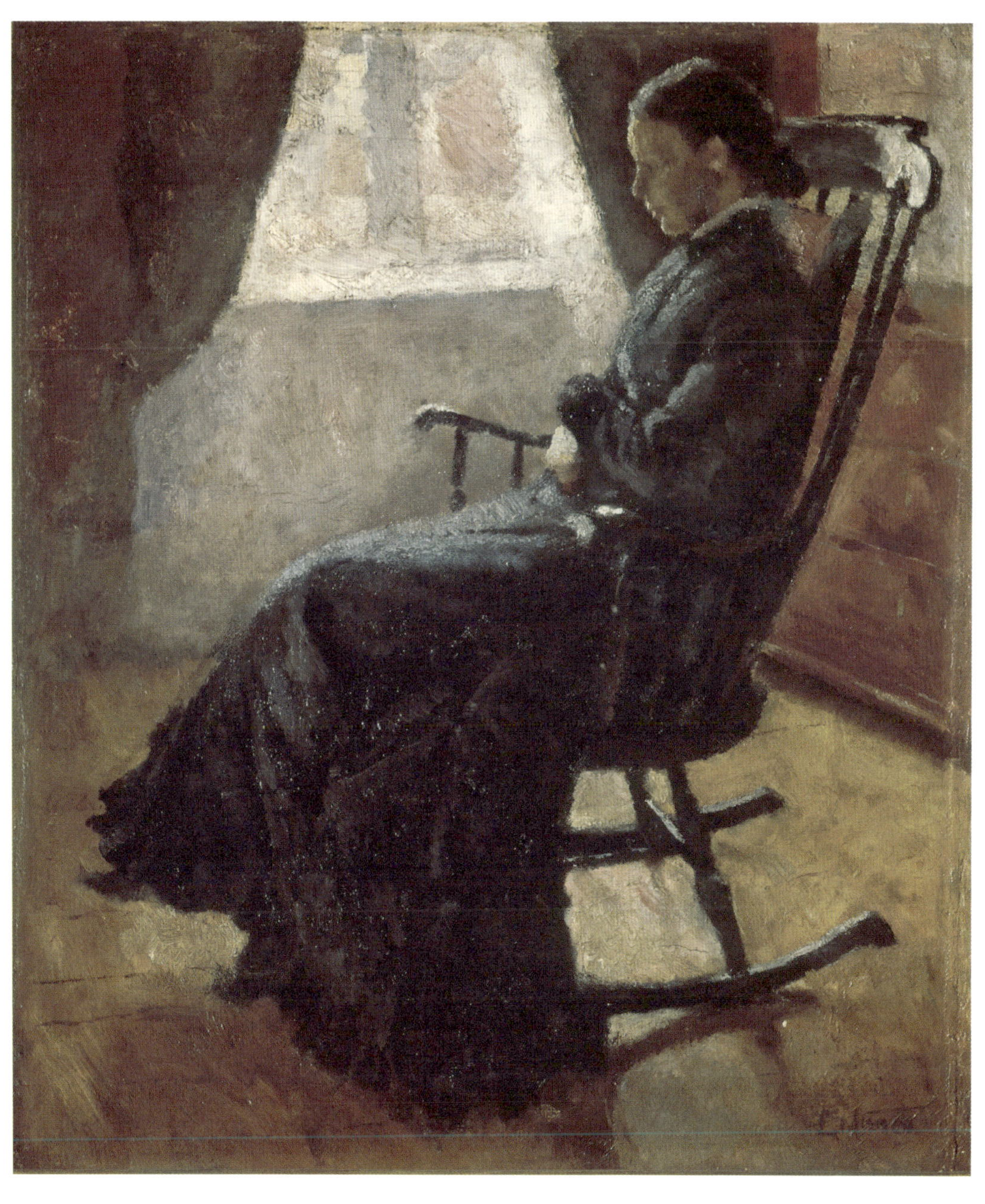

219. Edvard Munch, *Aunt Karen in the Rocking Chair*, 1883, oil on canvas

Yawning

Yawning is a strange action that has puzzled scientists for many years. There is no mystery about *when* it happens. It primarily occurs at moments of tiredness, when we feel the need to rest but perhaps cannot yet do so, although it can also be associated with boredom. Yawning involves a combination of opening the jaws to the maximum, while inhaling and then exhaling through the gaping mouth, and is often accompanied by stretching movements of the neck, chest and arms. It is highly contagious. When one person sees another yawning, they often find themselves drawn into performing the same action. This can sometimes spread to a whole group of people.

However, although we understand the context of the action and the form it takes, we don't fully understand *why* we yawn. One suggestion is that a sudden large intake of air into the lungs may help to keep us awake. Unfortunately for this theory, fish also yawn in water. Another ingenious explanation is that it helps to synchronize a group for sleeping, and is similar to certain pre-roosting activities of birds. Again, there is a weakness to this argument because yawning also occurs in solitary animals. A third possibility is that the essential feature of the yawn is the stretching of the jaw muscles, which is often accompanied by stretching of other parts of the body. This slightly increases the heart rate, and may help to reduce the feeling of tiredness. But, if this is the explanation, why is it that yawning often involves only the stretching of the jaw muscles? Research into the true function of yawning continues, but progress is slow. The discovery that people with autism spectrum disorders or schizophrenia are less likely to exhibit 'contagious yawning' has, however, added fresh insight into the topic.

Few artists have attempted to capture the moment of the yawn, probably because, for portraiture, it does not create a particularly becoming image. The 18th-century artist Joseph Ducreux, who had an interest in physiognomy and the extreme forms of facial expression, has provided us with arguably the most accurate depiction of this strange but familiar action. In *Self-portrait, Yawning* (1783) [220], he depicts himself at the peak of a massive yawn, which includes the characteristic asymmetrical stretching of the arms, as well as the gaping mouth.

Luigi i Montejano's *Yawning Men* (1850) [221] makes fun of the infectious nature of the action. The painting depicts a group of four young men: the two men in the centre of the composition appear to be suffering from an uncontrollable bout of contagious yawning, while their friends make fun of them in a light-hearted way.

In 1869, the Hungarian artist Mihály Munkácsy painted a portrait of an exhausted and overworked apprentice at the moment when his yawn was at its highest intensity [222]. Edgar Degas portrays a similar scene of exhausted workers in *Two Women Ironing* (*c.* 1884–86) [223]. In this depiction of two women toiling in the laundry, one of them has paused momentarily as a yawn overtakes her.

In more recent times, the Chinese artist Fang Lijun produced a remarkable image of a shaven-headed young man, mid-yawn, in a painting entitled *Series 2 No. 2* (1991–92) [224]. Lijun was one of the leading proponents of the Cynical Realism movement of the early 1990s, exploring such themes as the loss of direction in Chinese youth.

In 2015, the Chilean-born artist Sebastian Errazuriz took over a series of illuminated billboards in Times Square, New York, as part of an amusing installation called *A Pause in the City that Never Sleeps*. Between 23.57 pm and midnight throughout January, a black-and-white video of Errazuriz's yawning face was shown on approximately fifty screens, as a form of peaceful protest against the market system surrounding him. By inducing contagious yawning among the people in the streets below, the artist hoped to create a moment of pause and joint protest.

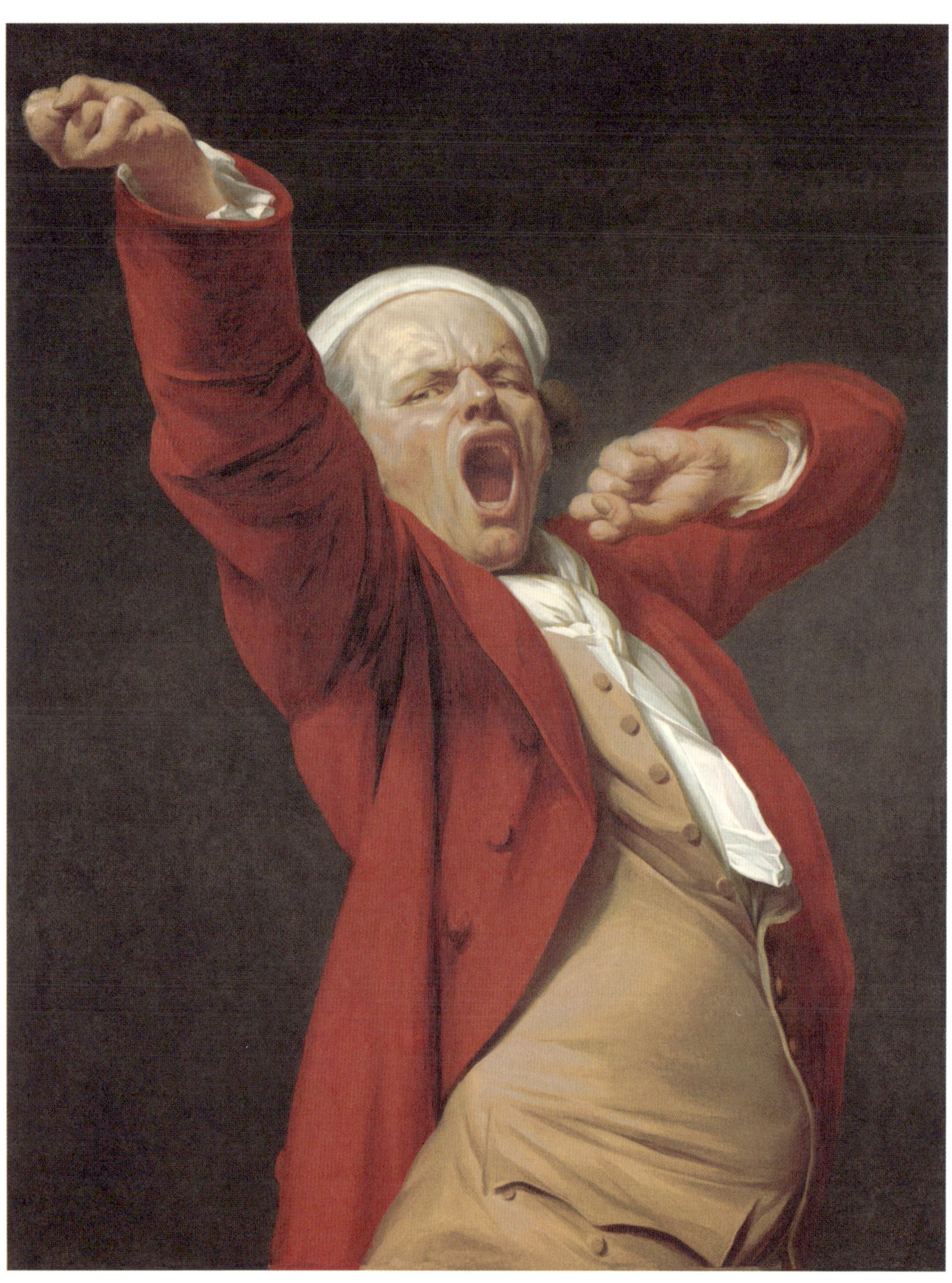

220. **Joseph Ducreux,**
Self-portrait, Yawning,
1783, oil on canvas

    At Rest / Yawning

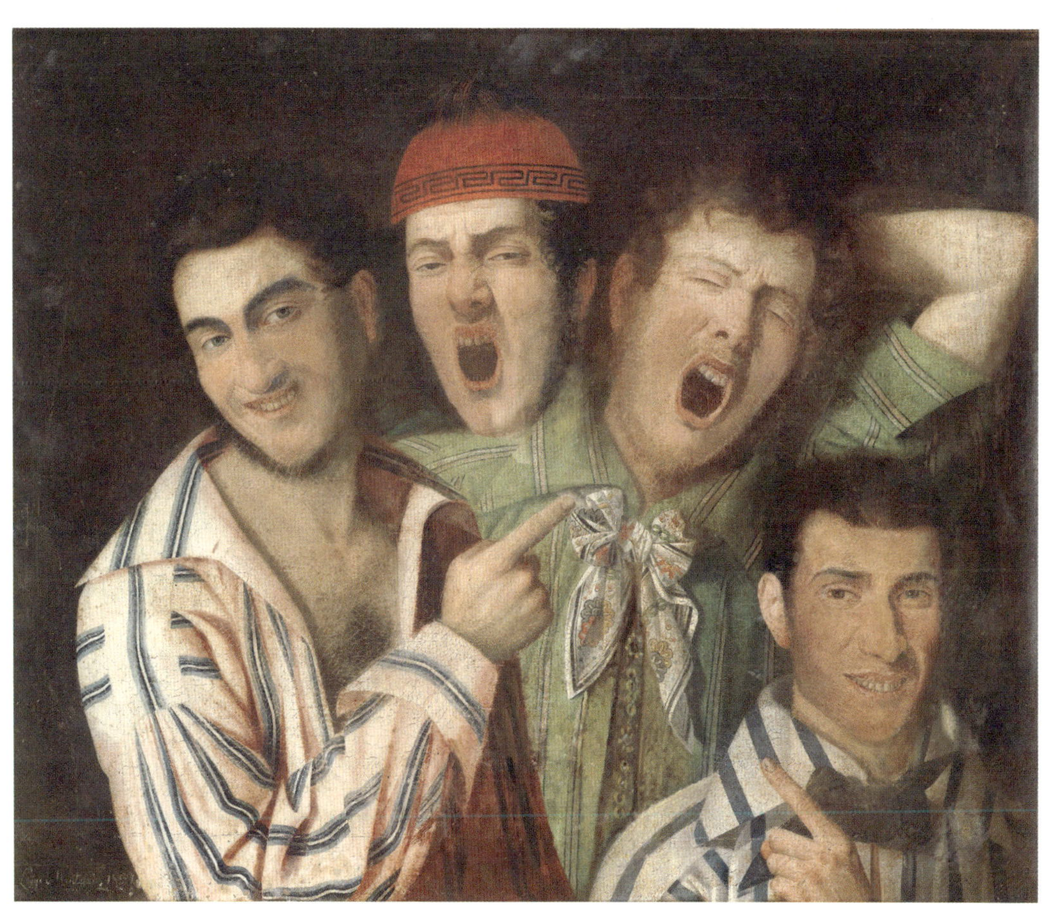

221. **Luigi i Montejano,**
Yawning Men, 1850,
oil on canvas

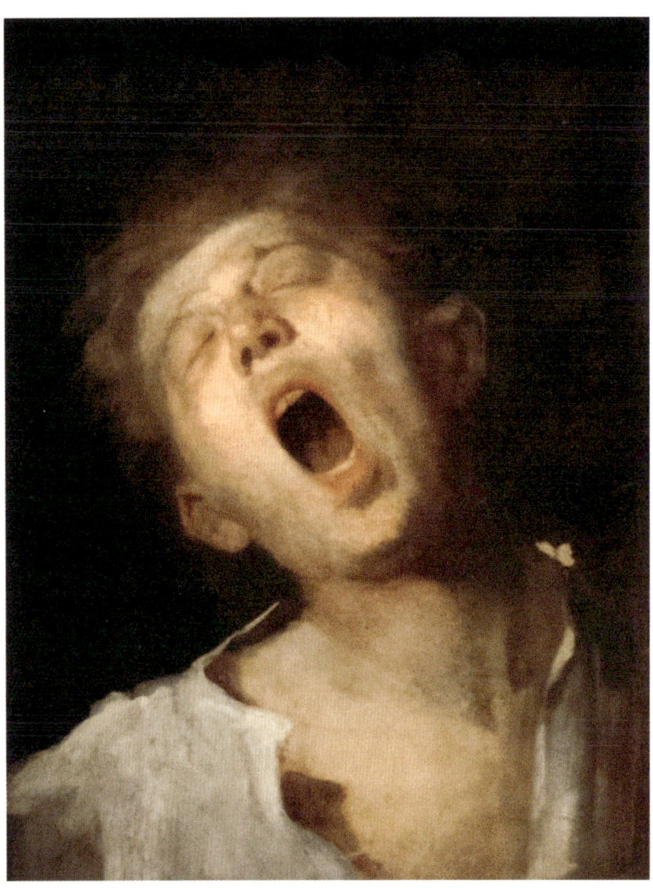

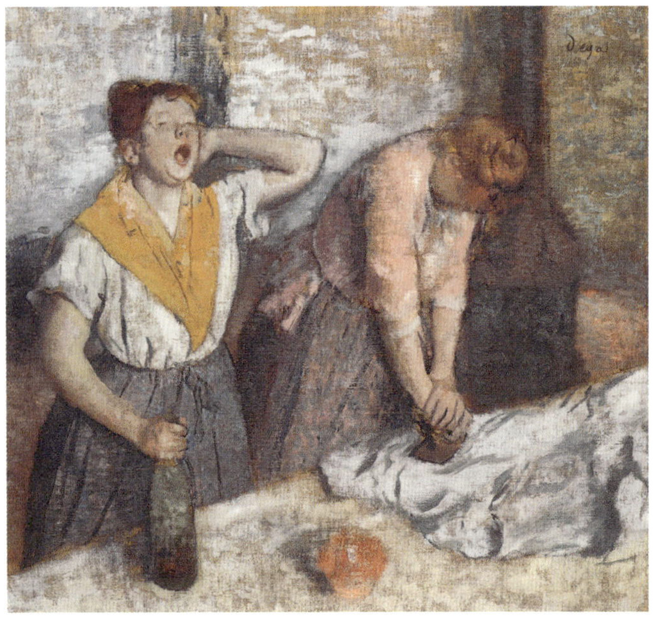

222. above **Mihály Munkácsy,**
***Yawning Apprentice*, 1869,**
oil on canvas

223. left **Edgar Degas, *Two Women
Ironing*, c. 1884–86, oil on canvas**

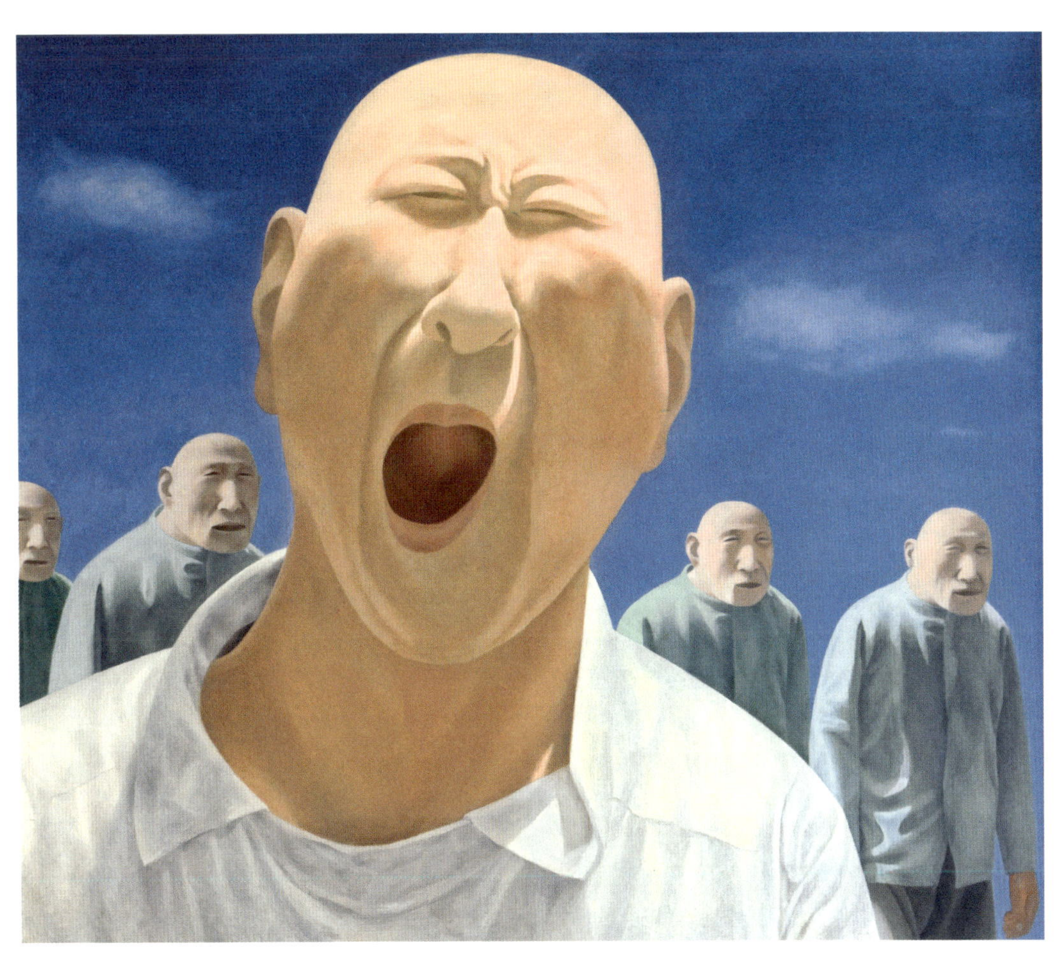

224. **Fang Lijun**, *Series 2 No. 2*,
1991–92, oil on canvas

Sleeping

Human beings spend, on average, about one third of their lives sleeping. While many of us value sleep as a blissful release from the daily grind, others view it as an appalling waste of time. As Edgar Allan Poe famously commented, 'Sleep, those little slices of death – how I loathe them.' Yet sleep is absolutely essential, not only because our bodies require physical rest, but also because our brains need time to organize and file away the information of the previous waking period. Prolonged sleep deprivation is known to have a detrimental effect on mental as well as physical health.

Sleeping postures can be separated into two distinct groups, depending on whether sleep is deliberate (i.e. we choose our position) or unintentional (i.e. we drift off in whatever position we happen to be in at the time). With deliberate sleep, psychiatrists have suggested that the particular posture we choose, when we settle down for the night, can be used to interpret our general mental state. The fetal position (lying on one's side with the knees drawn up) is widely known in this context, but many other sleeping postures have been recognized, including the royal (lying on the back with the arms down by the sides); the flamingo (lying on one's side, with one leg bent and one straight); the water-wings (on one's back, with the hands clasped behind the head); the Cyclops (on one's back, with one arm up and over the head, covering one eye); the Dutch wife (on one's belly or side, clasping a pillow); and the leaner (on one's side, resting the side of the head on one hand). Indeed, the initial sleeping position is likely to change between 40 and 70 times over the course of a night, owing to natural shifts that prevent cramping of limbs and other parts of the body.

There are countless examples of works of art that portray sleeping figures, dating from ancient civilizations up to modern times, but they are almost entirely absent from earlier, prehistoric art. There is, however, one remarkable exception. Known as the Sleeping Goddess of Malta [226], this small clay figure – which is thought to be about 5,000 years old – was discovered in a mysterious underground megalithic temple, the Hypogeum. She is shown sleeping on her right side with her head resting on what appears to be a stone pillow. Her posture is believed to be unique in prehistoric art: other early female figurines are depicted standing or sitting (or, occasionally, squatting in a birthing posture). Moreover, the figure is not stylized but is shown with her arms in a naturalistic, asymmetrical arrangement.

Among the most dramatic representations of a sleeping human figure are the huge statues of the reclining Buddha that can be seen all over Southeast Asia. The largest, erected near Mawlamyine in Burma, is about 180 metres (600 ft) long and 30 metres (100 ft) high. These colossal figures depict the Lord Buddha in his final moments of life on earth. Knowing that death was approaching, he lay down on his right side, with his right hand supporting his head, and his body facing west. In Buddhism, this posture is known as the Mahaparinirvana asana, and the statues are referred to as the Nirvana Buddhas.

Unintentional sleep can lead to a broad range of postures, depending on how we were sitting, crouching or reclining when we dozed off. For artists who decide to portray sleeping figures, this second type of slumber has tended to be more popular, probably because it creates more interesting compositions. *The Barberini Faun* [225], carved by an unknown Hellenistic artist in the late third or early second century BC, is a perfect example of this. It shows a naked male figure asleep on an animal skin that has been spread out on a rock. His sprawled limbs create a wonderfully angular composition. His left arm, which is missing, seems to be hanging down loosely, while his right arm is bent up and over to help cradle his tilted head against his left shoulder. A similar angularity of the limbs is seen in a portrait by the German artist Bernhard Strigel, *Sleeping Grave Guard* (1520) [227]. We feel the mixture of boredom and exhaustion that has led this lonely figure to slump against a tree and, with his head propped against his hand and his mouth open, drift away into a world of dreams.

In Western art, the story of *Sleeping Beauty* has proved a popular theme, but poses a particular problem for artists because she has to be shown in a deep, almost deathlike slumber, as if lying in state – a formal posture that can make the picture look rather boring. In a late Victorian depiction of the tale, *The Rose Bower* (1870–90) [229], part of a series of works on the subject by the Pre-Raphaelite Edward Burne-Jones, the artist solves the problem in two ways – allowing her head to loll sideways, so that her cheek rests on her pillow, and surrounding her with sleeping companions, whose informal postures create a more interesting composition.

There is a completely different mood in Henry Fuseli's famous painting of a woman having a restless night's sleep, *The Nightmare* (1781) [230]. Because we, the viewers of the painting, cannot see inside her tormented head, the artist has obligingly externalized her nightmare in the form of a sinister demon squatting on her stomach, while a blind, black horse (the night-mare?) in the background appears to look on menacingly. The woman's posture is appropriately melodramatic, with her head and arms hanging down over the end of her bed.

In *Sleep* (1937) [231], Salvador Dalí also explores the realm of the unconscious, reducing the slumbering body to little more than a huge head. The artist himself commented at the time, 'Sleep is a veritable chrysalitic monster whose morphology and nostalgia are leaning on eleven principal crutches...' These crutches do not look strong enough to hold up the great weight of the head, suggesting that Dalí sees the sleeper as dreamily floating in space and requiring only modest support.

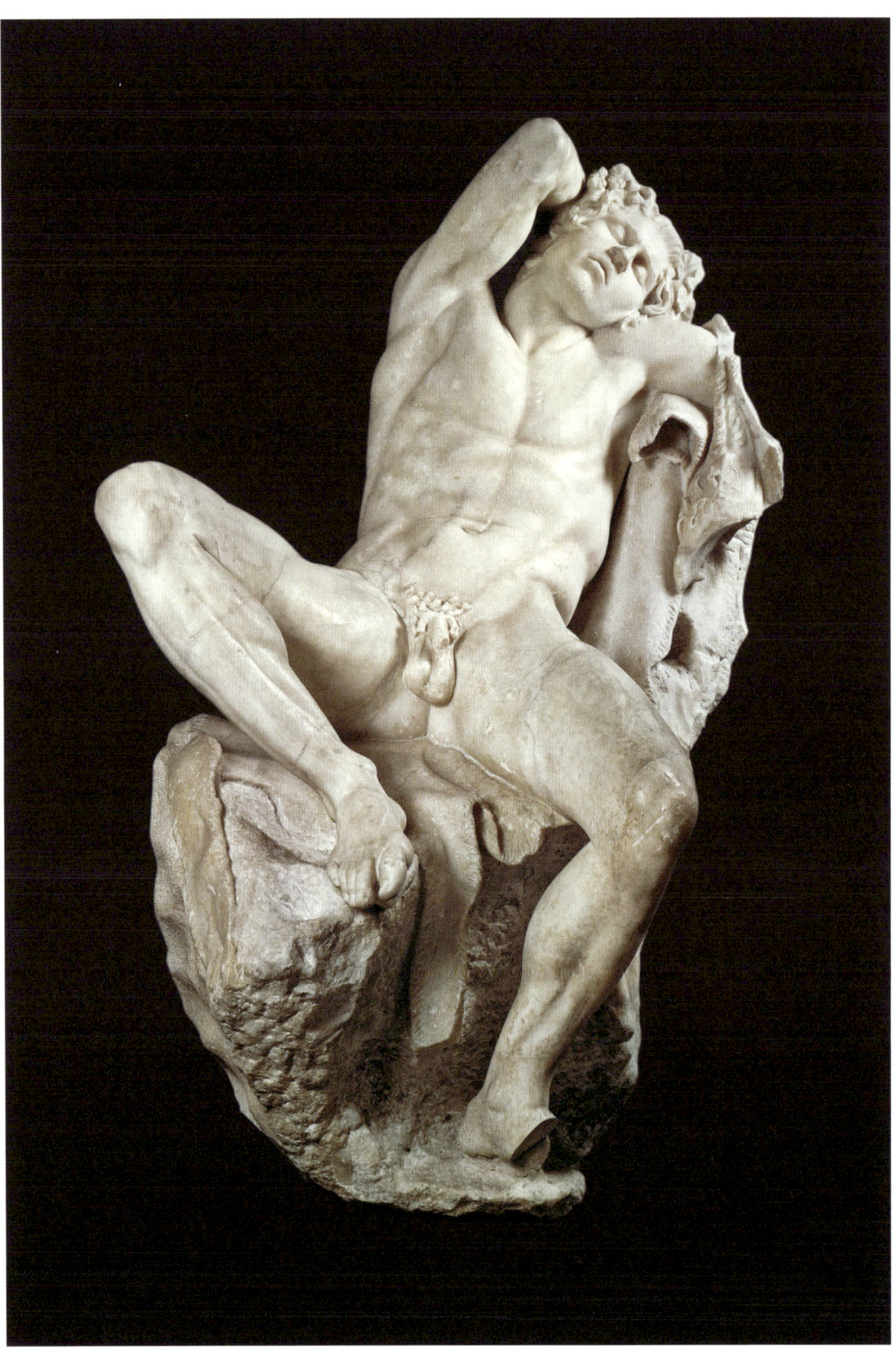

   At Rest / Sleeping

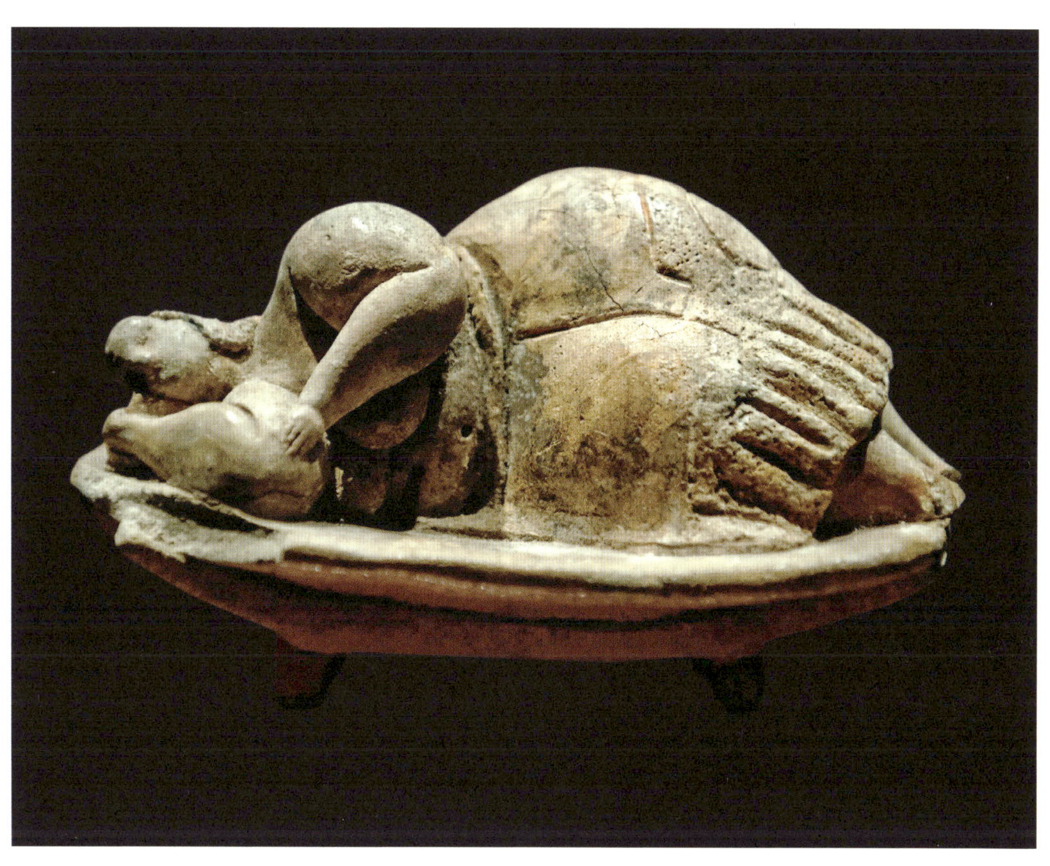

225. opposite **Unknown sculptor,
The Barberini Faun, 3rd–2nd
century BC, marble**

226. above **Sleeping Goddess
of Malta, clay figure from
the Hal-Saflieni Hypogeum,
Malta, 3000 BC**

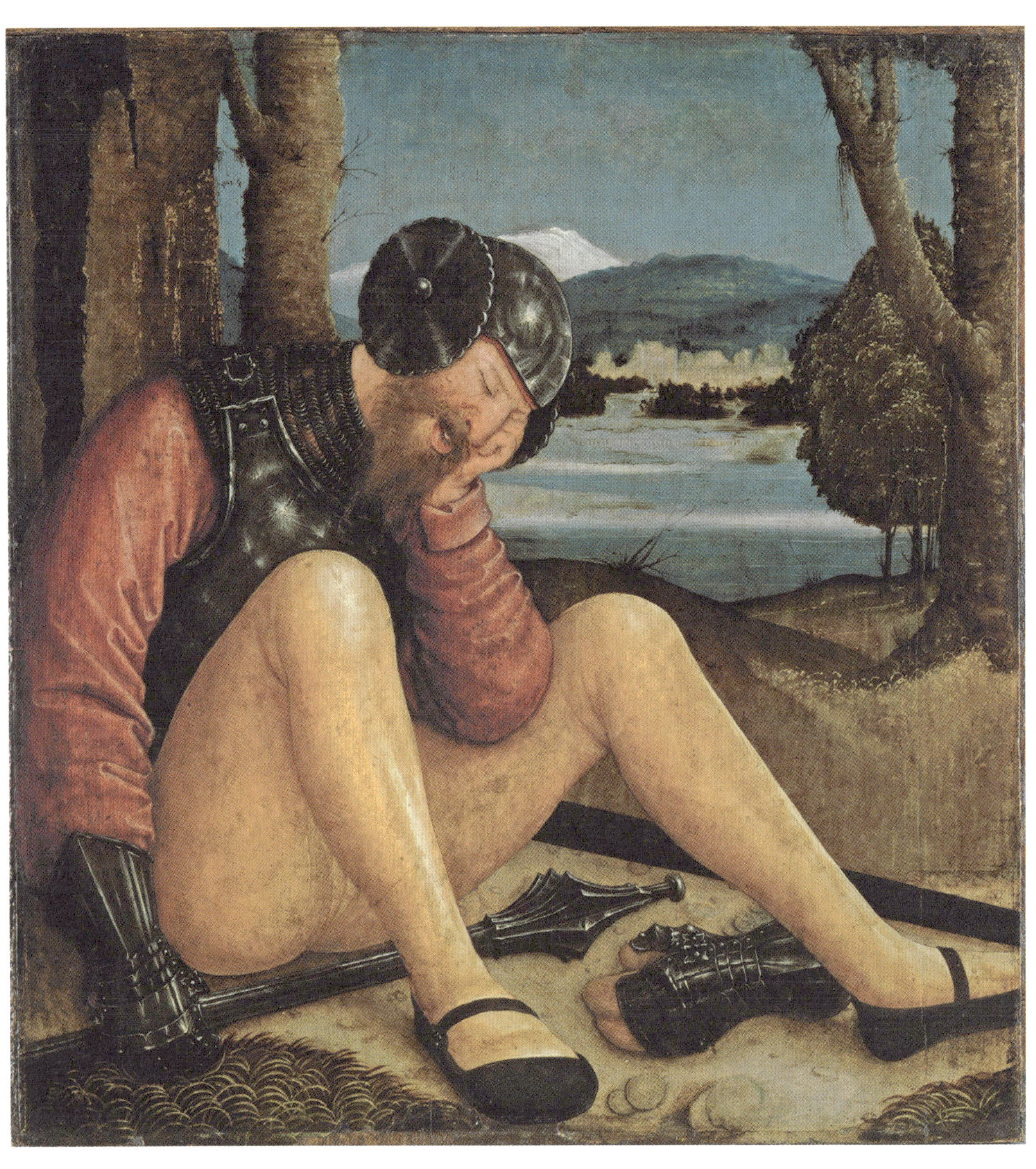

227. **Bernhard Strigel,**
Sleeping Grave Guard,
1520, oil on panel

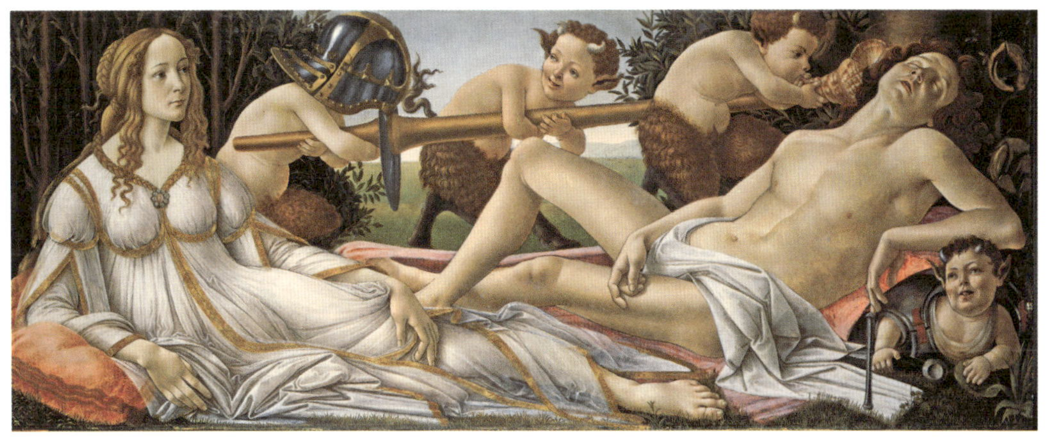

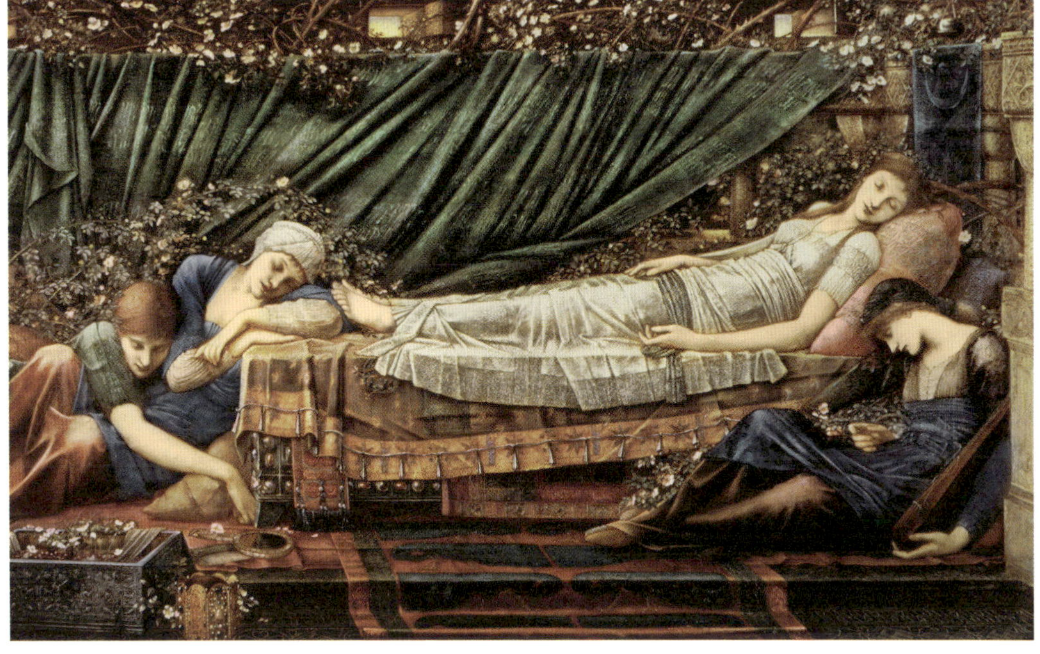

228. top **Sandro Botticelli,**
Venus and Mars, c. 1485,
tempera and oil on poplar

229. above **Edward Burne-Jones,**
The Rose Bower (detail), 'The
Briar Rose' Series, 1870–90,
oil on canvas

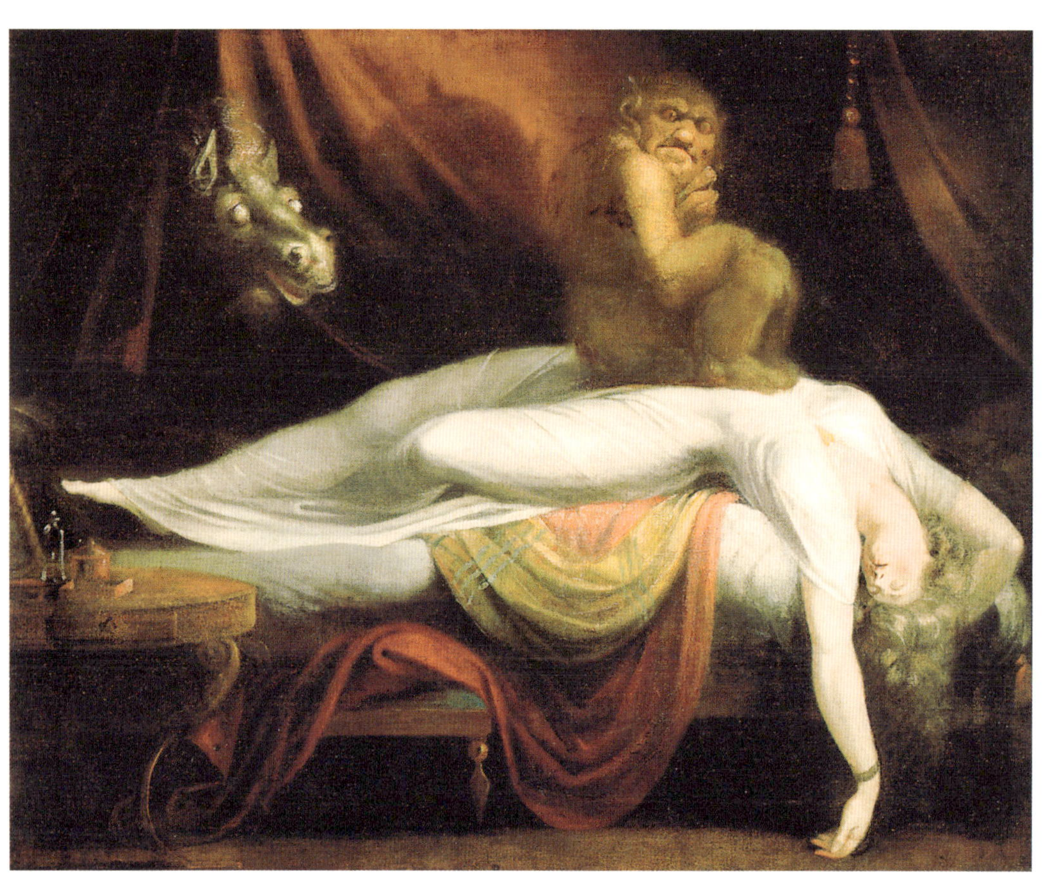

230. **Henry Fuseli,**
The Nightmare, 1781,
oil on canvas

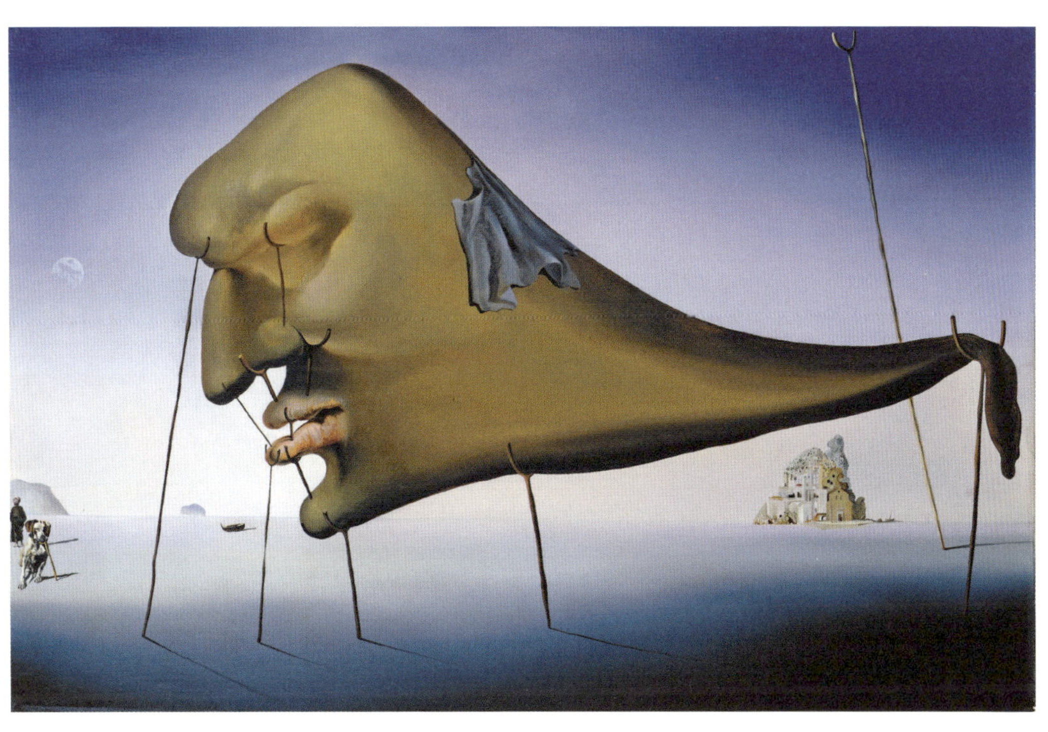

231. **Salvador Dalí,** *Sleep*,
1937, oil on canvas

Further Reading

Aldrete, Gregory S., *Gestures and Acclamations in Ancient Rome*, Baltimore: Johns Hopkins University Press, 1999

Allegro, John M., *The Sacred Mushroom and the Cross: A Study of the Nature and Origins of Christianity within the Fertility Cults of the Ancient Near East*, London: Hodder & Stoughton, 1970

Anon., *The Young Lady's Book*, London: Vizetelly, Branston & Co., 1829

Anon., *Charm of the Curtsey, The San Francisco Sunday Call*, vol. 111, no. 101, 10 March 1912

Barbaut, Jacques, *Histoires de la naissance à travers le monde*, Paris: Calmann-Lévy, 1990

Blue, Adrianne, *On Kissing: From the Metaphysical to the Erotic*, London: Gollancz, 1996

Bremmer, Jan, & Roodenburg, Herman (eds), *A Cultural History of Gesture: From Antiquity to the Present Day*, Cambridge: Polity Press, 1991

Corbeill, Anthony, *Nature Embodied: Gesture in Ancient Rome*, Princeton, NJ, & Oxford, UK: Princeton University Press, 2004

Craske, Matthew, *William Hogarth*, London: Tate Gallery Publications, 2000

De Jorio, Andrea, *La mimica degli antichi investigata nel gestire napoletano* (*Gesture in Naples and Gesture in Classical Antiquity*), Naples, 1832

Dunkell, Samuel, *Sleep Positions: The Night Language of the Body*, London: Heinemann, 1977

Elworthy, Frederick Thomas, *Horns of Honour: And Other Studies in the By-ways of Archaeology*, London: John Murray, 1900

Fryer, Peter, *Mrs Grundy: Studies in English Prudery*, London: Dennis Dobson, 1963

Grosbois, Charles, *Shunga: Images of Spring*, Geneva: Nagel, 1964

Harvey, Karen (ed.), *The Kiss in History*, Manchester: Manchester University Press, 2005

Holland, Evangeline. *Edwardian England: A Guide to Everyday Life, 1900–1914*, London: Plum Bun Publishing, 2014

Kunesh, Thomas Peter, *The Pseudo-zygodactylous Gesture of the Lactating Goddess: Evolution and Migration*, a thesis submitted to the faculty of the Graduate School of the University of Minnesota in partial fulfilment of the requirements for the degree of Master of Arts in Religious Studies, Minnesota, 1990

Marcardé, Jean, *Roma Amor: Essay on Erotic Elements in Etruscan and Roman Art*, Geneva: Nagel, 1961

Masséglia, Jane, *Body Language in Hellenistic Art and Society*, Oxford: Oxford University Press, 2015

Meyer, Arline, *Re-dressing Classical Statuary: The Eighteenth-Century 'Hand-in-Waistcoat' Portrait*, *The Art Bulletin* (College Art Association of America), vol. 77, no. 1, March 1995, pp. 45–63

Morris, Desmond, *The Naked Ape: A Zoologist's Study of the Human Animal*, London: Jonathan Cape, 1967

Morris, Desmond, *Manwatching: A Field Guide to Human Behaviour*, London: Jonathan Cape, 1977

Morris, Desmond, et al., *Gestures: Their Origins and Distribution*, London: Jonathan Cape, 1979

Morris, Desmond, *Bodywatching: A Field Guide to the Human Species*, London: Jonathan Cape, 1985

Morris, Desmond, *Bodytalk: A World Guide to Gestures*, London: Jonathan Cape, 1994

Morris, Desmond, *The Human Animal: A Personal View of the Human Species*, London: BBC Books, 1994

Morris, Desmond, *The Human Sexes: A Natural History of Man and Woman*, London: Network Books, 1997

Morris, Desmond, *Peoplewatching*, London: Vintage, 2002

Morris, Desmond, *The Naked Woman: A Study of the Female Body*, London: Jonathan Cape, 2004

Morris, Desmond, *The Naked Man: A Study of the Male Body*, London: Jonathan Cape, 2008

Morris, Desmond, *The Artistic Ape: Three Million Years of Art*, London: Red Lemon Press, 2013

Morris, Desmond, *The Lives of the Surrealists*, London: Thames & Hudson, 2018

Nivelon, François, *The Rudiments of Genteel Behavior*, 1737

Wasson, R. Gordon, *Soma: Divine Mushroom of Immortality*, New York: Harcourt, Brace, Jovanovich, 1972

Wildeblood, Joan, *The Polite World*, London: Davis-Poynter, 1973

Picture Credits

Page numbers are given in **bold**.
a = above b = below c = centre l = left r = right

2 Joseph Ducreux, *Self-Portrait, Yawning*, 1783, oil on canvas. J. Paul Getty Museum, Los Angeles **12a** Jean-Léon Gérôme, *Ave Caesar! Morituri te salutant*, 1859, oil on canvas. Yale University Art Gallery, New Haven, CT. Gift of Ruxton Love, Jr., B.A. 1925 (1969.85) **12b** Jacques-Louis David, *The Oath of the Horatii*, 1784, oil on canvas. Musée du Louvre, Paris **13** Thomas Cowperthwait Eakins, *Salutat*, 1898, oil on canvas. Addison Gallery of American Art, Phillips Academy, Andover, MA. Gift of an anonymous donor/Bridgeman Images **14** Gra Rueb, *Man Giving the Olympic Salute,* 1928, Olympic Stadium, Amsterdam. Photo Meunierd/Shutterstock **15** René de Saint-Marceaux, *Jean Sylvain Bailly*, 1881, plaster. Salle du Jeu de Paume, Château de Versailles. Photo RMN-Grand Palais (Château de Versailles)/Gérard Blot **19a** Assyro-Babylonian relief on throne pedestal, 9th century BC. Iraq Archaeological Museum, Baghdad. Photo DeAgostini/Getty Images **19b** Attic vase, 470BC. Harvard Art Museums, Cambridge, MA. Arthur M. Sackler Museum, Bequest of David M. Robinson (1960.339) **20** Bartholomeus van der Helst, *Banquet at the Crossbowmen's Guild in Celebration of the Treaty of Münster*, 1648, oil on canvas. Rijksmuseum, Amsterdam **21** Jennie Augusta Brownscombe, *Washington Greeting Lafayette at Mount Vernon*, early 20th century, oil on canvas. Kirby Collection of Historical Paintings, Lafayette College, Easton, PA **23** Giovanni di Paolo, *Paradise*, 1445, tempera and gold on canvas, transferred from wood. Metropolitan Museum of Art, New York. Rogers Fund, 1906 (06.1046) **24a** Angelos Akotantos, *The Embrace of the Apostles Peter and Paul*, 15th century, oil on canvas on panel. Ashmolean Museum, University of Oxford, UK. Bequeathed by James Campbell Thomson, 1982/Bridgeman Images **24b** Filippino Lippi, *Meeting of Joachim and Anne outside the Golden Gate at Jerusalem*, 1497, tempera on panel. National Gallery of Denmark, Copenhagen. **25a** Giotto, *Joachim and Anne Meeting at the Golden Gate*, 1305, fresco. Cappella degli Scrovegni, Padua, Italy. Photo Scala, Florence **25b** Benozzo Gozzoli, *Meeting of St Francis and St Dominic*, 1452, fresco. Church of San Francesco, Montefalco, Italy. Photo Scala, Florence **28a** Illustration from the *Chronicles by Sir John Froissart*, translated by Thomas Johnes (William Smith, 1839). Private Collection/Look and Learn/Bridgeman Images **28b** Suzuki Harunobu, *Pilgrims Bowing to Courtesan Chozan of the Chojiya*, c. 1767–68, woodblock print. Museum of Fine Arts, Boston. William Sturgis Bigelow Collection (11.19505) **29a** Henry Gillard Glindoni, *Fan Flirtation*, 1908, oil on canvas. Private Collection. Photo John Noott Galleries, Broadway, Worcestershire, UK/Bridgeman Images **29b** Unknown artist, illustration of a débutante performing a curtsey to King George V in 1914. Amoret Tanner Collection/Alamy Stock Photo **30a** Edgar Degas, *Dancer with Bouquet, Curtseying*, 1877, pastel on

paper. Musée d'Orsay, Paris **30b** Edgar Degas, *Dancers Bending Down*, 1885, pastel on paper. Private Collection/Photo Christie's Images/Bridgeman Images **31** William-Adolphe Bouguereau, *The Curtsey*, 1898, oil on canvas. Private Collection **35** Illustration from John Lydgate's *Troy Book* and *Siege of Thebes*, 1475. British Library, London (Royal 18 D. ii, f. 6). Photo British Library Board. All Rights Reserved/Bridgeman Images **36** Maurizio Cattelan, *Him*, 2001, wax, human hair, suit, and polyester resin. Installation view, 'Not Afraid of Love', at the Monnaie de Paris, 21 October 2016 to 8 January 2017. Photo Zeno Zotti, courtesy Maurizio Cattelan's Archive **37** Egyptian bronze of a kneeling man, probably a king, Late Period, c. 712–323BC. British Museum, London **38** Konrad Witz, *Abishai Kneeling before David*, c. 1435, mixed media on oak panelled with canvas. Kunstmuseum Basel. Donation Emilie Linder, Dienast Collection 1860 **39a** Thomas Stewart (after Hendrick Danckerts), *John Rose, the Royal Gardener, presenting a Pineapple to King Charles II*, 1787, oil on canvas. Ham House, Surrey, UK/National Trust Photographic Library/Bridgeman Images **39b** Henry Singleton, *The Proposal*, late 18th century, oil on canvas. Christie's Images, London/Scala, Florence **43** Assyrian black obelisk, 825BC. British Museum, London **44a** William James Müller, *Prayers in the Desert*, 1843, oil on canvas. Birmingham Museum & Art Gallery **44b** *Dipankara Jataka (The Story of the Ascetic Megha and the Buddha Dipankara)*, c. 2nd century, schist panel with gold leaf, Pakistan. Metropolitan Museum of Art, New York. Gift of Mr and Mrs Alan D. Wolfe, in memory of Samuel Eilenberg, 1998 (1998.491) **45** Luc-Olivier Merson, *The Soldier of Marathon*, 1869, oil on canvas. Heritage Image Partnership Ltd/Alamy Stock Photo **46** James Gillray, *The Reception of the Diplomatique and his Suite, at the Court of Pekin*, 1792, hand-coloured etching. British Museum, London **47** Kowtowing court official, early Tang dynasty, 7th–8th century, painted ceramic, China. Private Collection/Photo Christie's Images/Bridgeman Images **52a** Rembrandt, *Jacob Blessing the Sons of Joseph*, 1656, oil on canvas. Gemäldegalerie Alte Meister, Staatliche Museen, Kassel **52b** Govert Flinck, *Isaac Blessing Jacob*, 1638, oil on canvas. Rijksmuseum, Amsterdam **53** Icon of *The Baptism of Christ*, late 18th–early 19th century, painted gesso on wood, Volga region, Russia. British Museum, London **54** Ananias baptizing Paul, 12th century, mosaic. Cappella Palatina, Palermo, Sicily. Photo A. Dagli Orti/Scala, Florence **55** Pietro da Cortona, *Ananias Restoring the Sight of St Paul*, 1631, oil on canvas. Chiesa di Santa Maria della Concezione, Rome. Fine Art Images/age-fotostock **58** Leonardo da Vinci, *Salvator Mundi*, c. 1490, oil on walnut. Private Collection, New York. Photo Salvator Mundi LLC/Art Resource, NY/Scala, Florence **59** Alvise Vivarini, *Christ Blessing*, 1498, oil on panel. Pinacoteca di Brera, Milan **60a** Varrese Painter, Demeter extends her hand in benediction towards the kneeling Maetaneira, 340 BC, clay vase, Puglia, Italy. Antikensammlung,

Staatliche Museen, Berlin **60b** *Christ Pantocrator,*
mosaic, 6th century. Basilica of Sant'Apollinare Nuovo,
Ravenna. Photo Scala, Florence/courtesy of the Ministero
Beni e Att. Culturali e del Turismo **61** *Christ Pantocrator,*
Cypriot icon, 18th century, painted wood. Byzantine
museum, Pedoulas, Cyprus. Photo akg-images/Philippe
Lissac/Godong **63** Lingshan Grand Buddha, unveiled
1997, bronze, Jiangsu Province, China. Photo Henry
Westheim Photography/Alamy Stock Photo **65** Balage
Balogh, *Priestly Benediction,* 21st century, drawing.
© Balage Balogh/Art Resource, NY/Scala, Florence
66 Nazca textile panel, 2nd–3rd century AD, Peru. Photo
DEA/G. Dagli Orti/De Agostini/Getty Images **67** Stefan
Pabst, *Spock (Leonard Nimoy),* 2015, drawing. © Stefan
Pabst/Shutterstock **71** Graham Sutherland, *Somerset
Maugham,* 1949, oil on canvas. © Tate, London 2019
72 Unknown Flemish artist, *Queen Elizabeth I, c.* 1575, oil
on panel. National Portrait Gallery, London/Alamy Stock
Photo **73** Gerard ter Borch, *Memorial Portrait of Moses ter
Borch,* 1667–69, oil on canvas. Rijksmuseum, Amsterdam
77 El Greco, *The Nobleman with his Hand on his Chest
(El caballero de la mano en el pecho), c.* 1580, oil on canvas.
Museo del Prado, Madrid **78a** Sebastiano del Piombo,
Portrait of a Man, Said to be Christopher Columbus, 1519,
oil on canvas. Metropolitan Museum of Art, New York.
Gift of J. Pierpont Morgan, 1900 (00.18.2) **78b** Unknown
master of Bruges, *Nursing Madonna* (*Madonna Lactans*),
16th century, oil on wood. Museu de Aveiro, Portugal
79 Agnolo Bronzino, *Maria de' Medici,* 1551, tempera
on wood. Uffizi Gallery, Florence. Photo Scala, Florence/
courtesy of the Ministero Beni e Att. Culturali e del
Turismo **82a** Joseph Hiller, Sr. (after Charles Willson
Peale), *His Excellency George Washington Esq-r, c.* 1777,
mezzotint. Metropolitan Museum of Art, New York.
Bequest of Charles Allen Munn, 1924 (24.90.212)
82b Jean-Baptiste van Loo, *The Rt Honorable Stephen
Poyntz, of Midgham, Berkshire, c.* 1740, oil on canvas.
Yale Center for British Art, Paul Mellon Fund, New Haven,
CT (B1985.21) **83** Attributed to Johann Heinrich von
Dannecker, *Polyhymnia, Muse of Lyric Poetry, c.* 1785–89,
marble. Grand Palace, Pavlovsk, St Petersburg (216-VIII).
Photo akg-images **84** Robert Lefèvre, *Napoleon
Bonaparte,* 1812, oil on canvas. Collection of Apsley House,
London. Photo by English Heritage/Heritage Images/Getty
Images **85** Irakli Toidze, *Stalin Is Leading Us to Victory,*
1943, Soviet poster. Photo akg-images/Elizaveta Becker
88 Kehinde Wiley, *John Wilmot, 2nd Earl of Rochester,*
2013, oil on canvas. © 2013 Kehinde Wiley. Used by
permission **89l** Workshop of Hans Holbein the Younger,
Henry VIII, c. 1537, oil on panel. National Museums
Liverpool, Walker Art Gallery **89r** William Merritt Chase,
Lady in Black, 1888, oil on canvas. Metropolitan Museum
of Art, New York. Gift of William Merritt Chase, 1891
(91.11) **92** Adam Rabalais, *Cinematic Psychopaths –
A Clockwork Orange,* 2015, digital drawing. © Adam
Rabalais **93l** Parmigianino, *Pietro Maria Rossi, Count
of San Secondo,* 1535–38, oil on panel. Museo del Prado,
Madrid **93r** Alonso Sánchez Coello, *Infante Don Carlos,*
1564, oil on canvas. Kunsthistorisches Museum, Vienna.
Historic Images/Alamy Stock Photo **96a** Loyset Liédet,
wedding scene with the groom wearing long *poulaines,
c.* 1470, miniature. Bibiothèque Nationale de France,
Paris (Arsenal 5073 f.117v) **96b** Allan Ramsay, *Richard

Grenville, 2nd Earl Temple, 1762, oil on canvas. National
Gallery of Victoria, Melbourne/Art Collection 3/Alamy
Stock Photo **97** Hyacinthe Rigaud, *Portrait of Louis XIV,
King of France,* 1701, oil on canvas. Musée du Louvre, Paris
100 Vincenzo Campi, *Kitchen,* 1590–91, oil on canvas.
Pinacoteca di Brera, Milan. Photo Scala, Florence/courtesy
of the Ministero Beni e Att. Culturali e del Turismo
101a Jean-François Millet, *The Gleaners,* 1857, oil on
canvas. Musée d'Orsay, Paris **101b** Gustave Caillebotte,
The Floor Planers, 1875, oil on canvas. Musée d'Orsay, Paris
104a Pieter Bruegel the Elder, *The Wedding Dance,* 1566,
oil on panel. Detroit Institute of Arts (30.374) **104b** Pieter
Bruegel the Elder, *The Land of Cockaigne,* 1567, oil on panel.
Alte Pinakothek, Munich. Photo akg-images **105** William
Hogarth, *Gin Lane,* 1751, etching and engraving. National
Gallery of Art, Washington, DC, Rosenwald Collection
(1944.5.87) **110a** Hieronymus Bosch, *Christ Carrying the
Cross, c.* 1510, oil on panel. Museum of Fine Arts, Ghent,
Belgium **110b** Paul Klee, *Or The Mocked Mocker,* 1930, oil
on canvas. Museum of Modern Art, New York. Gift of J. B.
Neumann (637.1939)/Scala, Florence **111** Joseph Ducreux,
Self-portrait in the Guise of a Mocker, 1793, oil on canvas.
Musée du Louvre, Paris. Photo RMN-Grand Palais (Musée
du Louvre)/Jean-Gilles Berizzi **112** Adriaen Brouwer,
Youth Making a Face, c. 1632–35, oil on panel. National
Gallery of Art, Washington, DC, New Century Fund
(1994.46.1) **113a** Miniature from the *Gorleston Psalter,*
14th century. British Library, London (MS Addl 49622.
f.123r). Photo British Library Board. All Rights Reserved/
Bridgeman Images **113b** Gargoyle, 14th–15th century,
Guild Chapel, Stratford-upon-Avon, England. Photo
Septemberlegs/Alamy Stock Photo **116a** A woman
churning butter with the Devil, late 15th century, fresco.
Tingsted church, Denmark. Photo Stig Alenäs/Alamy Stock
Photo **116b** *Saint Nicholas's Day. The Krampus (Incubus
in Company of Saint Nicholas), c.* 1904, Hungarian
illustration. Photo CCI/Shutterstock **117** Attributed to
Roeloff van Zijl, *Elisha Mocked by Boys, c.* 1625–30, oil
on canvas. Rijksmuseum, Amsterdam **118** HoodGraff
team, *Albert Einstein,* 2014, spray paint on wall,
St Petersburg, Russia. Courtesy HoodGraff team
#myhoodisgood. Photo Lisa-Lisa/Shutterstock
119 Trenton Doyle Hancock, *Self-portrait with Tongue,*
2010, acrylic and mixed media on paper. Courtesy the
artist and James Cohan, New York **122** Pieter van der
Heyden (after Pieter Bruegel the Elder), *The Festival
of Fools,* 1559, engraving. Rijksmuseum, Amsterdam
123a *Trial by Battle,* mid-19th century, colour lithograph,
American School. American Antiquarian Society,
Worcester, MA/ Bridgeman Images **123b** *Thumbing one's
Nose from the Motor Tricycle,* 1900, advertisement for
the Automobiles de Dion-Bouton (illustration by Wilhio).
Musée National du Château de Compiègne, Musée de
la Voiture (Transport Museum). Photo DeAgostini/Getty
Images **127** Maurizio Cattelan, *L.O.V.E.,* 2010, hand:
White 'P' Carrara Marble; base: bright Roman travertine.
Installation view, *L.O.V.E.,* Piazza degli Affari, Milan, Italy,
2010. Photo Zeno Zotti, courtesy Maurizio Cattelan's
Archive **128a** *Statue of General Anira, one of the Twelve
Divine Generals,* Kamakura period, 12th–14th century,
Japan. Private Collection **128b** Dotmaster, *Rude Kids,*
2016, spray paint on wall, London. Courtesy the
dotmasters. #rudekids www.dotmaster.co.uk. Photo

OnTheRoad/Alamy Stock Photo **129a** Banksy, *Rude Copper*, *c.* 2002, print with spray paint. Photo Jan Fritz/Alamy Stock Photo **129b** Marion Peck, *Fuck You*, 2008, oil on canvas. © Marion Peck **134a** Etruscan fresco from the *Tomb of the Lioness*, 520 BC, Necropolis of Tarquinia, Lazio, Italy. Photo DeAgostini/Getty Images **134b** Illustration from the *Libro de los Juegos*, 1283. Real Biblioteca del Monasterio de San Lorenzo de El Escorial, Madrid **135a** 'Fig-and-phallus' Roman amulet, bronze. Collection of Desmond Morris **135b** Albrecht Dürer, *Studies of Dürer's Left Hand*, 1493–94, pen and ink on paper. Albertina Museum, Vienna (26327r) **136** Jan Massys, *The Ill-matched Pair*, 1566, oil on panel. Nationalmuseum, Stockholm (NM 508) **137** Felix Labisse, *La Fille d'Yemanja*, 1961, oil on canvas. Gustave J. Nellens Collection, Knokke, Belgium. © ADAGP, Paris and DACS, London 2019 **139** Walter Swennen, *Bras d'honneur*, 2003, oil on canvas. Courtesy the artist and Xavier Hufkens, Brussels **142a** Jehan de Grise, miniature from *The Romance of Alexander*, 1338–44. Bodleian Library, Oxford (MS Bodl.254 f.3) **142b** Michelangelo, *The Creation of the Sun and the Moon*, ceiling fresco, 1508–12. Sistine Chapel, Rome. Photo Peter Barritt/Alamy Stock Photo **143** Nick Walker, *Moona Lisa*, 2008, spray paint on wall, London. Photo Gonzales Photo/Alamy Stock Photo **148a** Stela of the God Bes, Ptolemaic or Roman Period, 4th century BC–1st century AD, paint on limestone, Egypt. Metropolitan Museum of Art, New York. Rogers Fund, 1922 (22.2.23) **148b** James Gillray, *Daniel Mendoza*, 1788, etching and aquatint. Metropolitan Museum of Art, New York. The Elisha Whittelsey Collection, The Elisha Whittelsey Fund, 1966 (66.683.9) **149** Rembrandt, *Samson Accusing his Father-in-law*, 1635, oil on canvas. Staatliche Museum, Berlin **150** Soviet propaganda poster, 1930s. Shawshots/Alamy Stock Photo **151** Joan Miró, *Aidez L'Espagne*, 1937, pochoir with lithographic inscription on paper. The Sherwin Collection. © Successió Miró/ADAGP, Paris and DACS London 2019 **153** Street art recreating the 'Santa Cruz screaming hand' by Jim Phillips, date unknown, spray paint on wall, Duisburg, Germany. Photo imageBroker/Alamy Stock Photo **154** Toyohara Kunichika, depiction of a Japanese kabuki actor, 1883–86, woodblock print. Metropolitan Museum of Art, New York. Gift of Eliot C. Nolen, 1999 (1999.457.2) **155** Toshusai Sharaku, *Kabuki Actor Otani Oniji III as Yakko Edobei*, 1794, woodblock print. Metropolitan Museum of Art, New York. Henry L. Phillips Collection, Bequest of Henry L. Phillips, 1939 (JP2822) **157** Kalejaye O.T., *Dare to Zlatan*, 2017, graphite and charcoal pencil on paper. © Kalejaye O.T. **158** WK Interact, *Portrait: Patrick (12 Angry Men)*, 2009, acrylic on canvas. © 2018 WK **159a** Carved *amo* (Maori housepost), *c.* 1800, wood, New Zealand. Metropolitan Museum of Art, New York. The Michael C. Rockefeller Memorial Collection, Bequest of Nelson A. Rockefeller, 1979 (1979.206.1508) **159b** Leonardo da Vinci, *Studies for the Heads of Two Soldiers in the 'Battle of Anghiari'*, *c.* 1505, charcoal on paper. Szépmüvészeti Múzeum, Budapest (1775) **162** Illustration by Alphonse-Marie-Adolphe de Neuville, from François Guizot's *The History of France from the Earliest Times to the Year 1789*, 1883. Chronicle/Alamy Stock Photo **163a** Illustration showing the Lords Appellant throwing down their gauntlets, 1864. The Print Collector/Alamy Stock Photo

163b After Henry Gillard Glindoni, *The Challenge*. Illustration for *The Boy's Own Annual*, 1898. Private Collection/Look and Learn/Bridgeman Images **165a** Gertrude Abercrombie, *The Courtship*, 1949, oil on Masonite. Collection of the Museum of Contemporary Art Chicago. Gift of the Gertrude Abercrombie Trust (1978.56). Photo Nathan Keay. © MCA Chicago **165b** Philip Guston, *Talking*, 1979, oil on canvas. Museum of Modern Art, New York. © The Estate of Philip Guston **170** Pablo Picasso, *Weeping Woman with Handkerchief*, 1937, oil on canvas. Los Angeles County Museum of Art. Gift of Mr and Mrs Thomas Mitchell (55.90). © Succession Picasso/DACS, London 2019 **171** Rogier van der Weyden, *The Descent from the Cross*, before 1443, oil on wood. Museo del Prado, Madrid **172** Andrea Mantegna, *Lamentation over the Dead Christ*, *c.* 1483, tempera on canvas. Pinacoteca di Brera, Milan **173a** Qiao Bin, *Par nirvana (Death and Transcendence of the Buddha) and Attendant Arhats*, 1503, earthenware with polychrome glaze, China. Metropolitan Museum of Art, New York. Fletcher Fund, 1925 (25.227.1) **173b** Olmec 'crying baby' figure, 1100–900 BC, ceramic, Mexico. Metropolitan Museum of Art, New York. The Michael C. Rockefeller Memorial Collection, Bequest of Nelson A. Rockefeller, 1979 (1979.206.1134) **175** Frederic, Lord Leighton, *Lachrymae*, 1894–95, oil on canvas. Metropolitan Museum of Art, New York. Catharine Lorillard Wolfe Collection, Wolfe Fund, 1896 (96.28) **176a** Annibale Carracci, *The Dead Christ Mourned ('The Three Maries')*, *c.* 1604, oil on canvas. National Gallery, London **176b** Attic funerary plaque, *c.* 520–510 BC, terracotta, Greece. Metropolitan Museum of Art, New York. Rogers Fund, 1954 (54.11.5) **177a** Funerary scene with mourning women, tomb of Ramose, XVIII Dynasty, *c.* 1550–1292 BC, Thebes, Egypt. Photo François Guénet/akg-images **177b** Émile Friant, *Study for 'La Douleur'*, *c.* 1898–99, charcoal on paper. Dahesh Museum of Art, New York/Bridgeman Images **179** Balthasar Permoser, *Marsyas*, *c.* 1680–85, marble. Metropolitan Museum of Art, New York. Rogers Fund and Harris Brisbane Dick Fund, 2002 (2002.468) **180a** Jusepe de Ribera, *Apollo and Marsyas*, 1637, oil on canvas. Museo Nazionale di Capodimonte, Naples **180b** Adriaen Brouwer, *Peasants Brawling over Cards*, 1630, oil on wood. Gemäldegalerie, Alte Meister, Dresden (1631). Photo akg-images **181** Francis Bacon, *Study of a Head*, 1952, oil on canvas. Yale Center for British Art, Gift of Beekman C. and Margaret H. Cannon (B1998.27). © The Estate of Francis Bacon. All rights reserved. DACS 2019 **183** Nicolas Poussin, *The Massacre of the Innocents*, *c.* 1625–29, oil on canvas. Musée Condé, Chantilly **184** Gustave Courbet, *The Desperate Man*, 1844–45, oil on canvas. Private collection. Photo Fine Art Images/Heritage Images/Getty Images **185a** Rogier van der Weyden, *The Last Judgment*, 1445–48, oil on wood. The Hôtel-Dieu, Hospices de Beaune, Beaune, Côte d'Or, Bourgogne, France **185b** Detail from the *Dionysiac Frieze*. Villa dei Misteri, Pompeii **187** Adriaen Brouwer, *The Bitter Potion*, *c.* 1636–38, oil on oak. Städelsches Kunstinstitut, Frankfurt am Main, Germany **188** Adriaen Brauwer, *Smell*, 1631, oil on panel. Gemaldegalerie Alte Meister, Dresden (1631). Photo akg-images **189** Franz Xaver Messerschmidt, *The Vexed Man*, 1771–83, alabaster. J. Paul Getty Museum, Los Angeles (2008.4) **191** Pierre

Reymond, *Plaque with Seven Sorrows of Mary*, 1541, enamel on copper. Photo Ligier Piotr/National Museum in Warsaw **195** Bernece Berkman, *Jews Fleeing War*, 1939, oil on canvas. Collection of Bernard Friedman. Photo Jamie Stukenberg **196** Henry Gibbs, *Aeneas and his Family Fleeing Burning Troy*, 1654, oil on canvas. Tate, London **197** Jacopo Tintoretto, *Saint George and the Dragon*, c. 1555, oil on canvas. National Gallery, London **199** Henri Rousseau, *Unpleasant Surprise*, 1901, oil on canvas. Barnes Foundation, Philadelphia, PA **200** Francisco Goya, *The 3rd of May 1808*, 1814, oil on canvas. Museo del Prado, Madrid **201a** Jean Michel Basquiat, *Untitled*, 1981, acrylic, oilstick and spray paint on canvas. Christie's Images, London/Scala, Florence. © The Estate of Jean-Michel Basquiat/ADAGP, Paris and DACS, London 2019 **201b** Wesley James Lock, *Scars and Stripes*, 2014, ink on paper. © Wesley James Lock **204a** Ancient Pueblo (Anasazi) rock art, c. 500 BC–AD 500, New Mexico, USA. Photo © Ira Block/National Geographic **204b** Caravaggio, *Portrait of Alof de Wignacourt and his Page*, c. 1608, oil on canvas. Musée du Louvre, Paris **205a** Detail from the *Alexander Mosaic*, c. 100 BC, originally from the House of the Faun, Pompeii. National Archaeological Museum, Naples. Photo Giannis Papanikos/Alamy Stock Photo **205b** Sydney Nolan, *Kelly and Horse*, 1946, enamel on composition board. ACT Museums and Galleries, Canberra. © Sidney Nolan Trust. All Rights Reserved, 2018/Bridgeman Images **206a** Scene from Trajan's Column (AD 113), showing Romans in *testudo* formation, 19th-century plaster cast of marble original in Rome. Museo della Civiltà Romana, Rome. Photo akg-images **206b** Henry Moore, *Warrior with Shield*, 1953–54, bronze on wooden plinth. Birmingham Museums and Art Gallery. Reproduced by permission of The Henry Moore Foundation **207** WK Interact, *Struggle*, 1992, mural, New York. © 2018 WK **211** Vincent van Gogh, *Sorrowing Old Man ('At Eternity's Gate')*, May 1890, oil on canvas. Kröller-Müller Museum, Otterlo, Netherlands **212a** Sandro Botticelli, *La Derelitta*, 1495, tempera on wood. Palazzo Pallavicini Rospigliosi, Galleria Aurora, Rome **212b** *Agony in the Garden of Gethsemane*, 1470, Book of Hours, Netherlands. The Walters Art Museum, Baltimore, MD (Ms W.918, fol. 104v) **213** Conor Harrington, *Hide and Seek*, 2016, oil on linen. © Conor Harrington **215** Paula Modersohn-Becker, *Old Peasant Woman*, c. 1905, oil on canvas. Detroit Institute of Arts. Gift of Robert H. Tannahill (58.385) **216** Netherlandish painter, *Portrait of a Man in a Turban*, 1440s, oil on wood. Metropolitan Museum of Art, New York. The Jules Bache Collection, 1949 (49.7.24) **217** Wyndham Lewis, *Stephen Spender*, 1938, oil on canvas. The Potteries Museum and Art Gallery, Stoke-on-Trent, UK/Bridgeman Images. © Estate of Wyndham Lewis/ Bridgeman Images **219** Francisco Goya, *Tiburcio Pérez y Cuervo, the Architect*, 1820, oil on canvas. Metropolitan Museum of Art, New York. Theodore M. Davis Collection, Bequest of Theodore M. Davis, 1915 (30.95.242) **220** Paul Cézanne, *Peasant Standing with Arms Crossed*, c. 1895, oil on canvas. Barnes Foundation, Philadelphia, PA **221** Paula Rego, central panel of the triptych *Vanitas*, 2006, pastel on paper. Fundação Calouste Gulbenkian, Lisbon. © Paula Rego. Courtesy Marlborough Fine Art, London **223a** Rembrandt, *Portrait of a Man with Arms Akimbo*, 1658, oil on canvas. Agnes Etherington Art Centre, Kingston, Ontario. Gift of Alfred and Isabel Bader, 2015 (58-008) **223b** Chaïm Soutine, *The Bellboy*, 1925, oil on canvas. Musée National d'Art Moderne, Centre Pompidou, Paris (AM 3611 P) **225** Nether, *The Fight for Building Blocks*, 2014, Baltimore, MD. © Nether **227a** John Phillip, *The Evil Eye*, 1859, oil on canvas. Smith Art Gallery and Museum, Stirling, Scotland/Bridgeman Images **227b** Detail from *Sacrifices of Abel and Melchizedek*, mid-6th century AD, mosaic. Basilica of San Vitale, Ravenna, Italy. Photo DeAgostini/Getty Images **229** Charles Rodius, two views of a tattooed Maori man, 1834–35, pencil, black chalk with stump, heightened with white. British Museum, London **232** Raffaelle Monti, *Veiled Vestal Virgin*, 1846–47, marble. Collection of the Duke of Devonshire, Chatsworth House, UK/Reproduced by permission of Chatsworth Settlement Trustees/ Bridgeman Images **233a** Jean-Léon Gérôme, *Veiled Circassian Woman*, 1876, oil on canvas. Christie's Images, London/Scala, Florence **233b** Edmund Blair Leighton, *Olivia*, 1887, oil on canvas. Private Collection/Photo Christie's Images/Bridgeman Images **240** Lucas Cranach the Elder, *The Three Graces*, 1531, oil on wood. Musée du Louvre, Paris. Photo RMN-Grand Palais (Musée du Louvre)/Stéphane Maréchalle **241a** Francisco Goya, *The Naked Maya*, 1797–1800, oil on canvas. Museo del Prado, Madrid **241b** Diego Velázquez, *The Rokeby Venus*, 1647–51, oil on canvas. National Gallery, London. Presented by the Art Fund, 1906 **242a** Jean-Léon Gérôme, *Phryne Revealed before the Areopagus*, 1861, oil on canvas. Kunsthalle, Hamburg. Freiherr Johann Heinrich von Schröder-Stiftung, 1910 (HK-1910). Photo Scala, Florence/ bpk, Bildagentur für Kunst, Kultur und Geschichte, Berlin **242b** François Boucher, *Louise O'Murphy*, 1752, oil on canvas. Bayerische Staatsgemäldesammlungen – Alte Pinakothek München (1166). Photo Scala, Florence/bpk, Bildagentur für Kunst, Kultur und Geschichte, Berlin **243** Amedeo Modigliani, *Reclining Nude*, 1917, oil on canvas. Private Collection **247** Venus of Hohle Fels, 38,000–33,000 BC, mammoth ivory. Institut für Ur- und Frühgeschichte und Archäologie des Mittelalters Abteilung für Ältere Urgeschichte und Quartärökologie. Universität Tübingen. Photo Hilde Jensen. **248a** Unknown artist, *Gabrielle d'Estrées and One of her Sisters*, c. 1594, oil on wood. Musée du Louvre, Paris **248b** Sarah Goodridge, *Beauty Revealed*, 1828, watercolour on ivory. Metropolitan Museum of Art, New York. Gift of Gloria Manney, 2006 (2006.235.74) **249** Raphael, *La Fornarina*, 1518–19, oil on wood. Galleria Nazionale di Arte Antica, Rome **251** Lucas Cranach the Elder, *Adam and Eve*, 1533, oil on wood. Gemäldegalerie, Staatliche Museen zu Berlin. Photo Scala, Florence/bpk, Bildagentur fuer Kunst, Kultur und Geschichte, Berlin **254** Titian, *Venus and Adonis*, 1554, oil on canvas. Museo del Prado, Madrid **255** Frederic William Burton, *Hellelil and Hildebrand, the Meeting on the Turret Stairs*, 1864, watercolour and gouache on paper. National Gallery of Ireland, Dublin **256** Frederic, Lord Leighton, *The Fisherman and the Syren*, 1856–58, oil on canvas. Bristol Museum and Art Gallery, UK. Given by the Hon. Mrs Charles Lyell, 1938/Bridgeman Images **257** Jean-Honoré Fragonard, *The Bolt*, c. 1777, oil on canvas. Musée du Louvre, Paris **260a** Auguste Rodin, *The Kiss*, 1888–98, plaster cast from marble after 1898.

 Picture Credits

Musée Rodin, Paris **260b** Henri de Toulouse-Lautrec, *In Bed: The Kiss*, 1892, oil on wood. Private Collection/ Photo Christie's Images/Bridgeman Images **261** Gustav Klimt, *The Kiss*, 1907–8, oil and gold leaf on canvas. Österreichische Galerie Belvedere, Vienna **264** Giuseppe Cesari, *Perseus and Andromeda*, *c.* 1592, oil on slate. Museum of Art, Rhode Island School of Design, Providence, Rhode Island, USA (57.167) **265a** William Johns, *A Foot Next to My Leg*, 2015, oil on canvas. © William Jones **265b** Pietro Perugino, *The Martydom of St Sebastian*, 1495, oil on panel. Musée du Louvre, Paris **270a** Chinese bodhisattva, probably Avalokiteshvara, AD *c.* 470–480, sandstone with traces of pigment. Metropolitan Museum of Art, New York. Gift of Robert Lehman, 1948 (48.162.2) **270b** Lucian Freud, *The Brigadier*, 2003–4, oil on canvas. Private Collection. © The Lucian Freud Archive/Bridgeman Images **271a** Anthony Brandt, *Nude with Crossed Legs*, 1959, oil on canvas. Reproduced with permission of the Anthony Brandt Foundation, www.anthonybrandt.com **271b** Shurooq Amin, *A Man of no Importance*, 2012, from the series, *Popcornographic*. *A Man of No Importance* (title based on Oscar Wilde's play *A Woman of No Importance*), 2013, mixed media on canvas mounted on wood. Ayyam Gallery, Dubai. © Shurooq Amin **273** Michelangelo, *Crouching Boy*, *c.* 1530–34, marble. Hermitage Museum, St Petersburg **274a** Egyptian block statue of Padimahes, *c.* 680–650 BC, granodiorite. Brooklyn Museum, New York. Charles Edwin Wilbour Fund (64.146) **274b** Huastec figurine, 16th century, Mexico, ceramic. Metropolitan Museum of Art, New York. The Michael C. Rockefeller Memorial Collection, Purchase, Nelson A. Rockefeller Gift, 1965 (1978.412.141) **275** Edgar Degas, *The Tub*, 1886, pastel on card. Musée d'Orsay, Paris **277** John Everett Millais, *The Woodman's Daughter*, 1851, oil on canvas. Guildhall Art Gallery, City of London/Bridgeman Images **278a** Fernand Pelez, *A Martyr: The Violet Vendor*, 1885, oil on canvas. Petit Palais, Musée des Beaux-arts de la Ville de Paris. Photo Roger-Viollet/Topfoto.co.uk **278b** Nicholas Hilliard, *A Young Man Leaning Against a Tree Amongst Roses, possibly Robert Devereux, 2nd Earl of Essex*, 1585–95, watercolour. Victoria and Albert Museum, London **279** Attributed to Peter Lely, *Countess of Dorchester*, late 17th century, oil on canvas. Bradford Art Galleries and Museums, West Yorkshire, UK/Bridgeman Images **280** Tai-Shan Schierenberg, *Portrait of Nicola Usborne*, 2010, oil on canvas. Courtesy Flowers Gallery London and New York. © Tai-Shan Schierenberg **281** Egon Schiele, *Seated Woman with Bent Knee*, 1917, crayon and gouache. Narodni Galerie, Prague **284** Titian, *The Venus of Urbino*, 1538, oil on canvas. Uffizi Gallery, Florence **285** Édouard Manet, *Olympia*, 1863, oil on canvas. Musée d'Orsay, Paris **286** Henri Matisse, *Large Reclining Nude*, 1935, oil on canvas. Baltimore Museum of Art. The Cone Collection, formed by Dr Claribel Cone and Miss Etta Cone of Baltimore, MD (1950.258). Photo Mitro Hood. © Succession H. Matisse/DACS 2019 **287** David Hockney, *Sunbather*, 1966, acrylic on canvas. Collection Museum Ludwig, Cologne. © David Hockney **288** Gustave Courbet, *Young Ladies on the Banks of the Seine*, 1857, oil on canvas. Petit Palais, Musée des Beaux-Arts de la Ville de Paris. Photo RMN-Grand Palais/Agence Bulloz **289** John William Godward, *Dolce Far Niente*, 1904, oil on canvas. History and Art Collection/Alamy Stock Photo **291** William F. Draper, *John F. Kennedy*, 1966, oil on canvas. National Portrait Gallery, Smithsonian Institution, Washington, DC (NPG.66.35). © January 1, 1966, Margaret Draper **292** James Tissot, *Young Woman in a Rocking Chair,* study for the painting *The Last Evening*, *c.* 1873, brush with gouache and watercolour, over graphite on brown paper. J. Paul Getty Museum, Los Angeles **293** Edvard Munch, *Aunt Karen in the Rocking Chair*, 1883, oil on canvas. Munch Museum, Oslo, Norway. Photo Scala, Florence **296** Joseph Ducreux, *Self-Portrait, Yawning*, 1783, oil on canvas. J. Paul Getty Museum, Los Angeles **297** Luigi i Montejano, *Yawning Men*, 1850, oil on canvas. Private Collection **298a** Mihály Munkácsy, *Yawning Apprentice*, 1869, oil on canvas. Museum of Fine Arts, Budapest **298b** Edgar Degas, *Two Women Ironing*, *c.* 1884–86, oil on canvas. Musée d'Orsay, Paris **299** Fang Lijun, *Series 2 No. 2*, 1991–92, oil on canvas. © Fang Lijun **302** Unknown sculptor, *The Barberini Faun*, 3rd–2nd century BC, marble. Glyptothek, Munich. Photo DEA Picture Library/De Agostini/Getty Images **303** Sleeping Goddess of Malta, clay figure from the Hal-Saflieni Hypogeum, Malta, 3000 BC. National Archaeological Museum, Valletta, Malta. Photo Dirk Renckhoff/Alamy Stock Photo **304** Bernhard Strigel, *Sleeping Grave Guard*, 1520, oil on panel. Alte Pinakothek München, Bayerische Staatsgemäldesammlungen, Munich (10066). Photo Scala, Florence/bpk, Bildagentur für Kunst, Kultur und Geschichte, Berlin **305a** Sandro Botticelli, *Venus and Mars*, *c.* 1485, tempera and oil on poplar. National Gallery, London **305b** Edward Burne-Jones, *The Rose Bower*, 'The Briar Rose' Series, 1870–90, oil on canvas. Faringdon Collection, Buscot, Oxon, UK/Bridgeman Images **306** Henry Fuseli, *The Nightmare*, 1781, oil on canvas. Detroit Institute of Arts. Founders Society Purchase with funds from Mr and Mrs Bert L. Smokler and Mr and Mrs Lawrence A. Fleischman (55.5A) **307** Salvador Dalí, *Sleep*, 1937, oil on canvas. Private collection. Christie's Images, London/Scala, Florence. © Salvador Dalí, Fundació Gala-Salvador Dalí, DACS 2019

Acknowledgments

I would like to acknowledge the tireless research that my late wife Ramona contributed to this book. She spent many hours pursuing images that illustrate perfectly a particular piece of body language. As an historian, she was also indispensable in tracking down obscure texts that explain the origins of the various postures and gestures. On a more general note, I would also like to record her immense, invaluable help with almost all the sixty books that I have written over the past six decades. Her death in November 2018 sadly robs me of the possibility of another wonderful collaboration, should I, at the age of ninety-one, embark on another volume.

As with my last book, *The Lives of the Surrealists*, Thames & Hudson have provided brilliant editing, design and picture research, and I am particularly grateful to Roger Thorp, Amber Husain, Susanna Ingram, Rebecca Pearson, Maria Ranauro, Alex Wright, Michela Parkin and Kate Wands.

Finally, I would like to thank my literary agent, Silke Bruenink, who, as always, has provided enormous encouragement and support.

Index

For Peter Collett, who for forty-five years has
shared with me the pleasure of pursuing the
origins and meanings of human gestures.

First published in the United Kingdom in 2019
by Thames & Hudson Ltd, 181A High Holborn,
London WC1V 7QX

Postures: Body Language in Art
© 2019 Thames & Hudson Ltd, London
Text © 2019 Desmond Morris

British Library Cataloguing-in-Publication Data
A catalogue record for this book is available from
the British Library

ISBN 978-0-500-02261-0

Printed and bound in China
by C & C Offset Printing Co. Ltd

To find out about all our publications,
please visit **www.thamesandhudson.com.**
There you can subscribe to our e-newsletter,
browse or download our current catalogue,
and buy any titles that are in print.